CIPA Guide to the Patents Acts

(3/4) Guide to the Patents Act

CIPA GUIDE TO THE PATENTS ACTS

THIRD CUMULATIVE SUPPLEMENT TO THE NINTH EDITION

EDITORS

PAUL COLE
Chartered Patent Attorney
Lucas & Co

RICHARD DAVIS
Barrister
Hogarth Chambers

FOR

THE CHARTERED INSTITUTE OF PATENT ATTORNEYS

CIPA THE CHARTERED INSTITUTE OF PATENT ATTORNEYS

SWEET & MAXWELL

THOMSON REUTERS

Published in 2023 by Thomson Reuters, trading as Sweet & Maxwell.
Thomson Reuters is registered in England & Wales. Company number
1679046.
Registered Office and address for service: 5 Canada Square, Canary Wharf,
London, E14 5AQ.

For further information on our products and services, visit
http://www.sweetandmaxwell.co.uk.

Computerset by Sweet & Maxwell.
Printed and bound by CPI Group (UK) Ltd, Croydon, CR0 4YY.
A CIP catalogue record for this book is available from the British Library.

NOTICE TO READERS

This book has been prepared mainly for use by patent practitioners in the
United Kingdom. It is truly intended as a "guide" and is not a substitute for the
exercise of professional judgment.

ISBN (print): 978-0-414-10948-3

ISBN (Proview e-book): 978-0-414-10951-3

ISBN (print and Proview e-book): 978-0-414-10949-0

TITLE HISTORY

First edition	1980
Second edition	1984
Third edition	1990
Fourth edition	1995
Fifth edition	2001
Sixth edition	2009
Seventh edition	2011
Eighth edition	2016
Ninth edition	2019

CIPA GUIDE TO THE PATENTS ACTS

EDITORS

Paul Cole
Chartered Patent Attorney
Lucas & Co

Richard Davis
Barrister
Hogarth Chambers

This supplement to the "Black Book" has been produced by a team of contributors acknowledged in alphabetical order below, each of whom has contributed subject matter for one or more individual sections. Barristers, solicitors and patent attorneys have all served as members of the team. The Editors named above have also contributed subject matter for certain sections.

James Anderson, Elkington and Fife LLP

Philip Barnes, Barnes IP

Richard Cooke, Elkington and Fife LLP

Zoe Butler, Powell Gilbert LLP

Sam Carter, Hogarth Chambers

Paul Casbon, Greaves Brewster LLP

Andrew Clay, Sonder & Clay Legal Limited

Trevor Cook, WilmerHale

Kristina Cornish, Kilburn & Strode LLP

Alison Firth, Professor Emeritus, University of Surrey

Nicholas Fox, Finnegan Europe LLP

Anna Hatt, Beck Greener

John Hull, Beck Greener

Dr Jonathan Markham, Beck Greener

Cara McGlynn, Brodies LLP

Jamie Muir Wood, Hogarth Chambers

David Pearce, Barker Brettell LLP

James Peel, J. P. Peel & Co Ltd

Thomas Phillips, Ministry of Defence

Dr Michael A. Roberts, Reddie & Grose LLP

Ashley Roughton, Barrister

Vicki Salmon, Impact Intellectual Property LLP

George Schlich, Schlich Ltd

Mike Snodin, Park Grove IP

Philip Walters, Celldex Therapeutics

Andrew Weaver, Impact Intellectual Property LLP

Simon Wright, Schlich Ltd

PREFACE

This Third Cumulative Supplement reviews legislative changes enacted and legal opinions handed down after the text for the Ninth Edition was finalised. It attempts to state the law comprehensively up to July 31, 2022, with coverage of more recent events where possible.

Although not now directly relevant to UK law, probably the most significant chain of events for our profession is the impending introduction of the unitary patent and the unified patent court, §83A.05. Also of great significance, especially for those practising in the life sciences, is the pending case before the Enlarged Appeal Board on the relevance of post-published evidence in case G 2/21 *Plausibility*, §3.18. A large number of pertinent decisions have been handed down on eligibility, notably *Renaissance Technologies v Comptroller* [2021] EWHC 2113 (Ch), §1.10, and T 0489/14 *BENTLEY SYSTEMS/Pedestrian simulation*, §§1.11 and 3.29. Two decisions on video games, *Sony Interactive Entertainment* BL O/599/21 and *NetEase (Hangzhou) Network* BL O/431/22 are found at §1.10. The relationship between novelty and obviousness was considered in *Fiberweb Geosynthetics v Geofabrics* [2021] EWCA Civ 854, §2.21. General principles concerning the *Windsurfing* approach were considered by Meade J. in *Optis v Apple* [2021 EWHC 3121 (Pat), affirmed [2022] EWCA Civ 792 with passing reference to T. A. Blanco-White's ludicrous example of designing two-hole Venezuelan razor blades, §3.07. Respective roles of skilled people within a group were considered in *Alcon v Actavis* [2022] EWCA Civ 845, §3.10. Issues of entitlement to priority e.g. where party A is named as applicant for the US and party B is named for other PCT contracting states are pending before the Enlarged Board, cases G 1/22 and G 2/22, §5.20. *Thaler's Application* on the naming of an AI machine as an inventor is now before the UK Supreme Court, §7.07A. Definition of an exclusive licence was considered in *Neurim v Generics* [2022] EWCA Civ 359, §67.03. An application for an interim injunction based on a divisional European patent application approved by the Appeal Board and proceeding towards grant but not yet granted was refused on *American Cyanamid* principles in *Novatis v Teva* [2022] EWHC 959 (Ch), §69.06. The interpretation of method and product claims relating to a transmit/receive system were considered in *Conversant Wireless Licensing v Huawei* [2020] EWHC 14 (Pat), §125.15.

Each entry in this Supplement has a marginal reference in bold type to the numbered section and paragraph number e.g. §125.23 of the Ninth Edition ["the Main Work"] to which it relates and is identified by headings (e.g. "Terms of degree" or "Claims containing a statement of purpose") corresponding to those in the Main Work. The Supplement also contains Supplementary Tables which are to be read in conjunction with the corresponding Tables in the Main Work.

It should once again be acknowledged that the Guide is a team effort. Special thanks are once again due to my co-editor Richard Davis. The Editors are, as ever, grateful for the help and encouragement of Kirsty Swain and the long-standing editorial team at Sweet & Maxwell, including in particular Lewis Ward. We are also grateful for the support of the Chartered Institute of Patent Attorneys through its Textbook and Publications Committee.

Paul Cole
November 2022

TABLE OF CASES

An additional table of EPO Decisions arranged in numerical order follows this Table.

These decisions are also included in the Table below, arranged under the proprietor's name.

TABLE OF EUROPEAN PATENT OFFICE DECISIONS

This Table is a list of decisions of the Appeal Boards of the European Patent Office and is arranged in numerical order. When the name of the patent proprietor is given, the decisions in this Table are also included within the alphabetical listing in the main Table of Cases.

TABLE OF STATUTES

Bold *type indicates a reprinted section.*

TABLE OF STATUTORY INSTRUMENTS

Bold *type indicates a reprinted article, regulation or rule.*

TABLE OF COURT RULES

Bold *type indicates a reprinted rule.*

TABLE OF INTERNATIONAL CONVENTIONS AND TREATIES AND RELATED RULES AND REGULATIONS

TABLE OF EUROPEAN PATENT OFFICE GUIDELINES

TABLE OF EC DIRECTIVES

TABLE OF EC REGULATIONS

Bold *type indicates a reprinted article or recital.*

UK RETAINED EU LAW

SECTION 1

Commentary on Section 1

Scope of the section

After the last paragraph, add new paragraphs:

An opinion which may be instructive to UK and European practitioners and which contains a lengthy   **1.04**
and detailed review of pertinent US decisions was handed down in response to a petition for rehearing
and rehearing *en banc* in *American Axle & Mfg. v Neapco Holdings LLC* (Fed. Cir. 2020) following an
earlier 2019 opinion. In the outcome, the following claim was held ineligible under s.101:

> "22. A method for manufacturing a shaft assembly of a driveline system, the driveline system further
> including a first driveline component and a second driveline component, the shaft assembly being
> adapted to transmit torque between the first driveline component and the second driveline component,
> the method comprising: providing a hollow shaft member; tuning a mass and a stiffness of at least
> one liner, and inserting the at least one liner into the shaft member; wherein the at least one liner is
> a tuned resistive absorber for attenuating shell mode vibrations and wherein the at least one liner is
> a tuned reactive absorber for attenuating bending mode vibrations."

The claim required use of a natural law relating frequency to mass and stiffness—i.e., Hooke's law—
but did not identify the "particular [tuned] liners" or the "improved method" of tuning the liners to
achieve the claimed result. Neither established processes nor "improved" processes for implementing
the underlying natural laws had been claimed. While AAM might have discovered patentable refine-
ments of the prior art process, such as particular uses of sophisticated finite element analysis models during its design process, neither the specifics of any novel computer modelling, nor the specifics of any
experimental modal analysis had been included as limitations in claim 22. These unclaimed features
could therefore not function to remove that claim from the realm of ineligible subject-matter. The
specification's concept of tuning was merely results-based. What was missing was any physical structure
or steps for achieving the claimed result. The focus of the claimed advance here was simply the concept
of achieving that result, by whatever structures or steps happened to work.

In contrast, the following claim was held arguably patent-eligible:

> "1. A method for manufacturing a shaft assembly of a driveline system, the driveline system further
> including a first driveline component and a second driveline component, the shaft assembly being
> adapted to transmit torque between the first driveline component and the second driveline component,
> the method comprising: providing a hollow shaft member; tuning at least one liner to attenuate at
> least two types of vibration transmitted through the shaft member; and positioning the at least one
> liner within the shaft member such that the at least one liner is configured to damp shell mode vibra-
> tions in the shaft member by an amount that is greater than or equal to about 2%, and the at least one
> liner is also configured to damp bending mode vibrations in the shaft member, the at least one liner
> being tuned to within about ±20% of a bending mode natural frequency of the shaft assembly as
> installed in the driveline system."

The patentees argued that invention was in the tuning of a liner in order to produce frequencies that
dampened both the shell mode and bending mode vibrations simultaneously, and it was held that because
the claim required "positioning" in addition to tuning and might reflect a broader definition of tuning,
the case should be remanded to the district court to address the eligibility of claim 1 and its dependent
claims in the first instance. Readers will note that a corresponding EP-A-1994291 is currently under
examination, and that it was objected under art.84 EPC and the Guidelines for Examination at F-IV 4.10
in the first examination report that an attempt to define the claimed subject-matter in terms of the result
to be achieved was not allowable because it appeared possible to provide a more specific definition of
how that effect was to be achieved. In their response, the patentees have argued that the technical effect of the features claimed were that both shell mode vibration and bending mode vibration and/or tor-
sion mode vibration could be attenuated in a single device using lightweight liners of inexpensive materi-

als so that shaft assemblies could be manufactured at reduced cost and weight. In both jurisdictions proceedings are on-going and future events may provide useful insights.

EPO Enlarged Appeal Board Decision in G 3/08 PRESIDENT'S REFERENCE and further references in G 1/19 Patentability of computer implemented simulation and G 3/19 Plants produced by essentially biological processes

Replace the last paragraph with:

1.08   A decision of the Enlarged Board in G 3/19 was issued on May 14, 2020 and is also discussed at §76A.05. The two questions were re-phrased by the Enlarged Board. The first was too general and unspecific since, if followed to its logical conclusion, it would effectively give the Administrative Council, as the authority empowered by the EPC to adopt the Implementing Regulations, a *"carte blanche"* to deviate from established case law and give a particular meaning to any Article of the EPC by means of the Rules of the Implementing Regulations and would open the door to circumventing the statutory procedures for amending the Convention itself. The second question likewise needed to be re-phrased to ensure that it was unencumbered by the opinion of the EPO President as the originator of the referral. The true object of the referral could be paraphrased as follows:

i.   With regard to the exception to patentability of "essentially biological processes for the production of plants and animals", does EPC art.53(b) permit only a single interpretation or could it bear a wider scope of interpretation?

ii.   Does EPC art.53(b) allow a dynamic interpretation in the sense that its meaning may change over time?

iii.   And if so, can an amendment to the Implementing Regulations give effect to a change of meaning resulting from a dynamic interpretation of EPC art.53(b)?

The following single question articulated the real issues at stake in the referral:

"Taking into account developments that occurred after a decision by the Enlarged Board of Appeal giving an interpretation of the scope of the exception to patentability of essentially biological processes for the production of plants or animals in Article 53(b) EPC, could this exception have a negative effect on the allowability of product claims or product-by-process claims directed to plants, plant material or animals, if the claimed product is exclusively obtained by means of an essentially biological process or if the claimed process feature define an essentially biological process?"

After a lengthy discussion of the legal issues including case law implementing G 2/12 *Tomato II* and G 2/13 *Broccoli II*, grammatical, systematic and teleological interpretations of EPC art.53(b), any subsequent agreement or practice under art.31(3)(a) and (b) of the Vienna Convention, national laws of the contracting states before and after decision G 2/12, and historical interpretation including the *travaux préparatoires* for EPC r.28(2), the single question above was answered as follows:

"Taking into account developments after decisions G 2/12 and G 2/13 of the Enlarged Board of Appeal, the exception to patentability of essentially biological processes for the production of plants or animals in Article 53(b) EPC has a negative effect on the allowability of product claims and product-by-process claims directed to plants, plant material or animals, if the claimed product is exclusively obtained by means of an essentially biological process or if the claimed process features define an essentially biological process.

This negative effect does not apply to European patents granted before 1 July 2017 and European patent applications which were filed before that date and are still pending."

Readers may note that despite the requirement of EPC art.52(1) which flows from art.27(1) of the TRIPS agreement that patents should be granted in all fields of technology, the opinion of the Enlarged Board is entirely silent about TRIPS, and there was no mention of the express provision in art.27(3)(b) that essentially biological processes for the production of plants or animals may be excluded from patentability. The opinion is criticised by Mike Snodin, "G 3/19: A need to improve the perception of independence of the EPO Boards of Appeal?" 2020 10 *CIPA* 7–12 and in a further article of his entitled "G 3/19: Do flaws in the EBA's reasoning amplify concerns regarding the perception of independence of the EPO Boards of Appeal?" 2020 10 *CIPA* 13–17.

Computer programs—further UK opinions

After the last paragraph, add new paragraphs:

1.10   In *Lenovo (Singapore)* BL O/017/20, which related to processing user handwriting strokes to determine possible words being input, spell-checking these and presenting the results to the user (where the results are determined from a combined weighting of the possible words and the spell-check), the Hearing Officer disagreed with the patent examiner and instead adopted the applicant's submitted broader definition of the contribution that the invention related to handwriting recognition generally and to include both the input and output (to the handwriting recognition "engine"). The Hearing Officer then considered whether the contribution was technical in nature, and again agreed with the applicant that signpost (iv) from *AT&T/CVON* as modified by *HTC v Apple* applied in that the contribution provided a better computer—the problem of improving a handwriting engine without improved OCR is solved by the claimed invention. As such, it was ruled that the claimed invention provided a technical contribution and was not excluded for defining a program for a computer *as such*.

In *Lenovo (Singapore)* BL O/305/20 however, which related to using context characteristics (such as location data or calendar data) for a user to refine search queries including ambiguous terms, the Hearing Officer did not consider providing more pertinent search results from a search query through the use of context characteristics to predict the user's actual intent and disambiguate query terms to be technical—instead ruling that the claimed invention was an exercise in data and information manipulation and selection and thus the claimed invention was excluded matter being a program for a computer as such.

In *Adobe Systems Incorporated* BL O/530/19, which related to an internet browser that created a "trigger area" around a link on a webpage such that when a cursor enters the trigger area the link content is preloaded and cached so that if the link is clicked then the content can be loaded from cache, no search had been performed by the patent examiner on the basis that the subject-matter of the application related to excluded subject-matter being a computer program as such. The Hearing Officer was passed the application to make a decision on the papers. The contribution was held to be a method of reducing web page loading times from the perspective of a user in a bandwidth-efficient manner by detecting user interactions with trigger areas and downloading content pre-emptively for faster display to a user should a link be clicked. The argument was rejected that the contribution was technical because it reduces network bandwidth usage and therefore had an effect outside of the computer (i.e. an effect on the network) and also the argument that the contribution was technical because cache memory was hardware—the effect was considered to be purely in software at the computer on which the software was executed. Further, the Hearing Officer considered that the invention circumvented the problem of bandwidth limitation by pre-loading content rather than providing a solution to the bandwidth limitation, so did not align with the respective signpost from *AT&T*. It was therefore concluded that the subject-matter was excluded because it related to a program for a computer as such.

In *Adobe Systems Incorporated* BL O/549/19, the claimed invention related to recommending actions to create an image and recommending images to demonstrate the effects of software actions in image editing/asset management software. For example, actions might include cropping or applying a filter to an image. The claimed invention represented actions and assets (i.e. media data) in a vector space in order to determine distances between actions and assets, which was then used to determine the recommendations output by the method. The contribution proposed by the applicants was "a means for autonomously determining a recommended set of actions for an asset representation based on analysis of the asset representation (including a distance in vector space between the asset representation and the set of actions) and pre-processing the asset representation with said set of actions while recommending the actions to a user". The Hearing Officer considered the *AT&T* signposts and concluded that the subject-matter of the claimed invention was excluded both for being a computer program as such and a mathematical method as such, rejecting the agent's argument that the technical contribution was the same as in *Vicom* as it related to speeding up image processing. Instead the contribution was considered to relate to recommending image processing rather than speeding up the actual image processing.

In *ION Geophysical Corp* BL O/774/19, the application related to a networked system for sharing data between multiple operators or entities in a maritime environment (such as marine installations or vessels, such as in an oil and gas marine field) where the shared data allows each operator to optimise its operations and complete tasks in a more efficient manner, each having various operational plans associated with them that can include task, positioning and/or timing information. The Hearing Officer indicated that the subject-matter was clearly technical, in that it related to the technical field of offshore exploration, drilling and production. The contribution was considered to include, as submitted by the agent, determining improvements to the operational plans, improving a physical operation and subsequently performing that operation—using (positive synergistic) "linkages" which are used to define and improve tasks to be performed by operators in a more co-ordinated and efficient manner. The Hearing Officer considered the inventive contribution to be technical in nature because it provided and implemented more efficient operations within a marine field, and thus decided that the subject-matter of the claimed invention was not excluded matter as it did not relate solely to either a computer program as such or a business method as such.

In *Google LLC* BL O/611/19, the claimed invention related to identifying a user at a particular location using facial recognition in order to provide payment processing for the user. The Hearing Officer adopted the agent's proposed contribution, being a new way of providing hands-free identification that is secure and efficient, and also agreed that the first *AT&T* signpost was met. The task of automatically identifying a user is not a task that is carried out solely within a computer but requires the retrieval and processing of images from the real world, and the issue of security and privacy for users when using computing devices is a technical problem which has an effect outside of the computer so that the claimed method makes a technical contribution by providing additional security and privacy benefits to users. The Hearing Officer also considered the contribution not to lie solely within the business method exclusion because of the provision of a new or more secure method of identification or authentication. Accordingly, the claimed invention was not excluded as a computer program or business method.

In *Suunto OY* BL O/461/19, the claimed invention related to a system/method whereby events can be created and joined using data collected from multiple sports watches. The Hearing Officer considered the contribution to be a computer-implemented method for receiving sport-specific data from two sports watches, including movement information collected in real-time, and notifying the users of the sports watches of an event based on a common context within the data, thus simplifying the creation of an event and enabling the sharing of sport-specific data in real-time. Following the summary in *AT&T* of the holding in *Vicom*, that if, ignoring the computer program, the claimed invention were patentable, collecting movement information in real time is a technical activity as this involves collecting real data from sensors and has technical significance in the real world. The Hearing Officer concluded that the computer program underlying the invention was being used to carry out a technical process (collection and comparison of real data) to improve the adaptability of sports watches, and thus the contribution was technical in nature and fell outside of the excluded matter of a computer program.

In *Lenovo (Singapore) PTE Ltd v Comptroller General of Patents* [2020] EWHC 1706 (Pat) (July 9, 2020), the claimed invention related to splitting payment between multiple payment cards in the event of "card clash" where multiple payment cards are presented to a contactless payment reader. In decision BL O/754/19 the Hearing Officer had concluded that the claimed invention was excluded from patentability on the grounds that it related to a computer program and a business method as such. Having considered the reasoning in the Hearing Officer's decision, it was ruled that the claimed invention was not excluded as either computer program as such or a business method as such because it was not considered trivial to automatically split payment between multiple cards without user confirmation being required (as in the cited prior art). Specifically, the effect of solving the problem of card clash without the user needing to take any further physical step at the point they use their contactless payment cards was considered to have a technical character and therefore not be excluded as either a computer program as such or a business method as such.

In *Lenovo (Singapore) Pte Ltd* BL O/007/21, the claimed invention related to a computer-implemented method for estimating the battery life of a computer or mobile phone. Specifically, the method receives user input to select the particular applications desired to be run and the duration it is desired to run them and then assesses what power consumption is made by user-selected applications running on the device and the baseline battery usage rate and outputs an estimated length of device operation time remaining. Considering the prior art cited, the contribution was accepted to be providing on a computing device a prediction of the time that the battery will power the device based on the expected battery usage of user submitted application information together with baseline battery usage and current remaining power. The Hearing Officer ruled that the mere selecting or entering of options on a computer was not a technical contribution, and because the method merely allowed a user to select and deselect applications for execution on the device in order to increase/decrease the battery life rather than, for example, automatically closing applications in order to extend battery life, it is the user that makes the choices rather than the invention and thus the user is interactive with the device but the invention is not providing a technical contribution nor having a technical effect on a process which is carried out outside of the device. The problem of battery life, which was accepted as a technical problem, was not therefore solved in a technical sense by the user deciding to run fewer applications based on the information provided by the system. Therefore the contribution was ruled to fall solely within the matter excluded as a program for a computer as such.

In *Smartglyph Ltd* BL O/037/21, the claimed invention related to a system for scanning two-dimensional codes that retrieves associated rich media content (such as videos, images and documents) for scanned codes identified in a database rather than simply provides a hyperlink or directs the device to a webpage. The construction of the term "two-dimensional" was debated but it was decided by the Hearing Officer to take a broad construction based on the normal understanding of the term by a notional skilled person, i.e. an indicator having two dimension such as a bar code or QR code, rather than a more specific construction put forward by the applicant based on an embodiment of the patent specification (to which the claim was not clearly limited, in the opinion of the Hearing Officer). Considering the *AT&T* signposts, the Hearing Officer decided that the first signpost was not met because the contribution was fully within the computer system in line with *Lantana Ltd v Comptroller-General of Patents, Designs and Trade Mark* [2014] EWCA Civ 1463 as there was no technical effect beyond

[4]

the retrieval of the rich media from the server and the transfer of files between the system components, which is entirely conventional. Considering *Lenovo (Singapore) PTR Ltd v Comptroller General of Patents* [2020] EWHC 1706 (Pat), the Hearing Officer ruled that the claims did not specify that user-specific rich media was retrieved so no user input would be saved and therefore this case law did not apply. Considering the fifth *AT&T* signpost, the Hearing Officer determined that the perceived problem as set out in the specification does not relate to a technical problem—while the invention avoids the need to provide additional scannable elements (i.e. existing barcodes or QR codes were sufficient) in order to provide users with access to rich media, this was done by no more than a computer program that is used to embody the database containing the link between scannable element and two-dimensional code, thus the fifth signpost was not met. In conclusion, the Hearing Officer noted that the scanning device and server are unchanged by the invention and the connection between computers was assumed to be conventional so the invention was implemented by a computer program and a database. Thus, the invention does not provide a technical solution to a technical problem as the problem relates to the access of rich media and the solution relates to a computer program and this is not technical in nature, therefore the application relates to a computer program as such and was excluded from patentability.

In *Renaissance Technologies LLC* BL O/045/21, the claimed invention related to a computer system/method for executing time synchronised trades at multiple exchanges. The underlying problem addressed was to overcome both (a) that a single exchange cannot always fulfil a large order for a financial instrument cost-effectively, and (b) if simply dividing the larger order into smaller orders at multiple exchanges then, due to latencies in the speed of execution per exchange, this opens up the possibility that high frequency traders can detect the order at one exchange and "front run" orders at another exchange. To address both these problems, co-located servers are placed at the multiple exchanges and an execution time is specified for all of the smaller orders such that they all execute at substantially the same execution time at each exchange. However, the Hearing Officer decided that, because the use of co-located servers was well known in the prior art the only contribution over prior art trading systems was an improved trading system and thus the claimed invention was still a system for doing business and therefore excluded from patentability. Further, after considering the *AT&T* signposts, the Hearing Officer decided that none of the signposts were met and thus the claimed invention was also excluded from patentability for being a computer program as such.

In *Fisher-Rosemount Systems Inc* BL O/141/21, the claimed invention related to a computer-implemented method of managing a "workflow" (typically a repair operation) in a process plant (such as a chemical or petroleum plant), where a set of operations (e.g. to fix equipment in the plant) for a task is generated and a nearby maintenance worker with the proper skill set to perform the set of operations is identified and sent a permission token (e.g. to allow access to the equipment) and instructions to perform the set of operations, after which the method verifies that the task is completed by communicating with the equipment on which the task is performed. The Hearing Officer considered the first *AT&T* signpost and decided that it was met due to the use of the permission tokens to allow (and then revoke upon verified completion of the task) correct access to only tasked maintenance workers, all of which are technical steps and which meant that enhancements to safety in a process plant were delivered by technical means, and so the claimed invention was not excluded from patentability for being a computer program or business method as such and remitted to examination.

In *Reaux-Savonte v Comptroller-General of Patents, Designs and Trade Marks* [2021] EWHC 78 (Ch), the claimed invention related to a structured array of data suitable for artificial intelligence applications which was determined by a Hearing Officer to relate to unpatentable subject-matter, being a computer program as such, and which was the subject of an appeal by the applicant for the Hearing Officer applying the *AT&T* signposts unduly restrictively. The technical contribution of the invention was determined to be a hierarchical data structure that facilitates evolution of code over time. Reconsidering the *AT&T* signposts it was ruled that the Hearing Officer was correct in their analysis that none of these were met by the invention (and it was noted that the description supporting the claimed invention did not provide sufficient technical detail to enable an understanding of the technical aspects of the claimed invention) and the Hearing Officer's decision to reject the application as excluded for being a computer program as such was upheld.

In *F-Secure Corp* BL O/420/21, the claimed invention related to a method using a proxy server to intercept network traffic from client devices which identifies any requests from client devices being sent to tracking services and allows a small number of these requests to be transmitted to the tracking services and the responses to these tracking requests is stored and analysed to generate a recipe that is then used to mimic the tracking data to be sent to tracking services for client devices while preventing real data from client devices from being sent to tracking services. The Hearing Officer determined the contribution to be an improved method of providing convincing fake tracking response to a tracking service for the purpose of increasing the prospect of websites loading without disruption on client devices while preserving the privacy of the users of the client devices, the method comprising a proxy server (i) to send some initial genuine requests from client devices to the tracking service; (ii) to analyse the responses

[5]

to the initial requests, and (iii) to use that analysis to generate the subsequent fake convincing responses. The Hearing Officer decided that this contribution was not technical because there was no technical effect on the user devices because it is not a technical problem to maintain user privacy, thus the claimed invention does not reveal a technical contribution to the state of the art and is excluded from patentability as it relates to a computer program as such.

In *Imagination Technologies* BL O/420/21, the claimed invention related to a system that receives a stream of data values and determines the median values of this data. It works by operating on these values and storing these as intermediate values. The data received is contiguous and by storing intermediate median values it allows the system to use some of the values already calculated to calculate the next median. Related divisional application had the data stream specifically limited to being pixel values, audio samples or signal samples thus relating to real world data and accepted as prima facie allowable. Due to the applicant's submission that the system would be implemented on fixed function circuitry the Hearing Officer accepted that there was no exclusion for being a computer program as such, but required the applicant to delete the claims from the application relating to computer programs for implementing the claimed method. Further, the Hearing Officer accepted that there was no exclusion for being a mathematical method as such because the fixed function circuitry was not conventional hardware component with a new set of instructions, and because there was a technical contribution in the reduction of physical size of silicon area of the hardware and power consumption for a median determining unit.

In *Imagination Technologies* BL O/296/21, the claimed invention related to method and systems for processing images in accordance with a traditional computer vision algorithm using a neural network accelerator. The contribution determined by the Hearing Officer was in performing two steps: (i) generating a neural network that represents a traditional computer vision algorithm; and (ii) processing images, via that neural network, using a neural network accelerator. Considering the fifth *AT&T* signpost, the Hearing Officer accepted that this was met as the technical problem addressed by the invention was how to process images in accordance with a traditional computer vision algorithm more efficiently, both in terms of silicon area and processing power and the subject-matter of the claims solves this problem rather than circumvents it.

In *ARM Ltd and Apical Ltd* BL O/519/21, the claimed invention related to image processing technology, whereby a sequential set of image frames representing a dynamic scene are processed. The objects in the frame are identified and classified by an object classifier in two subsequent cycles of object classification, the first a course classification and the second a finer classification. The object classifier may for example be used to detect the presence of a human face or animal in an image. The Hearing Officer decided that the contribution of the independent claims was in the administrative solution in selecting particular classification data based on control data from an external data source, implemented as a program for a computer, and therefore excluded from patentability being a computer program as such. However, dependent claims that specified that the control data is derived from the sensor data from external sensors and also that the sensor senses the availability of a state of charge of an electric battery to power the image processing system, an amount of available storage accessible by the image processing system, an amount of computer resource available or an amount of electrical power available to the image processing system would provide a link between the status of the hardware of the system and the operation of the image classification system which was considered to constitute a technical contribution and therefore these claims would not be excluded from patentability for being computer programs as such.

In *Lookout, Inc* BL O/701/21, the claimed invention related to a computer-implemented method of multi-factor authentication of access to a network resource via a server by a second authorising user after entering a first credential (e.g. user name and password). The Hearing Officer considered the technical contribution to be

"access control in which an access request made by a verified user is authorised by a second authorising user, the identity of the authorising user and a device associated with that user being determined by an authorising server, the authorising server sending a request for authorisation to the device and the authorising person responding with a credential, verified by the authorising server, to provide the authorisation."

The Hearing Officer found that this claimed invention provided a contribution that was technical using the first and fifth *AT&T* signposts, as it provided an effect outside of a single computer and didn't merely circumvent the problem of authenticating a user. The application was remitted to examination to attend to any other matters remaining prior to grant of the application.

In *Thunderhead Ltd* BL O/530/21, the claimed invention related to a computer-implemented method of testing multiple variants of content for delivery to content consumers, to assess the effectiveness of multiple variants of content displayed to users on a web page with a view to improving the content. The alleged advantage of the claimed invention was that it provided a more efficient method of generating multiple versions of content, avoiding the problem of the prior art where many of pieces of content had to be prepared manually for multi-variant testing. The argument that the claimed invention avoided "process clash" in a way that was broadly equivalent to the "card clash" found to be patentable in *Lenovo (Singapore) PTE Ltd v Comptroller General of Patents* [2020] EWHC 1706 (Pat) (July 9, 2020) BL O/754/19 (see above) was rejected by the Hearing Officer. Instead, considering *Aerotel* and the *AT&T* signposts, the Hearing Officer considered that steps 3 & 4 of *Aerotel* failed and that none of the signposts were met as the process occurred wholly within the computer, the process didn't change how the computer or any networked computer ran internally, the process provided a new method of content assembly but this was not a generally applicable method of operating a computer, any potential improvement to efficiency does not apply to the computer itself and finally the process circumvents the problem of "process clash" rather than solving or eliminating it (and it is noted from the text of the decision that perhaps process clash wasn't fully developed as a concept to the Hearing Officer, which may have contributed to the decision). In conclusion, the application was rejected as excluded from patentability as both a computer program as such and also a business method.

In *Jaguar Land Rover* BL O/609/21, the claimed invention related to a computer-implemented method for determining the time required for increased the state of charge of a vehicle battery to meet a minimum user requirement, to reduce "range anxiety" in drivers of electric vehicles. The Hearing Officer decided that the contribution was

"a computer implemented method of predicting the time required to charge an electric vehicle to meet first and second user requirements determined by taking into account the routine of use of charge of the energy storage means, and subsequently outputting together, indications of time requirements for increasing the state of charge of the energy storage means to a value at or above the minimum state of charge, for each of the first and second user."

This contribution was considered by the Hearing Officer not to have satisfied any of the five *AT&T* signposts, in particular the first signpost wasn't satisfied because the output was a prediction presented to a user via a user interface with no link to a technical step or control outside of the computer and the fifth signpost wasn't satisfied because the contribution provides a circumvention by telling the user how long to charge the battery for rather than solving the problem of battery charge. The Hearing Officer added that "range anxiety" was not a technical problem, and presenting charging scenario information to user was not a technical solution. The Hearing Officer suggested that adding a step of "charging the energy storage means to a value" would conceivably result in a claim being patentable and avoid the exclusion for being a computer program as such, as charging a battery was a technical step and would confer technical effect to the claimed invention. The application was remitted to examination as there was scope to amend to overcome the excluded matter objection and the Hearing Officer considered that the suggested amendment would also seem novel and inventive over the cited prior art.

In *Hitachi* BL O/877/21, the claimed invention related to a "water balance visualization system/ method" for activities in the water supply industry and provided a visualisation of the demand for water and forecasts how that demand might change (however it is noted that the term "water balance" was not well defined in the specification). The Hearing Officer determined the contribution to be

"a computer implemented method, and associated computer application, which provides a graphical visualisation of water balance for a water supply facility to facilitate more efficient management of the water supply facility as regards to any water losses in the water supply network, the visualisation based on calculations using values from a storage device which stores information on the details of water consumption by supply facilities and information on proposed known solutions"

and the arguments at the hearing focussed on whether there was any technical effect on a process carried on outside of a computer. Ultimately, the Hearing Officer refused the patent application as relating solely to a computer program as such/business method because while displaying information on screen might help make decisions to improve the financial efficiency of water supply management, it did not inherently improve water supply or its control, thus solving a business problem. The *AT&T* signposts were ruled not to have been met by the Hearing Officer.

In *Unanimous A.I.* BL O/018/22, the claimed invention related to procuring (vector) inputs from multiple users in response to a question and combined these to provide each user feedback as to what the other users have input, providing a "collective answer" to the question, by moving a pointer on a screen to the same position relative to a "target board" on screen. The applicant submitted that the contribution was

"a new mechanism which allows multiple users, in distributed locations, to interact together via vector inputs to their individual devices to collaboratively influence the position of a single, shared pointer and hence to make a collective selection, or in other words to make an input into a computer."

The Hearing Officer agreed and considered the contribution to be technical, as it could be defined in terms of an "input device", and referred the application back to the examiner to conclude the examination process.

In *Wally Tzara* BL O/303/22, the claimed invention related to tracking the trend in the value of a quantity that varies over time (against two suitably chosen threshold values), and more particularly about providing an alert upon detecting a reversal in the trend. The Hearing Officer ruled that the contribution was

> "identifying the onset of a trend reversal in a value of a quantity, by tracking the value and repeatedly comparing it against a first threshold, and if the first threshold is crossed then repeatedly comparing it against a second threshold, and triggering an alert if the value crosses the second threshold, wherein the two thresholds are defined so as to enable the identification of a trend reversal. Additionally the variable represents a value in the field of meteorology, climatology, seismology, economy, population dynamics or cosmology."

However, as the claimed invention did not relate to specific use in any number of potential fields in which it could be used (e.g. meteorology, climatology, seismology, cosmology), the application could not be granted as it was excluded as a program for a computer as such, a method of doing business and a mathematical method—however if limited to one or more of these fields it would be considered technical. In *Wally Tzara* BL O/410/22, an amended set of claims was considered, but the Hearing Officer remained unconvinced that the claimed used of technical data removed it from the excluded category of a business method, and again requested a limitation to an application or effect in a technical field and the application was refused.

In *International Business Machines Corp* BL O/390/22, the claimed invention related to a computer-implemented method of performing large scale "entity resolution" (data de-duplication of single, identifiable separate objects) using active learning (learning the composition of several matching functions together to create entity resolution rules) and using a "two-level memoing cache hierarchy comprising distributed memory cache and distributed disk cache". The Hearing Officer identified the contribution as "using a two-level cache hierarchy comprising distributed memory cache and distributed disk cache for storing link vector tables for intermediate results to be used as a memoing cache when performing active learning of large-scale entity resolution." The Hearing Officer did not consider large-scale entity resolution in itself as a technical process, nor as a technical form of indexing and did not agree that the invention related to using functional data (as per the EPO definition)—in particular noting that the data being processed was not limited in the claim to any specific form of data, noting the applicant's arguments (but dismissing them) that the data related to real-world entities. Considering the *AT&T* signposts: no technical contribution on a process outside a computer was found thus the first signpost was not met, the Hearing Officer noting that the data was not limited in any way to a real world entity/application; as the efficiencies of the claimed invention only arose in the specific use of distributed cache memory for entity resolution, there was deemed to be no contribution at the architecture level thus the second signpost wasn't met; the Hearing Officer noted that while the claimed method may be more efficient in removing redundant calculations, this was only to provide better entity resolution and not a better computer itself and thus the fourth signpost was not met; and as the invention circumvented the problem of improving efficiency of active learning for entity resolution using an improved algorithm thus the fifth signpost was not met. Thus the Hearing Officer refused the application as lying solely in the excluded field of a computer program as such.

In *Beijing Didi Infinity Technology* BL O/445/22, the claimed invention related to a computer-implemented method and system for queuing transportation/ride-hailing service requests in a geographical area. The Hearing Officer identified the contribution to be

> "a system used to prioritise and provide transportation service requests to users, that automatically activates a transportation request queue for transportation requests received from remote terminal devices when the number of transportation requests received is greater than a dynamic activation threshold, the dynamic activation threshold being dependent upon the number of activated queues in the area. The system determining when the number of transportation service requests is less than a deactivation threshold and as a result automatically deactivating the transportation request queue."

The Hearing Officer considered that the application did not meet any of the *AT&T* signposts as it was primarily a business method for activating/deactivating a queue of customer requests for transportation in order to prioritise the requests. Notably, considering the *AT&T* signposts, the Hearing Officer considered that the transport process outside the computer was unchanged (thus signpost one was not met); the computer and processor on which the system is run is entirely conventional (thus signposts two and three were not met; and while the system is more processor efficient, this was *due to a better program rather than a better computer* thus signpost four was not met); and as the problem identified in the application was "to provide a balance between non-priority requests and priority requests, the queue should be activated only when necessary", the problem was a business problem, thus overcoming this business problem did not provide a relevant technical contribution. The Hearing Officer ruled that the invention was therefore not technical in nature and that the claims were excluded as a method of doing business (and a program for a computer).

In *Zebra Technologies Corp* BL O/623/22, the claimed invention related to providing a computer-implemented central ledger that could be updated throughout a supply chain, making tracing easier, mentioning several use cases including pipeline inspection, traffic management, and public safety "citations". The Hearing Officer considered that the contribution was

"a computer implemented method for securely recording events on a distributed ledger wherein the ledger may be used with an end user application, the method comprising a networked data capture device, first terminal and distributed ledger, wherein one of the first terminal or data capture device is configured to apply a recordation flag to captured product data causing the product data to be recorded on a distributed ledger."

The Hearing Officer considered that the first signpost was not met as the effect, technical or otherwise, was not carried out outside the computer. However, the Hearing Officer considered that the second signpost was met as, regardless of the data being processed, the specific connectivity between the data capture assembly, first terminal and distributed ledger remained unchanged (and so the claimed technical effect operated at the "architecture level"). The Hearing Officer considered the third and fourth signposts not to apply. The Hearing Officer also considered the fifth signpost met—"I consider this to be a solution to the problem of providing a secure data acquisition and transmission network that is integrated with an existing data processing system. Does this relate to a technical problem? In as much as it relates to several physical devices and their particular interconnectivity, I believe it is." The Hearing Officer decided that the invention provided a technical contribution and remitted the application back to the examiner for final preparations to ensure compliance prior to grant.

In *Renaissance Technologies v Comptroller* [2021] EWHC 2113 (Ch), the invention related to a computer-based financial trading system that allowed orders to be broken up into smaller orders to be placed at multiple exchanges but synchronising the order executions to avoid front-running by other market participants. The claimed invention addresses this problem through a combination of co-located servers and utilising stored timing information. This enables the co-located servers to place orders at each of the exchanges substantially simultaneously. The original examiner's opinion was that the hardware was a conventional arrangement of networked computers and that the contribution lay in the functionality or method performed by the hardware not in the hardware itself. Following this, the Hearing Officer decided that the primary problem solved was that of "cost-effectively fulfilling large orders on financial exchanges" and that the claimed invention addressed the problem by "sending smaller orders to computers associated with each financial exchange and delaying all the smaller orders until a predetermined execution time." The Hearing Officer found the contribution to be

"a trading system to cost-effectively fulfil large orders in an electronic trading environment that includes a plurality of financial exchanges by: dividing a large order into a plurality of smaller orders; transmitting a plurality of trade instructions each containing one of the smaller orders and a transaction execution time to a plurality of servers each associated with one of the financial exchanges; receiving and storing the trade instructions at the plurality of servers; and, submitting the smaller orders to the associated exchange when the current time is the transaction execution time, whereby the smaller orders are placed substantially simultaneously."

The Hearing Officer decided that the claimed invention was excluded as a business method and a computer program as such. The court reviewed the Hearing Officer's decision and rejected the contention that the Hearing Officer had made an error in defining the technical contribution, and accepted most of the Hearing Officer's conclusions on the *AT&T* signposts but noted that on the fifth signpost that the claimed invention addressed a technical problem but however failed to provide a technical solution as the problem was circumvented by moving the servers closer to the exchange rather than solving the problem. The appeal was thus dismissed.

In *Michael Adewunmi Idowu* BL O/604/21, the invention related to a device and method of modelling a Collatz-based number dynamical system having a plurality of decision-based configurable functions and results thereupon by one or more other components. The Hearing Officer considered the contribution to be

[9]

"a method and system for understanding the dynamics of the Collatz function by determining rules to find the next odd number in the Collatz sequence from an input number using its congruence class modulo 18, and compiling the data on relationships between Collatz height values of input numbers in different congruence classes with the purpose of using the resulting system of rules to investigate the Collatz function and how it may be generalised to other mathematical functions."

The Hearing Officer concluded, in line with *Gale's Application*, that the claimed invention related to a mathematical method and therefore was excluded, and refused the application.

Computer programs—further EPO opinions

After the first paragraph, add new paragraphs:

1.11
On July 15, 2020, the Enlarged Board of Appeal held oral proceedings for the reference under T 489/14 now entitled G1/19 *CONNOR/Patentability of computer-implemented simulations*.

As previously explained, three questions were posed to the Enlarged Board of Appeal.

The first question asked whether the computer-implemented simulation of a technical system or process could solve a technical problem by producing a technical effect which goes beyond the simulation's implementation on a computer, if the computer-implemented simulation is claimed as such. The Enlarged Board of Appeal answered in the affirmative, saying that the computer-implemented simulation of a technical system or process that is claimed as such can, for the purpose of inventive step, solve a technical problem by producing a technical effect going beyond the simulation's implementation on a computer (e.g. the T 1227/05 *INFINEON/Circuit Simulation* case).

The second question posed was: what are the relevant criteria for assessing whether a computer-implemented simulation claimed as such solves a technical problem and, in particular, is it sufficient condition that the simulation is based, at least in part, on technical principles underlying the simulated systems or processes? In answer, the Enlarged Board stated that for this assessment it is not sufficient condition that the simulation is based, in whole or in part, on technical principles underlying the simulated process or system. In their written opinion, the Enlarged Board did not see a need to provide criteria and left this open for interpretation based on the details of each individual case, as the EPC does not define what "technical" means and its definition may be fluid in future. The Enlarged Board went on to clarify that the *COMVIK* approach should continue to be used.

The third question was whether the answers to the previous two questions remained the same if the computer-implemented simulation is claimed as part of a design process, in particular for verifying a design? In answer, the Enlarged Board stated that the answers to the first and second questions are no different if the computer-implemented simulation is claimed as part of a design process, in particular for verifying a design. In conclusion, computer simulations are not viewed by the EPO as a separate category from computer-implemented inventions and should continue to be assessed in the same way as computer-implemented inventions.

It should be noted that the application the subject of G 1/19 has reverted to the Appeal Board and a summons to oral proceedings on 26 November 2021 has issued. The accompanying communication refers to G 1/19 at [128] explaining that in accordance with *COMVIK*, calculated numerical data reflecting the physical behaviour of a system modelled on a computer usually cannot establish the necessary technical character, but only in exceptional cases e.g. if the potential use of the data is limited to technical purposes. In the present appeal, data reflecting the movement of a crowd moving through an environment does not contribute to a technical effect relevant to inventive step and the data could be used for non-technical purposes e.g. in computer games or obtaining knowledge about the environment and accordingly the claimed subject-matter lacks inventive step. It remains to be seen whether the applicants, now Bentley Systems (UK) Ltd, can devise arguments or amendments sufficient to reverse the present view of the Board and result in allowance corresponding to US patents 7188056 and 7389210.

For commentary, see Fennell and Worley, "G 1/19 on simulations—they're not special, but some are patentable" [2021] 4 *CIPA* 13. Subsequent to the above decision, in T 1746/16 *CAVATERRA/Method and apparatus for the transfer of a money amount by using a two-dimension image code*, the invention aimed to avoid the need for sensitive data to be sent from a merchant's device to a server using two mobile phones. A merchant's mobile phone transferred all data relevant for the payment transaction via QR code to the customer's mobile phone. The payment data was then transmitted from the customer's mobile phone to the server via encrypted SMS including the authorisation PIN. The invention had the advantage that only one request had to be transmitted via the mobile phone network without connection to the Internet or a similar network. The prior art cited was silent about details of the software implementation of the transaction method, handling the data, decoding and encryption. These features contributed to the technical effect of the invention, maintaining a high security standard and a high safety level for the transaction, though some of them might be considered as non-technical features (see G 1/19, point 85 and T 0697/17 *MICROSOFT/SQL extensions*, point 5.2.5) and the claimed subject-matter was held to be allowable.

After the last paragraph, add new paragraphs:

In T1924/17 *ACCENTURE GLOBAL SERVICES/Data consistency management*, the Board considered that the computer-implemented features of the claimed invention involved "further" technical considerations, as it is necessary to consider the technical properties of the implementations of query processing in different kinds of database management systems. In particular, it was considered convincingly argued by the applicant that the claimed system, using a NoSQL data store and a Relational Database Management System (RDBMS), provides a performance improvement over an RDBMS as a sole data source, and that this improvement is a consequence of the above-discussed "further" technical considerations, which are adequately reflected in the claimed data consistency management system.

In T 0489/14 *BENTLEY SYSTEMS/Pedestrian simulation*, the claimed invention related to a computer-implemented method of modelling pedestrian crowd movement in an environment (taking into account dissatisfaction, frustration and obstructions for each pedestrian). The main purpose of the simulation is its use in a process for designing a venue. It simulates foot traffic/pedestrian flow in a simulated design for a venue, and revisions to the design can be made after examining results. The Board concluded that the relevant inventive step could not be based upon the simulation's implementation on a general purpose computer and instead it had to be determined whether simulation of crowd movement qualified as a technical effect (in particular the provision of information about the movement of simulated pedestrians through a modelled environment). The Board considered that the provision of calculated information by the claimed method had no direct link with physical reality (such as a change in or a measurement of a physical entity) and therefore could not constitute a technical effect. The Board noted that if the result of the claimed process was specifically adapted for the purpose of controlling a technical device, the technical effect that would result from this intended use of the data would be considered "implied" by the claim (although the Board found no such technical effect in the claimed invention). The Board also made a distinction between real technical effects (of physical entities), which should be treated as technical effects for the purpose of assessing inventive step, and "virtual or calculated" technical effects which were not achieved through an interaction with physical reality versus potential technical effects that once put to their intended use became real technical effects. The Board decided that claim 1 and all auxiliary claims submitted where unallowable and dismissed the appeal.

—Scheme, rule or method for doing business—UK opinions

After the last paragraph, add new paragraphs:

In *Beijing Didi Infinity Technology and Development Co Ltd* BL O/719/19, the invention concerned providing a transportation service comprising one or more taxis or private cars where a processor receives a request for a user terminal and estimates both a time it will take to fulfil the request and a hypothetical time to fulfil the request if it were switched to a car pool request and a user is provided with a recommendation to switch to a car pool service if that time is shorter and if the user accepts the request a service request is sent to one of the taxis or private cars. The Hearing Officer rejected the submissions of the applicant and concluded that the contribution was a programme that receives a message, efficiently calculates two transport times by utilising historical data, recommends the shorter time, then sends a message. The Hearing Officer went on to decide that the contribution was therefore excluded as a business method as such and also as a computer method as such.

1.12

In *Motorola Solutions Inc* BL O/030/20, the invention related to the pursuit of fugitives by analysing various input data to predict the likely route of the fugitive and then outputting directions to direct pursuit assets to capture the fugitive at a determined capture location. The Hearing Officer considered the contribution to be a computer-implemented method of determining a capture location of a fugitive and outputting information to direct pursuit assets to that location wherein the method uses a number of sources of information such as real-time video information and is conducted across modules of a network comprising a main computer including a cornering strategy module, a mapping module, and a fugitive tracking/intelligence module, the method providing the advantage of improving the effectiveness and efficiency of the capture operation. The Hearing Officer concluded that the problem addressed by the claimed invention was purely logistical or administrative, with no technical content as it related to efficiently directing assets and therefore related to excluded matter as a program for a computer and a method of doing business.

In *Lenovo (Singapore) PTE Ltd v Comptroller General of Patents* [2020] EWHC 1706 (Pat) (July 9, 2020), the claimed invention related to splitting payment between multiple payment cards in the event of "card clash" where multiple payment cards are presented to a contactless payment reader. In decision BL O/754/19 the Hearing Officer had concluded that the claimed invention was excluded from patentability on the grounds that it related to a computer program and a business method as such. Having considered the reasoning in the Hearing Officer's decision, it was ruled that the claimed invention was not excluded as either computer program as such or a business method as such because it was not considered trivial to automatically split payment between multiple cards without user confirmation being required (as in the cited prior art). Specifically, the effect of solving the problem of card clash without the user needing to take any further physical step at the point they use their contactless payment cards was considered to have a technical character and therefore not be excluded as either a computer program as such or a business method as such.

In *Renaissance Technologies LLC* BL O/045/21, the claimed invention related to a computer system/ method for executing time synchronised trades at multiple exchanges. The underlying problem addressed was to overcome both (a) that a single exchange cannot always fulfil a large order for a financial instrument cost-effectively and (b) if simply dividing the larger order into smaller orders at multiple exchanges then, due to latencies in the speed of execution per exchange, this opens up the possibility that high frequency traders can detect the order at one exchange and "front run" orders at another exchange. To address both these problems, co-located servers are placed at the multiple exchanges and an execution time is specified for all of the smaller orders such that they all execute at substantially the same execution time at each exchange. However, the Hearing Officer decided that, because the use of co-located servers was well known in the prior art the only contribution over prior art trading systems was an improved trading system and thus the claimed invention was still a system for doing business and therefore excluded from patentability. Further, after considering the *AT&T* signposts, the Hearing Officer decided that none of the signposts were met and thus the claimed invention was also excluded from patentability for being a computer program as such.

In *Fisher-Rosemount Systems Inc* BL O/141/21, the claimed invention related to a computer-implemented method of managing a "workflow" (typically a repair operation) in a process plant (such as a chemical or petroleum plant), where a set of operations (e.g. to fix equipment in the plant) for a task is generated and a nearby maintenance worker with the proper skill set to perform the set of operations is identified and sent a permission token (e.g. to allow access to the equipment) and instructions to perform the set of operations, after which the method verifies that the task is completed by communicating with the equipment on which the task is performed. The Hearing Officer considered the first *AT&T* signpost and decided that it was met due to the use of the permission tokens to allow (and then revoke upon verified completion of the task) correct access to only tasked maintenance workers, all of which are technical steps and which meant that enhancements to safety in a process plant were delivered by technical means, and so the claimed invention was not excluded from patentability for being a computer program or business method as such.

—EPO, US and Australian decisions concerning business methods

After the fourteenth paragraph (beginning "TO144/11 SATO MICHIHIRO/ Security rating system"), add new paragraphs:

1.13   In T 1749/14 *MAXIM/Mobile Personal Point-Of-Sale*, the claimed invention related to the use of a paired point-of-sale terminal and mobile phone. The Board decided that while a notional business person might come up with the abstract idea of avoiding the customer having to provide a PIN and account information to a merchant, the invention required new infrastructure, new devices and a new protocol (involving technical considerations linked to modified devices and their capabilities) as well as security relevant modifications to the transfer of sensitive information using new possibilities achieved by the modifications to the previously known mobile POS infrastructure. The Board therefore concluded that this goes beyond what the normal business person knows and concerns technical implementation details which are more than straightforward programming of a business idea (and thus is in the sphere of the technical expert and subject to the assessment of inventive step).

In T 1798/13 *SWISS REINSURANCE/Forecasting the value of a structured financial product*, the claimed invention related to a method of forecasting the value of a weather-based structured financial product using a weather model. The Board considered that a system for weather forecasting would be considered to have technical character but, because the claimed invention used already measured data, this meant that the claimed invention could not be attributed this technical character. The Board decided that "weather" is not a technical system that the skilled person can improve (or simulate with the purpose of trying to improve it), instead taking the view that modelling of the weather is rather a discovery or a scientific theory and therefore the claimed invention did not involve an inventive step.

In T 232/14 *INDEXTO/Method and apparatus for identifying, authenticating, tracking and tracing manufactured items*, the invention related to a method and apparatus for labelling and tracking items. The Board decided that using ranges of unit identifiers to label a number of consecutive unit identifiers of manufactured items was, at the level of generality in the claimed invention, a business method and therefore related to non-technical subject-matter.

After the penultimate paragraph, add new paragraph:

An automated notification system was held ineligible in *Electronic Communication Technologies v ShoppersChoice.com* (Fed. Cir. 2020) on the ground that the claim was directed to the abstract idea of "providing advance notification of the pickup or delivery of a mobile thing." Business practices designed to advise customers of the status of delivery of their goods had existed at least for several decades, if not longer. Security enhancements referred to in the claim and described in the specification were at so high a level that they could be virtually anything and did not render the claim less abstract.

—Scheme, rule or method for performing a mental act

After the last paragraph, add new paragraph:

In T 2677/16 *QIAGEN/Drug Discovery Methods* the claimed invention related to a computer-implemented method for identifying a drug discovery target. The Board concluded that identification of genes or proteins as targets for a drug intervention unduly broadens the concept of a technical purpose to encompass any scientific endeavour in medicine, that a drug target is not a therapy nor has it a therapeutic effect, and that neither discoveries nor science have technical character as such. As the Board considered the modelling of the claimed invention an abstract intellectual activity, and not to serve a technical purpose, it decided that the claimed invention did not involve an inventive step. **1.14**

—Discoveries

After the ninth paragraph (beginning "The patent in Tate & Lyle v Roquette Frères [2010] F.S.R. 1"), add new paragraph:

In T 1798/13 *SWISS REINSURANCE/Forecasting the value of a structured financial product*, the claimed invention related to a method of forecasting the value of a weather-based structured financial product using a weather model. The Board considered that a system for weather forecasting would be considered to have technical character but, because the claimed invention used already measured data, this meant that the claimed invention could not be attributed this technical character. The Board decided that "weather" is not a technical system that the skilled person can improve (or simulate with the purpose of trying to improve it), instead taking the view that modelling of the weather is rather a discovery or a scientific theory and therefore the claimed invention did not involve an inventive step. **1.17**

After the last paragraph, add new paragraph:

More recently in *Illumina v Ariosa Diagnostics* (Fed. Cir. 2020) claims of two Sequenom patents directed to methods for detecting fetal DNA in maternal blood were found to satisfy the subject-matter eligibility requirements of s.101. The inventors found that cffDNA was significantly smaller (300–500 bp) than the "interfering" maternal DNA, and thus using admittedly conventional techniques of size separation the cffDNA could be isolated and enriched compared to the vast bulk of circulatory extracellular DNA and thereby rendered detectable. The basis of the decision was that "this is not a diagnostic case. And it is not a method of treatment case. It is a method of preparation case." The preparative steps included size discrimination and selective removal.

—Mathematical methods

After the thirteenth paragraph (beginning "Another question was whether an improvement"), add new paragraph:

In T 1924/17 *ACCENTURE GLOBAL SERVICES/Data consistency management*, the Board considered that the computer-implemented features of the claimed invention involved "further" technical considerations, as it was necessary to consider the technical properties of the implementations of query processing in different kinds of database management systems. In particular, it was considered convincingly argued by the applicant that the claimed system, using a NoSQL data store and a RDBMS, provided a performance improvement over an RDBMS as a sole data source, and that this improvement was a consequence of the above discussed "further" technical considerations, which were adequately reflected in the claimed data consistency management system. **1.19**

To the end of the last paragraph, add:

On somewhat the same lines, a claim to improving the known laboratory technique of real-time discrimination of sperm cells or other particles by flow cytometry using the application of the mathematical formula was held eligible in *XY, LLC v Trans Ova Genetics, LC* (Fed. Cir. 2020).

After the last paragraph, add new paragraph:
In *Communisis Plc v Tall Group of Companies Ltd* [2020] EWHC 3089 (IPEC), the claimed invention relates to the use of a printed code as a security feature on a cheque or other credit slip to prevent fraud by fraudulent alteration of personal details and addition of new, fraudulent details relating to a different account. By combining the numbers printed on each cheque (sort code, account number and cheque number) and converting these to a different base and printing the resulting security code on each cheque, tampering with the account number or sort code can be detected as these will no longer match the security code. The alleged contribution was determined to be the conversion of the combined numbers from base 10 to a higher base to create a security code (as all of the other elements were either common general knowledge or known from the prior art) and so ruled to be excluded subject-matter due to being a mathematical method as such.

—Scheme, rule or method for playing a game

After the last paragraph, add new paragraphs:

1.20   A patent allegedly covering the video games Ingress and Pokémon Go and relating to a computer system for providing a virtual thematic environment (VTE) was held invalid at the US District Court level in *Barbaro Technologies v Niantic* (N.D. Cal. 2020). The court held that improvement offered by the patent was directed to a result—integrating the real and virtual worlds—rather than to any particular method of achieving it, citing *Interval Licensing v AOL* 896 F.3d 1335, 1342 (Fed. Cir. 2018) and that the lack of technological details in the claims and specification—i.e. any details beyond mere instructions to apply a "pre-Internet abstract idea" using generic computer components—was fatal to validity.

In *Sony Interactive Entertainment Inc* BL O/599/21, the applicant's claimed invention related to a computer-implemented launcher for loading computer video games which allowed users to load video games in an immediately playable state thus speeding up the launch of video games. The claimed invention also allowed for pre-loading of one or more common components of the video game before the user chooses to launch the game. The Hearing Officer ruled that the contribution was "a quicker and more efficient method of launching a video game application", but that the claimed invention lay solely in the excluded category of being a computer program as such. Specifically, the Hearing Officer considered that the technical effect of the claimed invention was only at the application level as opposed to the architecture level and that the technical problem of (reducing) processing time was not solved, only circumvented (in line with the final *AT&T* signpost).

In *NetEase (Hangzhou) Network Co)* BL O/431/22, the claimed invention related to online battle games played on mobile terminals, such as a multiplayer online battle arena, which sought to overcome a problem with conventional game scene displays in which a specific resource appears in the game scene in a different relative position for players belonging to different factions, by presenting a game scene to players of a second faction that is a mirror image of the game scene presented to players of a first faction. The Hearing Officer considered whether the claimed invention was excluded as a method for playing a game, but decided that it wasn't excluded as the game was not altered by the claimed invention. The Hearing Officer however decided that the claimed invention was excluded as a computer program as such or as a presentation of information because the effect produced during data processing by the claimed invention is specific to the data and couldn't be considered a technical effect operating at the level of architecture of the computer (thus not meeting signpost two of *AT&T*) and noting that none of the other signposts were of any assistance, and the application was refused.

SECTION 2

Commentary on Section 2

Scope of the section

Replace the ninth paragraph with:

2.03   The preliminary step of construing the extent of protection provided by claimed subject-matter (for which see the commentary on s.125) is crucial to the determination of novelty, as the same claim construction must be applied to anticipation as to infringement, see *Novamedix v NDM* BL C/78/97, noted I.P.D. 20108 CA and *Horne Engineering v Reliance Water Controls* [2000] F.S.R. 90. An example of the importance of claim construction to the outcome of a decision as to novelty is provided by *Glaverbel v British Coal* [1994] R.P.C. 443; and [1995] R.P.C. 255 CA where the Court of Appeal adopted a wider construction of the claims than had been adopted by the Patents Court and then found the claims to lack novelty. The court held as established law in *Interdigital Technology v Lenovo Group* [2021] EWHC 2152 (Pat) that the date at which a patent specification must be interpreted is it priority date or application date if there is no valid priority date rather than the date of publication of the granted patent, see §§76.07 and 125.06. Construction of a prior art document is considered at §§2.17–2.18.

The state of the art (subss.(1)–(2))

—Documents in public places and/or that can be inspected as of right—Internet publications

After the ninth paragraph (beginning "Where the URL of a web document had not"), add new paragraphs:

In T 13/20 *QUALCOMM/Proof of the publication date*, the examining division introduced a cited document D2 into the examination proceedings and did so without an explanation as to how it was retrieved, in particular as to how D2's publication date was actually determined. It considered the "nominal" date indicated on the first page of D2 to be this document's publication date, but on appeal the Board held that this "nominal" date might bear no relation with this document's publication date: it could, for instance, refer to the point in time when a particular internal draft of D2 was started or finalised. In any case, it could not be regarded as an "explicit publication date" in the sense of the Guidelines. The applicants' concern regarding the ability of a commercial tool such as the Google search engine used by the examining division to provide a reliable proof of a publication date was legitimate, given the lack of verifiability of the tool's functioning and its associated collection of search results. The evidence provided in the decision under appeal to support the examining division's assessment of D2's publication date was inadequate, which led the Board to conduct its own investigations to assess whether or not D2 could be taken into account as a prior-art document. These investigations could only confirm the appellant's doubts regarding D2's publication date and accordingly the document could not be considered to be part of the state of the art.

2.04

In T 3071/19 *BLACKBERRY/Searching data* it was held that a decision open to appeal is not reasoned within the meaning of EPC r.111(2) if it does not enable the Board of Appeal to review its correctness. A decision should therefore not rely on evidence accessible only at a web page which is not guaranteed to remain accessible and unchanged. Rather, it should be ensured that a person inspecting the file could reliably access the cited evidence. In T 3000/19 *BLACKBERRY/Searching data with registered applications* which concerned a parallel application in the same family, it was held that when a video retrieved from the internet is used as prior-art evidence for refusing a patent application, its content, in a form suitable for reviewing the decision, and metadata evidence demonstrating when and how it was made available to the public should be preserved and made accessible over time to interested parties and judicial bodies. The prior-art evidence cited by the examining division referred to a video retrieved from the YouTube website and a screenshot of a web browser visiting that website. However, the web page corresponding to the URL indicated in the citation was no longer functioning, so the Board could not assess on its own the relevant parts of the video evidence. It could not review the correctness of the contested decision's reasoning in so far as it relies on what had been shown in the YouTube video evidence. Nor could the Board assess the appellant's arguments that this online video was not an enabling disclosure and that there were further distinguishing features other than those recognised in the decision under appeal.

Prior public use

To the end of the third paragraph, add:

However, in *Claydon Yield-O-Meter v Mzuri* [2021] EWHC 1007 (IPEC) the invention concerned a seed drill, a prototype of which had been made in a farm workshop and tested at 6.30 in the morning in the corner of a field close to a footpath. The experts' evidence suggested that there would have been periods when a passer-by would have been able to see the prototype in action and been able to deduce from its appearance and from the appearance of soil left in its wake features of construction of the prototype including all the relevant claimed features. If the inventor had noticed such a person, he could not have taken action that would have prevented the skilled person from seeing or inferring each of those features. The inventor had to test his prototype, nobody saw any of the testing and it was understandable why he believed that his invention had not been publicly disclosed. Unfortunately for him, in law the prototype had been made available to the public and the relevant claim therefore lacked novelty because of the prior use.

2.07

To the end of the thirteenth paragraph (beginning "It was explained in T 2048/12 AIR PRODUCTS/PU catalysts"), add:

Similarly in T 1409/16 *PROCTOR & GAMBLE/Blocky CMX 1* following the reasoning in G 1/92 extrinsic characteristics of an allegedly novelty-destroying commercial composition were held to be accessible only by subjecting that composition to a kind of reverse engineering based on hindsight, deliberate choices having been made with specifically chosen outside conditions in order to obtain a particular result.

Prior non-public use

In the penultimate paragraph, after "In E Mishan & Sons v Hozelock [2019] EWHC 991", add:

2.08   (compare *Claydon Yield-O-Meter v Mzrui* [2021] EWHC 1007 (IPEC) §2.09)

The requirement for a novelty-destroying disclosure to have an "enabling" character

After the last paragraph, add new paragraph:

2.09   A seed drill prototype tried on a farm adjacent a footpath was considered in *Claydon Yield-O-Meter v Mzuri* [2021] EWHC 1007 (IPEC). As to the extent to which a passer-by would have gained potentially enabling information, HHJ Hacon held that the relevant features could have been seen by a passer-by and observed:

"It seems to me that there is no absolute bar in law to the enablement of an invention by reason of the hypothetical skilled person having gained an understanding of it with the assistance of technical equipment. There are, though, potential difficulties which may prevent such enablement. I give two examples in a contemporary context. If enablement required a phone with a sufficient zoom facility and the evidence showed that at the relevant time and place a member of the public could reasonably have been expected to carry such a phone and use the zoom and could have done so lawfully, then it may be that the hypothesis will go forward on the basis that the information made available included information obtained using the phone, whether seen at the time or recorded and discerned later. On the other hand, it will not be often that evidence will establish that the skilled person would have had a swarm of drones to hand at the relevant time and place and even if they did, use of the swarm may be liable to give rise to issues of privacy and breach of confidence. Both examples assume that the skilled person is a passer-by, in that he or she is not to be taken to have planned the observation in advance.

To my mind the evidence in the present case did not sufficiently explore what equipment a member of the public might reasonably have been expected to carry and use to observe Claydon's prototype without being in breach of an implied obligation of confidence. Brief speculation by Mr Wright was not enough. Nor did it explore what could have been discerned in the prevailing conditions using binoculars or a video camera typically available in August 2002. In my view, therefore, enablement in the present case must be assessed by reference to hypothetical observation with the naked eye."

Confidentiality

After the eleventh paragraph (beginning "Whether or not a prior use"), add new paragraph:

2.10   *The Janger Ltd v Tesco Plc* [2020] EWHC 3450 (IPEC) concerned the showing of a previously uncommercialised clothes hanger by a designer to M&S in the basement of their head offices rather than in a public place. The evidence was that it was pointless to have asked customers to sign NDAs before meetings because they would not have signed them. The meetings would either not have happened, or been delayed while customers consulted their legal departments (which the customers would not have wanted to do). However, there was evidence that those participating at the meeting would not have expected the clothes hanger to be disclosed to third parties. Held that the disclosure was made under conditions of confidence, based on both the circumstances of the meeting itself and on the evidence of the participants.

After the twelfth paragraph (beginning "The EPO has held that an express secrecy agreement"), add new paragraphs:

Similarly, according to the jurisprudence of the EPO Boards of Appeal a relationship between two companies which contract to develop and deliver prototypes and products for test purposes cannot be treated as equivalent to that between a dealer and a customer and in these cases an obligation to maintain secrecy applies, see T 72/16 *ROCKWOOL/Pipe section* and T 1847/12 *FORD GLOBAL/ Zylinderkopf* in which evidence of an employee of a contractor was held to be irrelevant because it is the client placing a contract, not the contractor, that decides whether the prototypes' development and delivery is to be treated as secret.

Confidentiality of working documents that had been submitted to an MPEG working group by MPEG members involved in the elaboration of a particular new standard was in issue in T 2239/15 *FRAUNHOFER-DOLBY/MPEG input documents*. It emerged that the MPEG set-up did not guarantee or even envisage absolute confidentiality within the relatively small groups present at meetings, but in fact envisaged a wider discussion among experts in the elaboration of standards fit for purpose. The arrangements were designed to guarantee a certain "privacy" of data by controlling access and transmission while at the same time being sufficiently pragmatic and flexible to allow such transmission to other parties in order for the mission to be satisfactorily fulfilled. Accordingly, public availability of the documents was established.

Replace the penultimate paragraph with:

For a further decision where confidentiality in a sale of samples (throttle valves to a motor vehicle manufacturer) was not established see T 1511/06 *HITACHI/Air flow rate control apparatus*. The patentees argued that in the highly competitive automotive industry a parts manufacturer and a vehicle manufacturer were both interested in maintaining information confidential before production had started. However, in the present case the throttle valves were a generic product of the valve supplier which might be sold to other manufacturers, and although the vehicle manufacturer might have wanted the fact of sale kept secret to avoid leakage of information about its engines, this could not be equated with maintaining secret the constructional details of the throttle valve as such. Similarly in T 2702/18 *DYNAPAC/Road pavers or feeders*, ACE, a supplier of dampers, had been requested to supply products to meet the requirements of a particular customer (Dynapac). It had found that the product originally requested did not meet those requirements and so developed an alternative solution. However, from the point of view of ACE, no new product had been developed that was worthy of protection but only a product that had existed for some time and had been adapted to customer specifications and sold. ACE had no interest in selling this product exclusively to Dynapac, but on the contrary wanted to sell the product to as many customers as possible. The intellectual performance lay in the adaptation of the structural damper to specification and there was no reason for assuming that Dynapac had an interest in protecting a possible joint development, since Dynapac only set the task in the present case which ACE then solved for it. The Board observed that;

> "The assumption of an actual presumption that the partners in a joint further development in the field of vehicle construction want to commit themselves to secrecy in a binding manner up to the publication of the developed product presupposes at least the determination of the awareness that it is a joint development of both partners, and that both sides will be interested in secrecy." (headnote §3)

Comparison of earlier disclosed matter and subsequently claimed matter

—The UK approach to construction of a prior art document

Replace the fifth paragraph with:

Where a document cited as a prior publication is susceptible of two possible interpretations, the onus of proof is on an applicant for revocation to establish what is the correct disclosure, i.e. whether there truly is an anticipatory disclosure, see *James Industries' Patent* [1987] R.P.C. 235. Therefore, in ex parte proceedings, an applicant should be given the benefit of the doubt in such a circumstance. A somewhat similar situation arose in the context of a point-to-multipoint digital micro-cellular communication system, where it was held that even though stated in the context of obviousness, the notion that one cannot strip out inconvenient detail from the prior art applies also/especially in the context of anticipation, citing *Philips v Asustek* [2019] EWCA Civ 2230:

2.17

> "The task for the party attacking the patent on the ground of obviousness is to show how the skilled person would arrive at the invention claimed from the disclosure of the prior art. If the invention claimed is, as it is here, a simple idea, then it is correct that this simple idea is the target for the obviousness attack. That does not mean, however, that the court is entitled to assume that the skilled person takes a different approach to the prior art, stripping out from it detail which the skilled person would otherwise have taken into account, or ignoring paths down which the skilled person would probably be led: see the passage from *Pozzoli* cited above. The nature of the invention claimed cannot logically impact on the way in which the skilled person approaches the prior art, given that the prior art is to be considered without the benefit of hindsight knowledge of the invention."

In *Commscope v SOLiD* [2022] EWHC 769 (Pat), the cited prior art disclosed a particular multichannel arrangement in its preferred embodiment, the Skilled Person would have appreciated that its teaching could be implemented in a single channel system. What maximised the efficiency of the signal transmission was the basic teaching of converting the IF signals from analog to digital, sending the digital signals over the optic line and converting them back to analog after that transmission. The point here was that the Skilled Person would understand this teaching as of general application: both to a single channel arrangement or to a multi-channel arrangement. Although digital summing was a point of significance in the circumstances of this case, the prior art did not consider it necessary to mention it in the context of Figure 1 (although it was covered in the more detailed description of the multichannel arrangement because individual functional components were described). The reason was that the Skilled Person would automatically have understood that the signals were to be digitally summed. Accordingly the claimed subject-matter had been clearly and unambiguously disclosed in the relevant prior art.

After the sixth paragraph (beginning "A disclosure includes implicit features"), add new paragraph:

In *Optis v Apple* [2021] EWHC 1739 (Pat) Meade J. commented in relation to a priority document and a more polished finalised specification at [149]–[150]:

"There was also no dispute that where a method claim is in issue, what must be disclosed by the prior art is all the method steps of the claim. It is not enough that a prior art method has the same result as the claimed method. Navigation by the stars and by a compass might both result in heading due North, but they are different methods. Although Apple accepted this principle, its arguments later lost sight of it.

Apple reminded me of the decision of the House of Lords in *Merrell Dow v. Norton* [1996] RPC 76 at 88 that an anticipating piece of prior art does not have to have equivalence of language, but of teaching, so that Amazonian Indians would refer to quinine as that which came from cinchona bark while chemists used its chemical name. I agree with this (and I also agree that rearranging a mathematical equation may do no more than describe the same thing in a different way). The question in the present case is the application of this principle."

Subsequently at [158]–[159]:

"More importantly, Apple stressed that the disclosure of the earlier document can include implicit teaching; if there is something that is disclosed by inevitable implication in the earlier document then it is disclosed, and the fact that the later application made the same information explicit cannot alter that. I agree.

Apple also argued in its closing written submissions that the prior art document must be considered through the eyes of a skilled reader seeking to understand, not to misunderstand. I agree with this to some extent, and synthetic confusion generated by a patentee seeking to avoid anticipation should be ignored, but in the context of novelty-only art and anticipation it could be pressed too far: if the novelty-only prior art is genuinely unclear or ambiguous then anticipation is not made out, and the ambiguity cannot be resolved in favour of the party attacking the patent by arguing that the reader would set about solving the ambiguity by doing tests, or analyses, or thinking about what the best approach within the envelope of uncertainty might be. In other contexts, such as insufficiency, patent law requires the skilled addressee to make practical progress despite a lack of clarity in a document. That is a different matter, and I note that none of the cases cited by Apple was specifically about anticipation. They were about ambiguity under the 1949 Act, or claim interpretation."

And in conclusion at [203]–[205]:

"First, relevant to claim 1, is there a sufficiently clear disclosure of using byte counting and PDU counting together in the same method, so as to trigger a status report if either exceeds a predefined value?

In my view there is not. I agree that there is a clear disclosure of byte counting and triggering a status report by polling once a byte threshold is passed. And although perhaps not articulated explicitly, the reader would clearly understand that the PDU counting of UMTS was being preserved, with the associated parameters needed for it. But that does not mean that there is a disclosure of using them at the same time in one method as required by claim 1. I have considered each passage relied on by Apple with that in mind and am not persuaded by any of them. The attention to the parameters provided and/or needed is not helpful and tends to confuse, but in any case I accept Optis' case that certain of them were being repurposed for byte counting, and that does not necessarily imply the two counts being done at the same time in the way required.

Apple forcefully urged the point that it would not be sensible for the skilled addressee who saw that the window-based J (PDU) and K (byte) parameters were used together in the section on RLC Status Reporting not to envisage combining the equivalent counters. I think this is the wrong side of the line: it is an obviousness argument (quite possibly a very strong one) and Pani is a novelty-only citation."

—The EPO approach to construction when deciding on novelty

After the penultimate paragraph, add new paragraph:

It was noted in T 1943/15 *VALLOUREC/Tubular connection* that patent drawings in the field of mechanical engineering, especially cross-sectional views, often reveal the complete structure of a device to a high degree of detail and go beyond a mere schematic representation of the essential features. Yet this does not mean that such drawings are to be regarded on a par with construction drawings, which may generally be relied on to show dimensions and proportions of elements to scale. As to whether the relative size of dimensions or of ratios between dimensions can be inferred from patent drawings merely by visual perception it is impossible to lay down general rules and each case will depend on the knowledge of the person skilled in the art and the way in which the feature in question is shown in the drawing. In the present case, the claim in issue was dimensionally complex and anticipation by the relevant figures of the various cited documents was not established. **2.18**

—The general test for anticipation

After the last paragraph, add new paragraph:

In *Alcon v Actavis* [2021] EWHC 1026 (Pat) Meade J. rejected [138] an anticipation attack against a second medical use claim on the principle that such a claim can only be anticipated by a disclosure which makes plausible, so as to enable, the treatment effect claimed. **2.19**

—Completeness as a necessary attribute of anticipation

Add new paragraph at the beginning:

It was observed in T 2635/16 *4SC AG/Acrylamide salts* at 4.10 in the context of selection from lists that the same "gold standard" of disclosure applies to novelty (EPC art.54), validity of a claimed priority (EPC art.87) and added subject-matter (EPC art.123(2)). These standards had been established in inter alia G 2/88 *MOBIL III/Friction reducing additive* (Reasons, 8.4), G 3/89 *Correction under Rule 88* (Reasons, 3), G 1/03 *PPG/Disclaimer* (Reasons, 2.2.2) and G 2/10 *SCRIPPS RESEARCH INSTITUTE/ Disclaimer* and confirmed in G 1/16 *OLED/Disclaimer III* (e.g. Reasons, 17). Applying this standard, it was held that a hypothetical amended claim in the citation directed to the subject-matter of the claim at issue would contravene the requirements of EPC art.123(2). In order to arrive at the compound claimed it was necessary (i) to select an individual compound from a list in the relevant citation of 121 compounds, (ii) to select a salt rather than the free acrylamide compound and (iii) to select toluenesulphonic acid from a long list of possible acids. As a selection was required in the citation from two lists of considerable length in combination with the further selection of a salt rather than the free compound the claimed subject-matter was novel following the two-list principle in T 12/81 *BAYER/ Distereoisomers*. **2.20**

After the second paragraph, add new paragraph:

It was observed in *Fisher and Paykel v Flexicare* [2020] EWHC 3282 (Pat) at [150] that the fact that something unmentioned is not expressly ruled out does not mean that it is disclosed, still less to the standard required for anticipation.

After the last paragraph, add new paragraph:

In *InterDigital Technology Corp v Lenovo Group Ltd* [2022] EWHC 10 (Pat), Mellor J. explained that:

"Lenovo's case is also based on a misunderstanding of the role of pieces of knowledge which are (or might be) CGK. CGK is not a reservoir from which pieces of information can be plucked to supplement an alleged anticipation where the document in question is lacking. It is only if that piece of knowledge would come to the skilled person's mind directly during or on their reading of the document, that it can be taken into account. As already indicated, in the circumstances of Filiatrault, what Lenovo requires would not."

—Certainty as a necessary attribute of anticipation

To the end of the third paragraph (beginning "In the present case, the question was whether"), add:

2.21   However, in *Fiberweb Geosynthetics Ltd v Geofabrics Ltd* [2021] EWCA Civ 854 Birss L.J. held that although anticipation is legally possible in the absence of obviousness, in the present case it was difficult to see how the question whether following the directions of a prior art reference would inevitably result in a product falling within claim 1 of the patent could be answered in the affirmative when the answer to the question whether that reference made it obvious to produce such a product has been answered in the negative.

—Novelty of purpose

After the ninth paragraph (beginning "Similarly, in T 151/13 BLUE CUBE/ Conversion process"), add new paragraphs:

2.23   Absence of conflict between T 848/93 and T 304/08 was confirmed in T 1931/14 *GE ENERGY/ Combined cryogenic air separation*. The claimed process involved producing oxygen to fuel an integrated gasifier combined cycle power generation system at a rate which corresponded to the demand during peak periods while maintaining peak efficiency when operating at varying power production. Liquid oxygen more than that required by the gasifier system was collected and stored in a liquid oxygen cold storage vessel and during an increase in power demand was withdrawn and vaporized. The Board observed that according to established case law, where a claim concerns an apparatus differing from a known apparatus only as regards the use indicated, then the use is not an apparatus feature, meaning that two apparatuses (differing only in the intended use) are structurally identical. If the known apparatus is suitable for the claimed use, the claimed apparatus lacks novelty. If, however, the claim is for a process, the situation is not comparable and it is important to differentiate between different types of stated purpose, namely those that define an effect arising from the steps of the method and implicit therein and those that define the application or use of a method. Where the purpose merely states a technical effect which inevitably arises when carrying out the other remaining steps of the claimed method (e.g. the malodor is inherently reduced as in T 304/08) and is thus inherent in those steps, such a technical effect is not limiting because it is not suitable for distinguishing the claimed method from a known one. But where the stated purpose defines a specific application of the method, in fact it requires certain additional steps which are not implied by or inherent in the other remaining steps defined in the claim, and without which the claimed process would not achieve the stated purpose (e.g. no actual re-melting of a galvanic layer would occur as in T 848/93). In this manner the stated application represents a genuine technical limitation of the method and the claimed method must be interpreted in that manner. In the present case the relevant steps related to the specific application of oxygen production to IGCC power generation system. The relevant parts of the claim thus defined functional features of that process i.e. physical activities that the process had to perform in order to fuel the IGCC as a function of its power demand: on the one hand during low demand to collect and store the excess oxygen produced, and during increased power demand to operate in two different operation modes defined in the claim. The claimed process was novel because the citation which concerned a steel mill did not teach application to IGCC power systems and did not teach more effectively employing liquid oxygen storage to alleviate or dampen fluctuations in a cryogenic rectification plant operating rate.

     The main claim in T 1385/15 *PROCTOR & GAMBLE/Machine disinfection of objects* was directed to the use of a surfactant-based cleaning agent selected for killing microorganisms in the mechanical disinfection of objects. A first prior art document disclosed the use of surfactants for mechanical disinfection. A second disclosed that the surfactants claimed could be used to kill microorganisms. The Opposition Division had found the patent invalid for lack of novelty on the basis that the technical effect described in the prior art need not have been disclosed in combination with the other features of the claim within a single document. The TBA disagreed with this approach and held that all the technical features must be disclosed in combination in one document. Furthermore, treatment of technical effect should follow G 6/88 where it was not considered in isolation, but instead in the manner of use claimed. In this case the functional technical feature was antimicrobial activity in combination with the mechanical disinfection of the objects, and that combination of features was not disclosed in the second prior art document, so that the finding of lack of novelty should be set aside.

     In T 1930/14 *ROCHE/Purification of antibodies* the Board observed (Reasons, 7) that

> "the finding in decision T 1931/14 (see Reasons, 2.2.4) that – '[w]here the stated purpose defines the specific application of the method, in fact it requires certain additional steps which are not implied by or inherent in the other remaining steps defined in the claim, and without which the claimed process would not achieve the stated purpose' - can only hold in cases where it is unambiguously

clear that the purpose implies such steps and where it is also unambiguously clear what those steps in fact are."

In the present case, the Board could identify no indication, either in the claim itself or in the description, that would lead the skilled person to understand that the stated purpose "for purifying a monoclonal antibody from aggregates thereof", implied that the claimed method contained any additional steps. It was the Board's view that the skilled person would consider that the claim specified all the essential features of the invention in line with EPC r.43 and hence would consider that carrying out the process steps set out in the claim necessarily achieved the stated purpose, i.e. the separation of monomers from aggregates of IgG monoclonal antibodies.

Selection inventions

After the penultimate paragraph, add new paragraph:

In T 1085/13 *RECORDATI/ Amorphous Lercanidipine Hydrochloride* it was held that a claim defin- **2.24**
ing a compound as having a certain purity will only lack novelty over a prior-art disclosure describing the same compound if the prior art discloses the claimed purity at least implicitly, for example by way of a method for preparing said compound, the method inevitably resulting in the purity as claimed. Such a claim, however, does not lack novelty if the disclosure of the prior art needs to be supplemented, for example by suitable (further) purification methods allowing the skilled person to arrive at the claimed purity. The question of whether such (further) purification methods for the prior-art compound are within the common general knowledge of those skilled in the art and, if applied, would result in the claimed purity, is not relevant to novelty, but is rather a matter to be considered in the assessment of inventive step (Reasons, 3.7, 3.8), it being observed that these conclusions are in line with G 2/88 *MOBIL OIL/ Friction reducing additive* and T 1523/07 *NIPPON SHOKUBAI/ Washing a device for the production of meth(acrylic)acid or esters.* It was further observed that the rationale of T 990/96 *NOVARTIS/ Erythro compounds* (holding that a document disclosing a low molecular chemical compound and its manufacture makes normally available this compound to the public in the sense of EPC art.54 in all desired grades of purity) and the similar decision in T 728/98 *ALBANY MOLECULAR RESEARCH/ Pure terfenadine* are no longer compatible with the case law developed by the Enlarged Board and subsequent decisions.

SECTION 3

Commentary on Section 3

Introduction and background

—Scope of the section

After the last paragraph, add new paragraphs:

Floyd L.J. observed in *Koninklijke Philips v Asustek* [2019] EWCA Civ 2230 that in general, a case **3.03**
of obviousness ought to be capable of being stated shortly, and a complex step-by-step argument is unlikely to succeed. However, the present case was complex and the length of a party's closing submissions was a crude and misleading guide to their merit.

A useful summary of the current law was given by Arnold J. in *Allergan v Aspire* [2019] EWHC 1085 (Pat) at [96]–[102]:

"The Supreme Court has recently reviewed the law as to obviousness in *Actavis Group PTC EHF v ICOS Corp* [2019] UKSC 15. The overall tenor of the judgment of Lord Hodge, with whom the other members of the Court agreed, is to confirm the approach which had previously been adopted by the courts to this question. For present purposes, it is sufficient to note five points.

First, at [60] and [93]–[96] Lord Hodge endorsed, while not mandating, the use of the structured approach set out in *Windsurfing International Inc v Tabur Marine (Great Britain) Ltd* [1985] RPC 59 as reformulated in *Pozzoli SPA v BDMO SA* [2007] EWCA Civ 588, [2007] FSR 37 at [33].

Secondly, at [63] Lord Hodge endorsed, while emphasising that it was not exhaustive, the statement of Kitchin J (as he then was) in *Generics (UK) Ltd v H Lundbeck A/S* [2007] EWHC 1040 (Pat), [2007] RPC 32 at [72]:

'The question of obviousness must be considered on the facts of each case. The court must consider the weight to be attached to any particular factor in the light of all the relevant circumstances. These may include such matters as the motive to find a solution to the problem the patent addresses, the number and extent of the possible avenues of research, the effort involved in pursuing them and the expectation of success.'

Thirdly, at [65] Lord Hodge agreed that it was relevant to consider whether something was 'obvious to try', saying that '[i]n many cases the consideration that there is a likelihood of success which is sufficient to warrant an actual trial is an important pointer to obviousness'. He nevertheless endorsed the observation of Birss J at first instance that 'some experiments which are undertaken without any particular expectation as to result are obvious'.

Fourthly, at [69] Lord Hodge said that 'the existence of alternative or multiple paths of research will often be an indicator that the invention ... was not obvious', but nevertheless endorsed the statement of Laddie J in *Brugger v Medic-Aid Ltd (No 2)* [1996] RPC 635 at 661:

'[I]f a particular route is an obvious one to take or try, it is not rendered any less obvious from a technical point of view merely because there are a number, and perhaps a large number, of other obvious routes as well.'

Although Lord Hodge did not explicitly make the point, it is implicit in his endorsement of this statement that it remains the law that what matters is whether the claimed invention is obvious from a technical point of view, not whether it would be commercially obvious to implement it.

Fifthly, at [70] Lord Hodge confirmed that the motive of the skilled person was a relevant consideration. As he put it:

'The notional skilled person is not assumed to undertake technical trials for the sake of doing so but rather because he or she has some end in mind. It is not sufficient that a skilled person could undertake a particular trial; one may wish to ask whether in the circumstances he or she would be motivated to do so. The absence of a motive to take the allegedly inventive step makes an argument of obviousness more difficult.'"

A European patent (UK) that described an improved wireless communication system by an improved mechanism for polling within the wireless communication network was one in a series of trials in a multi-patent action and had already been litigated and held valid in *Unwired Planet v Huawei* [2015] EWHC 3366 (Pat) before Birss J. and before the Court of Appeal at [2017] EWCA Civ 266, see inter alia §§3.23, 3.32. The same patent was relitigated before Meade J. in *Optis v Apple* [2021] EWHC 1739 (Pat), Apple's attacks being different from those of Huawei with a new construction point, new prior art and different expert evidence so that the trial started with a "clean sheet of paper". However, the patent was held valid, and no amendment was necessary.

—Historical development of the concept of obviousness—tests used by the UK and US within the common law and problem/solution analysis (PSA) used by the EPO

After the eleventh paragraph (beginning "The current test for inventive step in the UK"), add new paragraphs:

3.04   Meade J. in *Optis v Apple* [2021] EWHC 1739 (Pat) described basic legal principles as to obviousness as to which there was no dispute as being set out in the decision of the Supreme Court in *Actavis v ICOS* [2019] UKSC 15 at [52]–[73], with its endorsement at [62] of the statement of Kitchin J. as he then was in *Generics v Lundbeck* [2007] EWHC 1040 (Pat) at [72]. See also *Brugger v Medicaid* [1996] R.P.C. 635 at 661, approved by the Supreme Court in *Actavis v ICOS* to the effect that an obvious route is not made less obvious by the existence of other obvious routes, and *Pozzoli v BDMO* [2007] EWCA Civ 588 where Jacob L.J. reformulated the *Windsurfing* approach as follows:

(1)(a)   Identify the notional "person skilled in the art";

(1)(b)   Identify the relevant common general knowledge of that person;

(2)   Identify the inventive concept of the claim in question or if that cannot readily be done, construe it;

(3)   Identify what, if any, differences exist between the matter cited as forming part of the "state of the art" and the inventive concept of the claim or the claim as construed;

(4)   Viewed without any knowledge of the alleged invention as claimed, do those differences constitute steps which would have been obvious to the person skilled in the art or do they require any degree of invention?

In argument, Apple relied on *Brugger v Medicaid* [1996] R.P.C. 635 at 661, approved by the Supreme Court in *Actavis v ICOS* [2019] UKSC 15 to the effect that an obvious route is not made less obvious by the existence of other obvious routes. Apple relied on this (a) to seek to head off an argument that it perceived Optis would make that the only obvious thing to do over InterDigital would be exactly what it taught, and (b) to seek to minimise any importance of Optis' expert's review of contemporary TDocs as a "Simpkins list" (see *Brugger*, ibid.). Apple also relied on the same passage in *Brugger* for the closely related and well-known principle that what other workers did is not likely to be of assistance if they did not know about the pleaded prior art. These arguments were accepted by Meade J.

After the last paragraph, add new paragraphs:
In *A Ward Attachments v Fabcon* [2021] EWHC 2145 (IPEC) at [64]–[68], Judge Melissa Clarke noted the reformulated first *Improver* question in *Actavis UK Ltd v Eli Lilly & Co* [2017] UKSC 48 and commented that since *Actavis* there has been judicial consideration about the meaning of the "inventive concept", as it is not a phrase that is found in any of the relevant UK or European patent legislation. Lord Kitchin described it in *Icescape v Ice-World International* [2018] EWCA Civ 2219 at [72] as *"the problem underlying the invention and the patent's inventive core."* In *EValve Inc v Edwards Lifesciences Ltd* [2020] EWHC 514 (Pat), Birss J. (as he then was) said at [315] that *"one should examine what is the problem underlying the invention and how does the patent solve that problem."* (emphasis in the original)

A posting by Cole, *Hindsight Bias, An Ovine Survey* on IPWatchdog on November 24, 2021 and republished in the CIPA Journal, September 2022, page 20 explained that what started as a joke has become a research exercise based on the question: 'How do sheep send messages to one another in this digital age?' The answer, of course, is that they do so by baa code. Almost nobody can make the connection without prompting, few people do so when it is pointed out that the sound that sheep typically make is a baa, and most still not do so when it is subsequently pointed out that the sheep send coded messages. Disclosure of the answer almost invariably gives rise to amusement, much of that arising from the contrast between the enigmatic nature of the problem and the hindsight obviousness of the answer. Examination of patent validity is invariably with hindsight knowledge of the invention, and personal experience that can be gained by putting this question to friends and colleagues prompts caution when considering obviousness objections, the article having been prompted by a US Office Action citing six references allegedly disclosing some of the claimed features but still needing a small amount of purposeful prior art redesign by the examiner to arrive at the full set of features claimed.

Evidence and arguments covered by the structured enquiry

The preliminary question—field of the invention

—The art or field of endeavour in which the invention arises—disclaimer practice

After the first paragraph, add new paragraph:
In *Conversant v Apple* [2019] EWHC 3266 (Pat), Birss J., quoting *Schlumberger* (above), said that the person skilled in the art is a legal construct used to provide an objective legal standard by which various legal questions can be answered. A sceptical editor might argue at this point that the identity and scope of the relevant art is an issue of fact based on and derivable from the disclosure of the specification and claims and that the categorical identity of the relevant skilled person(s) is essentially a factual issue to be determined. However, Birss J. then observed that the court will always have regard to the reality of the position at the time and continued:

3.06

> "Apple's case seems to involve a point of principle that the way to identify the skilled person as a matter of law is to look at the field the patent itself locates the invention in and posit a person in that field as the relevant person. The problem with that approach is that one could end up in this case with a person working in the field of (say) PDAs, even though they are no longer within the claims. The point is wrong because a patent is taken to be directed to those with a practical interest in its subject-matter (*Catnic v Hill & Smith* [1982] RPC 183). Its subject-matter is the invention, and the invention is what is defined in the claims (s125 of the Act). It follows that while it will be unusual, there is nothing wrong in principle for the effect of a claim amendment to mean that the notional person skilled in the art relevant to an amended claim may be different from the one applicable to the unamended claim."

Replace the fourth paragraph (beginning "In Blue Gentian LLC v Tristar Products (UK) Ltd") with:
Unusually, the same patent came before the Court of Appeal on successive occasions with opposite results. In *Blue Gentian LLC v Tristar Products (UK) Ltd* [2013] EWHC 4098 (Pat), affirmed on appeal [2015] EWCA Civ 746, the invention concerned an expandable garden hose. A pleaded reference related to a self-elongating oxygen hose for a stowable aviation crew oxygen mask. The defendants submitted that a skilled person would have recognised the principle of hose construction exhibited in

the aircraft hose and would have seen that it could have been adapted with choice of appropriate ready to hand materials to the field of garden hoses. However, in cross-examination their expert doubted that a practical hose designer would have used the aircraft hose as the basis for a new product. Birss J. held that a garden water hose designer presented with the aircraft hose reference and reading it with interest would be interested in the space-saving quality of the idea but would also see a document which was not addressed to him or her and was concerned with something used in an environment and context a very long way from garden water hoses and subject to considerations that the garden water hose designer would have known little about. Therefore the designer would not have been confident that the idea would have been practical if applied to a garden water hose. Although a person skilled in the art could have arrived at a garden hose as now claimed if presented with the aircraft hose reference, given that the hoses function in the same way, an unimaginative skilled person working without hindsight would not have done that, so that obviousness over the hose reference had not been established. The second case was *E Mishan & Sons Inc v Hozelock Ltd* [2020] EWCA Civ 871. It was noted that in *Blue Gentian* neither of the experts had experience in the design or manufacture of hoses. Here, Mishan's expert was an engineer with particular experience in water systems, but no personal experience in the design or manufacture of hoses, which limited his ability to give evidence as to the attributes of the skilled person, and the common general knowledge that such a person would possess. Hozelock's expert was an engineer with a postgraduate degree specialising in plastics and polymers who had considerable experience in the design and manufacture of both garden hoses, which are sold to consumers, and what were described as "technical" hoses, which were sold for commercial use. On appeal, Arnold L.J. and Floyd L.J. had opposing views, and the decisive vote in favour of obviousness was by Henderson L.J. who disagreed with Floyd L.J.'s repeated dismissal of a prior art US patent known as McDonald as "a mere paper proposal" and observed:

"So it was, in the limited sense that there was no evidence that McDonald had ever been translated into a working model in the eight (in fact nearer nine) years between its publication in the USA on 2 January 2003 and the first claimed priority date of the Patents on 4 November 2011. But the important point, to my mind, is that McDonald unambiguously disclosed the same basic concept of an extensible and retractable hose as Mr Berardi's later invention. That concept was clearly expressed, both verbally and visually, in the original patent application for McDonald. Bearing in mind that the notional skilled person was a designer of hoses in general, not just of garden hoses, and that he was familiar with the transposition of a hose structure from one application to another (see the judgment at [177]), it seems to me only a small step, and not an impermissible exercise in hindsight, to conclude that the skilled person would at once have seen the potential for use of the same basic idea in the construction of a garden hose. The question of how to make the idea work in practice would not then have been a problem, because as every gardener knows the operation of a garden hose depends on nothing more sophisticated than its attachment at one end to a pressurised supply of water through an ordinary household tap."

The skilled person or team and his or their characteristics

—The person skilled in the art

After the fourth paragraph (beginning "The inventor himself may not be representative"), add new paragraphs:

3.07 The applicable law relating to the skilled person was considered by Meade J. in *Optis v Apple* [2021] EWHC 3121 (Pat) (appeal dismissed at [2022] EWCA Civ 792), concerning one of three European (UK) patents owned by Optis, which had been declared as essential to the LTE telecommunication standards, the outcome also being relevant to the other two patents. Apple's counterclaim was that the patents were obvious in view of two documents, referred to as Ericsson and Knuth respectively, the latter being a standard reference work. Meade J. referred to *Illumina v Latvia* [2021] EWHC 57 (Pat) (affirmed at [2021] EWCA Civ 1924) at [68]–[70] and to *Alcon v Actavis* [2021] EWHC 1026 (Pat) at [31]. In *Illumina*, Birss J. explained the following approach at [68]:

"I conclude that in a case in which it is necessary to define the skilled person for the purposes of obviousness in a different way from the skilled person to whom the patent is addressed, the approach to take, bringing *Schlumberger* and *Medimmune* together, is: i) To start by asking what problem does the invention aim to solve? ii) That leads one in turn to consider what the established field which existed was, in which the problem in fact can be located. iii) It is the notional person or team in that established field which is the relevant team making up the person skilled in the art."

Meade J. quoted Birss J. (as he then was) in *Illumina* that blindly applying an approach based on the definition of the problem to be solved could lead to a very narrowly defined skilled person and that could create its own difficulties. These were well described by Peter Prescott QC in *Folding Attic Stairs v The Loft Stairs Company Ltd* [2009] EWHC 1221 (Pat) at [33]:

"Common general knowledge is quite different. It is what people skilled in the art actually do know, or ought to know, provided that knowledge is regarded as sound. Common general knowledge is not a phrase used in the Patents Act or the European Patent Convention. It would be difficult to define the person skilled in the art in this case, or the common general knowledge, because so far as I know there is no recognised profession or calling of designing folding attic stairways. At the date of the patent nobody seems to have done it in the British Isles except the Claimant and perhaps one other company. There must have been one or more companies in America, I suppose. It is unfair to define an art too narrowly, or else you could imagine absurd cases e.g. 'the art of designing two-hole blue Venezuelan razor blades', to paraphrase the late Mr T.A. Blanco White. Then you could attribute the 'common general knowledge' to that small band of persons who made those products and say that their knowledge was 'common general knowledge' in 'the art'. That would have the impermissible result that any prior user no matter how obscure could be deemed to be common general knowledge, which is certainly not the law."

He therefore intended to apply the *Illumina* approach, taking particular note that:

"(i)   The requirements not to be unfair to the patentee by allowing an artificially narrow definition, or unfair to the public (and the defendant) by going so broad as to 'dilute' the CGK. Thus, as Counsel for Alcon accepted, there is an element of value judgment in the assessment.

(ii)   The fact that I must consider the real situation at the priority date, and in particular what teams existed.

(iii)   The need to look for an 'established field', which might be a research field or a field of manufacture.

(iv)   The starting point is the identification of the problem that the invention aims to solve."

He explained that in the present case, the problem that the invention aimed to solve was not in dispute: it was a narrow one of how to allocate PDCCH search spaces. The established field in which this problem was in fact located was RAN1. The PDCCH was not a field in its own right. Professor Lozano accepted that no one would have had a scope of work that matched it. Thus Apple's argument should be rejected that the skilled person would have been a PDCCH person in the sense Apple meant that. It was a "blue Venezuelan razor blade" kind of argument, though not nearly as extreme in degree as that imaginary example. Optis' view of the skilled person had the benefit that RAN1 clearly was an established field, and that the problem that the invention aims to solve was within its scope. He went on to explain at [36]–[38] and [42]:

"However, in my view Optis treated the analysis that the skilled person is a RAN1 person as an opportunity to carry out some inappropriate dumbing-down through dilution, of the kind deprecated in *Mayne v. Debiopharm* [2006] EWHC 1123 (Pat) and cited by Birss J in *Illumina* and recognised by me in Alcon. RAN1 is a broad umbrella and probably no one real person had the knowledge, skills and experience to cover the whole of its field. One can see that by the number of people participating in the discussions, and by the fact that major companies had teams on RAN1, either attending as delegates or participating in the background.

Where this is of potential practical importance in the present case is in Optis' contentions that the skilled person would not be comfortable with, for example and in particular, modular arithmetic, or hashing functions/random numbers. This was basically a submission that the skilled person would lack the basic tools to do the task which Ericsson set - to assess its function and then improve it if necessary. The submission was rather grounded in the idea of the skilled person being an individual spread so thin across RAN1 that their CGK on any particular aspect of it must be very shallow. For the reasons I have just given, I reject this as a matter of principle and on the facts.

My conclusion in this respect is supported by the principle expressed by Pumfrey J in *Horne v. Reliance* [2000] FSR 90 (also cited in *Illumina*) that the attributes of the skilled person may often be deduced from assumptions which the specification clearly makes about their abilities. In the present case the specification of the Patents gives the skilled person some parameters for use as A, B and D in the LCG of the claims, but it assumes that with only the modest amount of help that the specification gives, the skilled person would be able to find more options for the parameters if they wanted to."

In the outcome, the patents, as to all the claims in issue, were held obvious over Ericsson.

—The skilled team

After the third paragraph, add new paragraph:

3.09   An electrically heated smoking system with improved heater was the subject of *Nicoventures v Philip Morris* [2021] EWHC 1977 (Pat) and the design team would require expertise in various fields, including cigarette/tobacco development, material science and mechanical and electronic engineering. It was argued that the skilled person should be identified as a lead project engineer, but it was held that this distinction between a skilled person leading a team, and the skilled team was unhelpful. There should be no difference between a team led by a non-heating engineer (say a technically unskilled manager) and a team led by a heating engineer. The fact was that the team was a construct—just as is the skilled person—and to focus on who led the team would begin to place a premium on precisely those sort of skills (inventiveness; curiosity; good communication) that an assembly of skilled persons might not have. However, it was the common general knowledge vesting in the "product engineer" that would be critical in this case. That was not, in any way, to diminish the general importance of (for example) tobacco chemists. It was simply—given the fact that the case turned on the engineering questions of heating and insulation—that the primary focus must be on the product engineer and his or her knowledge.

—Different teams for different situations

After the second paragraph, add new paragraphs:

3.10   In *Illumina Cambridge Ltd v Latvia MGI Tech SIA* [2021] EWHC 57 (Pat) which concerned DNA sequencing technology, Birss J. acknowledged the distinction between the two potentially relevant teams, the first kind of which is the person skilled in the art to whom the patent is addressed and whose attributes, skills and common general knowledge will be necessary to implement the patent and the second kind is relevant to obviousness. He explained that:

"66.   In the present case Illumina proposed, based on *Medimmune*, that a sensible test was to require something which could properly be called an established field at the priority date. Depending on the facts the field could be a research field as in *Medimmune* or a field of manufacture as in *Folding Attic Stairs*.

67.   The advantage of this test is that it provides a principled way of solving the problem identified in *Folding Attic Stairs*. If the design and manufacture of folding attic stairs in particular was an established field then there is nothing unfair in defining the skilled person that way. But if not then the wider definition (general carpenter plus metal fabricator) is appropriate. In other words the width of the field in which the skilled person operates for the purposes of obviousness (aka the 'art in which the problem lay' (per *Schlumberger*)) is ultimately governed by what was actually going on up to the priority date. It is not primarily a function of the invention itself, the problem to be solved, nor the patent's text.

68.   I conclude that in a case in which it is necessary to define the skilled person for the purposes of obviousness in a different way from the skilled person to whom the patent is addressed, the approach to take, bringing *Schlumberger* and *Medimmune* together, is:

(i)   To start by asking what problem does the invention aim to solve?

(ii)   That leads one in turn to consider what the established field which existed was, in which the problem in fact can be located.

(iii)   It is the notional person or team in that established field which is the relevant team making up the person skilled in the art.

69.   Sub-paragraph (i) is phrased as it is rather than referring to a problem the patentee was trying to solve, because although those words are in *Schlumberger*, I do not believe the Jacob LJ was there intending to suggest that the identification of the problem is anything other than an objective exercise.

70.   Sub-paragraph (ii) is phrased as it is for two reasons. First, there always will be some established field in which the problem would have been located. How wide the definition of that field should be will depend on the facts and what was going on in reality. Second, the field is the one in which the problem can be located, looking back from today as an exercise in hindsight. It does not matter at this stage if those in that field at the priority date did not perceive the particular problem or did not perceive it in the manner it is now characterised."

On the facts before him, however, Birss J. held that the person skilled in the art for one of the patents in issue was a team working on research into sequencing by synthesis, the team having two members: one having a background in molecular biology or genetics, with a focus on DNA sequencing and the other having a background in organic chemistry, both with a post-graduate degree, probably a PhD but perhaps a Master's, and some years' research experience. For other patents, an additional member who was a fluorescence chemist might be added. Having defined the team in this way, it would be the same skilled team to whom the patent is addressed and which would be relevant for sufficiency and all other issues.

The technical problem in *Alcon Research v Actavis Group* [2021] EWHC 1026 (Pat) was that although natural prostaglandins and the derivative PGF2a-IE had been found to be capable of lowering intraocular pressure, they had unacceptable side-effects that had stopped efforts to use them. Synthetic analogues were needed to maintain the activity while avoiding the side effects. To meet this need, the medical team would include a medicinal chemist and a pharmacologist. There was no dispute about the characteristics of the medicinal chemist, but the parties differed on the characteristics of the pharmacologist. Alcon contended that the skilled pharmacologist had a general interest in finding new treatments for glaucoma, and further that since existing treatments did not include prostaglandins or prostaglandin analogues, the notional skilled pharmacologist would have no knowledge or interest in them. Actavis contended that the skilled pharmacologist would be someone with an interest in using prostaglandins (or analogues) in the treatment of glaucoma. It was held that the established field in which the problem was located was prostaglandins having ocular therapeutic potential, and that any solution to the problem lay in the field of a pharmacologist who was a prostaglandin specialist. That finding was affirmed on appeal [2022] EWCA Civ 845, Arnold L.J. commenting that nature of each member's role, and the relationship between them, was inevitably fact-specific. In some cases, this might involve one member taking the lead: see e.g. *KCI Licensing Inc v Smith & Nephew Plc* [2010] EWHC 1487 (Pat); [2010] F.S.R. 31 at [103] and *Generics (UK) Ltd v Warner-Lambert Co LLC* [2015] EWHC 2548 (Pat); [2016] R.P.C. 3 at [118]–[119]. In the present case, although the skilled team would be led by the pharmacologist it did not follow that the medicinal chemist would have no role in deciding what steps to take in the light of the prior art. On the contrary, the evidence showed that, as would be expected, this would be a matter for discussion between the two members of the skilled team so that the input of the medicinal chemist could not be ignored. The compound fluprostenol was a highly potent FP-receptor agonist but was very selective and was known as a diagnostic in establishing whether FP receptors exist in any particular tissue. The claimed compound travoprost (fluprostenol isopropyl ester) involved incorporation of a double bond, replacing a carbon atom with oxygen and providing a trifluoromethyl substituent on a phenyl ring, the question being how to get the same or better efficacy as latanoprost with reduced or the same side effects. At first instance it was held that the skilled team would not without invention have tried fluprostenol in the first place since it was only known as an analytical tool, and there was no definitive way for the medicinal chemist to predict how these differences would affect the its pharmacological profile and its suitability for the treatment of glaucoma, so that the allegation of obviousness was rejected.

The knowledge attributed to the skilled team

—Common general knowledge in the art

After the first paragraph, add new paragraphs:

In *Fisher & Paykel Healthcare v Flexicare Medical* [2020] EWHC 3282 (Pat), Meade J. noted that **3.11** in the present case there was no primer and nor was there anything in the nature of a textbook to which the parties could direct the court for its pre-reading as a source of agreed common general knowledge (CGK). At the same time, the parties' respective opening skeleton arguments contained statements that there was much agreement about the CGK, but they had not got together to provide a joint list or a summary for the court of what was agreed and what was not. At his request the parties conferred during the evidence and during the time allowed for writing closings and provided a joint summary of the CGK which was extremely useful and had saved a lot of time in the preparation of this judgment. Because this was a relatively simple case the absence of a primer, textbook or agreed CGK summary during the court's reading and the oral evidence was not too much of a problem but in a more complex case it would have been. It was to be hoped parties will ensure that at least one of these is available by trial in future cases.

In *Tate and Lyle Technology Ltd's Application* BL O/035/21 the Hearing Officer quoted the following passage from the opinion of Luxmore J. in *British Acoustic Films v Nettlefold Productions* (1935) 53 R.P.C. 221:

"In my judgment it is not sufficient to prove common general knowledge that a particular disclosure is made in an article, or series of articles, in a scientific journal, no matter how wide the circulation of that journal may be, in the absence of any evidence that the disclosure is accepted generally by those who are engaged in the art to which the disclosure relates. A piece of particular knowledge as disclosed in a scientific paper does not become common general knowledge merely because it is widely read, and still less because it is widely circulated. Such a piece of knowledge only becomes general knowledge when it is generally known and accepted without question by the bulk of those who are engaged in the particular art; in other words, when it becomes part of their common stock of knowledge relating to the art."

In *Illumina Cambridge v Latvia MGI Tech SIA* [2021] EWHC 57 (Pat) the court referred to a classic statement of the law on common general knowledge is in *General Tire v Firestone* [1972] R.P.C. 457 at 482 and to a more recent summary by the Court of Appeal in *Idenix v Gilead* [2016] EWCA Civ 1089 at [72], citing *General Tire* and explaining the correct approach as follows:

"It follows that the common general knowledge is all that knowledge which is generally regarded as a good basis for further action by the bulk of those who are engaged in a particular field. It is that knowledge which those working in that field will bring to bear when they are reading or learn of a piece of prior art. It is not necessary that those persons have that knowledge in their minds, however. The common general knowledge includes material that they know exists and which they would refer to as a matter of course if they cannot remember it and which they understand is generally regarded as sufficiently reliable to use as a foundation for further work."

A point arose on the principles. The reference to a "good basis for further action" does not mean only things which work can be common general knowledge. The common general knowledge of a skilled person will often be as much about knowing what does not work as it is about knowing what does. Both are examples of a "good basis for further action" in that they are ideas which are worth acting upon. In a similar vein, in *Merck v Ono* [2015] EWHC 2973 (Pat) at [24], the court held that the common general knowledge includes contradictions as long as the information was sufficiently well known to be common general knowledge. So the fact a given technique was something which had been proposed for some years, tried out by a number of groups, but not (yet) shown to work, would not in and of itself preclude information about that technique being held to be part of the common general knowledge. A technique like that which was sufficiently well known could be common general knowledge.

In *Alcon Research v Actavis Group* [2021] EWHC 1026 (Pat), Meade J. commented at [75]–[76]:

"... it is not necessary or realistic to prove exactly by what route the skilled addressee would find or access CGK, and it may well be enough to show that the information is contained in a number of well known reference-type works. I found this observation particularly relevant to the Coleman classification system.

I also reject Alcon's approach of seeking to rule out general publications merely on the basis that they were general. For example, Rang & Dale's *Pharmacology* (2nd Ed, 1991) was a general pharmacology work, and Shields' *Textbook of Glaucoma* (3rd Ed, 1992) was a relatively general medical work about glaucoma, but that does not mean that the skilled addressee would not look to them, in addition to more specialist works, or that they could not form part of the evidence proving common general knowledge."

In *Lufthansa Technik v Astronics Advanced Electronics Systems* [2020] EWHC 1968 (Pat) the court referred to a negative aspect of common general knowledge represented by a negative mindset, or prejudice, against taking a particular course as in *Dyson Appliances Ltd v Hoover Ltd* [2001] R.P.C. 26 at [156]. A similar view was expressed by Floyd L.J. in *Wyeth v Merck Sharp and Dohme (UK)* [2021] EWCA Civ 1099 in which he explained [42] that it is not unknown for an obviousness case to be rejected on the basis that, with the passing of time, a prior art document comes to be seen as a dead end as opposed to a useful starting point for further development. Such a treatment of a prior art document must, however, be supported by the evidence that this is how the skilled person would treat the document, based on the common general knowledge.

Mitsubishi Electric Corp v Oneplus Technology (Shenzen) [2021] EWHC 1639 (Pat) concerned the use of pilot or reference signals which are sent in telecommunications networks for various purposes and the relevance of certain technical reports each of which had been published and was available to the public to download at the priority date. The court held that each of these reports would have been consulted by a skilled person given any reason to do so and in other words it would have been obvious for the skilled person to obtain the information, given any need to do so. This did not make the contents of these technical reports common general knowledge—see *KCI v Smith & Nephew* [2010] EWHC 1487 (Pat); [2010] F.S.R. 31, Arnold J. at [112].

After the last paragraph, add new paragraphs:

In *Tate and Lyle Technology Ltd's Application* BL O/035/21 the claimed invention related to a protein having psicose 3-epimerase activity useful in producing allulose which is a C3 epimer of fructose and is useful as a zero-calorie sweetener. The examiner had found documents designated D3–D8. The applicants argued that these documents might well have been found by the examiner in database searching, but there is a significant difference between what might have been found and references that form part of the common general knowledge. Otherwise they explained there is a danger of inadvertently mosaicking lots of references together, which is not the correct approach to inventive step and so it would not be correct to sweep them together into the common general knowledge. Furthermore, it was not apparent that the enzymes described in these documents were direct substitutes for each other. In the outcome, the Hearing Officer agreed that the skilled person, whilst having a general knowledge and understanding of ketose epimerases, would not be readily aware of the teaching of each of the documents D3–D8 and in particular all the enzymes and their sequence similarities. He would not go as far as accepting the suggestion such knowledge is only to be found in a textbook. Consequently, the skilled person might well be aware that epimerases are diverse and do not necessarily display great sequence similarity, but there was not a clear and consistent teaching that could be drawn from these disclosures such that it would form part of the common general knowledge over and above these broad assumptions about these enzymes. Modifying the sequence of D3 to a large degree to arrive at the claimed invention would require an inventive step and would not be obvious to the skilled person, nor would the skilled person be motivated to do so.

In *Teva v Astellas* [2022] EWHC 1316 (Pat) which concerned the compound mirabegron, which was sold by Astellas under the name Betmiga as a treatment for overactive bladder it was noted [176] that the claimants' case was a little unusual in that the CGK did nearly all the heavy lifting and provided all the rationale and motivation; the function of the cited prior art was simply to provide the identification of mirabegron to be plugged into an argument which could apply to any selective β3-AR agonist. Although at the priority date the β3-AR agonism mechanism had "momentum" relevant to OAB arising from the recent advances in understanding, the claimants' case suffered from the two defects of overstating the confidence that that would give the skilled addressee since it had not been used successfully in any drug for any condition, and it had failed for diabetes, and of oversimplifying the situation, in particular to the effect that any β3-AR agonist would be likely to succeed as a treatment, and also the poor quality of the examples in a reference relied on and the poor quality of the data given. Accordingly the patent was held valid.

In T 2759/17 *KAO CORPORATION/Composition of biofilm control agent* it was commented that a disclosure within a prior art document can only be considered to represent a suitable starting point for assessing inventive step if the skilled person would have realistically started from it. An important consideration in this assessment generally is whether this disclosure aims at the same or a similar purpose or effect as that underlying the patent in question. However, on the relevant facts, the Board in T 574/19 *KRKA/Process for forming solid oral dosage forms of solifenacin* concluded that such an approach would not lead to an objective assessment of inventive step because it would amount to disregarding the solvent-free method of the main citation on the ground that it did not represent the most promising—or a realistic—starting point for addressing the additional problems of content uniformity and stickiness, even before assessing whether these problems were actually solved by the claimed method itself. The respondent could not foreclose an assessment of inventive step starting from that reference just because the patent mentioned, among others, also these technical problems.

Prior art acknowledged in the specification

—Prejudice (an aspect of common general knowledge)

After the fourth paragraph (beginning "In Dyson v Hoover [2002] R.P.C. 465"), add new paragraphs:

In *E Mishan v Hozelock* [2020] EWCA Civ 871 which concerned an expandable garden hose and a prior art expandable oxygen hose for aviation use, it was held that there was no mindset in the garden hose industry comparable to that in *Dyson* and there was no evidence that the hose industry was resistant to innovation so that a finding of obviousness was not based on impermissible hindsight.

In *Add2 Research v Dspace* [2021] EWHC 1630 (Pat), Meade J. observed at [65]:

> "I would also comment that a mindset is usually about an attitude of the notional skilled addressee that something *must* (bags) or *should not* be done. It is not satisfied merely because a state of affairs is in fact common. In the context of the present case, the fact (if it were so) that those in the art always did make the interfaces bespoke does not necessarily mean that they thought that they *had to*."

3.17

In *Insulet v Roche Diabetes Care* [2021] EWHC 1933 (Pat) which concerned a portable infusion device, the plaintiff's evidence was that "Most companies which had successful pumps on the market would begin their work on the next generation of pump by building on the existing technology that they already had" and that this was driven at least in part by patient confidence and trust in pumps that they knew and by safety considerations. The defendants agreed that when beginning such a task the skilled person or team would have as part of their mental equipment the information that could be gleaned from existing products of a similar type. In the light of this evidence, the court concluded that part of the common general knowledge at the priority date would be the design choices, functionality and technology utilised in similar devices. For those with products already on the market, they might begin the design process from those specific products, but it did not follow that the skilled team would necessarily start with the specific attributes of a single existing product or family of products.

After the last paragraph, add new paragraph:

In *Koninklijke Philips v Asustek* [2019] EWCA Civ 2230 it was observed at [133] that if a particular prejudice is to prevent the skilled person from having a technically obvious idea, it needs to be a strong one. Sedley L.J. in *Dyson* said that the relevant skilled person was "functionally deaf and blind" to the relevant development, but nothing like that sort of mental block had been established here. Following *Dyson v Hoover* (above), a commercially driven mindset can be a relevant aspect of the skilled person's common general knowledge. Thus, what the skilled person does in the light of a given prior disclosure has to be decided with that mindset in mind. If the technical differences from the prior art to the invention are trivial, then the mindset may not matter, but if more substantial changes are involved, the court may conclude that the reluctant and prejudiced skilled person would not make them. However, if the court reaches the conclusion that the claimed invention would be arrived at by the skilled person, there is no further hurdle to be crossed concerned with whether the invention would be perceived as likely to lead to sufficient commercial success to make its manufacture worthwhile. The defendants argued that if a patent is devoid of implementation details, and concerned only with a particular idea, the pleaded prior art should be treated at a comparable level of generality from the perspective of the skilled person. However, this was not accepted as a general principle. The task for the party attacking the patent on the ground of obviousness is to show how the skilled person would arrive at the invention claimed from the disclosure of the prior art. If the invention claimed was, as it was here, a simple idea, then it was correct that this simple idea was the target for the obviousness attack. That did not mean, however, that the court was entitled to assume that the skilled person takes a different approach to the prior art, stripping out from it detail which the skilled person would otherwise have taken into account, or ignoring paths down which the skilled person would probably be led: see *Pozzoli* at [37]. The nature of the invention claimed cannot logically impact on the way in which the skilled person approaches the prior art, given that the prior art is to be considered without the benefit of hindsight knowledge of the invention. On the facts here [72], it is quite possible for the detail of a prior art document to operate as a set of technical blinkers which prevents a skilled person from going in an alternative direction. Prior to the invention the skilled person might think that in order to implement the prior art he/she needs to take in all of a reference's details, whereas once the blinkers are taken off by the patent, with its clear suggested proposals, the skilled person can see how the invention is to be implemented when he/she would not have done so merely starting from that reference. In the outcome, obviousness was not established.

The inventive concept

—Identifying the inventive concept

Replace the first paragraph with:

3.18

This section discusses the established caselaw on inventive concept from a validity perspective. How much these cases are applicable to the identification of inventive concept for the purposes of the doctrine of equivalents, or remain good law at all is open to debate. See §125.01 and following. Note as also mentioned in §2.03 that HHJ Hacon held in *Interdigital Technology v Lenovo Group* [2021] EWHC 2152 (Pat) that the date at which a patent specification must be interpreted is its priority date or application date if there is no valid priority date rather than the date of publication of the granted patent, see §§76.07 and 125.05.

After the eighth paragraph (beginning "Especially in empirical research fields it may not be possible"), add new paragraphs:

In *SRJ Ltd and SRG Technologies Group Plc v Per-Christian Irgens* BL O/429/22 it was held that the skilled person had no reason to use the cited prior art device for the patentees' purpose, citing *Vernacare v Environmental Pulp Products* [2012] EWPCC 41, *Inhale v Quadrant* [2002] R.P.C. 21 and *Actavis v ICOS* [2019] UKSC 15.

In a recent EPO decision in T 116/18 *SUMITOMO/Insecticide compositions* the patent proprietor submitted experimental data to prove a technical effect, that data being post-published evidence. The following questions have been referred to the Enlarged Board of Appeal:

1. Should an exception to the principle of free evaluation of evidence (see e.g. G 3/97, Reasons 5, and G 1/12, Reasons 31) be accepted in that post-published evidence must be disregarded on the ground that the proof of the effect rests exclusively on the post-published evidence?

2. If the answer is yes (the post-published evidence must be disregarded if the proof of the effect rests exclusively on this evidence), can the post-published evidence be taken into consideration if, based on the information in the patent application in suit or the common general knowledge, the skilled person at the filing date of the patent application in suit would have considered the effect plausible (*ab initio* plausibility)?

3. If the answer to the first question is yes (the post-published evidence must be disregarded if the proof of the effect rests exclusively on this evidence), can the post-published evidence be taken into consideration if, based on the information in the patent application in suit or the common general knowledge, the skilled person at the filing date of the patent application in suit would have seen no reason to consider the effect implausible (*ab initio* implausibility)?

The reference is currently pending as G 2/21 *Plausibility*. In a brief filed by CIPA, it has been argued that the answer to the first question should be negative, see the CIPA Journal, June 2022 at page 8. The EPO's approach to inventive step involves formulating a technical problem—based on technical effects achieved vis-à-vis an objectively chosen "closest prior art", of which the applicant may not have been aware when drafting the application. As a result, it is inevitable that in some (many) cases, the data needed to make the necessary comparison is not in the application as filed. The referring decision T 116/18 recognised this very problem (Reasons 13.7.2). Also, in a huge number of cases, the patent application must be filed relatively early in a research program, before all of the data and evidence relating to the invention has been collected. For example, this may be because of a planned disclosure, not necessarily in the control of the applicant—it could be for regulatory reasons, or in view of known competitor activity. It has hence been established EPO practice for many, many years to accept post-filing evidence in support of inventive step. It would be unfair on applicants to change that now, and it might have undesirable consequences for already-granted EP patents. In relation to the second question, it was submitted that any requirement for information in respect of plausibility (or lack of implausibility) at the filing date should be minimal. A review article by Giliani and Gill, *Where next for plausibility?* focuses on T116/18 and was published in the CIPA Journal, October 2021 at pages 18–21.

The Enlarged Board issued a communication in advance of the oral proceedings scheduled for November 24, 2022. In relation to the first question it was noted that the principle of free evaluation of evidence is a key rule of procedural law governing patent grant proceedings (see G 1/12 *Admissibility of appeal* at [31], G 3/97 *INDUPAK/Opposition by a third party* and G 4/97 *GENENTECH/Opposition on behalf of a third party* at [5]). Disregarding such evidence would deprive the party submitting and relying on such evidence of a basic legal and procedural right generally recognised in the contracting states and enshrined in EPC arts 113(1) and 117(1). The core issue rests with the question what a skilled person, with the common general knowledge in mind, understands as the teaching of the invention at the original filing date of the application. The technical effect relied on, even at a later stage, needs to be encompassed by that technical teaching and embody the same invention. It is then to be considered whether a skilled person, having the common general knowledge in mind, would have any significant reason to doubt it. In the absence of such doubts, post-published evidence such as experimental data, would be a potential source for a body when deciding on inventiveness to decide whether or not it is convinced of the technical effect. However, it appears questionable whether such technical effect can be relied on if the skilled person, on the basis of the application as originally filed together with the common general knowledge, has significant doubts.

A factual situation materially different from that in T 1329/04 *JOHNS HOPKINS/Factor 9* in which it was held that no plausible solution of the technical problem had been provided was found in T 184/16 *GALENICUM/Novel compounds* in which post-filing experimental evidence was considered pertinent notwithstanding the absence of such examples in the application as filed. The relevant facts appear from the following explanation by the Board:

"In the case underlying T 1329/04, claim 1 was directed to a polynucleotide sequence encoding a polypeptide denoted as GDF-9. The problem to be solved was isolating a further member of the TGF-beta superfamily. However, GDF-9 lacked the most striking structural feature which served to establish whether or not a polypeptide belonged to the TGF-beta superfamily, namely the presence of seven cysteine residues, and furthermore had only 34% sequence homology with known members of the TGF-beta superfamily. Those seven cysteine residues played a fundamental role in the tertiary structure of the protein, which was in turn to a very large extent responsible for its functional activity. The board held that accordingly, any change in the pattern of the seven cysteine residues would be expected to have significant repercussions for the function of a TGF-beta family member. The board therefore considered that any compound which did not exhibit those residues could not clearly and unambiguously be considered a member of the TGF-beta superfamily unless further evidence was available to that effect. Plausibility was therefore denied and post-published evidence not taken into account.

In the present case, however, the core structure of the claimed compounds of formula (I) conforms to that of the C-aryl glucoside family identified in D7. The situation in the present case is thus different from that in T 1329/04.

In view of this, the post-published evidence D4 can be taken into consideration to support the disclosure in the patent application."

—The collocation/combination test and its relevance to inventive concept

To the end of the third paragraph (beginning "In Nokia v IPCom [2009] EWHC 3482 at [108]"), add:

3.19   A similar finding was made in *Nicoventures v Philip Morris* [2021] EWHC 1977 (Pat), there being no synergistic effect between heating of the tobacco product and the insulation (whether to keep the device efficient or to protect the user), the insulation feature being so blindingly obvious that it was quite clear that this was a non-inventive combination of what may be (or what may not be) two inventions, given that there was literally nothing apart from heat linking the two features. Accordingly the obviousness of each feature was evaluated separately and both were held to lack inventive step so that the allegation of invalidity succeeded.

After the eighth paragraph (beginning "The SABAF approach was not followed"), add new paragraph:

The main claim of one of the patents in issue in *Illumina Cambridge Ltd v Latvia MGI Tech SIA* [2021] EWHC 57 (Pat) related to a conjugate molecule consisting of a nucleotide, a cleavable linker and a fluorescent dye. The collocation argument was that in the conjugate molecule there was no extra technical effect or benefit, over and above the known effects of those components acting independently. The claimants replied that the compound claimed was useful, that its utility derived from the compound as a whole and could not be parsed down to be nothing more than the sum of the parts, and also that the successful use of the compound in a 20-cycle sequencing reaction with a 1% error rate represented a technical advance over the prior art and an answer to the collocation case. They also pointed out that despite the research of their legal team, there had been no case in which the collocation principle had been applied to a case concerning a chemical molecule. They submitted that this was not an accident: it was because the argument could not succeed when applied to that sort of invention. On the evidence it was held that the case was about unwelcome interactions. The dye fluoresced because the linker and the nucleotide did not interact in an unfavourable way. The dye part was not a priori immune from the effects of the linker or the nucleotide. The skilled person would have hoped the molecule worked satisfactorily because the two elements did not interact, but that would need to be demonstrated by an experiment testing the combination as a whole, which meant that the collocation principle did not apply. The molecule claimed was a single invention. Its beneficial properties derived from the functional relationship which included non-interference between the constituent parts. Accordingly the claim was held valid [514]. The decision was affirmed by Arnold L.J., [2021] EWCA Civ 1924, commenting that even assuming that the collocation principle is applicable to an invention consisting of a class of molecules, the application of the principle must take account of that technical context. Although the molecules claimed are made up of building blocks, those building blocks are incorporated into single molecules. The judge found that the skilled team would know from their common general knowledge that, when joined together, these building blocks were capable of interacting adversely with each other in various ways and that the skilled team could not predict in advance whether this would occur or not. If it did occur, the claimed molecules would not be useful in sequencing by synthesis. The patent demonstrated that there is no such adverse interaction, and thus the claimed molecules are useful for that purpose, so that the patent claimed a single invention that made a technical contribution to the art which neither cited reference makes even when taken together, so that the objection of obviousness was rejected.

Individual references and combinations of references

Teachings, or combinations of teachings, that may be relied on

—**Citable disclosures and combinations of disclosures**

After the last paragraph, add new paragraphs:

Suitability of an item of prior art as a starting point was considered in *Adolf Nissen Elektrobau v* **3.20**
Horizont [2019] EWHC 3522 (IPEC) following *Eli Lilly v Human Genome Sciences* [2008] EWHC 1903
(Pat); [2008] R.P.C. 29, at [295] which made it clear that whether the skilled person takes the view that
an item of prior art is a promising or unpromising solution to the problem, he or she will consider it with
exactly the same care and interest. HHJ Hacon commented at [29]–[31]:

> "Moving away from the particular facts of *Eli Lilly*, it is possible for the subject-matter of the prior
> art to be too remote from the nature of the problem to suggest the claimed solution to the skilled
> person. Sometimes such prior art is characterised as being not a worthwhile starting point. But this
> sort of remoteness is really just one of many alternative reasons why a skilled person may, having
> carefully considered the prior art, fail to spot the invention.
>
> In the present case it was said of one of the cited items of prior art that the skilled person would
> have thought that implementing its content would result in making a product that was dangerous to
> users and that therefore the prior art would have been of no interest as a starting point. I think that
> characterising prior art as a good or bad starting point can be a distraction. Whatever the prior art
> may be, the skilled person is invariably required to start with it in the sense that he or she is deemed
> to have considered it carefully. Having done so, the skilled person either will or will not find the
> invention in suit technically obvious.
>
> The perception of a dangerous outcome might be relevant on certain facts. To take an example, a
> line of investigation may not be pursued by the skilled person because of expected dangers involved
> and this might make a difference to the obviousness of the end-product of such an investigation.
> However, such circumstances must be distinguished from a situation in which the skilled person
> believes a variant of the prior art to be technically obvious but of limited or no commercial value
> because the result may be dangerous or otherwise unattractive to users. Such unattractive qualities
> would not make the variant any less obvious from a technical standpoint. The unattractive qualities
> may affect whether the variant falls within a claim, but that is a separate matter."

Where a cited document discloses numerous embodiments, it fell to be decided in *Evalve v Edwards
Life Sciences* [2020] EWHC 514 (Pat) whether it was necessary for the skilled person to prefer that
particular embodiment over the others before taking it forward, and whether that might be an inappropriate focus. The defendants argued that it was irrelevant whether a discrete piece of information had been
disclosed in isolation (e.g. in a single paper) or as part of a series (e.g. a book chapter) or as part of a
document (e.g. a paragraph in a patent), citing *Brugger v Medic-Aid* [1996] R.P.C. 635 at 661 about
multiple avenues. However, that argument was rejected, the court observing:

> "In my judgment Edwards' submission about the law is wrong. There is nothing in the legislation
> which requires that the context in which a discrete piece of information has been disclosed should
> be ignored, as a matter of law, when considering it as a starting point for an obviousness analysis.
> As a matter of fact a piece of information disclosed in isolation may well be regarded differently by
> skilled people from the same piece of information disclosed as part of a larger work. Although the
> obviousness analysis is necessarily artificial in a number of ways and the skilled person is a legal
> construct, there is nothing in the law which precludes that result or renders it necessarily irrelevant.
> Both sides must take the prior art as they find it.
>
> The skilled person is presented with the prior art and reads it with interest. As a matter of law they
> read it all and they never tire when doing this. That satisfies the policy identified by Edwards because
> it means that all the words, pictures, paragraphs and embodiments in a document, even those buried
> a long way inside, are part of the state of the art and are available as potential starting points, in
> principle. This is so even if in the real world actual skilled people would never have read the docu-
> ment or would have started skimming after the first page. However once the notional skilled person
> has read the whole document, including what is (with hindsight) the important paragraph, what they
> do then will be a question of fact. They may put the whole thing down and walk away. There may
> be a number of obvious avenues to take forward. The obvious avenues may include the one the
> defendant wants or it may not. The perceived qualities of one route may or may not have an effect
> on the attractiveness of another route as a place to start. The fact one route is a very attractive and
> obvious place to start does not, either as a matter of law or in fact, mean that other routes may not
> be obvious places to start too."

In the outcome, the claimed subject-matter was held to involve an inventive step over the relevant embodiment.

—Obviousness having regard to a single reference and common general knowledge

After the last paragraph, add new paragraph:

3.22   In *Commscope v SOLiD* [2022] EWHC 769 (Pat) the claimants contended that a cited reference came with all the baggage disclosed in the preferred embodiment. However, that contention was only possible if the more general teaching in that reference was ignored, and the reference was not read as a skilled person would have done. Accordingly the relevant claims were held to be obvious over that reference.

Evaluation of the differences—additional evidence and arguments commonly adduced

—Allegedly trivial or arbitrary differences

After the third paragraph (beginning "In Actavis v Novartis [2010] F.S.R. 18, [2010] EWCA Civ 82"), add new paragraph:

3.26   In *Philip Morris Products v RAI Strategic Holdings* [2021] EWHC 537 (Pat) it was argued that the allegedly novel feature (a change from extruded to gathered sheet reconstituted tobacco) was arbitrary and made no technical contribution, citing *Optis v Apple* [2020] EWHC 2746 (Pat) at [207]–[208]. It was not disputed that a claim which lacks all technical contribution is uninventive in law; however, it was said that there was a technical contribution in the present case. It was argued that there is no requirement in law that an invention be better than the prior art because a valid invention can lie in providing an alternative. The reply was that there still had to be a technical contribution which in the case of an alternative could lie in providing a new and inventive way to get to the same result. The patentees argued that it was the product claimed which was new and not obvious simply because the prior art did not suggest it. The court observed that to argue that because a choice is arbitrary and so would not be thought of, therefore it is non-obvious, and therefore a technical contribution of a new and non-obvious product is made, was circular. In terms of technical contribution, the claimed product had the tangible (but minor and obvious) advantage over the prior art that it was easier to handle the tobacco for a cigarette. There had been conflation between the added matter and obviousness arguments. The standard is different and while added matter concerns what choice (by way of claim narrowing) might be made from e.g. a grandfather application, inventive step concerns what choice might be made from the prior art and common general knowledge. Squeezes could arise, and the EPO case law recognised that a technical effect not disclosed in the application cannot be relied on for inventive step. However, that did not justify a general mixing of the two issues. In the outcome, objections of lack of inventive step succeeded.

After the eighth paragraph (beginning "The EPO also takes the position that features"), add new paragraphs:

In T 2314/16 *RAKUTEN/Distributing rewards by assigning users to partial advertisement display areas* the claimed business method ended with how to determine the reward distribution ratio. Dividing the advertisement display area into partial areas and allocating each partial area to a user such that when the partial area was clicked on the user got a reward, were based on technical considerations of the web page system and was not motivated by any business considerations. In order to come up with this idea, it was necessary to understand how a website is built, and in particular how an image map works. Thus, this feature could not be part of the non-technical requirements. Instead it was part of the solution that had to be evaluated for obviousness.

This decision may be contrasted with T 550/14 *SWISS REINSURANCE/Catastrophe relief* which concerned a computer-implemented method for managing funding of catastrophe relief efforts associated with a special purpose vehicle that defined a corporate body to isolate financial risks. A valid starting point was held to be a networked computer system comprising a control module and several functional modules. Such a "networked" system could be interconnected with other networked computers via a telecommunications network and not just be a stand-alone system and followed from the business requirements in a straightforward and obvious manner. The remaining claimed features related to the business method and were non-technical. Similarly in T 1234/17 *ADIDAS/Customization based on physiological data* the claimed method of customising a piece of footwear involved receiving gait data based at least in part on data characterising a category of human gait and generated by a sensor including an accelerometer and determining a customized design for the piece of footwear based at least in part on the gait characterising data which included a time series of acceleration vectors. The question was whether the mere idea of mapping this acceleration data to gait category was technical, involving any technical considerations or having any overall technical effect. The Board's conclusion was negative, citing T 1798/13 *SWISS REINSURANCE/Forecasting the value of a structured financial product* and T 2079/19 *SWISSRE/Control of cellular alarm systems* where the invention was seen to lie in the improvement of the measurement technique itself, involving technical consideration about the sensors and their positions.

—Solution to a "technical problem"—"AgrEvo obviousness"

Replace the last paragraph with:

Arguments for *AgrEvo* obviousness were rejected in *TQ Delta v Zytel* [2019] EWHC 562 and similarly in *Optis v Apple* [2021] EWHC 1739 (Pat) where Meade J. observed at [283] that:

    3.28

"In my view, Apple's case represents a considerable oversimplification of the real-world position. The notional skilled addressee would be aware of counter-based and window-based triggers, with their similarities and differences. That does not mean that there was a perception in the art that they were interchangeable, or that which to use was merely a matter of taste. Switching between them was not perceived as merely a workshop modification in the way that the choice of glue or nails might be when two physical items have to be fixed to each other."

At [290] he held that:

"These arguments are quite finely balanced and there are valid points both ways. However, overall I prefer Optis' position. In particular, there is nothing in InterDigital to suggest or motivate a change to a counter-based system, or, as it were, to revisit the choice presented by the Editor's note. Lack of motivation is not fatal to an obviousness case and indeed in a true workshop modification case there may be no motivation at all, yet the change is obvious in law. However, Apple has failed to make out that this is a workshop modification."

—New or improved result flowing from a claimed combination of features; relationship to technical problem

After the last paragraph, add new paragraphs:

Whether there was invention in a bottle closure having a flexible valve retained more securely in place by a crimping flange on the circular wall which was an upstanding wall and which was capable of being bent from an uncrimped position to a crimped position to retain the valve in the device by engaging a peripheral flange on the valve was considered in *Obrist Closures Switzerland's Application* BL O/554/21. Lengthening the crimping flange of a prior product to provide the needed security was seen as obvious but patentability was conferred on the basis that the claimed length of 1.4mm was alleged to be the optimum in terms of benefits achieved. The description explained that: "It has been found that this flange length gives particular benefits to the force required to pull the valve out of a sub-assembly, by greatly increasing the force required, in some embodiments by in excess of a 300% increase in valve pull-out force." The application was allowed to proceed on the basis that the applicant should receive the benefit of the doubt, see *Blacklight Power Inc v The Comptroller-General of Patents* [2009] R.P.C. 6.

    3.29

European practitioners, especially in the chemical and life sciences fields, should be aware of the limited supportive value of predictive or "prophetic" examples in the eyes of the USPTO and US courts. In *Ex parte Nico L.M. Callewaert et al.,* 2021 WL 795084, 25 February 2021, an applicant relied upon an example in the specification to help prove an unexpected result (that the living cell would create certain "unnatural glycan structures"). The example was written in the present tense and therefore assumed to be prophetic, see *Atlas Powder Co v E.I. du Pont De Nemours & Co,* 750 F.2d 1569, 1578 (Fed. Cir. 1984). The PTAB observed that it was well settled that unexpected results must be established by factual evidence. "Mere argument or conclusory statements in the specification does not suffice": see *In re De Blauwe,* 736 F.2d 699, 705 (Fed. Cir. 1984). The relevant example which was prophetic and not evidence of results obtained did not provide the *factual* evidence needed to support unexpected results (emphasis in the opinion).

Following the decision in G 1/19 *CONNOR/Patentability of computer-implemented simulations* (see §1.11), the case returned to the Appeal Board in T 489/14 *BENTLEY SYSTEMS/Pedestrian simulation* (March 2021). In the outcome, the main request was refused on the grounds that in a computer-implemented invention, a technical effect relevant for the assessment of inventive step exists if the features of the claim directly achieve a (real) technical effect on physical reality (including both external physical reality and the "internal" physical reality of the computer system in which the invention is implemented). In addition, an "implied" technical effect relevant for the assessment of inventive step is present if the claimed invention or the data produced by it necessarily achieves a real technical effect when it is put to its intended (and only relevant) use. In contrast, merely providing calculated data which corresponds closely to technical effects of physical entities is not a technical effect relevant for the assessment of inventive step. Therefore the claimed method which reflected the behaviour of a crowd moving through an environment did not contribute to a technical effect for the purpose of assessing inventive step. Indeed, the potential use of such data was not limited to technical purposes, as it could be used in computer games or presented to a human for obtaining knowledge about the modelled environment, to give just two examples of non-technical uses that were within the scope of the claim. The many auxiliary requests directed e.g. to design methods or measurement methods were also refused.

Ticagrelor for use in a treatment of Acute Coronary Syndrome or myocardial infarction, in combination with acetyl salicylic acid and a computer program product comprising instructions causing a computer to present questions to a patient and generate patient-specific feedback information was considered in T 752/19 *INTELLECTUAL PROPERTY ENABLER STOCKHOLM/Ticagrelor, acetylsalicylic acid and a computer program.* In refusing the application, the Board held that:

> "In the case at hand, the pharmaceutical composition is indeed not new. Since the computer program of claim 1 does not interact with the intrinsic properties of the pharmaceutical composition, it can be ruled out that it leads to an overall technical effect in terms of improved patient compliance. Any improved patient compliance in the case at hand, as apparently demonstrated by D4 or D5, is instead the result of a 'broken technical chain' (see T 1670/07, point 11 of the Reasons), namely an alleged chain of technical effects starting with information provided to a patient which is then broken by the patient's mental activities. In the case at hand, the possible final technical effect of improved patient compliance brought about by a computer program generating and presenting patient-specific feedback is conditional on the patient's mental activities and thus cannot be used to establish an overall technical effect. This is analogous to the information provided on a package insert, which would also not produce any technical effect in an unbroken technical chain. In fact, D6, an extract from a textbook on therapeutics, which was cited in the contested decision and also discussed by the appellant, lists several such techniques involving a broken technical chain, such as labelling prescriptions with clear directions, encouraging the use of stickers or calendars to remind patients to take medications, providing feedback to patients, establishing a positive relationship with them or rewarding them for taking medications. While the board does not dispute that such techniques may have the effect of improved patient compliance, such an effect is conditional on the patient's mental activities and thus does not contribute to the technical character of the invention."

—Obvious to try—reasonable expectation of success

To the end of the third paragraph, add:

3.30
However, in *Promptu Systems v Sky UK* [2021] EWHC 2021 (Pat), Meade J. commented at [185] that in assessing obviousness the number of possible options available may be a relevant factor (see the statement of Kitchin J. as he then was in *Generics v Lundbeck* [2007] EWHC 1040 (Pat) at [72], also approved in *Actavis v ICOS* [2019] UKSC 15).

After the nineteenth paragraph (beginning "In Medimmune Ltd v Norvartis Kitchin L.J. explained"), add new paragraph:

Use of travoprost (fluprostenol isopropyl ester, FIE) for the treatment of glaucoma and ocular hypertension was the subject of *Alcon Research v Actavis Group* [2021] EWHC 1026 (Pat). It was the defendants' case that FIE was obvious to try based on its affinity and selectivity for the FP receptor and not structure. Their case suffered from the problem that the common general knowledge of fluprostenol was as an analytical tool, not a medicament. Insofar as it was known as a medicament, its use was only in an unrelated field (luteolysis in animals) and it was not mentioned in the relevant standard textbook on prostaglandin research. It was observed that hope for a positive result sufficient to justify research being done does not necessarily imply an expectation of success (see e.g. *MedImmune v Novartis* [2012] EWCA Civ 1234 at [90]–[91], referred to in *Actavis v ICOS* [2019] UKSC 15). Even if the skilled team thought of trying fluprostenol in animal models to assess its possible use to treat glaucoma, they would have regarded it as very uncertain what advantage it would have from the standpoint of side effects. Even if they had thought that initial animal experiments with fluprostenol would have needed such low resources that it could be justified as a gamble, that would not make it obvious. Much more attractive options consistent with the overall teaching and direction of the standard prostaglandin textbook were available.

—Delay—"If obvious, why was it not done before?"

Add new paragraph at the beginning:

3.34
In *Kwikbolt v Airbus* [2021] EWHC 732 (IPEC) HHJ Hacon observed at [177]:

"Even if a piece of prior art is old, the hypothesis is still that the skilled person will read it with care at the filing or priority date. If an obvious modification to the prior art would occur to the skilled person, such a modification is not taken out of consideration for inventive step solely because the skilled person would believe that modified or not, this old piece of prior art would have little practical or commercial use as of the filing or priority date."

Avoidance of hindsight

After the second paragraph, add new paragraphs:

However, a somewhat contrary position was set out in *E Mishan v Hozelock* [2020] EWCA Civ 871 at [76] per Arnold L.J. and Henderson L.J., Floyd L.J. dissenting:

3.40

"In simple terms ... the patent system aims to incentivise technical innovation, and investment in and disclosure of such innovation, by conferring limited monopolies. Monopolies are generally contrary to the public interest, however, because they prevent competition. Patent law contains a number of mechanisms which are designed to strike a balance between these conflicting considerations. Amongst these mechanisms are the requirements of novelty and inventive step (i.e. non-obviousness): in order not to fetter competition unduly, the public is deemed to have the right to do anything which is disclosed by, or obvious in the light of, any item of prior art, no matter how obscure, which was made available to the public anywhere in the world before the relevant date, without infringing a patent. For that reason, when attacking the validity of a patent, the party doing so is allowed to select the prior art used as the foundation for the argument with 20/20 hindsight. To that extent (but only to that extent), hindsight is not merely permitted, but an inherent feature of the current design of the European patent system (and indeed, of most patent systems worldwide). It inevitably follows that some patents turn out to be invalid because, unbeknownst to the inventor, or indeed other persons skilled in the relevant art, prior art emerges when sufficient searches are carried out which anticipates or renders obvious the claimed invention. The judge concluded that this was such a case so far as obviousness over McDonald was concerned, and I see no basis on which this Court is entitled to interfere with that conclusion."

The above discussion on the patent bargain was approved by Marcus Smith J. in *Nicoventures v Philip Morris* [2021] EWHC 1977 (Pat) at [66].

The tosylate salt of a drug called sorafenib was the subject of *Teva v Bayer* [2021] EWHC 2690 (Pat). A published article reported a clinical trial of oral tablets of sorafenib with encouraging preliminary clinical data but without mention of an appropriate salt to use. The evidence of an expert for the patentee Bayer was that tosylate would not have been included in a salt screen seeking improved solubility because the reported solubility of sorafenib tosylate was low. Mellor J. held that the skilled person would not have been aware of the real solubility of sorafenib tosylate until the salt form had in fact been made and tested and dissuasion by solubility data from the EMA regulatory documents necessarily involved hindsight. The claim to sorafenib tosylate was therefore found obvious in view of the clinical trial disclosure. Mellor J. commented at [113]:

"In this case, there were accusations of hindsight from both sides. It is axiomatic that hindsight must be eliminated, but hindsight can infect both sides of the analysis. It is naturally critical that the obviousness attack must not be influenced or tainted by hindsight, but equally, hindsight must not infect the response to that attack. Hindsight can infect the response to an obviousness case if, for example, a witness (knowing of the 'target') appears to be looking for ways to avoid taking a particular step or making a particular choice towards the target, when the Court assesses that the Skilled Person would consider the step or choice differently and, having considered it dispassionately, would decide to take the step or choice."

In contrast, in *Saint-Gobain Adfors v 3M Innovative Properties* [2022] EWHC 1018 (Pat) which related to producing shaped abrasive particles the allegation of obviousness relied on the skilled person chancing on a combination of conditions within a multi-dimensional space. While there may have been reasons why the skilled person would have considered making changes to certain variables, the defendant's expert did not identify why the particular combination of variables would be arrived at by the skilled person. Once the combinations of variables which produced planar/concave dish-shape was known, it was possible to explain how the skilled person could have arrived at those combinations of variables, and to produce reasons why each change of variable could have been made. However, this evidence was a classic step-by-step analysis infected by hindsight knowledge of the answer.

To the end of the thirteenth paragraph (beginning "It should, therefore, be borne in mind that, in choosing expert witnesses"), add:

In *Conversant v Apple* (above) it was observed at [127] that:

"The skilled person when they read the cited prior art is not being told or being given a hint that a solution to a problem might be found in that document. Otherwise there is a real risk of injecting hindsight into the analysis."

Problem/solution analysis at the EPO

—The EPO problem and solution approach to consideration of inventive step

After the first paragraph, add new paragraphs:

3.42
A published decision in the field of biotechnology cited inter alia in T 1450/16 *SHURE/Acoustic port of a hearing device* contains significant pointers to what might be expected of a skilled person considering a prior art reference, see T 455/91 *GENENTECH/Expression in yeast* OJ EPO 1995, 684. The appropriate approach was set out in *GENENTECH* as follows:

"The Board considers it useful for the purpose of the present decision to make some considerations on what is believed to be the attitude of the said person skilled in the art vis-à-vis possible changes, modifications and/or adjustments in known products (e.g. a plasmid) or procedures (e.g. an experimental protocol). This with a view to provide a possibly objective answer to the question whether or not the introduction of a given change in a structure or in a procedure can be seen as obvious for the skilled person, avoiding any ex post facto analysis.

In the Board's view, the skilled person in this field is well aware of the fact that even a small structural change in a product (e.g. a vector, a protein, a DNA sequence) or in a procedure (e.g. a purification process) can produce dramatic functional changes. Therefore, the said expert would constantly be conditioned by the prior art and, before taking action, would carefully ponder any possible modification, change or adjustment against the background of the existing knowledge. Under these circumstances, in the Board's view, the skilled person would adopt a conservative attitude. However, this must not be seen in the sense of being reluctant or opposed to modify or adjust a known product or process, but rather in the sense of being cautious. For example, the skilled person in question would neither go against an established prejudice nor try to enter into "sacrosanct" or unpredictable areas nor take incalculable risks. However, within the normal design procedures, the said expert would readily seek appropriate, manifest changes, modifications or adjustments which involve little trouble or work and no risks or only calculable risks, especially for the sake of obtaining a more handy or convenient product or of simplifying a procedure. In particular, the skilled person working in one field (e.g. expression in yeast) would regard a means conveniently adopted in a neighbouring field (e.g. the bacterial art) as being readily usable also in that field, if this transfer of technical knowledge involves nothing out of the ordinary.

Taking the above considerations into account, the proper question to ask is not whether the skilled person could have tried to modify the technical teaching disclosed in document (24'), but whether he or she would have done so. In seeking an answer to this question it should be borne in mind that the skilled person in the field of expression of polypeptides in yeast had good reasons to move in the direction of the technical teaching of the patent-in-suit, because the skilled person knew how to adjust the technical teaching in (24') from an adjacent neighbouring field, namely the bacterial art. This was a sufficient incentive for an expert at least to try to transform knowledge from the bacterial art to yeast. It is observed that in this respect the expert in the bacterial art and for yeast is the same."

As explained in T 441/93 *GIST BROCADES/Cloning in kluyveromyces*, with reference to T 500/91 *BIOGEN/Alpha-interferon* and T 455/91 *GENENTECH/Expression in yeast* the development of the art normally expected by the skilled person does not include solving technical problems by performing scientific research in areas not yet explored. The notional skilled person will perform a transfer of technology from a neighbouring field to his/her specific field of interest if this transfer involves routine experimental work comprising only routine trials. In the present case, inventive step was acknowledged. in the absence of any suggestion from the prior art that the cell walls of both yeasts might behave in a similar fashion, the skilled person would not have reasonably expected to transfer the technology developed for permeablizing *Saccharomyces* cell walls to *Kluyveromyces* by simple routine experimentation but might rather have expected that scientific research would be necessary to succeed.

T 441/93 was considered distinguishable on the facts in *Sun Pharmaceutical Industries Australia's Application* BL O/320/20 firstly because there was no transfer of technology and secondly because the skilled person reading the relevant citation would be minded to use the technology on other *P. somniferum* cultivars, including those that produced noscapine, in order to attempt to manipulate the morphine biosynthesis pathway and increase the yield of codeine and would arrive at a plant as claimed.

Selection of the starting-point prior art

After the first paragraph, add new paragraph:

The appropriate person or body to select the primary reference was considered in T 1450/16 *SHURE/ Acoustic port of a hearing device*. It would not be in line with the objective approach of the Boards for this to be entrusted to a person skilled in the art since that would mean that the same (fictitious) person as the one who finally assessed the obviousness of a certain claimed subject-matter had already selected their "favourite" prior-art document in order to conduct that assessment. The person skilled in the art within the meaning of EPC art.56 enters the stage only when the objective technical problem has already been formulated. The skilled person under EPC art.56 is the person qualified to solve the established objective technical problem and not necessarily the person versed in the field of the underlying application or in the field of the selected closest prior art. It must be the respective deciding body (whose members cannot be equated with the skilled person as a notional entity; see T 1462/14 *WISeKey SEMICONDUCTORS/Contactless circuit* at [14], [15])—be it the examining division, the opposition division or the relevant Board of Appeal—who selects the closest prior art rather than the skilled person mentioned in EPC art.56, see T 855/15 *WONDERWARE/Security architecture* at [8.4]. In the latter case, the Board observed: **3.44**

"For this assessment, the deciding body will select one or more documents for consideration. However, no argument is required as to whether the skilled person would select a document. In fact, the board considers that a consideration of what the skilled person would do, in particular whether the skilled person 'would select' a document, in order 'to arrive at the invention as claimed' would amount to hindsight reasoning, because the skilled person would have to be assumed to know the invention before an argument could be made as to what he would do in order 'to arrive at' it."

After the second paragraph, add new paragraph:

Principles for selection of the primary reference are set out in T 797/17 *OVD KINEGRAM/ Multilayer body*:

"The board cannot agree with the submission that this embodiment does not constitute a realistic starting point because it does not provide the skilled person with any indications as to how to proceed to solve the problem. In principle, any element of the prior art in the field of invention which discloses an object developed for the same purpose or with the same objective is a possible starting point. A special justification, e.g. based on considerations of the skilled person, is not required.

In particular, the question whether such an element contains a reference to the solution of the objective technical problem is irrelevant for its choice as a starting point. This is already evident from the fact that the objective technical problem can only be defined on the basis of the starting point. Whether a prior art contains a reference to the solution of the objective technical problem is usually only important in two respects. On the one hand, such a reference, if it is found in the nearest prior art itself, is relevant for the examination of the obviousness of the solution according to the invention. If, on the other hand, the reference is found in another element of the prior art, then it is important for answering the question of whether the skilled person would consider this prior art to solve the objective technical problem (and therefore possibly combine his teaching with that of the nearest prior art).

Nor is there any need to justify why the skilled person would assume a particular embodiment within a pre-published document comprising a large number of embodiments. Each of the embodiments represents an element of the prior art, which as such is known to the (fictitious) skilled person and can therefore also serve as a starting point."

After the sixth paragraph (beginning "A generically different document does not qualify"), add new paragraph:

These decisions may be contrasted with *E Mishan v Hozelock* [2020] EWCA Civ 871 in which the invention concerned a garden hose having an outer tube and an expandible inner tube. The most important reference described a self-elongating oxygen hose for a stowable aviation crew oxygen mask. Arnold L.J. held that there was no error in the judge's decision that the earlier hose was relevant, whether of hindsight or otherwise, and his conclusion was one that was open to him. The invention in the earlier reference was a self-elongating hose. The evidence established that the same hose was frequently used for multiple applications, including transporting both gases and liquids. No technical reason was identified leading the skilled person to think that the earlier hose would (or even might) be unsuitable for use as a garden hose.

Combining references—the EPC approach

—Advantages must be demonstrated

Replace the first paragraph with:

3.49
It may be necessary to rely on reports of experiments contained in the specification of a patent in support of an alleged technical result or advantage. The plausibility requirement for inventions in pharmaceuticals and similar life sciences inventions should be noted, see the pregabalin litigation, *Warner-Lambert v Generics* [2018] UKSC 56 discussed at §14.29 and *Alcon Research v Parmathen* [2022] EWCA Civ 845 concerning fluprostenol isopropyl ester for use in the treatment of glaucoma and ocular hypotension in a dosage range between 0.05 and 10 μg per eye, in which Arnold L.J. explained at [90] in relation to insufficiency (but arguably equally relevantly to obviousness) that:

"Since the Patent is a patent for a second medical use of a known medicinal compound, the Patent must plausibly disclose the effect that it claims. The criterion for plausibility is stated by Lord Sumption in *Warner-Lambert Co LLC v Generics (UK) Ltd* [2018] UKSC 56, [2019] Bus LR 360 at [36]: 'the specification must disclose some reason for supposing that the implied assertion of efficacy in the claim is true'."

SECTION 4A [ADDED]

Commentary on Section 4A

Unpatentability of medical and veterinary treatment (subss.(1) and (2))

—The meaning of treatment of the human or animal body and diagnosis practised on the human or animal body

In the penultimate paragraph, replace "T 611/09" with:

4A.04
T 611/09 *ASH ACCESS TECHNOLOGY/Catheter lock solution*

—The meaning of "therapy"

In the seventh paragraph (beginning "Whereas therapeutic treatment has the purpose"), replace "T 774/89 (unreported)" with:

4A.05
T 774/89 *BAYER/Eformycine as a performance enhancer* (unreported)

—The meaning of "surgery"

After the sixth paragraph (beginning "In T 663/02 METHOD FOR MAGNETIC IMAGING OF ARTERIES/PRINCE"), add new paragraphs:

4A.06
In T 2699/17 *COLTÈNE/Retraction of sulcus*, when assessing whether the method involved a substantial health risk, the Board preferred to consider the "more abstract risk criterion" suggested by T 1695/07 rather than the "risk matrix" approach of T 663/02. In particular, the Board in T 2699/17 agreed with the Board in T 1695/07 that use of a fact matrix would require "absolute scale" risk analysis, but the data required to perform that analysis were not normally available. The Board were of the view that the applicant's fears that a malicious choice of patient, for whom even a minor procedure could result in considerable risk were unfounded. The Enlarged Board had required that the assessment of risk was made when the method was carried out with the "required professional care and expertise", which precluded use on a contraindicated patient. The specific training necessary for performing the method was minimal, as was the medical expertise required from the person applying the method.

"Moreover, sulcus retraction is one step in the preparation of an impression which is subsequently used e.g. for the manufacture of a dental crown. In other words, it belongs to the context of manufacturing a dental implant and is thus not at the core of the dental practitioner's freedom to choose the best treatment for the patient, which is rather in deciding that the patient needs a crown, to prepare the tooth accordingly, and to apply the crown. There is thus no need to exclude the claimed method to guarantee the freedom of the medical profession to apply the treatment of choice."

See also T 467/18 *COLTÈNE/Dental set for sulcus retraction.*

After the seventh paragraph (beginning "In T 775/97 EXPANDABLE GRAFTS/ Surgical Device"), add new paragraphs:
The principles of T 775/97 were applied in T 1731/12 *FORSCHUNGSZENTRUM JÜLICH/Implant* where the claim related to a device comprising at least two electrodes and a control means "for the desynchronization of activity of pathologically active brain areas" (English translation of the German claims) comprising two electrodes and a control means to control the electrodes. The Board noted that such devices were known, and that the distinguishing feature of the claimed device was the additional requirement for the control means to be designed such that the electrodes provide stimuli to cause phase resets of the neuronal activity of two subpopulations of the neuron population to be desynchronized, so that the at least two subpopulations have different phases after the phase resets.
The Board noted that art.53(c) prohibited patentability of methods of surgery. However, although products for use in such methods were not excluded from patentability, the Board furthermore noted that T 775/97 explained the exclusion applied to products that could only be manufactured in the human body by a surgical step. Although T 775/97 was decided under EPC 1973 art.52(4), in the Board's view the law was not changed by incorporating the provision into EPC 2000 art.53(c). The Board found a difference between surgical products which could, after purchase, be freely used by the medical professional and those which required manufacture by the medical professional using a surgical step, for which the medical staff would then require a licence under the patent. In the present case, the patent explained that the adaptation of the control means to allow the claimed phase resetting of subpopulations to be carried out took place after implantation to the patient, and in particular that the stimulation parameters were crucially dependent on the positioning of the electrodes. Therefore, a surgical step was required to produce the claimed device, which was excluded from patentability.
T 1631/17 *MÜHLBAUER TECHNOLOGY GMBH/Process and material set for manufacturing tooth replacement parts* explained that an explicitly claimed surgical step was not required to be caught by art.53(c). In addition, essential steps that would be required to perform the invention, even if not claimed, were relevant. The relevant claim related to a method for the production of a dental prosthesis involving the use of two impressions of the teeth. Although not claimed, the description explained that the first impression was prepared after temporarily filling the gap in the patient's teeth. The Board explained that this step represented the contribution to the art, because it allowed the shape of the replacement tooth to be performed on the patient by the dentist, thereby simplifying the task of the dental technician. Therefore, although not explicitly claimed, the Board explained that the claimed method implicitly required the addition of the missing tooth substance to prepare the first impression and then its removal before preparing the second impression. As the patentee accepted that these steps were surgical, and it did not matter that they were not explicitly recited in the claim, the patent contravened art.53(c).

—The meaning of "diagnosis"

After the third paragraph (beginning "In T 1255/06 EXERGEN CORP/Radiation detector"), add new paragraph:
In *Perspectum Diagnostics Ltd* BL O/446/22, the Hearing Officer considered an application relat- **4A.07** ing to a method for assessing liver health involving the analysis of an MRI scan. The Hearing Officer noted the test as defined by the Enlarged Board of Appeal in G 1/04 held that a diagnostic method fell within the scope of the prohibition only if it included the specific interactions with the human or animal body which occurred when carrying out the steps of a technical nature. The Hearing Officer also noted that the Enlarged Board of Appeal had explained that the requirement for these steps to be performed "on" the human or animal body required its presence. The first step of the method claim was "obtaining a volumetric map of organ health generated from one or more MRI scan data sets", which the examiner held was a step of technical nature requiring interaction with the human or animal body. The Hearing Officer disagreed, noting that the invention was not intended to include collection of the MRI data and rather was restricted to manipulation of that data once obtained. The Hearing Officer sympathised with the examiner, because in order to analyse an MRI at some point such a scan must have been obtained, thereby requiring interaction with the human or animal body. However, the Enlarged Board of Appeal had explained that the exclusion was to be construed narrowly, preventing patents for methods performed on the body but not carried out, for example, in a laboratory. Therefore, the Hearing Officer concluded that, although an interaction with the human body was required, that step was not claimed and therefore the method was not excluded.

—*Patents for the protection of the second (or further) medical indications*

Replace the tenth paragraph with:

4A.09   In contrast, in T 1570/09 *PROTISTA/Alpha-ketoglutaric acid … for use in increasing HDL plasma levels*, the Board held that Protista could not obtain a patent which contained two independent claims, one in "Swiss form" and one in EPC 2000 form, and noted that the claims were to the same indication and same substance, and the "medicament" aspect of the "Swiss form" claim did not convey any novelty. Only the EPC 2000 claim was permitted. However, the Board in T 1021/11 *BOEHRINGER INGELHEIM/PCV2 composition* disagreed, and allowed the presence of both claim forms in a single set of claims, noting that a consequence of the transitional provisions adopted by the Board in G 2/08 was that a time period was created in which the old and new formats could be used.

Replace the eleventh paragraph with:

A claim to the use of an implantable strip of biocompatible material could not benefit from the novelty provisions of EPC art.54(4) and (5) because these covered only substances or compositions having a medical effect, see T 1099/09 *COLOPLAST/Implantable apparatus*. The MOPP has been updated at para.4A.28.3 to explain that in T 1099/09 it was held that second medical use claims can only be used to protect the use of a known substance or composition as an active agent. The use of a known substance or composition as an inactive carrier or excipient for a therapeutic agent cannot therefore be protected by a second medical use claim.

After the fourteenth paragraph (beginning "The two-part test set out in the EDWARDS decision"), add new paragraphs:

In T 264/17 *DR MED GÖTZ VON FORESTER/Synthetic lubricant*, the application related to the use of certain known lubricants for use as a replacement for synovial fluid in diseased joints. The application was refused by the Examining Division on the basis that the lubricants were not a substance or composition within the meaning of EPC art.54(5), because this required some pharmacological interaction with the body i.e. the term substance or composition was limited to an active ingredient in the classic sense. However, in the Examining Division's view, the relevant lubricants worked through purely physical mechanisms, and the EU's regulatory classifications suggested that the lubricants were a device.

The Board disagreed. The lubricants were not a device because they did not form a defined shape either before or after entry to the body. Therefore T 1758/15 *INCEPT/Fillers and methods for displacing tissues to improve radiological outcomes* and T 2136/15 *CARDIOPOLYMERS/Intramyocaardial patterning for global cardiac resizing and reshaping*, in which an effect was provided by a macroscopic form of the substances in the body, were irrelevant, and so was the Examining Division's reference to the EU's definitions of medical devices because regulatory procedures involved assessments using different principles. Moreover, the two-part test set out in the *EDWARDS* decision was satisfied. For step (a), the means by which the therapeutic effect was achieved was by the material properties of the lubricants. In particular, the effect was caused by their omniphobic properties that resulted in a repellent effect on hydrophilic and hydrophobic liquids and thereby the formation of lubricating film. Whether this effect was labelled physical was purely a matter of nomenclature—the ligand-immunogloblin interaction in T 2008/08 *EDWARDS/Dilated cardiomyopathy* was also ultimately physical. For step (b), the therapeutic effect was undoubtedly achieved by a chemical composition, namely the defined lubricants. The Board of Appeal did not need to decide on the applicant's argument that the scope of EPC art.54(5) was not limited to active ingredients in the classic sense, because they reached the view that the lubricants did provide a therapeutic effect.

After the last paragraph, add new paragraphs:

The Boards of Appeal have also accepted novelty based on a purposive selection of a new patient group from a larger group already known to be treated. In T 0694/16 *NV NUTRICIA/Food composition for prodromal dementia patients* the Board evaluated the novelty of a claim to a particular composition for use in preventing onset of dementia in a person having characteristics of a prodromal dementia patient including two defined cerebrospinal fluid (CSF) markers. It noted that the aim of personalised medicine was to move away from a one-size-fits-all approach and to provide treatment tailored to specific groups of patients. Accordingly, the skilled person would understand that the purpose of the treatment was to target the particular patients selectively, implying a functional relationship between the markers and the therapeutic effect sought and meaning that the purposive selection of patients was an essential technical feature of the claim that had to be taken into account when assessing novelty.

The Board dismissed the opponents' arguments that the claimed patients would inevitably have been treated amongst previously treatment patients. The concept of inherency did not arise under EPC art.54, and the claimed methods allowed treatment to be targeted, following the screen, precisely at the defined patients.

The Board also dismissed the opponent's reliance on T 0233/96 *MEDCO RESEARCH/Adrenaline*, in which case the Board interpreted earlier decisions T 0019/86 *DUPHAR/Pigs II* and T 0893/90 *QUEEN'S UNIVERSITY KINGSTON/Controlling bleeding* to mean that novelty could not reside in a new group if (i) the group overlapped with the previously treated group and (ii) if the choice of the novel group was arbitrary in that there was no functional relationship between the particular physiological or pathological status of this group of subjects and the therapeutic or pharmacological effect achieved. In T 2699/17, the Board agreed with T 1399/04 *HCV/SCHERING/Combination therapy* that the situation in T 0233/96 was a special case, because the patients were characterised by being "unable to exercise adequately" which was vague, unsuitable for defining the claimed subject-matter and not related to the therapeutic effect. In the Board's view, those facts had no relevance to their case, in which patients with the CSF markers could be identified by clearly testable criteria, and therefore the opponents' objection that the claim lacked novelty due to overlap with the previously treated patients was not convincing. The Board also dismissed the opponents' arguments that the defined patient group was arbitrary, because the CSF markers were strong indicators of the risk of the development of clinical Alzheimer's disease.

The relevant principle in T 0694/16 is summarised in the Catchwords published with the decision:

"If a claim is directed to a known compound or composition for use in a therapeutic method of treatment or prevention of a disease, and the claim specifies that the subject to be treated displays a clearly defined and detectable marker, which is not displayed by all subjects affected by or likely to develop that disease, then the purposive selection of the patients displaying the marker for the specified treatment is a functional feature characterising the claim. (Points 5.1–5.21 of the Reasons)"

In *Nymox Corporation's Application* BL O/552/21 the claim related to the use of a particular peptide for treating benign prostatic hyperplasia (BPH) in treatment naïve patients i.e. patients who had not previously been treated for the relevant condition, as opposed to patients who had unsuccessfully been treatment by another therapy. The examiner was of the view that the application was insufficiently disclosed, because the examples did not identify the peptide that had been used. Furthermore, the examiner was of the view that the application lacked an inventive step.

The Hearing Officer did not agree with the objection of insufficiency of disclosure. There was no dispute that the examples showed treatment of the relevant disease, but they did so using an active agent referred to as "DRUG", and this term was not explicitly identified in the application. Contrary to the view of the examiner, the Hearing Officer took the view that the skilled person would conclude that "DRUG" was likely, although not certain, to be one of four preferred compounds identified in the application, which included the relevant peptide and close analogs that would be expected to have similar properties. This provided enough for the skilled person to believe it was worth trying the relevant peptide, which was enough to render the therapeutic effect plausible.

However, the Hearing Officer agreed with the examiner that the application lacked an inventive step. The applicant and Hearing Officer agreed that the inventive concept was the use of the peptide to treat BPH in treatment naïve patients. The Hearing Officer agreed with the examiner that the only difference between the animal models in the prior art and the claim was that the prior art did not disclose treatment of BPH in treatment naïve patients. The Hearing Officer did not accept the applicant's argument that treatment of humans was also a distinction, because the point of animal models was to reflect human treatment. The Hearing Officer accepted the applicant's argument that treatment naïve patients could represent a new patient group, and that the skilled person could not have predicted that these patients were treated more effectively than patients who had been treated unsuccessfully using another therapy. However, the Hearing Officer found that after reviewing the prior art, the skilled person would expect the therapeutic effect of treating BPH in humans and would be motivated to undertake further investigations. In doing this, the most straightforward starting point would be naïve patients, so the effect could be linked to the particular peptide, in particular because BPH was not a life-threatening condition for which treatment-failure patients would be a more likely starting point. Accordingly, even if unexpected, the improved treatment of naïve patients was a bonus effect that would inevitably be discovered when taking the obvious step to investigate human treatment.

SECTION 5

Commentary on Section 5

The prima facie priority date (subs.(1)) and the onus of proof

After the last paragraph, add new paragraph:

See also *Illumina Cambridge Ltd v Latvia MGI Tech SIA* [2021] EWCA Civ 1924, where Arnold L.J., **5.15** citing *Evans Medical*, stated that the legal burden lies upon the patentee to justify its claim to priority but that the evidential burden may shift to the party attacking the validity of the patent. He found that MGI had not discharged that burden in challenging Illumina's priority claim.

Filing a late declaration of priority post-January 1, 2005

In the third paragraph, replace "(see Formalities Manual, ch.6, para.6.23)" with:
(see Formalities Manual, ch.6, para.6.26)

5.19

In the fifth paragraph (beginning "To satisfy s.5(2C)(b), the applicant must"), replace "see also Formalities Manual, ch.6, para.6.25" with:
see Formalities Manual, ch.6, para.6.28

Replace the seventh paragraph (beginning "However, the Formalities Manual notes") with:
However, the Formalities Manual notes at para.6.29 that, if the applicant intended to file a PCT application claiming priority but failed to do so within the 12-month period, he may file his PCT application within 14 months and request that a late declaration be allowed under the PCT rules (late declarations to priority are permitted on international applications under PCT r.49 ter.2, see also paras 13.71 to 13.73 of the Formalities Manual). Alternatively, the applicant may wait until the international application enters the national phase and, provided the international application was filed within 14 months of the priority date, make the request using form PF 3 within 1 month of entry (r.66(3); see paras 6.30, 13.71 to 13.73 of the Formalities Manual, see also r.7(5)).

In the last paragraph, replace "para.6.28 of the Formalities Manual" with:
para.6.32 of the Formalities Manual

Person with right to make a declaration of priority

To the end of the fourth paragraph, add:
Of note, T 205/14 *TEVA/Ibandronate sodium* made a distinction between matters of entitlement (a matter for national law and explicitly not for the EPO) and matters outside entitlement e.g. whether an assignment has effectively transferred the right to claim priority (see also §76A.06).

5.20

Replace the ninth paragraph (beginning "Although there has not yet been a decision") with:
Since the last update, the EPO Board of Appeal decision in T 844/18 *BROAD INSTITUTE/CRISPR-Cas* has been issued. To recap: the first EPO opposition hearing for a patent relating to CRISPR gene editing technology, which was heard in January 2018, attracted much attention with the opposition division revoking the patent based on lack of novelty having found that the patent was not entitled to the claimed priority date ("The Broad Institute, Application No. 13818570.7" [2018] 5 *CIPA* 31). The loss of priority arose because the Opposition Division ("OD") found that the right to claim priority had not been assigned before the filing date from certain individuals named on the priority documents (each being US provisional applications) to the applicants named on the PCT patent application. A key issue was whether the EPO had the power to decide on entitlement to priority. The patentee considered that national law (here US law) should apply and that essentially this assessment was best left to national courts. The OD dismissed this, noting that, if it were presumed that any person filing a later application is entitled to claim priority, the EPO would grant patents based on an unreliable state of the art (i.e. because the presumed effective date of an application might be incorrect). The patentee also argued that in cases of multiple applicants for a first application, the term "any person" under EPC art.87 should be interpreted as meaning "one or more indiscriminately" of the co-applicants. The OD agreed that such an interpretation was not excluded by the wording of the EPC or Paris Convention but considered it inappropriate to deviate from the EPO's established practice. The decision was appealed with a request that a series of questions concerning entitlement to claim priority be referred to the Enlarged Board of Appeal. On January 17, 2020 the TBA rejected the request for a referral and upheld the decision of the OD.

After the ninth paragraph, add new paragraphs:
Decision T 844/18 was issued on November 6, 2020 and held: (1) the Board is empowered to and must assess the validity of a priority right under EPC art.87(1), (2) the EPO's interpretation of "any person" as per its "all applicants" approach is confirmed as the correct interpretation, and (3) the Paris Convention, not national law, determines who is "any person". In relation to (1) there is a difference between entitlement and the right to claim priority, and the EPO has the power to examine the latter. In

relation to (2), where applicants A and B file a first application then, absent a transfer of the right to claim priority from (i) A and B to (ii) A, A cannot file a later application and validly claim priority from the first application. Lastly, the Board were able to deal with all matters in the appeal beyond doubt, so no EBA referral was necessary. On (1), see below regarding the subsequent referral to the EBA in case T 1513/17 (consolidated with T 2719/19)—G 1/22 and G 2/22 *Entitlement to priority*.

In T 725/14 *FURANIX/Synthesis of organic acid esters of 5-hydroxymethylfurfura* a priority claim was held invalid in view of the transfer of the priority right within the priority year. A priority application had been filed in the name of Avantium on March 10, 2006. Opponents averred that by a declaration of assignment dated March 1, 2007, all rights pertaining to the priority application were transferred from Avantium to the respondent, Furanix. The parent application, a divisional application of which led to the opposed patent, was filed on March 12, 2007 in the name of Avantium and claimed priority based on this priority application. However, on that date Avantium was no longer entitled to claim priority as the right had already been assigned to Furanix. The priority claim in the parent application was therefore invalid. Since a valid right to claim priority must exist when an application is filed, a subsequent assignment of the parent application to Furanix did not remedy the deficient priority claim. As a result, the opposed patent was not entitled to priority either, and the relevant date for assessing novelty and inventive step was therefore its filing date of March 12, 2007. The patentees argued that the priority application had been transferred to Furanix only after the filing of the parent application, specifically on October 24, 2007, the date in which a request was sent to the EPO to register the transfer of the priority application. However, the Board held that EPC r.22 and decisions T 1751/07 *ELAN PHARMA/ Nanoparticulate compositions* and T 976/97 *SOLVAY/Schaumstoffen* which deal with that rule have no relevance to the present case. The rule concerns procedural aspects of the registration of a transfer of a European patent application and the effect of a transfer vis-à-vis the European Patent Office only. It has no bearing on the establishment of the right to priority. The assignment clearly pointed to the assignment of the priority right to Furanix and the counterevidence put forward by the respondent was not convincing, so that the priority claim of the opposed patent was invalid.

To the end of the tenth paragraph (beginning "Where the later application is filed by joint applicants"), add:

See also the commentary at §76A.06 regarding the EPO's "joint applicants" approach to who has the right to claim priority where there are multiple applicants named on a PCT application and a reduced number of applicants for the priority filing.

After the tenth paragraph, add new paragraph:

In January 2022, the TBA referred two questions to the Enlarged Board of Appeal regarding entitlement to claim priority, the first concerning whether the EPO has the power to decide on entitlement to a priority claim and the second concerning how the "joint applicants" approach is to be applied to PCT applications where different applicants are listed for different states (G 1/22 and G 2/22 *Entitlement to priority*, referrals from consolidated appeals T 1513/17 and T 2719/19 *ALEXION/Prolongation of survival of an allograft*). On the first question, the Board acknowledged that this issue had been addressed (and answered in the affirmative) by the TBA in T 844/18 *BROAD INSTITUTE/CRISPR-Cas* discussed above. However, although the present Board was inclined to agree with that previous decision, they considered that this power had been questioned *ex officio* in communications from other Boards as well as in commentaries and was, therefore, likely to be raised again. They decided, therefore, that it was appropriate to refer this question. As regards the second question regarding the application of the "joint applicants" approach, the question essentially asks whether naming the applicant for the first filing (i.e. the claimed priority document) as applicant for the US only in a PCT application claiming priority thereto (and naming a different party, who was not named as applicant on the first filing, as applicant for all other designated states including the European patent) is enough for the purposes of a valid claim to priority under EPC art.87(1). This scenario is not uncommon where, for example, a US provisional application is filed in the name of the inventors and the subsequent PCT application is filed naming those inventors as applicants for the US but someone else as applicant for all other designated states. The appellant argued that the applicant for the non-US states should be regarded as a joint applicant with the applicant for the US designation (and therefore benefit from the "joint applicants" approach referred to above). However, the counterargument was that none of the applicants on the priority document were applicants for the European patent designation and therefore they could not be considered as joint applicants. The Board agreed that this was an important issue requiring guidance from the EBA.

After the last paragraph, add new paragraph:

See discussion at §5.22 below regarding transferability of partial priority.

According multiple priorities or a partial priority

In the seventh paragraph (beginning "So, for example, if a claim is drafted"), final sentence, replace "See also EPO Guideline C-V, 1.5" with:

5.22   See also EPO Guideline F-VI, 1.5

To the end of the penultimate paragraph, add:

See also T 1879/15 *NESTLÉ/Oligosaccharide Ingredient* for a further application of G 1/15.

After the last paragraph, add new paragraph:

In the March 2022 update to the EPO Guidelines, a paragraph has been included to note that partial priority may also be transferable separately (see EPO Guideline F-VI, 1.5).

Test of "supported by matter disclosed" (subs.(2)(a))

After the fourteenth paragraph (beginning "The question of what constitutes an enabling disclosure"), add new paragraph:

5.24   *Illumina, Inc v Latvia MGI Tech SIA* [2021] EWHC 57 (Pat) is another example of a case where the court considered the question of plausibility of the disclosure of the priority document in the context of whether the disclosure constituted an enabling disclosure, and Birss J. (now Birss L.J.) referred to the enunciation of the legal test for priority set out at [38]–[42] of the Court of Appeal judgment in *Icescape v Ice-World* [2018] EWCA Civ 2219 discussed further in §5.27. On appeal, Arnold L.J., who gave the leading judgment of the Court of Appeal, considered in some detail the law on the test for priority and in particular whether, as a matter of law, plausibility is required. Illumina had argued that Birss J. was correct to find that its patents were entitled to priority on the facts but argued, in the alternative, that the judge had been wrong to proceed on the basis that plausibility is always required for priority as a matter of law. Illumina argued that plausibility is only a requirement where the claims involve "predictive claiming" (where the applicant predicts that a class of compound and/or methods would have utility across the breadth of the class). They contended that the patents in suit did not involve "predictive claiming" and hence plausibility was not required. Arnold L.J. disagreed with the premise of this submission: he said the judge had proceeded on the basis that the claimed invention did not lie merely in identifying a class of compounds, but in identifying their utility in sequencing by synthesis, and hence in the claimed method. Therefore, on the facts of the *Illumina* case, the test for priority included a requirement for plausibility.

According priority under the EPC

After the last paragraph, add new paragraph:

5.26   T 1583/16 *Cell Group Detection* [2021] is a recent example of a TBA decision emphasising that, in accordance with the jurisprudence of the Boards of Appeal, the entitlement to priority is subject to the same principles as for assessing compliance with art.123(2) and that therefore, in accordance with the so-called "gold-standard", the claimed subject-matter must be directly and unambiguously derivable from the priority document, explicitly or implicitly, taking account of common general knowledge. See further discussion under §5.27.

Regenerating the priority date (subs.(3))

In the ninth paragraph (beginning "If the first application was filed before the normal 12-month period"), replace "EPO Guideline C-V, 1.4" with:

5.30   EPO Guideline F-VI, 1.4

Practice under Section 5

Filing of application number and copy of priority application

Replace the last sentence of the second paragraph with:

5.33   The Formalities Manual at paras 6.41 to 6.42 sets out the correct numbers for Belgian and Hungarian priority documents.

Supply of translation of copy of priority application

In the second paragraph, replace "Formalities Manual, para.6.54" with:

5.34   Formalities Manual, para.6.55

Delete the penultimate paragraph.

RIGHT TO APPLY FOR AND OBTAIN A PATENT AND BE MENTIONED AS INVENTOR [SECTIONS 7–13]

SECTION 7

Commentary on Section 7

AI as the inventor

Replace paragraph §7.07A with:

A question as to whether an artificial intelligence system can be an inventor is becoming a practical question and not merely theoretical (although note the comment by Laddie J. in *University of Southampton's Application* [2004] EWHC 2107 (Pat); [2005] R.P.C. 11 at [39] that the inventor was a "natural person").

7.07A

Since then, patent applications based on two concepts have been filed at patent offices around the world (see e.g. GB1816909.4 and GB1818161.0 published as GB-A-2574909 and GB-A-2575131 respectively). Both UK applications have been provisionally accepted as meeting the requirements of patentability following early examination and the question now is whether the AI system (named "DABUS") that allegedly developed these concepts can lawfully be named as the inventor on PF 7.

A UK-IPO decision in *Thaler's Application* BL O/741/19 was appealed to the Patents Court as *Thaler v Comptroller* [2020] EWHC 2412 (Pat) and further appealed to the Court of Appeal (Arnold, Elisabeth Laing and Birss, L.JJ.) whose decision [2021] EWCA Civ 1374 was handed down in September 2021. This is the first case in which the UK-IPO and courts considered whether the naming of an AI system as inventor complied with the requirements of the Act. The Hearing Officer noted that the AI system is not a person within the meaning of the Act and thus cannot be considered an inventor and stated that it was settled law that a body corporate could not be named as an inventor, but without identifying any case, this decision being upheld by the patents court.

The three judges in the Court of Appeal held unanimously that only persons can be inventors and that the Hearing Officer and the judge were correct to hold that DABUS does not qualify as an "inventor" within the meaning of the 1977 Act because it is not a person. Birss L.J. explained that within the meaning of the 1977 Act the "inventor" is the person who actually devised the invention and at [55] that:

"That conclusion is arrived at without any need to examine the policy arguments raised by both parties. Machines are not persons. The fact that machines can now create inventions, which is what Dr Thaler says happened in this case, would not mean that machines are inventors within the meaning of the Act. Assuming the machine is the entity which actually created these inventions, it has no right to be mentioned as the inventor and no right to employee's compensation under s39 (which no doubt it never had anyway)."

Laing L.J. observed at [102] that rights are a constant theme that runs through s.7. Only a person can have rights including the right to be named as an inventor (s.13(1)). A machine cannot. Arnold L.J. explained at [116] that:

"In my judgment it is clear that, upon a systematic interpretation of the 1977 Act, only a person can be an 'inventor'. The starting point is section 130(1) which provides that '"inventor" has the meaning assigned to it by section 7 above'. Section 7(3) provides that '"inventor" in relation to an invention means the actual deviser of the invention'. A dictionary definition of 'deviser' is 'a person who devises; a contriver, a planner, an inventor' (*Shorter Oxford English Dictionary*, 5th edition, Oxford University Press, 2002). Section 7(2) provides that a patent may be granted (a) 'primarily to the inventor or joint inventor', (b) 'to any person or persons who ...', (c) 'the successor or successors in title of any person or persons mentioned in paragraph (a) or (b) above', but 'to no other person'. As Lord Hoffmann explained in *Yeda Research and Development Company Ltd v. Rhone-Poulenc Rorer International Holdings* [2007] UKHL 43, [2007] Bus LR 1796 at [20], this is 'an exhaustive code'. It is clear from this code that category (a) must consist of a person or persons, just as much as categories (b) and (c) do. Section 7(4) creates a presumption that 'a person who makes an application for a patent shall be taken to be the person who is entitled under subsection (2) above to be granted a patent'. Again, it is plain that only a person can be entitled under section 7(2), and thus only a person can fall within paragraph (a)."

Dr Thaler's submission that he was entitled to the property of the invention under s.7(2)(b) was rejected by Arnold and Laing L.JJ., Birss L.J. dissenting. The starting point was that an invention is a piece of information, *Merrell Dow Pharmaceuticals Inc v HH Norton & Co Ltd* [1996] R.P.C. 76 at 86 (Lord Hoffmann) and that there is no property in information even if it is confidential, citing decisions from *Jefferys v Boosey* (1854) 4 H.L.C. 814 at 966 (Lord Brougham) to *Celgard LLC v Shenzhen Senior Technology Material Co* [2020] EWCA Civ 1293; [2021] F.S.R. 1 at [56]. The common law doctrine of accession, see *Blackstone's Commentaries on the Laws of England* (Clarendon Press, 1766), Book II, Ch.26, para.6, pp.404–405 concerned new tangible property which is produced by existing tangible property and did not translate to intangible property produced by existing tangible property and there was no rule that the property contemplated by s.7(2)(b) in an invention created by a machine is owned by the owner of the machine so that the Hearing Officer and the judge were correct to hold that Dr Thaler was not entitled to apply for patents in respect of inventions allegedly made by DABUS.

In the outcome, the Hearing Officer was correct to hold that the applications were deemed to have been withdrawn by virtue of s.13(2) of the 1977 Act, see §13.08.

Dr Thaler has been granted permission to appeal to the Supreme Court and the outcome is awaited.

Particularly in the areas of formal requirements and eligibility it is often the case that major and substantial issues are not considered. Readers are invited to download GB-A-2574909 which has a main claim as amended reading:

"A food or beverage container comprising:

a generally cylindrical wall defining an internal chamber of the container, the wall having interior and exterior surfaces and being of uniform thickness;
a top and a base either end of the generally cylindrical wall;
wherein the wall has a fractal profile with corresponding convex and concave fractal elements on corresponding ones of the interior and exterior surfaces;
wherein the convex and concave fractal elements form pits and bulges in the profile of the wall; wherein the wall of the container is flexible, permitting flexing of the fractal profile thereof; the fractal profile of the wall permits coupling by inter-engagement of a plurality of said containers together; and the flexibility of the wall permits disengagement of said or any coupling of a plurality of said containers."

A main claim of GB-A-2575131 in its amended form reads:

"A method for attracting enhanced attention, the method comprising the steps of:

(a) generating a lacunar pulse train having characteristics of a pulse frequency of approximately four Hertz and a pulse-train fractal dimension of approximately one-half generated from a random walk over successive 300 millisecond intervals, each step being of equal magnitude and representative of a pulse train satisfying a fractal dimension equation of ln-(number of intercepts of a neuron's net input with a firing threshold)/ln(the total number of 300 ms intervals sampled);

(b) transmitting said input signal to at least one controllable light source; and

(c) pulsatingly operating said at least one controllable light source to produce a neural flame emitted from said at least one controllable light source as a result of said lacunar pulse train."

It may be instructive to consider whether it is credible that the subject-matter of either of these claims was in truly the invention of a digital device rather than a human, in this instance Dr Thaler. It also may be instructive to consider whether the disclosure of either published specification meets the requirement of enablement.

This issue has also been pursued in other jurisdictions. Both the USPTO and the EPO have rejected corresponding applications. In J 8/20 *DABUS/Designation of inventor*, the Board of Appeal of the European Patent Office held that a machine cannot be an inventor, as under the EPC the inventor has to be a person with legal capacity—given the ordinary meaning of the word "inventor". In addition, they stated that they are not aware of any case law which would prevent the user or the owner of a device involved in an inventive activity to designate himself as inventor under European patent law. The Board of Appeal appears to have differed from the English courts in suggesting that the rules for derivation of title might be different under the EPC, notwithstanding that they have to be decided by national courts and so left open that the appellant could derived title as owner and creator of the machine. However, this was not enough, as the failure to name a human inventor meant that the applicant had not complied with the requirements of EPC art.80.

SECTION 8

Commentary on Section 8

Raising of questions of entitlement

After the second paragraph, add new paragraph:
    In *Kwix UK Ltd v Matthew Murphy and Joint Trustees of the Bankruptcy Estate of Matthew Murphy* BL O/563/20, summary judgment was entered against Mr Murphy's claim that he was the owner of the applications. Although the story was far from clear, any rights which Mr Murphy had held before his bankruptcy now belonged to the Joint Trustees in Bankruptcy (JTIB) and had not been returned to Mr Murphy following his discharge. He therefore had no interest in the ownership. The JTIB had stood back from the case, expecting Mr Murphy to run his defence, but were given permission to change that stance. Mr Murphy's late amendment, that he held the applications (and US patent) on trust for his mother, could not proceed as she had not filed a counter statement when invited to do so and was therefore taken, by virtue of r.77(9), as supporting Kwix's case.

8.05

SECTION 12

Commentary on Section 12

Application of section 12 in practice

To the end of the tenth paragraph (beginning "In Zincometal's Application BL O/469/12, the Comptroller again held"), add:
    In *Drayson Technologies Application* BL O/205/20, the Comptroller's order declared the entitlement of the employer to the grant of the US application and "hereby assigned" any rights of the inventor to the employer. The employee had neither signed the confirmatory assignments sent to him nor filed any counter-statement in the proceedings before the Comptroller.

12.04

SECTION 13

Commentary on Section 13

Declaration of inventorship (PF 7)

After the last paragraph, add new paragraphs:
    Inventors are natural persons. Though applicants may be non-natural persons and thus entitled to ownership of a patent under s.7, this does not extend to the rights derived as an inventor under the Act. In *Thaler's Application* BL/O/741/19, and [2020] EWHC 2412 (Pat), an AI system named "DABUS" was listed as the inventor on two applications. Drawing comparisons with the "settled law that an inventor cannot be a corporate body", the Hearing Officer concluded that as DABUS is a machine and not a natural person, it cannot be regarded as an inventor for the purposes of s.7 and s.13 of the Act. See also discussion at §7.07A including whether or not this is "settled law". Note, the UK-IPO cannot refuse an application for a failure to file an acceptable PF 7. However, the application will be deemed withdrawn if this is not done in the relevant time frame. This differs from the effect at the EPO and USPTO of failing to file forms which comply with their requirements. Although argued on appeal that s.13 had been deployed unjustifiably to sanction Dr Thaler, the High Court found this misconceived and focussed on the requirements of s.7, which were not fulfilled.
    On appeal, [2021] EWCA Civ 1374, Arnold L.J., with whom Laing L.J. agreed, Birss L.J. dissenting, held that the requirement of s.13(2)(b) cannot be ignored and that if not complied with then an application is deemed to be withdrawn, see *Nippon Piston's Applications* [1987] R.P.C. 120. The Comptroller's function under s.13(2) is to check whether the prescribed statements have been filed in time, and if so whether the statements filed appear to comply with the statutory requirements or are defective on their face. Identification of a non-person an inventor was a legal impossibility and the Comptroller's

13.08

analysis did not involve determination of factual accuracy but merely consideration of the statement at face value, see *Aerotel Ltd v Telco Holdings Ltd* [2006] EWCA Civ 1371 at [5]. Since the applications did not comply with the statutory requirements that the named inventor must be a person and that an applicant who was not named as the inventor must be able to establish right to apply.

It would not be right to allow the applications to proceed, particularly since the statute provides no other mechanism for addressing the non-compliance.

Time for filing PF 7

To the end of the last paragraph, add:

13.09   Following *Thaler's Application*, filing an unacceptable designation of inventor does not abridge that time.

Inventor designation in international and European applications (UK)

To the end of the last paragraph, add:

13.10   In the co-pending PCT application filed by Thaler, WIPO published the application with DABUS named as inventor. However, this route was not to survive entry into the national phase. In *Thaler's Application* BL O/447/22, the formalities officer informed the applicant that the national phase entry into the UK did not meet the requirements of the Patents Rules and a Statement of Inventorship needed to be filed. The applicant argued that s.89B(1)(c) of the Act mean that the Statement of Inventorship filed during the international phase was adequate. In essence, the applicant attempted to bypass the requirements of s.13(2) by arguing that the formalities officer was incorrect in their application of s.89B(1)(c), which should have resulted in any Statement of Inventorship filed during the international phase not being subject to further preliminary examination. The Hearing Officer found that, regardless of the interpretation of s.89B(1)(c), the Comptroller has explicit power under s.89B(5) of the Act to undertake its own examination in this regard. When no new Form 10 or appeal was filed, the application was taken to be withdrawn.

Practice under Section 13

Filing of declaration of inventorship on PF 7

To the end of the third paragraph, add:

13.15   In *Thaler's Application*, the application was published without the name of the AI inventor.

Amendment of named inventors(s)

To the end of the first paragraph, add:

13.17   In *Gillian Taylor v Lanarkshire Health Board* BL O/556/21, the Board had tried to file a form PF 7 to add a second inventor, when they should have made an application under r.10(2). In the end, the Hearing Officer regarded this as a "formal omission having no material consequence" and in the interest of dealing with the case expeditiously, deemed the request made on PF 7 to be an application under r.10(2).

APPLICATIONS [SECTIONS 14–16]

SECTION 14

Commentary on Section 14

Filing of application (subss.(1) and (2))

After the last paragraph, add new paragraph:

14.10   Where an application is accompanied with a sequence listing, in accordance with Rule 13, it is now a requirement that the sequence listing is compliant with new WIPO standard WIPO ST.26. This applies to all new patent applications filed on or after July 1, 2022 except for new divisional applications where the parent application was filed before July 1, 2022. If the sequence listing does not comply with WIPO ST.26, the applicant has until 15 months from the filing date to provide a compliant sequence listing.

Sufficiency of description (subs.(3))

—General requirements for sufficiency

After the fifth paragraph (beginning "The difference in the effects of subss.(3) and (5) is that"), add new paragraphs:

Where there is an objection of insufficiency or lack of plausibility, the importance of positive and **14.24** timely pleading in revocation proceedings is highlighted by *Rockwool v Knauf* [2020] EWHC 1068 (Pat) which was an appeal from revocation proceedings before the IP Office. Following claim amendments, applicants for revocation sought to rely on lack of plausibility, this having been raised in supplemental grounds for revocation filed only a few days before the first instance hearing and without the ground having been formally pleaded. In their reply, Knauf submitted that:

"... Rockwool has never pleaded any allegation of lack of plausibility against the granted patent; and a narrowing amendment cannot by its nature create any lack of plausibility. Rockwool should certainly not be allowed to advance an unpleaded plausibility objection (or any other insufficiency objection) at this late stage, after the evidence rounds have been completed."

They further submitted that a point on sufficiency/plausibility requires evidence and (if the point had the slightest force) would have required evidence from the patentee to rebut it. It would have been a procedural unfairness if the Hearing Officer had upheld the objection, given the lack of opportunity for Knauf to adduce evidence on it. On appeal it was held that the only basis on which the Hearing Officer could properly have considered plausibility was to satisfy himself that, on their face, the amendments to the patents were not so obviously defective on the ground of plausibility that they could not be permitted. The Hearing Officer had rejected the insufficiency issue, and that decision was affirmed on appeal.

In *Illumina v MGI* [2021] EWCA Civ 1924, it was confirmed that for a priority claim to be valid, the priority document must also make the invention plausible.

After the last paragraph, add new paragraphs:

In T 2773/18 *VESTAS/Wind turbine*, the Board of Appeal sought to differentiate the case law for mechanical inventions from the case law developed in the field of chemistry. The decision noted:

"This argument fails to convince the Board, not least because it misapplies case law developed in the field of chemistry, where a claimed invention resides in a compositional range or other range of values but the associated effect may not be proven or plausible for large parts of that range, to a claimed invention in the mechanical field, even if it claims no ranges. By its very nature a claim in this field, which - often in functional or other generic terms - attempts to capture the essence of some concrete machine or mechanical structure (or its operation), is schematic allowing for some breadth of interpretation. It may be that on clever construction subject-matter can be found to be covered within that breadth that may not solve the problem or achieve the desired effect. However, this is normally not an issue of lack of disclosure, but rather of claim construction. Whether claims, description and figures provide the skilled person with sufficient information to carry out an invention, is a purely technical question, that is separate from that of what reasonably falls within the ambit of claim wording. In the Board's view if the skilled person upon consideration of the entire disclosure possibly using common general knowledge can infer what will and what will not work, a claimed invention is sufficiently disclosed, even if a broad construction might also encompass what doesn't work. Indeed that inference from the whole disclosure might lead to a more limited construction of the claim."

The issue of support for an invention in the pharmaceutical field by post-filing data is now the subject of a referral to EPO Enlarged Appeal Board G 2/21 *Plausibility* following a decision in October 2021 in T 116/18 *SUMITOMO/Insecticide compositions*. The patent in issue, EP-B-2484209 claims an agrochemical composition comprising the broad-spectrum neonicotinoid insecticide thiamethoxam and a further compound represented by a Markush formula, the compounds in combination exhibiting an allegedly synergistic effect enabling reductions in the rate or number of applications to be realised. The referring decision resulted from an opposition by Syngentia and extensively reviews case law on plausibility, including the decision of the UK Supreme Court in *Warner-Lambert v Generics* [2018] UKSC 56. In the present case, the relevant data was contained in a letter filed during the appeal procedure. In explaining the need for a referral, the Appeal Board commented at 13.7.1 onwards:

"The three lines of case law discussed above contain two extreme positions, one being a strict application of the *ab initio* plausibility standard and the other one applying the no plausibility standard. These two extremes illustrate that different results are obtained depending on which plausibility standard is applied. On the one hand, by applying the *ab initio* plausibility standard strictly, the ultimate result would be that patent applicants receive a patent only for embodiments for which experimental data or other substantiation is contained in the application as filed that makes the effect invoked for inventive step plausible for these embodiments. Hence, any extension of the claimed scope over what has been experimentally shown or otherwise substantiated in the application as filed would lead to refusal of the application. If, on the other hand, no plausibility standard were applied at all, a patent applicant could claim whatever it thinks might possibly be proven later to bring about a purported technical effect. This would give rise to what is often referred to in the case law as 'speculative patenting' or 'armchair inventions' where a monopoly is conferred to a patent applicant for mere speculation rather than a true invention. The *ab initio* implausibility standard in terms of its results appears to lie somewhere between these two extreme lines of case law.

On the other hand, requiring plausibility or at least the absence of implausibility to access post-published evidence can be particularly problematic in cases where an effect needs to be established *vis-à-vis* a prior-art document that has not been, and perhaps could not have been, considered by the patent proprietor/applicant. For instance, if a patent proprietor is confronted with a new closest prior document which makes a reformulation of the objective technical problem necessary, in particular under the *ab initio* plausibility line of case law, the patent proprietor would be barred from providing any evidence in support of the reformulated technical problem. This would mean a basically insurmountable hurdle for patentability once an opponent invokes a new closest prior-art document in opposition proceedings. Furthermore, such an approach would go against decades of case law which has allowed the reformulation of the technical problem in view of new closest prior-art documents and the reliance on post-published evidence in support of the newly formulated problem. In fact, the only hurdle applied in this case law has been that the newly formulated problem must be within the spirit of the invention as originally disclosed. See, for instance, T 1397/08 *L'OREAL/ Composition pour la teinture d'oxydation*, where it is stated in the catchword (translation provided and emphasis added by the current board; see also T 184/82 *MOBIL/Poly (p-methylstyrene) articles* (point 5 of the Reasons)) that:

'According to the problem-solution approach for assessing inventive step in the field of chemistry, the technical problem can be reformulated, and in certain circumstances must even be reformulated, since for the objective determination of the problem, only the result actually achieved in relation to the closest state of the art counts. Nothing prevents, even at the appeal stage, the modification of the problem initially posed, provided that the spirit of the original statement of the invention is preserved ...'

The same follows from decision T 1422/12 *TEVA/Tigecycline crystalline forms*. In the case underlying that decision, a certain compound, namely crystalline tigecycline, was claimed. The effect relied upon was based on an improved stability with respect to epimerisation. This effect was not even mentioned in the application as filed. The board stated (point 2.3.2 of the Reasons, insertion in squared brackets by the current board) that:

'In this connection [i.e. well-established case law], any effects may be taken into account, so long as they concern the same field of use and do not change the character of the invention.'

On this basis, the board took post-published evidence into account, concluded that the effect of improved stability was credibly shown and acknowledged inventive step.

An additional tension exists between the ab initio plausibility and ab initio implausibility standards on the one hand and the principle of free evaluation of evidence on the other hand (see G 3/97 *Opposition on behalf of a third party* (OJ EPO 1999, 245), point 5 of the Reasons and G 1/12 *ZENON/ Water filtration* (OJ EPO 2014, A114), point 31 of the Reasons). It is not immediately clear what could be the legal basis for preventing the patent proprietor from relying on a particular type of evidence of a fact relevant to the outcome of the proceedings. Likewise, it is not clear on what basis a board would be prohibited from taking into account evidence it finds convincing and decisive.

In this respect, it should be stressed that, in accordance with Article 56 EPC, an invention must be considered as involving an inventive step if, having regard to the state of the art, it is not obvious to a person skilled in the art. There can thus be no doubt that inventive step can only be judged in relation to the prior art. The rationale developed in the *ab initio* plausibility line of case law is, however, that the invention had not been made on the filing date. This finding has been, and can only be, arrived at without considering any prior art. So it may be questionable whether Article 56 EPC is a proper legal basis for plausibility. Indeed, the legal basis for the requirement of plausibility has also been questioned elsewhere. In this respect, the current board would like to refer to the opinion expressed in the UK Supreme Court decision that plausibility 'is a court-invented pre-condition to validity' (point 192 of the decision). In R. Jacob, "Plausibility and Policy", *Bio-Science Law Review* 17(6), 223, the author goes even a step further and states (page 223, first paragraph under "The Statutory Language") that:

'If one actually looks at the words of the EPC a purist would say it is straining the meaning of words beyond breaking point to get plausibility out of them - positively Humpty Dumpty-ish. I suppose it is for that reason that none of the judicial reasoning for getting the notion of plausibility out of either the definition of inventive step (obviousness) or sufficiency has much, or indeed anything, to do with the actual words in the statute. And the word plausibility itself is not in the statute - indeed is not, and never has been, in any patent statute anywhere.'

Also in A. Slade, "Plausibility: a *conditio sine qua non* of patent law?", *I.P.Q.* 2020, 3, 180-203, the author considers Articles 56 and 83 EPC not to be a proper legal basis for the application of any plausibility standard. She advocates for Article 52(1) EPC as a legal basis since a speculative use of a known compound must fail the initial requirement of this article of being an invention. In this author's view, only if the requirement of Article 52(1) EPC is met can secondary requirements such as lack of inventive step be examined.

In the outcome, the following questions have been referred to the Enlarged Board:

If for acknowledgement of inventive step the patent proprietor relies on a technical effect and has submitted evidence, such as experimental data, to prove such an effect, this evidence not having been public before the filing date of the patent in suit and having been filed after that date (post-published evidence):

1. Should an exception to the principle of free evaluation of evidence (see e.g. G 3/97, Reasons 5, and G 1/12, Reasons 31) be accepted in that post-published evidence must be disregarded on the ground that the proof of the effect rests exclusively on the post-published evidence?

2. If the answer is yes (the post-published evidence must be disregarded if the proof of the effect rests exclusively on this evidence), can the post-published evidence be taken into consideration if, based on the information in the patent application in suit or the common general knowledge, the skilled person at the filing date of the patent application in suit would have considered the effect plausible (*ab initio* plausibility)?

3. If the answer to the first question is yes (the post-published evidence must be disregarded if the proof of the effect rests exclusively on this evidence), can the post-published evidence be taken into consideration if, based on the information in the patent application in suit or the common general knowledge, the skilled person at the filing date of the patent application in suit would have seen no reason to consider the effect implausible (ab initio implausibility)?"

—Classical insufficiency

To the end of the seventh paragraph (beginning "A legally straightforward if scientifically complex example"), add:

However, the Supreme Court overturned the decision of the Court of Appeal in *Regeneron Pharmaceuticals Inc v Kymab Ltd* [2020] UKSC 27 based on a finding of insufficiency due to the breadth of claim, as discussed at §14.29. **14.28**

After the fifteenth paragraph (beginning "In Merck v Ono [2015] EWHC 2973 (Pat)"), add new paragraphs:

In *Sandoz v Bristol-Myers Squibb* [2022] EWHC 822 (Pat), the patent related to a compound called apixaban which is used for thromboembolic disorders. The judgment included a summary of the relevant law on plausibility. The judge concluded that the patent did not provide enough guidance that apixaban would have a particular level of binding as apixaban was not specifically identified as having this property. Even if it had been, the judge concluded, on the facts, that this was not sufficient to make it plausible that apixaban would be useful in therapy.

In *4D Pharma Research Ltd's Application* BL O/202/21, the Hearing Officer considered the low hurdle set by the Supreme Court in *Warner-Lambert* and found that the examiner had taken too strict an interpretation when requiring experimental evidence in support of all conditions claimed to be treated.

Similarly, in *Nymox Corp's Application* BL O/552/21, the Hearing Officer found that, although the Examples did not specify which of the 116 disclosed peptides were the drug actually used, the skilled person would consider it likely that it would be one of the preferred, claimed peptides and therefore the application made it plausible that the peptide of claim 1 would have the claimed therapeutic activity.

After the seventeenth paragraph (beginning "In T 1868/16 NOVARTIS AG/mTOR inhibitors in the treatment of endocrine tumours"), add new paragraph:

In T 2015/20 *ALMIRALL/Aclidinium for treatment of asthma* the Board took the view that a statement in the application was a significant technical teaching and did not prima facie lack plausibility. That statement was falsifiable and open to challenge and no serious doubts had been raised in the proceedings.

To the end of the twenty-sixth paragraph (beginning "In Anan Kasei v Molycorp [2018] EWHC 843 (Pat) it was argued that"), add:

This decision was upheld by the Court of Appeal in *Anan Kasei v Neo* [2019] EWCA Civ 1646.

After the last paragraph, add new paragraphs:

In T 1285/15 *De La Rue International Ltd/Security device and its production method*, the Board responded to an objection by the appellant that it was taking an atomistic treatment of different objections of lack of sufficiency. The Board considered that in practical terms, there was no other way to tackle the multiple issues and this was what the skilled person would have done. A more holistic approach would have to have been based on an overall impression and so would have lacked objectivity.

In T 161/18 *ARC SEIBERSDORF/Equivalent aortic pressure*, the Board considered that an application which required the training of an artificial neural network was not sufficient as the application did not disclose which input data were suitable for training the artificial neural network according to the invention, or at least one data set suitable for solving the technical problem at hand. The training of the artificial neural network cannot therefore be reworked by the person skilled in the art, and the person skilled in the art cannot therefore carry out the invention.

In T 983/18 *MEYN FOOD PROCESSING/Residual fat remover*, the Board agreed that it might not always be necessary to provide a theory as to why an invention worked. However, it considered that there must be sufficient information in the patent for the skilled person to be able to reproduce the invention, without undue burden. In this particular case, the Board found the patent insufficient.

—Insufficiency by breadth of claim

After the second paragraph, add new paragraphs:

14.29   In *Regeneron Pharmaceuticals Inc v Kymab Ltd* [2020] UKSC 27, the Supreme Court overturned a finding of the Court of Appeal that patents relating to mice genetically modified to possess human antibody genes were sufficient. The relevant claims covered the insertion of different lengths of DNA. It was accepted that it was not possible at the priority date to produce mice with large sections of DNA inserted. However, the Court of Appeal considered that this was not important as the invention was one of general application, which taught the method of introducing the human DNA which would yield the benefit of reduced murine immunological sickness for all products. The Supreme Court disagreed, finding that for a product claim, it was necessary to be able to produce products across essentially the whole scope of the claim, in this case for most of the range of 1 to 125 human DNA segments that were covered. The Supreme Court considered that the Court of Appeal had not correctly applied the law as it stood and its analysis could not be regarded as a legitimate analysis of the law. The Supreme Court decision therefore reaffirms that a patent must be capable of being worked across the whole scope of the claim at the priority date.

The conclusion in *Regeneron* followed a detailed analysis of a number of UK and EPO Appeal Board decisions. Relevant UK decisions were *May & Baker v Boots* (1950) 67 R.P.C. 23; *Chiron Corp v Organon Teknika Ltd (No.3)* [1994] F.S.R. 202; *Biogen v Medeva* [1995] R.P.C. 25 and [1997] R.P.C. 1; *Rockwater v Coflexip SA* [2004] EWCA Civ 381; [2004] R.P.C. 46 at [7] and [10]; *Kirin-Amgen Inc v Transkaryotic Therapies Inc (No.2)* [2004] UKHL 46; [2005] R.P.C. 9; *Generics (UK) v H Lundbeck* [2008] EWCA Civ 311; [2008] R.P.C. 19 at [30] and [2009] R.P.C. 13 at [86]; and *Actavis v ICOS* [2019] UKSC 15; [2019] Bus. L.R. 1318 at [57]. Relevant EPO Appeal Board decisions were T 226/85 *UNILEVER/Stable bleaches*; T 292/85 *GENENTECH/Polypeptide expression*; T 361/87 *NABISCO/Microorganisms*; T 409/91 *EXXON/Fuel Oils*; T 435/91 *UNILEVER/Detergents*; T 694/92 *MYCOGEN/Modifying plant cells*; and G 1/98 *NOVARTIS II/Transgenic plant*. Lord Briggs (joined by Lords Reed, Hodge and Sales, Lady Black dissenting) derived the following principles from these earlier cases:

- The requirement of sufficiency imposed by EPC art.83 exists to ensure that the extent of the monopoly conferred by the patent corresponds with the extent of the contribution which it makes to the art.

- In the case of a product claim, the contribution to the art is the ability of the skilled person to make the product itself, rather than (if different) the invention.
- Patentees are free to choose how widely to frame the range of products for which they claim protection. But they need to ensure that they make no broader claim than is enabled by their disclosure.
- The disclosure required of the patentee is such as will, coupled with the common general knowledge existing as at the priority date, be sufficient to enable the skilled person to make substantially all the types or embodiments of products within the scope of the claim. That is what, in the context of a product claim, enablement means.
- A claim which seeks to protect products which cannot be made by the skilled person using the disclosure in the patent will, subject to de minimis or wholly irrelevant exceptions, be bound to exceed the contribution to the art made by the patent, measured as it must be at the priority date.
- This does not mean that the patentee has to demonstrate in the disclosure that every embodiment within the scope of the claim has been tried, tested and proved to have been enabled to be made. Patentees may rely, if they can, upon a principle of general application if it would appear reasonably likely to enable the whole range of products within the scope of the claim to be made. But they take the risk, if challenged, that the supposed general principle will be proved at trial not in fact to enable a significant, relevant, part of the claimed range to be made, as at the priority date.
- Nor will a claim which in substance passes the sufficiency test be defeated by dividing the product claim into a range denominated by some wholly irrelevant factor, such as the length of a mouse's tail. The requirement to show enablement across the whole scope of the claim applies only across a relevant range. Put broadly, the range will be relevant if it is denominated by reference to a variable which significantly affects the value or utility of the product in achieving the purpose for which it is to be made.
- Enablement across the scope of a product claim is not established merely by showing that all products within the relevant range will, if and when they can be made, deliver the same general benefit intended to be generated by the invention, regardless how valuable and ground-breaking that invention may prove to be.

It will be familiar to readers that many inventions arise in empirical research fields at least partly from Edisonian trial and error. In his Caltech 1974 commencement address, *http://calteches.library.caltech.edu/51/2/CargoCult.htm*, Cargo-Cult Science, "Some remarks on science, pseudoscience, and learning how to not fool yourself", Richard Feynman emphasized the importance of fully understanding the conditions under which an experiment is carried out so that the results obtained are under the control of the experimenter. Inventors have a long history of exaggerating what they have under their control, while not always clearly defining what they have brought into the realm of predictability. Thus, in relation to T 435/91 *UNILEVER/Detergents*, the relevant "Richard Feynman" question that the inventors should have asked themselves when instructing their patent attorney was: "What materials have we got under our control that force the detergent into a hexagonal phase?"

The *Regeneron* inventors might well respond that the principle that they had allegedly devised rendered their research systematic, or not less than semi-empirical and that the claim scope for which they sought was reasonable in the circumstances. However, that position is difficult to maintain in the face of the finding of Carr J. at first instance [2016] EWHC 87 (Pat) at [257]:

"The difficulty does not relate to some hypothetical puzzle at the edge of the claim, but rather to the central disclosure of the specification, and the amounts of genetic sequence of which it contemplates the deletion and insertion. *None of the methods of the 287 Patent for achieving this, as disclosed in Example 3 would have worked.* The task contemplated was unprecedented and could not have been achieved, if at all, without a great deal of creative thinking at the priority date. I do not accept that all embodiments within the claim are unified by a single principle of a reverse chimeric locus. This is not a principle that enables the method to be performed, rather it is the result of successfully carrying out the method. Accordingly, the insufficiency objection succeeds in respect of claim 1 of the 287 Patent" (emphasis added).

Example 3 of the patent in issue appears to be a predictive example and little actual experimental work appears to be reported. The proposition that a skilled reader confronted with an unworkable predictive example would necessarily seek a remedy from the common general knowledge rather than simply dismissing it is not to be taken for granted. In the Editors' opinion, the Feynman address is something that all concerned with the drafting of patent applications would benefit from reading at regular intervals.

Readers should be aware of corresponding developments for the patents on these inventions at the

EPO and their relationship to the UK litigation on this subject. A parent application was granted as EP-B-1360287 (*Regeneron*) claiming a method of modifying an endogenous immunoglobulin heavy chain variable region gene locus in an isolated mouse embryonic stem (ES) cell and also a genetically modified eukaryotic cell or a mouse comprising a genetically modified immunoglobulin heavy chain variable region locus obtainable by the method of any one of the preceding claims in situ in place of the endogenous immunoglobulin heavy chain variable region gene locus. A decision of the EPO Appeal Board in T 2220/14 *REGENERON/VelocImmune mouse* issued in November 2014, before the first instance UK decision [2016] UKHC 87 in February 2016, inter alia holding that the disclosure was sufficient, see the Reasons at [55]–[72] and a second appeal on the same patent was held to be inadmissible, see T 1716/17 *REGENERON/VelocImmune mouse II*. There is also a granted divisional patent EP-B-2264163 claiming a transgenic mouse that produces hybrid antibodies containing human variable regions and mouse constant regions, wherein said mouse comprises an in situ replacement of mouse VDJ regions with human VDJ regions at a murine chromosomal immunoglobulin heavy chain locus and an in situ replacement of mouse VJ regions with human VJ regions at a murine chromosomal immunoglobulin light chain locus, and also a method of making a human antibody. A decision of the Opposition Division maintaining the patent issued in April 2018, after the UK Court of Appeal decision but before that of the Supreme Court. In rejecting arguments on insufficiency the Opposition Division pointed out that the contested main claim was directed to a product, not to a method of producing it, that the techniques described in the patent were not new in themselves but merely extended known techniques in a new way and that since the main claim was to a product it was irrelevant whether the patentee actually used the method of Example 3 to prepare the mouse of claim 1. A letter dated September 8, 2020 from J.A. Kemp on behalf of Regeneron argues that the different forms of evidence considered in the UK proceedings does not in itself amount to different facts for the purposes of EPC art.83 and that the results of witness cross/examination/expert reports do not meet the standard of "serious doubts supported by verifiable facts" used by the EPO in relation to art.83 but instead can be considered as non-verifiable personal opinions, see T 488/16 *BRISTOL MYERS SQUIB/Dasatinib*, reasons at [80]. One of the three opponents, Novo Nordisk, withdrew from the opposition in January 2021 but the other two opponents including Kymab remain, and the opposition remains pending at the time of writing.

In *Illumina Cambridge Ltd v Latvia* [2021] EWHC 57 (Pat), Birss J. noted that the principles proposed by Lord Briggs were not limited to product claims, but the language used was so limited. Therefore, he proposed the following principles:

i)   When examining any aspect of claim scope for the purposes of the enablement it is necessary to distinguish between ranges relevant in the *Regeneron* sense and other ranges.

ii)   For ranges relevant in the *Regeneron* sense, to be sufficient, there must be enablement across the whole scope of the claim within that relevant range (subject to de minimis exceptions) at the relevant date. If a type or embodiment within such a range is not enabled at that date then the fact it could be made later, as a result of further developments not enabled by the patent, even though it never could have been made without the invention, will not save the claim from insufficiency.

iii)   Not all claims will necessarily contain a range relevant in the *Regeneron* sense but if they do, then this principle applies to that range.

iv)   An example of another range, not relevant in the *Regeneron* sense, will be a descriptive feature in a claim (whether structural or functional) which can cover a variety of things, but for which that variety does not significantly affect the value or utility of the claimed product or process in achieving its relevant purpose. The relevant purpose is judged in all the circumstances, starting from the terms of the claim itself but also, where appropriate, by reference to the essence or core of the invention.

v)   For a claim feature which amounts to a range in this other sense, the skilled person must still be able to make a suitable selection, without undue burden, in order for the claim to be sufficiently disclosed. However, provided that is so at the relevant date, such a claim feature will not be insufficient simply because it is capable of also covering within its scope things which had not been invented at that relevant date.

vi)   When examining enablement of any kind, the test is always about what the skilled person is able to do without undue burden. The patentee is entitled to expect that the skilled person, in seeking to make the invention work, will exercise that skill. If need be that exercise will involve testing and experiments, as long as it is not unduly burdensome.

Replace the fifth paragraph with:

In *Merck Sharp and Dohme v Shionogi* [2016] EWHC 2989 (Pat), the allegedly infringing antiviral agent raltegravir had not been disclosed as an individual compound in the patent in issue, but was alleged to fall within two generic Markush claims in Swiss form. There was experimental evidence that some of the claimed compound were ineffective. More significantly, on the issue of plausibility it was estimated that one of the relevant claims covered some 10^{39} compounds which exceeded the total number of unique chemical substances ever registered in the American Chemical Society CAS Registry by a factor of approximately 10^{31}. It was irrelevant that the claim was functionally limited to compounds that "worked". The upshot was that the patent presented the skilled team with a vast research project with a high likelihood of failure, but claims the results if they happen to succeed—even if (as in the case of raltegravir) such success had nothing to do with the teaching of the patent. This approach had been followed by Arnold J. in *Idenix Pharmaceuticals Inc v Gilead Sciences Inc* [2014] EWHC 3916 (Pat), finding it implausible that all compounds covered by the claim had the alleged activity and subsequently in *Akebia v FibroGen* [2020] EWHC 866 (Pat). The position in *Idenix* was upheld by the Court of Appeal in a lead judgment by Kitchin L.J. [2016] EWCA Civ 1089. Similar reasoning was applied by the UK-IPO in *The Hong Kong University of Science and Technology's Application* BL O/326/17 in which a single compound had been isolated from the root of the herbal plant *Rhodiola Rosea* and was said to be useful in the management of pain and type 2 diabetes, but in which a genus of compounds had been defined by a Markush formula with substituents from R_1 to R_{11} some of which were defined by open-ended terms e.g. "alkyl" and "aryl". The Examiner identified from *Biogen Inc v Medeva Plc* [1997] R.P.C. 1 and *Pharmacia v Merck* [2001] R.P.C. 41 three necessary conditions for sufficiency: (a) when a range of compounds is claimed the specification should contain sufficient information on how to make them; (b) the compounds covered by the claim must all have the advantage or avoid the disadvantage that characterizes the selected group; and (c) sufficiency must be demonstrated at the date of filing. Disclosure of starting materials and synthetic routes was lacking, and the postulated structure-activity relationship (SAR) was not an inevitable consequence and necessarily predictable absent any evidence in the specification that there was clearly a SAR arising from the core scaffold structure provided in the Markush formula. In the outcome, the only amendment that might result in grant was restriction to the single novel compound that had been disclosed.

After the fifth paragraph, add new paragraphs:

A significant departure from the above line of cases is found in the decision of the Court of Appeal in *FibroGen v Akebia* [2021] EWCA Civ 1279 on appeal from the decision of the Patents Court (Arnold L.J.) above, although the possibility of a further appeal to the Supreme Court remains. The decision is remarkable for the number of earlier cases cited including a decision of the German Supreme Court in *Dipeptidyl-Peptidase-Inhibitoren X ZB 8/12* (September 11, 2013), *Idenix v Gilead* [2016] EWCA Civ 1089, *Conor v Angiotech* [2008] UKHL 49, *Generics v Lundbeck* [2009] UKHL 12, *Regeneron v Genentech* [2013] EWCA Civ 93 at [95]–[103] and *Kirin-Amgen v Hoechst Marion Roussel* [2004] UKHL 46 and the depth of the legal discussion. The claimed subject-matter was the use of a heterocyclic carboxamide compound that *inhibited hypoxia inducible factor (HIF) prolyl hydroxylase enzyme activity* in the manufacture of a medicament for *increasing endogenous erythropoietin* in the treatment of anaemia associated with chronic kidney disease, the two functional limitations given weight in the appeal opinion being italicised. On general principles, the opinion of Birss L.J. referred to the *Inhibitoren* decision at [19]:

"Subject to this, it may be admissible to recite a group of substances in a generalised form, even if not all substances that belong to this group are suitable for the purpose of the invention, provided the skilled person is easily able to determine the suitability of the individual substances by experiments ([*citations*]). That a claim worded in this manner also covers substances that do not yet exist or that have not been discovered yet, is no cause for concern. As long as using them makes use of the invention, it is not problematic that substances are also covered that cannot be found without an inventive effort."

The court explained that the two functional features limited the class of claimed compounds, that these functional features did not themselves create a breadth of claim problem, and that:

"Putting claim construction and the law together, contrary to the finding [of Aldous L.J.] at paragraph [376], the patent does not promise that substantially all compounds which satisfy the structural definitions in the claims will have the claimed therapeutic activity. The classes were not said to be new compounds. They had previously been described in earlier patents and scientific literature. They were known as inhibitors of other members of the enzyme family to which HIF-PH belongs. Contrary to [376] the technical contribution of the Family A patents resides not in the identification of a novel class of molecules per se, but in the teaching that certain classes are HIF-PH inhibitors and may be used in the treatment of anaemia associated with CKD, by increasing the endogenous production of epo."

[57]

In the outcome on sufficiency, it was held that:

> "[95] … The right test is as follows. If one has a claim with a functional feature which defines the claimed compounds, or a mix of such structural and functional features, it must be possible, without undue burden, both to identify compounds which satisfy the relevant test, and to find out whether any given compound satisfies the test. However it is not necessary as a matter of law, for sufficiency (or for *Agrevo*), simply because a claim contains functional features (or a mix of functional and structural features) to establish that the skilled person can identify all or substantially all the compounds which satisfy the test.
>
> 96. Finally, if the law does not require the identification of substantially all such compounds, the question remains, how many is enough? Take the facts of the present case. The claims like claim 8A with structural and functional language at step one clearly claim a wider class than the particular compounds C, E, F, J and K identified in the patent as likely to have therapeutic efficacy. Even if one adds on the 100 or so compounds identified in the patent at paragraphs [0072]–[0077], the claim is plainly intended to be much wider than that too. In terms of a promise, the wider claim is a promise or assertion that there are more useful compounds within the class than the ones identified by name in the patent. Bearing in mind the ultimate issue is all about breadth of claim, in such a case the question is how many is enough?
>
> 97. I believe the answer is in two parts. For claims of this type, it must be possible for the skilled person, without undue burden, to identify some compounds beyond those named in the patent, which are within the claimed class and therefore are likely to have therapeutic efficacy. Otherwise the contribution is no more than the named compounds and the wider claim is too wide and unsupported by the disclosure. Second and separately, it must also be possible for the skilled person to work substantially anywhere within the whole claim (*Kymab* is one example, in which inventive step was needed to be able to work in a part of the claim which was not otherwise available to the skilled team from the specification, and another is the non-functional 2'-methyl-up-2'-fluoro-down sub-class of the Markush formula in *Idenix*). So it must be possible for the skilled person, given any sensible compound within the structural class (or substantially any), to apply the tests without undue burden and work out if it is a claimed compound."

A further reason why the judgment did not approach the third step in the right way was because, at [376], it was held that the patent implicitly promised that substantially all the compounds which satisfied the structural definitions would have the claimed therapeutic efficacy. That was not correct and was an error of construction of the patent specification. The patent did not promise that explicitly or implicitly. Its promise was that it was compounds which satisfied both the structural definitions and the functional features that were the ones which would have the claimed therapeutic activity. Allegations of undue burden were also rejected:

> "Standing back, the finding was that although it would be a great deal of work, the skilled team would be able to find some compounds which were effective. The judgment does not expressly state that this result would be reached without undue burden but I believe that is the only answer. It would take a great deal of work but it would be routine for the medicinal chemist and iterative in nature. What made the whole process an undue burden below was the number of compounds in the claim and the fact the exercise would not scratch its surface."

And accordingly the appeal on sufficiency was allowed.

After the last paragraph, add new paragraphs:

The Board in T 2340/12 *LEE/Space energy implosion unit* reaffirmed the principle that in an empirical research field an application should contain all the details required for an effect relied to be achieved and commented:

> "Concerning the burden of the proof, the following should be noted. It is not contested that it is for the organ raising the objection of lack of sufficiency to justify its view. It is, therefore, in ex-parte proceedings, up to the examining division or the board of appeal to substantiate the objection raised. A different approach would be tantamount to incorporate further conditions for the grant of a patent for which no legal support can be found in the EPC. Such objection should rely on concrete and verifiable knowledge or facts that question the reality of the effects provided for by the claimed invention. The lack of credibility may result, for example, from a conflict with established laws of physics or merely because the nature or intensity of the effects relied upon may appear rather 'surprising' in view of what is generally achieved by the prior art.

It is then for the applicant/appellant to provide the arguments or evidence that convince the examining division or board to change its position. This may be achieved, for example, by way of a plausible theoretical explanation of the phenomena involved, or by providing results from experimentation or simulation. Reference is made, in this respect, to decision T 1842/06 (cf. point 3) of the present Board (in a different composition) where similar issues were discussed.

There is no provision in the EPC according to which the grant of a patent depends on the filing by the applicant of evidence that the claimed invention performs satisfactorily in the form of results of experimentation. It follows that the filing of such results is not to be seen as an obligation imposed on the applicant but, in contrast, as a right, recognised by the practice and the case law of the boards of appeal, providing the applicant with the opportunity to convince the examining division or board of appeal that it erred in its initial findings."

It was explained in T 1943/15 *VALLOUREC/Tubular connection* at [2.5] that an open-ended range in a claim does not necessarily result in a lack of sufficiency of disclosure due to the absence of a second boundary to the range. Where it is clear for a skilled person that an open-ended range is limited in practice, depending on the surrounding circumstances, such that the claimed values should be only as high as can be attained above the lower limit, then such open-ended ranges are normally not objected to. In support of that proposition the Board cited T 487/89 *ASAHI KASEI/High tenacity polyhexamethylene adipamide fiber* at [3.5], *AKZO/Fibre* T 129/88 OJ EPO 1993, 598 at [2.2.4] and T 1018/05 *SANGO/Forming an end portion of a cylindrical member* at [2.3].

Change title from "Sufficiency by ambiguity" to: **14.30**

—Sufficiency by ambiguity (or uncertainty)

After the second paragraph, add new paragraph:

In *Anan Kasei v Neo* [2019] EWCA Civ 1646, the Court of Appeal considered whether the term "consisting essentially of" rendered the claim insufficient. It concluded that it did not in this case because it was only a "fuzzy boundary" of the claim which was unclear. The judges noted that this type of sufficiency should properly be called uncertainty rather than ambiguity. Lewison L.J. noted:

"Something is ambiguous when it is capable of having two (or more) meanings, and ultimately the court will be able to decide which of them is the correct meaning. Rather, in my judgment, the issue here is that of uncertainty. If the court cannot ascertain the boundary, having used all the interpretative tools at its disposal, it must conclude that the specification does not disclose the invention clearly enough and completely enough for it to be performed by a person skilled in the art."

After the eighth paragraph (beginning "In the present case, however, the skilled person"), add new paragraphs:

In T 1845/14 *BASELL POLYOLEFINE/Copolymers of ethylene with alpha-olefins*, the Board of Appeal noted that the term "invention" for sufficiency has the same meaning as for priority, novelty and inventive step, namely the specific claimed features. Therefore, where there is an unclear parameter defined in a claim whose values are essential to solving the problem underlying the patent at issue, the ability of the skilled person to solve that problem by reproducing what is claimed is not a suitable criterion for assessing sufficiency of disclosure when the problem or an effect derivable from it are not explicitly or implicitly part of the definition of the claimed subject-matter.

The Board noted in T 383/14 *PELLNEC/Sorting table with roller sorter* that although a claim seeks to define a device under ideal conditions, the person skilled in the art readily understands that the practical operating conditions are not the ideal ones defined by the claim.

After the ninth paragraph (beginning "In INEOS/Polymerisation process (above) [2009] CIPA 483"), add new paragraphs:

In T 250/15 *RHODIA/Composite polyamide article*, the Board found that a limitation to a range of number average molecular mass (Mn) without identifying the method of measurement did not render the claim insufficient. The Board considered that the case law predominantly ruled that an imprecise definition of the scope of protection, as was the case here, fell under EPC art.84. Therefore, the Board refused an application by the Respondent to refer to the Enlarged Board of Appeal the question of whether the difficulty that a person skilled in the art might have in determining whether an object falls within the scope of the protection covered by a claim concerned clarity of the claim or sufficiency of the disclosure of the invention.

In T 1583/17 *TAGHLEEF/Use of coated films*, the Board found that the absence of an indication of a method for measuring the thickness of a film did not prevent the skilled person from practicing the claimed invention.

The claims (subs.(5))

—Claims to be clear and concise (subs.(5)(b))

After the last paragraph, add new paragraph:

14.37   In T 3003/18 *CORNING/Fiber optic plug*, objection was raised to the definition of claimed subject-matter by reference to standards or norms and so the claims were unclear. The Board found that the clarity depended on the specifics of the case and that in this case, the connectors specified designated a well-known, standardized family of connectors and that the person skilled in the technical field would understand what was meant in the claimed context.

—Claims to be supported by description (subs.(5)(c))

After the fourteenth paragraph (beginning "In Glatt's Application [1983] R.P.C. 122, it was observed"), add new paragraphs:

14.38   In *The Scripps Research Institute's Application* BL O/604/19, the Hearing Officer noted the overlap between s.14(3) and s.14(5)(c). He quoted Dillon L.J. in *Genentech Inc's Patent* [1989] R.P.C. 147 at 236–237 that:

"The Patent Office ought to have very clearly in mind that it is undesirable to allow claims the object of which is to cover a wide and unexplored field or where there is no disclosure in the specification which is in any way coterminous with the monopoly indicated in the claims"

and also Aldous J. in *Schering Biotech Corp's Application* [1993] R.P.C. 249 at 252–253:

"I do not believe that the mere mention in the specification of features appearing in the claim will necessarily be a sufficient support. The word 'support' means more than that and requires the description to be the base which can fairly entitle the patentee to a monopoly of the width claimed."

Accordingly, it was necessary to determine, based on the information in the application and taking account of the views of the examiner and applicant during the examination process, whether the application provided enough detail to support the invention as claimed. The claimed invention concerned a method of detecting subclinical acute rejection (subAR) in a kidney transplant recipient in which at least four genes of interest were extracted from the blood of the transplant recipient, the genes being listed in a table and providing a negative predictive value (NPV) for subclinical acute rejection (subAR) of at least 75%. It was held that although one way of performing the invention had been disclosed the technical contribution in this case was in the identification of a specific set of genes that enabled the distinguishing of subAR between transplant patients with an NPV of greater than 75% and some disclosure in the specification would be expected to support a claim that all the genes listed in in the table could be used in a combination of four or more to distinguish subAR with an NPV of greater than 75%. There was not enough information in the application to tell the skilled person that any four or which sets of four genes listed had the claimed property. Given that the applicant pointed to this prior art to illustrate how difficult it was to achieve the invention as claimed, this also pointed to the fact that the limited disclosure in the application as filed did not provide the skilled person with enough information to work the invention across the breath claimed.

In *Anan Kasei v Neo Chemicals* [2019] EWCA Civ 1646, Floyd L.J. considered *Biogen v Medeva* and *Generics (UK) Ltd v Lundbeck* [2009] UKHL 12; [2009] R.P.C. 13 and concluded as follows [52], these conclusions also now being quoted in the MOPP at para.14.80.01:

"1.   The principle in *Biogen* is concerned with permissible scope of claim in the light of the patentee's contribution to the art.

2.   In general, that principle is that the claim must not extend to embodiments which owe nothing to the patentee's contribution to the art.

3.   In the case of a claim to a single novel chemical compound [as in *Generics v Lundbeck*], the patentee's technical contribution is that compound. Such a claim will not be insufficient if the single compound is enabled by a method in the specification, notwithstanding the fact that there may be other methods of making it which owe nothing to the disclosed method.

4.   The same must be true of a claim to a class of compounds, each of which can be made by the application of a method disclosed in the specification. There is no requirement that the patentee disclose more than one method, where one method will do.

5.   This does not mean that all claims to a class of products by definition comply with the *Biogen* principle. The conclusion in *Biogen* shows that a claim which is formally to a class of products may cover embodiments which owe nothing to the patentee's technical contribution.

6.   The reason why the claim in *Biogen* offended the principle was not because it had "process components" but because the language of the claim was so generalised (both in relation to the manner in which the product was made and in relation to its function) that it extended to embodiments which owed nothing to the patentee's contribution to the art. A claim to a product defined by its function (e.g. any heavier than air flying machine referred to by Lord Hoffmann at p.52 in *Biogen*) is capable of extending to subject-matter which owes nothing to the patentee's contribution to the art."

Section 15

Commentary on Section 15

Missing parts of documents (subss.(5)–(8) and r.18)

Replace the second paragraph with:
The MOPP indicates that the description and/or drawings must be "manifestly incomplete" for these provisions to be applicable. It is not possible, for example, to replace a drawing which was already present under these provisions. In BL O/769/18 the wrong description had been filed. An auxiliary request under subs.(5)(c) to replace the application text with the text of the priority application was refused because the description was not manifestly incomplete.

15.13

Replace the third paragraph with:
Missing parts may be identified either by the UK-IPO or by the applicant. The MOPP indicates that the UK-IPO Documents Reception will check for missing parts, although it is not required to do so. A sequence listing which is mentioned in the application but not included will be treated as a missing part (*https://www.gov.uk/government/publications/changes-for-patent-applications-with-biological-sequence-listings/changes-for-patent-applications-with-biological-sequence-listings*). Where the UK-IPO identifies missing parts, it will notify the applicant. The notification may be either part of a formal preliminary examination report (s.15A(4)) or a separate notification (s.15A(9)(b)). It may be included in the notification of a date of filing and outstanding requirements (under subs.(4)(a) and (b)).

Divisional and replacements applications (subs.(9))

—Late filing of divisional applications

Replace the second paragraph with:
The extension possibilities are as follows (MOPP para.15.21):

15.21

•   If the compliance period of the parent application is due to expire in more than one month but less than three months, the r.19 period for filing a divisional application can be extended with discretion using r.108(1), or alternatively the r.30 compliance date of the parent can be extended as of right using r.108(2). The latter option is more reliable. The Formalities Manual indicates that a situation may arise where a discretionary extension under r.19 for late filing of a divisional application is refused, but the compliance period of the parent application can be extended as of right and the divisional application can then be re-filed.

•   If the compliance period of the parent application is due to expire in one month or less, either the r.30 compliance period of the parent application can be extended using r.108(2) and the r.19 period allowed for filing a divisional application can be extended under r.108(1); or the r.30 compliance period of the parent application can be extended twice (once under r.108(2) as of right and a discretionary further extension under r.108(3), Sch.4 Pt 2).

Note that extension under rr.19 and 30 is restricted because they are Sch.4 Pt 3 rules (as discussed in §15.17). Rule 30 (but not r.19) is a Sch.4 Pt 2 rule, extendable as of right by two months with a further discretionary extension of time possible.

After the third paragraph (beginning "In Akron Brass Company's Application BL 0/012/19"), add new paragraph:

In *4D Pharma Research Ltd* BL O/794/21 a request to extend the r.30 compliance period for the parent application was allowed, so that divisional applications were validly filed. There were exceptional circumstances because the applicant was a pre-revenue start-up business which could not incur the costs of divisional applications until objections requiring a hearing on the parent application were resolved. Although there were errors in the requests for extensions of time, the applicant had been diligent.

In the fourth paragraph (beginning "The cases discussed below were decided"), after "Their principles are still relevant", add:

(see *4D Pharma Research Ltd* above)

In the tenth paragraph (beginning "In Knauf Insulation Ltd's Application"), replace "a divisional application was late, filed following several rounds of examination" with:

a divisional application was late-filed following several rounds of examination

—*Content of divisional applications*

After the fourth paragraph (beginning "There is no obligation for a cross-reference"), add new paragraph:

15.23   Sequence listings in a divisional application are subject to the same standard requirements as for the parent application i.e. WIPO ST.26 applies only if the parent application was filed on or after July 1, 2022.

SECTION 15A [ADDED]

Commentary on Section 15A

Preliminary examination

To the end of the penultimate paragraph, add:

15A.06   , and for applications with a filing date from July 1, 2022 will check whether the standard WIPO ST.26 is complied with.

Replace the last paragraph with:

The Formalities Manual indicates that the formalities examiner will check whether there are over 25 claims and, if so, whether the correct excess claims fee element of the search fee has been paid on Form 9. Similarly, if Form 10 has been filed, the formalities examiner will check whether there are over 35 pages and, if so, whether the correct excess pages fee element has been paid on Form 10.

SECTION 16

Commentary on Section 16

"Contents of published application"

To the end of the fifteenth paragraph (beginning "As the search under s.17(5) is carried out"), add:

16.04   If a report is issued under s.17(5)(b) that a search would not serve a useful purpose and no response is received, the application will be published in the usual way but the front page will indicate that no search was possible (MOPP para.17.95).

Accelerated publication

Replace the fourth paragraph with:

16.06   For accelerated publication to take place, the claims and abstract must have been filed, a report must have been issued under s.17(5) and the formal requirements must have been met (see ss.14 and 15A). The report under s.17(5) may be either a search report (under s.17(5)(a)) or a report that a search would not serve a useful purpose (under s.17(5)(b)). Where accelerated publication is requested, there is unlikely to be time after the search report for amended claims to be filed for publication, or for the application to be withdrawn before publication.

Commentary on Section 18

Corresponding identical patents (subs.(5))

After the seventh paragraph (beginning "In LG Chem/Lithium battery use T 1765/ 13"), add new paragraphs:

Whilst an apparent majority of EPO Technical Board of Appeal Decisions confined double patenting issues before the EPO to substantially identical subject-matter only (see, for example, T 2461/10 *BOEHRINGER INGELHEIM VETMEDICA/mat MOLECULES* and T 2563/11 *F Hoffmann-La Roche/ Double patenting*), there was sufficient divergence in the case law to warrant the Technical Board of Appeal on T 318/14 *BIOFER/Trivalent iron complexes with polysaccharide sugars* to refer three questions on legal prohibition on double patenting to the Enlarged Board of Appeal. The questions which were referred were as follows: **18.12**

"1. Can a European patent application be refused under Article 97(2) EPC if it claims the same subject-matter as a European patent granted to the same applicant which does not form part of the state of the art pursuant to Article 54(2) and (3) EPC?

2.1 If the answer to the first question is yes, what are the conditions for such a refusal and are different conditions to be applied where the European patent application under examination was filed

a)   on the same date as, or

b)   as a European divisional application (Article 76(1) EPC) in respect of, or

c)   claiming the priority (Article 88 EPC) in respect of a European patent application on the basis of which a European patent was granted to the same applicant?

2.2 In particular, in the latter case, does an applicant have a legitimate interest in the grant of the (subsequent) European patent application in view of the fact that the filing date and not the priority date is the relevant date for calculating the term of the European patent under Article 63(1) EPC?"

The referral culminated in decision G 4/19 *NESTLÉ/Double patenting*. The Enlarged Board of Appeal interpreted EPC art.125 in line with the principles of arts 31 and 32 of the Vienna Convention and took the EPC "*travaux préparatoires*" into account as a supplementary means of interpretation. It held that the term "procedural provisions" in EPC art.125 may extend to provisions requiring a substantive examination of the subject-matter claimed. It stated that the prohibition on double patenting constitutes a principle of procedural law within the meaning of EPC art.125 and is generally recognised in the Contracting States. It further held that the prohibition on double patenting is not limited to applications directed to the same subject-matter which were filed on the same day—it also extends to parent and divisional applications, and to applications claiming the same priority. It also confirmed that the prohibition only applies where the application under examination and the patent already granted have common designated Contracting States. The Enlarged Board of Appeal answered the referred questions as follows:

"1. A European patent application can be refused under Articles 97(2) and 125 EPC if it claims the same subject-matter as a European patent which has been granted to the same applicant and does not form part of the state of the art pursuant to Article 54(2) and (3) EPC.

2.1 The application can be refused on that legal basis, irrespective of whether it:

a)   was filed on the same date as, or

b)   is an earlier application or a divisional application (Article 76(1) EPC) in respect of, or

c)   claims the same priority (Article 88 EPC) as the European patent application leading to the European patent already granted.

2.2 In view of the answer to Question 2.1 a separate answer is not required."

After the ninth paragraph (beginning "It went on to set out guidelines for when a double patenting objection"), add new paragraphs:

In *Motorola Solutions, Inc's Application* BL O/030/20 the question arose as to whether the refusal of a parent application in proceedings before the Comptroller gave rise to any form of estoppel in respect of a subsequent divisional application which was filed in the period between the hearing on the parent and the issuing of the decision refusing the parent application.

In the parent case, BL O/800/18, the claimed invention was found to fall solely within matter excluded under s.1(2) as a program for a computer as such and a method of doing business as such. The applicant's representative suggested a saving amendment but this did not persuade the Hearing Officer. Finally, the Hearing Officer carefully considered the specification as a whole but did not see anything that could be reasonably expected to form the basis of a valid claim.

The Hearing Officer found that in principle a decision of a tribunal such as the Comptroller in ex-parte proceedings was not excluded from being subject to a form of estoppel on the grounds that the decision was made within the clear framework of the Patents Act and, absent any further route for challenging the decision other than by appeal, was a final decision of a competent tribunal. Nevertheless, the Hearing Officer, considering his "careful consideration of the specification as a whole", concluded that in this instance it did not give rise to an estoppel:

"That i[t] was not essential to my earlier decision does I believe give rise a legitimate question as to whether that particular part of my decision could indeed give rise to any estoppel. As such without a more thorough consideration than was possible at the hearing in this instance, together with the outstanding questions of whether estoppel can really arise in an ex-parte hearing and in the absence of a specific pleading to that effect, I conclude that it would be inappropriate to deny the applicant consideration of the divisional application for reasons of a possible estoppel."

The Hearing Officer then considered whether the filing of the divisional constituted an abuse of process. His view was that it would have been preferable to present the divisional claims as an auxiliary claim set at the hearing of the parent not least to provide certainty to third parties. However, whilst the Hearing Officer noted that this behaviour leant towards being abusive, he noted it was not so abusive that he would be justified in refusing the consider the divisional claims. Nevertheless, the Hearing Officer issued a final warning:

"Should other applicants however seek to exploit that window between hearing and decision by filing further divisionals, and it is feasible for that to happen multiple times for the same parent, then the IPO will need to consider in more depth whether any estoppel arises or whether the behaviour of the applicant does amount to an abuse of process that would justify a stronger response."

SECTION 21

Practice under Section 21

Replace the first paragraph with:

21.07   By r.33(1), subject to r.33(2), a copy of any observations filed under s.21 has to be sent to the applicant, whether or not a request for substantive examination under s.18(1) has yet been filed. The applicant will also be supplied with copies of any documents referred to in the observations, unless the Comptroller considers any such document will already be available to the applicant or if the document is not, for some reason, suitable for photocopying (see r.33(3) and the MOPP para.21.04).

After the first paragraph, add new paragraph:

For a document to be considered as observations under s.21, it should be filed between s.16 publication and grant. Where observations are received before the application is published under s.16, a copy will nevertheless be sent to the applicant but the observer will be informed that these will not be considered by an examiner before publication, as only afterwards is the file open to public inspection, see the MOPP para.21.10. If termination action has been taken on the application in question or is appropriate when observations are received, the observations will be copied to the applicant and placed on the file, see the MOPP para.21.11. If the terminated application has been published, the observations will be open to public inspection.

At the end of the second paragraph, replace "para.21.02.1" with:

para.21.03

After the second paragraph, add new paragraph:

Observations on patentability filed in relation to one application can, where appropriate, be considered in relation to any other application relating to the same invention. In particular, where observations are filed on a priority document, if they appear relevant to the later application, the observations should be considered for that later application.

Replace the third paragraph with:

Although there is no express right to comment on observations made under the section, it may be assumed that the applicant may do so during that examination. The examiner may himself comment on the observations in his/her initial report under s.18(3), or in a later additional report also having the effect of a further report under s.18(3), see the MOPP para.21.12. The MOPP at para.21.12 specifies that the examiner should consider any alleged prior art in exactly the same way as they would if it had been found in the course of the search. However, if the date at which any alleged prior art was published, used or otherwise made available to the public is not given or cannot be established, the examiner should not raise an objection.

Nevertheless, if an applicant denies material facts contained in observations made under s.21, for example an allegation of prior use or prior publication, and the examiner considers it probable that the third party could provide evidence to substantiate his/her allegation, then the examiner may invite the third party to do so. Any such invitation is not a direct request for evidence or information. Rather the examiner will indicate that an objection cannot be raised or pursued unless such material is available.

There is considerable merit in submitting well-reasoned observations because, as set out in the MOPP at para.21.12, if the examiner fully agrees with well-argued observations, they can raise an objection of lack of novelty or inventive step by formally citing the relevant documents and then drawing the applicant's attention to the supporting argument as set out in the observations. Thus the third party observer may have a limited ability to control the nature of the objections raised to the applicant, although of course they are not, and cannot be, a party to the proceedings.

The applicant in his/her own interest ought to reply to any examination report so raised, as otherwise the application may be refused (s.18(3)). If the examiner considers that there is no substance in the observations, he/she need make no reference to them. If observations are received at a time when the application is in order for grant, the MOPP para.21.21 indicates that the applicant should be informed of the observations and that the application will not be sent for grant for two months (in order to enable him/her to file voluntary amendments) unless he/she requests that the application may be so sent earlier. No action on s.21 observations can be taken once the s.18(4) report has issued indicating that the application is to proceed to grant, but it is possible that this report could be rescinded, see the MOPP para.21.22.

Replace the fifth paragraph with:

All observations submitted under s.21 should be placed on the public file 14 days after submission, see §118.10 and §118.14. The MOPP para.21.08 indicates that an application by the informant for confidentiality under r.53 should be referred to the relevant group head who will consider the issue of public interest (see the MOPP at para.118.13). However, objections to patentability should only be made on the basis of documents which are open to public inspection. The MOPP at para.21.08 notes that, having regard to the terms of r.33(1), observations on patentability should be sent to the applicant irrespective of any request under r.53 that the observations be treated as confidential. Nevertheless, it is possible for parts of the observations to be treated as confidential to the extent that they are not laid open to public inspection on the file. *Central Research Laboratories' Application* BL O/419/00 is an example of a confidentiality order being made on observations containing commercially sensitive information.

Replace the eighth paragraph with:

The UK-IPO will accept s.21 observations that are submitted anonymously, see the MOPP, para.21.09. In this way an applicant could submit observations on his/her own application. Note that if the examiner identifies observations filed anonymously but which contain personal data mixed in with observations on patentability, the examiner may write to the third party observer giving them an opportunity to withdraw their observations so that they are not made available and are not considered under s.21. If no response is received within two weeks the observations will be processed under s.21 in the normal way.

SECTION 22

Commentary on Section 22

Power to give prohibition directions (subss.(1) and (2))

In the penultimate paragraph, replace "Secretary of State for Business, Innovation and Skills" with:

22.03 Secretary of State for Business, Energy and Industrial Strategy

Notice of directions to Secretary of State (subss.(5) and (6))

Replace the second paragraph with:

22.05 The UK-IPO previously also had obligations to communicate information relating to applications concerning atomic energy to the European Commission under the Euratom Treaty (Cmnd.4865), but such obligations have now ceased to apply following the UK's withdrawal from the European Union (see the Appendix to section 22 of the MOPP).

Practice under Section 22

Procedure on imposition, and effect, of prohibition order

In the second paragraph, replace "should not be filed by fax" with:

22.09 should not be filed by fax or online

Replace the sixth paragraph (beginning "Where the subject-matter of the invention relates to the production") with:

Where the subject-matter of the invention relates to the production or use of atomic energy, or research into matters connected with such production or use, the Security Section will refer the application to the Secretary of State which may itself inspect the application and may authorise a government body or a person appointed by such a government body for inspection of the application under subs.(6)(a)(i) and (6)(a)(ii).

The previous procedure requiring the applicant to also give their consent to the inspection of applications relating to nuclear matters by the European Commission under the terms of the Euratom Treaty is no longer relevant to applicants for UK patents following the withdrawal of the UK from the European Union (see §22.05). These procedures may however still be relevant for applicants who also wish to seek protection in the remaining Euratom member states.

After the seventh paragraph (beginning "Although a prohibition order imposes a blanket prohibition against disclosure"), add new paragraph:

Where an applicant seeks to assign an application that is subject to security restrictions, in addition to seeking permission for the disclosure from the Comptroller, they must also now consider whether it is necessary to make a notification under the National Security and Investment Act 2021. Such notifications are voluntary in the case of transfer of assets (such as intellectual property) but may be mandatory if the associated business entities are also being transferred.

Effect of other statutes

—Export of Goods (Control) Order

In the first paragraph, replace "Export Control Organisation, 3rd Floor, 1 Victoria Street, London SW1H 0ET (Tel: 020 7215 4594 Fax: 020 7215 2635.)" with:

22.14 Export Control Joint Unit, Department for International Trade, Old Admiralty Building, Admiralty Place, London SW1A 2DY (Tel: 020 7215 4594 e-mail: exportcontrol.help@trade.gov.uk).

Add new paragraph §22.15:

—National Security and Investment Act

The National Security and Investment (NSI) Act 2021, which came into force on January 4, 2022, **22.15**
sets out the powers granted to the Government to scrutinise and intervene in business transactions, such
as takeovers, mergers and acquisitions, in order to protect UK national security. For the first time, the
regime extends these powers to cover transfers of assets, including intellectual property assets, and may
result in the application of sanctions where those transfers are considered to pose a national security risk.

It seems likely that patent applications that are subject to prohibition orders under s.22 on the grounds
of national security, and the know-how and information associated with such applications, may also be
subject to restrictions under the NSI Act. Applicants who are considering transferring such patents and
technology to a third party may therefore wish to consider making a voluntary notification under the Act
to be sure that no restrictive measures will be applied by the Government. In the event that the relevant
business entity is to be transferred along with the intellectual property a notification under the Act may
be mandatory. Further information can be obtained if required from the Investment Security Unit (ISU)
within the Department for Business, Energy and Industrial Strategy, who may be contacted at
investment.screening@beis.gov.uk.

SECTION 23

Commentary on Section 23

Similar laws in other countries

Replace the last paragraph with:

For inventions made in China, applicants must submit the subject-matter of the invention to the China **23.06**
National Intellectual Property Administration (CNIPA) for a "confidentiality examination" prior to filing any patent application overseas (see art.20 of Patent Law of the People's Republic of China). A patent will not be granted for any invention that has been filed abroad without such scrutiny and there is
the further risk of a criminal penalty. Those engaged in collaborative research with Chinese individuals or institutions will need to exercise care to ensure that such requirements are complied with.

PROVISIONS AS TO PATENTS AFTER GRANT [SECTIONS 24–29]

SECTION 27

Practice under Section 27

Effect of amendment (subs.(3))

Replace the first paragraph with:

By subs.(3) an amendment once allowed is considered to have had effect from the grant of the patent. **27.15**
This suggests that if an invalid patent is infringed, and the invalid patent as subsequently amended into
valid form is still infringed, infringement can be considered to have taken place during the time when
the claim was in invalid form; and conversely, if a patent is not infringed after amendment, there will
have been no infringement at any time. For a consideration of the application of s.27(3) in the context
of an argument of infringement under the doctrine of equivalents following *Actavis UK Ltd v Eli Lilly
& Co* [2017] UKSC 48, see *IPCom GmbH & Co KG v Vodafone Group Plc* [2020] EWHC 132 (Pat);
[2020] Bus. L.R. 514, in particular at [169]. However, amendment may have an effect on an award of
monetary relief for infringement prior to amendment. Thus s.62(3) (discussed in §62.05) states that
where a patent has been amended, the court or tribunal shall, when considering damages or an account
of profits for pre-amendment infringements, take into account inter alia whether the specification as
published was framed in good faith and with reasonable skill and knowledge. Section 58(6) applies
similar restrictions to Crown user compensation.

SECTION 28

Commentary on Section 28

Term for filing the application for restoration

To the end of the sixth paragraph (beginning "The period for filing an application for restoration"), add:

28.06   Such an attempt was unsuccessful in *IT-ACS Limited's Application* BL O/444/22.

PROPERTY IN PATENTS AND APPLICATIONS, AND REGISTRATION [SECTIONS 30–38]

SECTION 30

Commentary on Section 30

Scope of the section

In the second paragraph, after "includes an interest in it", add:
(and further includes the right to apply for a patent—see *Jones v Irmac Roads Ltd* [2022] EWHC 495 (IPEC)) **30.02**

Practice under Section 30

Transfer of rights by companies

After the last paragraph, add new paragraph:
An assignment of a patent by a company to a shareholder at an undervalue may be ultra vires, and **30.08** therefore void as an unlawful distribution at common law, on the basis that it constitutes a distribution/ dividend paid out of the company's capital (rather than profits), and therefore a "fraud on the company's creditors"; see, to that effect, *Add2 Research and Development Ltd v DSpace Digital Signal Processing & Control Engineering GmbH* [2021] EWHC 1630 (Pat). Assignments of patents by companies will also need to comply with the provisions of the Companies Act 2006.

SECTION 31

Commentary on Section 31

Grant of security under Scots law

Replace the second paragraph with:
It is important to note that the whole area of assignations and security over incorporeal moveable **31.05** property including intellectual property (and therefore patents) was the subject of a review by the Scottish Law Commission, as part of its *8th Programme of Law Reform* (SCOT LAW COM No. 220 paras 2.4–2.6). A Discussion Paper was published in the second half of 2011 (SCOT LAW COM No.150 paras 7.16–7.28 and 19.10). Following publication of the Discussion Paper the Commission published its Report on December 19, 2017. The Report was in three volumes and included in Volume 3 a draft Moveable Transactions (Scotland) Bill. The main recommendations of the Report included a new statutory scheme for moveable transactions law, as well as a change to the law of assignation, such that registration of an assignation would be an alternative to intimation, with a new Register of Assignations being created. It also proposed the introduction of a new "fixed" security called a "statutory pledge", which would be created by registration of the pledge in a new Register of Statutory Pledges—without the need for delivery or transfer of the underlying asset which is subject to the security. See the article by H. Patrick and A. Steven, "Moveable transactions law reform coming in Scotland?" (2018) B.J.I.B. & F.L. 71–73.

Replace the third paragraph with:
In November 2019, the Scottish Parliament's Economy, Energy and Fair Work Committee took evidence from the Scottish Law Commission as part of its inquiry into reform of the law on moveable transactions.

After the third paragraph, add new paragraph:
On May 25, 2022, the Moveable Transactions Bill was introduced. The main provisions of the Bill are aligned with the recommendations of the Scottish Law Commission's Report referred to above. However, as at the end of July 2022, the Bill was only at the first stage of the parliamentary process.

Replace the fourth paragraph with:
At present, therefore, whilst the Bill, if passed, will in some way move Scots law more in line with

English law, Scots law remains notably different and must be followed to ensure securities over intellectual property assets are valid.

At the start of the fifth paragraph, replace "At present therefore, the" with:
The

SECTION 37

Commentary on Section 37

Raising questions of entitlement

To the end of the first paragraph, add:

37.06   Entitlement was raised as a defence in *Price v Flitcraft Ltd* [2020] EWCA Civ 850. The Recorder had granted the claimant's summary judgment application, even though they had indicated that they would adduce evidence, but had failed to do so, the defendant also having not submitted copies of documents relied upon. This was set aside on appeal and the defendant allowed to adduce further evidence and amend its pleading.

Types of relief available under sections 8 and 37

To the end of the fifth paragraph (beginning "However, subsequently in Hughes v Paxman"), add:

37.07   However, there are limits to what the Hearing Officer can deal with. In *Gillian Taylor v Lanarkshire Health Board* BL O/864/21, the Hearing Officer felt that an order as to how royalties were split between proprietors was beyond the scope of the sections; see also §37.07.

Powers of the Comptroller and court to determine entitlement disputes

At the end of the nineteenth paragraph (beginning "In Nut Security Products Limited v SafetyTrim Worldwide Holdings Ltd"), replace "BL O/683/18" with:

37.08   BL O/151/19

Relief granted under sections 8, 12 and 37

After the second paragraph, add new paragraph:

37.10   In *Jones v Irmac Roads Ltd* [2022] EWHC 495 (IPEC), Jones, the sole inventor, had agreed verbally to assign all intellectual property rights in relation to an invention, for which a patent was eventually granted, to Irmac in exchange for consideration. Jones retained an option in a written agreement to have the rights reassigned to him should Irmac not commence active trading within six months of the patent being allocated an application number. HHJ Hacon followed *Hartington Conway Ltd's Patent Applications* [2004] R.P.C. 7 and concluded that the right to apply for a patent is within the meaning of s.30(6)(a) and can only be assigned in writing. As such, the legal interest was never assigned. However, the equitable interest passed to Irmac by virtue of the verbal agreement. Jones exercised his option and thus the equitable right was assigned back to him making him the owner of the legal and equitable right, and as such he was declared the true proprietor of the patent (notwithstanding that the original application had been dropped and a new one filed after the option had been exercised).

After the fifth paragraph (beginning "In Statoil v University of Southampton BL O/204/05"), add new paragraph:

In *Close Brewery Rentals Ltd v Geco Holdings Ltd* BL O/264/21, the Hearing Officer ordered that the claimant's employees be named as the only inventors, the claimant be named as the sole proprietor of the relevant patent and any foreign or international patents applications claiming priority from the relevant UK patent should proceed on like basis. The Hearing Officer having found that Close Brewery Rental's employees had come up with the inventive concept and that, if the employees of the original applicant (MD Engineering Solutions Limited) had made inventions in working the concepts into a product, their contributions had not been set out in the patent and they were not the inventors—discussed also at §7.08 and §7.10.

After the eighth paragraph (beginning "In Szucs' Application BL O/4/86 a declaration was made"), add new paragraph:

In *Gen-Probe and Stratec Biomedical's Application* BL O/647/19, Stratec had consented to be removed as a co-owner of the EP(UK) patent. Certain inventors had been deleted from the EP patent in post-grant correspondence with the EPO, by consent, following pre-grant amendment of the claims. The patent was to proceed in Gen-Probe's name alone.

After the twenty-third paragraph (beginning "In Advanced Extrusion's Patent BL 0/76/98"), add new paragraph:

However, it is a different matter where the Comptroller is asked to settle terms as between two co-owners as part of an entitlement dispute. Following the finding in *Gillian Taylor v Lanarkshire Health Board* BL O/556/21 (discussed at §37.11 below), in *Gillian Taylor v Lanarkshire Health Board* BL O/864/21 the Hearing Officer was asked to give effect to his findings on the claimant's entitlement to the patent. In the prior case, it had been held that the claimant was time barred from having all or part of the patent transferred to her by virtue of s.37(5) of the Act (although that did not apply to the foreign applications where relief was sought under s.12). Both parties asked that the Hearing Officer order a particular value of royalty rate to the claimant. Given the lack of similar authorities he declined to accept that he had jurisdiction to do so on the basis of s.12 of the Act. Instead, he ordered registration of the claimant as proprietor or joint licensor in related overseas applications and applicable licences, and encouraged both sides to come to a suitable commercial settlement. The Hearing Officer stated (at para.15),

> "it seems to me that the claimant is entitled to an equal share of all royalties, both backdated and going forward, arising from licenses granted in respect of the applicable applications, but that an adjustment would need to be made for the costs incurred by the defendant in prosecuting the applications and in developing the inventions to a licensable product (as well as the very many other commercial consideration set out by both sides in their submissions). However, these adjustments are commercial factors that I believe are beyond the scope of section 12, and the comptroller cannot meddle in such disputes beyond answering the baseline question as to entitlement and thereby establishing a starting point for commercial negotiation between the two sides."

After the penultimate paragraph, add new paragraph:

In the sorry tale of *Nut Securities v Safetytrim Worldwide* BL O/151/19, the Comptroller ordered the claimant to pay the defendant's wasted costs from a late adjournment of a hearing and late amendment. This order for off the scale costs was upheld on appeal ([2019] EWHC 2836 (Pat)).

Time bar for orders under section 37 (subss.(5) and (9))

To the end of the fourth paragraph (beginning "Subsection (9) is not cited in s.130(7)"), add:

The second sentence in this paragraph was approved in *Gillian Taylor v Lanarkshire Health Board* BL O/556/21, where the Hearing Officer was prepared to make a variety of orders, including that Mrs Taylor should have been named as an applicant, even though the claim for transfer of the granted UK patent was time-barred, and therefore it would not be transferred.

37.11

After the thirteenth paragraph (beginning "At the stage the proceedings had reached"), add new paragraph:

The test for knowledge was also discussed in *Gillian Taylor v Lanarkshire Health Board* BL O/556/21, both in relation to knowledge as to whether the Board had any knowledge as to either sole entitlement or entitlement as a joint proprietor, and concluded that Board did not have the relevant knowledge.

EMPLOYEES' INVENTIONS [SECTIONS 39–43]

SECTION 39

Commentary on Section 39

The status of the inventor as employee

After the last paragraph, add new paragraph:

Questions may also arise where two companies work together and one seeks to argue that there is an "implied" employment contract. This arose in *Gillian Taylor v Lanarkshire Health Board* BL O/556/21, where the Lanarkshire Health Board sought to argue that it had an employment relationship with

39.06

Mrs Taylor, even though her contract of employment was with another organisation. The issue of the "implied" employment contract was not rejected—the Hearing Officer being prepared to ask whether "Mrs Taylor was subject to the control of [the Board] in a sufficient degree to make it her 'master'", but the existence of any implied employment contract was not made out on the facts.

Ownership of employee inventions by an employer

The basic rule

After the last paragraph, add new paragraph:

39.07   In *Gillian Taylor v Lanarkshire Health Board* BL O/556/21, it was found that Mrs Taylor's employer was CHSS. Her original idea had been made whilst working for the Board (but was agreed by the parties not to be the "invention"). The interactions between her original employment by the Board, her work for CHSS, but deployed to educate staff employed by the Board, who part-funded her post, had led to the Board thinking that it owned all IP in her invention and told her so. So whilst the investment made in helping her to develop her invention should only have been made available to Board employees, no-one had correctly investigated the situation. It was agreed that she was not employed to invent. An assessment was made as to whether her involvement in the development process had then amounted to assigned duties, but Mrs Taylor had done much of the development work in her spare time. As noted above, there was no "implied" employment by the Board and Mrs Taylor was entitled to own her invention. As there was a second inventor, the Board remained as joint owner.

CONTRACTS AS TO PATENTED PRODUCTS, ETC. [SECTIONS 44–45]

SECTION 44 [REPEALED]

Commentary on Repealed Section 44

Add new paragraph §44.09:

Brexit

44.09   Some three and a half years after the Brexit vote on June 23, 2016, the UK officially left the EU with effect from 23:00 on January 31, 2020. It then entered a transition period under what is widely called simply the Withdrawal Agreement (available in the *Official Journal of the European Union* at L 29/7), which expired on December 31, 2020. The Withdrawal Agreement has effect in UK law due to the provisions of the European Union (Withdrawal Agreement) Act 2020, which received royal assent on January 23, 2020. The principal effects of the Withdrawal Agreement are to (a) govern the relationship between the UK and the 27 remaining EU member states until December 31, 2020 and (b) in effect to ensure that almost all EU law continues to have effect in the UK until that time. This means that EU competition law continued to apply until December 31, 2020 to agreements relating to patents in substantially the same manner as it did prior to January 31, 2020.

Whatever happens after the transition period comes to an end, practitioners should not assume that EU competition law can simply be ignored after December 31, 2020. Many agreements relating to patents (even those between only UK based entities) will continue to have an effect within the EU and may thus be subject to the jurisdiction of EU competition authorities: see for example the Court of Justice of the European Union's well-known effects doctrine set out in its decision in *A Ahlstrom Osakeyhtio v Commission of the European Communities* (C-89/85) EU:C:1988:447; [1988] 4 C.M.L.R. 901 (joined cases 104/85, 114/85, 116-117/85 & 125-129/85)).

SECTION 45 [REPEALED]

Commentary on Repealed Section 45

Add new paragraph §45.05:

Brexit

45.05   Attention is drawn to the comments made in relation to the effects of Brexit on EU competition law set out in the guidance under Section 44.

Licences of right and compulsory licences [Sections 46–54]

Section 46

Commentary on Section 46

Assessment of royalty terms

—By considering "comparables"

Replace the first paragraph with:

Of the three approaches to the assessment of the appropriate royalty rate for a licence of right outlined **46.10**
in §46.09, the "comparables" approach is regarded by the courts as the most reliable guide to what would
be agreed between a willing licensor and willing licensee (*Smith Kline & French's (Cimetidine) Patents*
[1990] R.P.C. 203 CA), particularly where the patented invention, or one of a similar commercial nature,
has been licensed on such a basis at a proved royalty rate. This approach is best seen in relation to inventions which the proprietor exploits only by licensing, when the licence of right will be settled on terms
providing the proprietor with an equivalent royalty and rates of royalty voluntarily accepted under the
patent in suit by others, as in *Syntex's Patent* [1986] R.P.C. 585. In *American Cyanamid's (Fenbufen)
Patent* [1990] R.P.C. 309 and [1991] R.P.C. 409 CA, the "comparables" approach was applied in respect
of royalties previously settled under s.46(3) for similar drugs, themselves also the subject of voluntary
licences though these were supply contracts which justified a slightly lower royalty than would otherwise
be agreed for a voluntary licence. In *Cabot Safety's Patent* [1992] R.P.C. 39, a licence granted under a
corresponding United States patent was held not strictly comparable because it arose in the settlement
of litigation and was the subject of a lump sum payment.

Import and Export prohibitions

Replace the first paragraph with:

In the past, it was held that settled licence terms could, on request, include a prohibition on importa- **46.15**
tion of the patented product from outside the EEA, but prohibition on importation was imposed only if
the proprietor worked the invention within the EEA. A prohibition against importation from elsewhere
within the EEA was, however, not permissible (*Allen & Hanbury v Generics* (C-434/85) [1988] 1
C.M.L.R. 701; [1988] F.S.R. 312 ECJ); and see *Generics v Smith Kline & French* (C-191/90) [1993]
R.P.C. 333; [1993] 1 C.M.L.R. 89 ECJ where it was held to be contrary to what are now arts 28–30
TFEU for a prohibition on importation to depend on whether the proprietor manufactured the patented
product in one EEA State rather than another. Notwithstanding the withdrawal of the UK from the
European Union, these decisions form part of UK law as retained EU law, and will continue so unless
legislation provides, or the UK Supreme Court (or another specified court, in certain limited
circumstances) decides, to the contrary.

Effect of "licences of right" register entry (subss.(3)(c) and (d), (3A), (3B), (4) and (5))

*In the first paragraph, replace "Except in case of importation from outside the
European Community" with:*

Except in case of importation from outside the EEA **46.17**

Section 48 [Substituted]

Commentary on Section 48

The provisions for the grant of compulsory licences

In the first paragraph, replace "Competition Commission" with:

Competition and Markets Authority **48.02**

Scope of the section

In the first paragraph, replace "Competition Commission" with:

Competition and Markets Authority **48.03**

In the second paragraph, replace "Competition Commission" with:
Competition and Markets Authority

In the second paragraph, replace "art.12 of the European Biotechnology Directive" with:
art.12 of the EU Biotechnology Directive

In the fifth paragraph, replace "The amendments to ss.48–54 also have the consequence of bringing the statute into compliance with European law" with:
The amendments to ss.48–54 also had the consequence of bringing the statute into compliance with EU law

Replace the eighth paragraph with:
It is to be noted that the CJEU has decided that the "exhaustion of rights" doctrine, under which parallel imports of a patented article may not be prevented when that article has first been put on the market within the EU by the proprietor or with his/her consent (as discussed in §D15), does not apply where the first marketing within the EU or EEA took place under a compulsory licence, because this was not with the "consent" of the proprietor (*Pharmon v Hoechst* (19/84) [1985] E.C.R. 2281; [1985] 3 C.M.L.R. 775; [1986] F.S.R. 108, for case comment on which see D. Guy, [1986] E.I.P.R. 252).

Delete the last paragraph.

Other relevant provisions in other sections

In the third paragraph, replace "Competition Commission" with:
48.07 Competition and Markets Authority

At the beginning of the fifth paragraph, replace "Article 12 of the Biotechnology Directive" with:
Article 12 of the EU Biotechnology Directive

At the beginning of the sixth paragraph, replace "The Regulations require that" with:
The 2002 Regulations require that

After the last paragraph, add new paragraph:
The 2002 Regulations will be amended as from IP completion day on December 31, 2020 as provided for by the European Union (Withdrawal Agreement) Act 2020 by virtue of the Patents (Amendment) (EU Exit) Regulations 2019 (SI 2019/801) in a number of respects, such as deleting references to the Community plant variety right. Although the Regulations state that such amendment will come into force on exit day (which was on January 31, 2020) this expression is to be read as IP completion day by virtue of the European Union (Withdrawal Agreement) Act 2020 Sch.5 para.1(1).

SECTION 48A [ADDED]

Commentary on Section 48A

Scope of the section

Replace the tenth paragraph with:
48A.04 In *EC Commission v United Kingdom* (C-30/90) [1993] R.P.C. 283; [1992] 1 E.C.R. 829; [1992] 2 C.M.L.R. 709, the CJEU ruled that it is contrary to what is now art.34 TFEU (for which see §§D03 and D13) to permit the grant of a compulsory licence on the ground of insufficiency of exploitation of the patent within only part of the European Union, when the demand for the patented product is satisfied by importation from other Member States. The main reason for this view is, apparently, that a reference to working (or lack of it) merely within the United Kingdom, as distinct from the EU as a whole, acts as a disguised restriction on trade between Member States. Thus, s.48A(1) has to be interpreted to meet this criterion, as extended to apply to all EEA States. However, it appears that care has been taken over the wording of the section to see that this requirement has been achieved, particularly as all the EEA Member States are WTO members. Such decision forms part of retained EU law in the UK after

December 31, 2020 and will so continue unless legislation, or the UK Supreme Court (or another specified court, in certain limited circumstances) specifies the contrary.

No licence in field of semi-conductor technology (subs.(3))

In the second paragraph, replace "Competition Commission" (two occurences) with:

Competition and Markets Authority   **48A.06**

Exploitation of another patent prevented or hindered (subss.(1)(b)(i), (4) and (5))

Replace the second paragraph with:

Subsection (1)(b)(i), by referring to the exploitation of a patented invention "in the United Kingdom" **48A.08**
was not contrary to EU law (e.g. as laid down in *EC Commission v United Kingdom* (C-30/90) [1993]
R.P.C. 283; [1992] 1 E.C.R. 829) because the purpose of EU law is to abolish barriers to trade within
the single market of the EEA and the grant of a compulsory licence assists in achieving this overall aim.

Prejudice due to imposed licence conditions (subs.(1)(c))

In the second paragraph, replace "this provision meets the rationale of the ECJ decision" with:

this provision met the rationale of the CJEU decision   **48A.10**

Restrictions on terms of licences ordered under the section (subs.(6))

Replace the third paragraph with:

Thirdly, the licence is to be "predominantly for the supply of the market in the United Kingdom" **48A.11**
(subs.(6)(c), in conformity with TRIPS art.31(f) which states that "any such use shall be authorized
predominantly for the supply of the domestic market of the Member authorizing such use". However,
it is arguable that the words "domestic market" in the TRIPS provision should have been construed as
referring to the "single market" of the EEA in accordance with the prior CJEU decisions in *Allen &
Hanbury v Generics* (C-434/85) [1988] F.S.R. 312; [1988] 1 C.M.L.R. 701 and *EC Commission v United
Kingdom* (C-30/90) [1993] R.P.C. 283; [1992] 1 E.C.R. 829; [1992] 2 C.M.L.R. 709. As observed above
such decisions form part of retained EU law in the UK after December 31, 2020 and will so continue
unless legislation, or the UK Supreme Court (or another specified court, in certain limited circumstances)
specifies the contrary.

In the last paragraph, replace "Competition Commission" with:

Competition and Markets Authority

Section 48B [Added]

Commentary on Section 48B

Scope of the section

Replace the fifth paragraph with:

However, in conformity with the CJEU decisions in *EC Commission v United Kingdom* (C-30/90) **48B.02**
[1993] R.P.C. 283; [1992] 1 E.C.R. 829; [1992] 2 C.M.L.R. 709 ECJ and *Allen & Hanbury v Generics*
(C-434/85) [1988] F.S.R. 312; [1988] 1 C.M.L.R. 701, the grounds now specified in subs.(1)(b)(ii) and
(1)(c)(i) include limitations in order to avoid the creation of some barrier to trade with another "member
State". Although the term "member State" as used in these provisions is not defined as such, their
underlying purpose (in accordance with these CJEU decisions) is to refer to any Member State of the
European Economic Area, that is to give this term the same meaning as one specifically set out in
s.46(3)(c), as amended, and as effectively further amended (see the Note to §46.01). This remains so
notwithstanding the UK withdrawal from the EU, as such decisions form part of retained EU law in the
UK and will so continue unless legislation, or the UK Supreme Court (or another specified court, in
certain limited circumstances) specifies the contrary.

SECTION 49

Commentary on Section 49

Effect of treaty obligations

Replace the first paragraph with:

49.03   Section 49 is governed by the further provisions of s.53 and therefore, by virtue of s.53(5), as discussed in §53.05, no compulsory licence can be granted which would offend the provisions of any international treaty to which the UK is a party, which will exclude the TFEU as from December 31, 2020. It would appear that this provision also requires compliance with the TRIPS Agreement so that any defect in the wording of ss.48 and 48A (but not s.48B) in relation to the wording of this Agreement would have to be ignored, see *Allen & Hanbury v Controller of Patents* [Ireland] [1997] F.S.R. 1.

SECTION 50

Commentary on Section 50

Scope of the section

Replace the second paragraph with:

50.02   Whether or not the proprietor is a "WTO proprietor", the objects and principles set out in either of the subsections must be exercised in conformity with the overriding principle of European Union law (enshrined in arts 34–36, 101 and 102 of the TFEU, reprinted in §§D03–D07 and discussed in §§D13–D16) that there should be free trade between the Member States of the European Economic Area, notwithstanding the UK withdrawal from the EU, as such considerations form part of retained EU law and will so continue unless legislation, or the UK Supreme Court (or another specified court, in certain limited circumstances) specifies the contrary. However, the wording of ss.48A and 48B does seem to be in compliance with this principle as indicated in the commentaries on these sections, but should there be doubt on any point this principle must prevail under the wide powers given to the Comptroller, particularly that of s.53(5), discussed in §53.05. This provides that no order may be made under s.48 or s.50 which is at variance with any treaty or international convention. This, of course, includes the TFEU, but only until the end of the implementation period on December 31, 2020 under the European Union (Withdrawal) Act 2018 as amended. Thus, although the principle of free trade between the EEA States could previously have been expected to be incorporated into the terms of any compulsory licence, whether granted under s.48A or s.48B, the need to do so after December 31, 2020 is open to question, notwithstanding that the free movement of goods provisions of the TFEU remain part of retained EU law in the UK.

Grant of compulsory licences (subs.(1))

Replace the second paragraph with:

50.03   Although the words "United Kingdom" have been retained in subs.(1)(a) and subs.(1)(c), it was probable that, in practice, these words should have been notionally replaced by "the European Economic Area" for the reason explained in §50.02. This is because a clear preference for United Kingdom manufacture over foreign manufacture would have been likely to be taken as contrary to the terms of the EU and EEA Treaties unless by "foreign manufacture" was meant manufacture which has taken place outside the EEA. Whether this remains the case after December 31, 2020 is, as also discussed in §50.02, open to question, notwithstanding that the free movement of goods provisions of the TFEU remain part of retained EU law in the UK.

SECTION 50A [ADDED]

Replace subs.(2) with:

50A.01   **(2)   The Competition and Markets Authority or (as the case may be) the Secretary of State may apply to the comptroller to take action under this section.**

Commentary on Section 50A

Scope of the section

Replace "Competition Commission" (two occurences) with:
Competition and Markets Authority

50A.02

Practice under Section 50A

Applications under subs.2

Replace "Competition Commission" (two occurences) with:
Competition and Markets Authority

50A.03

Section 51 [Substituted]

Replace subs.(2A) with:

[*(2A) Where—*

51.01

   (a) on a reference under section 5 of the Competition Act 1980, a report of the Commission, as laid before Parliament, contains conclusions to the effect that—

     (i) any person was engaged in an anti-competitive practice in relation to a description of goods which consist of or include patented products or in relation to a description of services in which a patented product or process is used, and

     (ii) that practice operated or might be expected to operate against the public interest; or

   (b) on a reference under section 11 of that Act, such a report contains conclusions to the effect that—

     (i) any person is pursuing a course of conduct in relation to such a description of goods or services, and

     (ii) that course of conduct operates against the public interest,

the appropriate Minister or Ministers may, subject to subsection (3) below, apply to the comptroller for relief under subsection (5A) below in respect of the patent.]

Commentary on Section 51

Scope of the section

Replace the last paragraph, first sentence with:
While under s.90 of the Fair Trading Act 1973 (c.41) (repealed by the Enterprise Act 2002 (c.40)) a Minister had a general power to declare monopoly situations and mergers unlawful if found contrary to the public interest and to prohibit the carrying out of existing agreements relating to these, he/she was not permitted thereby to cancel or modify conditions in licences granted by the proprietor of a patent or registered design, or to require licences to be available as of right (s.90(5) of that Act).

51.02

Change title from "Relevant conclusions of the Competition Commission (subs.(1))" to:

51.03

Relevant conclusions of the Competition and Markets Authority (subs.(1))

Replace the first paragraph with:
Subsection (1) now operates when a report of the Competition and Markets Authority has been laid before Parliament containing conclusions which arise from a reference to that Commission of one of the following types:

(a)   a "competition reference," under either Ch.I or II of Pt 1 of the Competition Act 1998 (c.41); or

(b)   a reference under s.11 of the Competition Act 1980 (c.21), as this section stands amended by various subsequent statutory provisions.

In the second paragraph, after "case of a", replace "reference under (c)," with:
competition reference,

In the third paragraph, after "Such a report", delete "from the Competition Commission".

Procedure under section 51

At the beginning of the paragraph, replace "When a Competition Commission report" with:

51.04   When a Competition and Markets Authority report

Practice under Section 51

In the first paragraph, replace "Competition Commission" with:

51.06   Competition and Markets Authority

SECTION 53

Commentary on Section 53

Scope of the section

Replace paragraph with:

53.02   Section 53 contains certain supplementary provisions relating to compulsory licences arising from ss.48–51, but, as the CPC did not come into force, subs.(1) was never itself brought into force and was ultimately deleted.

53.03   *Change title of paragraph:*

Reports of Competition and Markets Authority (subs.(2))

Replace "Competition Commission" with:
Competition and Markets Authority

Conformity with treaties and international conventions (subs.(5))

Replace the first paragraph, second sentence with:

53.05   Such agreement could be the Paris Convention, EPC, PCT or the TRIPS Agreement (under the GATT Treaty).

Replace the second paragraph with:

However, even though the subsection appears to have this automatic effect, the CJEU did not consider its terms to be sufficient to avoid a finding that certain of the provisions of the original forms of ss.48 and 50 were contrary to EU law (*EC Commission v United Kingdom* (C-30/90) [1993] R.P.C. 283; [1992] 1 E.C.R. 829; [1992] 2 C.M.L.R. 709 ECJ), see §48.03. This decision continues to form part of retained EU law and so will continue to apply in the UK notwithstanding the UK withdrawal from the EU, unless legislation, or the UK Supreme Court (or another specified court, in certain limited circumstances) specifies to the contrary. However as the UK is not to be a party to the TFEU as from December 31, 2020 these treaties no longer fall to be considered under this subsection, being replaced for this purpose by the EU-UK Trade and Cooperation Agreement, which was signed on December 30, 2020, applied provisionally as of January 1, 2021 and entered into force on May 1, 2021.

SECTION 54

Commentary on Section 54

In the second sentence, replace "Section 54 originally contemplated reciprocal ar-
rangements between the United Kingdom and non-EEC countries" with:

Section 54 originally contemplated reciprocal arrangements between the United Kingdom and **54.02**
non-EU countries

USE OF PATENTED INVENTIONS FOR SERVICES OF THE CROWN [SECTIONS 55—59]

SECTION 55

Commentary on Section 55

Scope of the section

Replace the first paragraph with:

Section 55 is the first of a group of sections, ss.55–59, which concern the use by the Crown of **55.09**
patented inventions, including those of European patents (UK). Section 55 is supplemented by the provisions of ss.122 (Crown's right to sell forfeited articles) and 129 (Application of Act to Crown), for which
see the commentary on those sections.

Principles of Crown use

After the second paragraph, add new paragraphs:

The meaning of the requirement for Crown use to be "authorised in writing by a government depart- **55.11**
ment" was considered by the Court of Appeal in *IPCom GmbH & Co KG v Vodafone Group Plc* [2021]
EWCA Civ 205, with particular reference to the form of authorisation that was required and whether
such an authorisation had to be expressly given or whether it could be implied from the facts.

The case related to the alleged infringement by Vodafone of a patented method for determining access rights to a telecommunications network. There was no dispute that Vodafone had been authorised
in writing by a government department to provide priority access to their network for emergency
responders, but the authorisation in question did not specify the method to be used to provide such
prioritised access and said nothing about the patent in suit (or indeed about patents in general). It was
also common ground that it would have been technically possible for Vodafone to provide the requested
prioritised access without infringing the patent in suit. The court therefore had to consider the extent to
which express authorisation to do a specific act could thereby imply an authorisation to use a specific
patented invention, and so provide a defence of Crown use.

Replace the third, fourth and fifth paragraphs with:

In deciding the issue, the court considered three possible interpretations of "authorised in writing by
a government department":

i)   it requires an express authorisation to work the patent in question (or an express authorisa-
     tion to use any patent);
ii) it requires either an express authorisation to work the patent or an authorisation to do a
     particular act in circumstances where that act necessarily infringes the patent;
iii) it extends to an authorisation to do a particular act even if that does not necessarily involve
     infringing the patent.

In a reversal of the decision at first instance, the court held that the third interpretation was not correct, stating that "the authorisation must be an authorisation to do acts in relation to a patented invention, not merely an authorisation to do acts".

Whilst the court was not strictly required to decide whether the first or second interpretations was
correct, it expressed a clear preference for the second interpretation. In his judgment Arnold L.J. drew
parallels with the law of agency, stating at [151]:

"... although section 55(1) extends beyond agents of the Crown, the concept of authorisation is one
which is familiar from the law of agency. In that context actual authority may be either express or

implied. The usual basis for implication is necessity (as it is in the case of implied terms in contracts). It is difficult to see why section 55(1) should exclude an authorisation to do an act which necessarily infringes a patent. It is equally difficult to see why it should extend to an authorisation to do an act which does not necessarily infringe a patent"

The court also observed that the burden to ensure that goods are non-infringing or properly licensed falls on the supplier of those goods rather than on the purchaser, and that this position should be no different for a Crown purchaser, provided that the Crown does not authorise use of the patent either expressly or by necessary implication. This was true even in technical fields that involved complex patent landscapes and multiple Standards Essential Patents, such as standardised telecommunications networks.

This decision has thus confirmed that it is not safe for government contractors to assume that a defence of Crown use will be available to them should they choose to use a patented invention to fulfil a UK government requirement. Such contractors would therefore be advised to identify any need to use such inventions in advance wherever possible, and to secure an express authorisation from the relevant government department where necessary, noting that such departments are likely to encourage their contractors to pursue commercial licensing solutions in preference to the exercise of Crown user rights wherever possible.

The defence of Crown use has been rarely used prior to this case and, notwithstanding the clear limitations placed on the use of the defence by the Court of Appeal, it is possible that this decision will encourage greater use of the defence in future. It also seems likely that this decision may cause government departments to be more cautious when issuing functional instructions to their suppliers in future, and they may seek to protect their financial position by way of contractual indemnities against unanticipated claims for Crown use of patents.

The judgment in *IPCom GmbH v Vodafone* [2020] EWHC 132 (Pat) also confirmed that an implied Crown use authorisation would also extend to acts that were ancillary but necessary to the main purpose of the authorisation, in this case to the keeping and testing of the relevant network equipment against the possibility of a Crown request to use it. This interpretation was not challenged on appeal.

Acts for services of the Crown (subss.(1) and (2))

After the first paragraph, add new paragraph:

55.13   The definition of "use for the services of the Crown" given in s.56(2) was considered in *IPCom GmbH v Vodafone* [2020] EWHC 132 (Pat) where it was confirmed that the examples provided were non-exhaustive (see §56.04).

Retrospective authorisation (subs.(6))

After the last paragraph, add new paragraph:

55.21   In *IPCom GmbH & Co KG v Vodafone Group Plc* [2021] EWCA Civ 205 the Court of Appeal considered the compatibility of retrospective authorisation under s.55(6) with the provisions of art.31(b) of the TRIPS agreement that require prior negotiation with the rights holder. Arnold L.J. concluded that, to the extent authorisations permitted under s.55 extend beyond the exceptions for "national emergency or other circumstances of extreme urgency" and "public non-commercial use" provided in art.31(b), retrospective authorisation under s.55(6) would be inconsistent with TRIPS. This matter was not considered in any depth, but such an interpretation may have implications for future authorisations by government under this section.

Notification to proprietor (subs.(7))

After the first paragraph, add new paragraph:

55.22   In the light of the decision in *IPCom GmbH & Co KG v Vodafone Group Plc* [2021] EWCA Civ 205 that a Crown use authorisation may be implied from an authorisation to perform a given act, where that act necessarily involves use of a patented invention, and irrespective of any knowledge of the existence or relevance of the patent, it appears possible that in some circumstances the government department concerned may not actually be aware that any authorisation has been given, and so presumably would be unable to notify the proprietor until this information came to its attention (whether as a result of proceedings for infringement or otherwise).

Section 56

Commentary on Section 56

Definition of "services of the Crown" (subs.(2))

At the end of the last paragraph, replace "Secretary of State for Health" with:
Secretary of State for Health and Social Care   **56.04**

After the last paragraph, add new paragraph:
In *IPCom GmbH v Vodafone* [2020] EWHC 132 (Pat) it was argued that s.56(2) provided an exhaustive list of the acts that may be considered as "for the services of the Crown", but this interpretation was rejected by the court. The word "includes" plainly indicated that the examples provided in this sub-section were intended to be non-exhaustive. Furthermore, the closing wording of the sub-section merely confirmed that the words "use for the services of the Crown" were to be construed as covering, but not limited to, the examples given. It was noted that this interpretation was consistent with that provided in the UK-IPO's Manual of Patent Practice.

Section 58

Notes

Delete item "7." from the list.   **58.01**

Commentary on Section 58

Scope of the section

Replace the second paragraph with:
The provision formerly present in s.48(2) of the 1949 Act that, in the event of a dispute being brought   **58.02**
before the court, the Crown can put the validity of the patent in issue, is now to be found in s.74(1)(e).
Thus, as formerly, a proprietor wishing to have a dispute resolved by the court must face the possibility of the expense of full validity proceedings. If validity is put in issue then s.75(1) operates, and the court may allow the specification to be amended.

Section 59

Commentary on Section 59

Scope of the section

To the end of the paragraph, add:
At the time of publication, no declaration of emergency has been made or proposed for the purposes   **59.02**
of this section in relation to the coronavirus pandemic.

Extension of powers

After the first paragraph, add new paragraph:
It was confirmed in *IPCom GmbH v Vodafone* [2020] EWHC 132 (Pat) that s.59 does not expressly   **59.03**
or impliedly limit the scope of "use for the services of the Crown" as defined in s.55 and s.56:

"On the contrary s 59 provides a separate defence for a much broader list of acts including those which would not generally be regarded as being 'use for the services of the Crown' even on the widest view of these words: see e.g. 59(b) to 59(f)."

INFRINGEMENT [SECTIONS 60–71]

SECTION 60

Commentary on Section 60

Direct (or substantive) infringement (subs.(1))

Scope of subsection (1)

After the last paragraph, add new paragraph:

60.04   In *IPcom v Vodafone* [2020] EWHC 132 (Pat), the court considered the concept of de minimis infringement in slightly unusual circumstances, namely the position where particular acts are only ever intended to be undertaken on a small scale, in abnormal performance of a method. The court concluded that such acts could not benefit from the de minimis exclusion, despite only occurring rarely, since the defendant benefited from the ability to perform them. This was upheld on appeal [2021] EWCA Civ 205.

Infringement of product invention (subs.(1)(a))

Replace the last paragraph with:

60.05   In *Illumina v Premaitha* [2017] EWHC 2930 (Pat), the court considered whether a process invention was infringed in the United Kingdom where one step was carried out on computers located in Taiwan. By analogy with *Menashe v William Hill* [2002] EWCA Civ 1702, the court found that the substance of the process was taking place in the UK, notwithstanding the fact that a computer undertaking a particular automated computer process was located elsewhere. In *Promptu v Sky* [2021] EWHC 2021 (Pat), the court distinguished *Menashe*, finding that the patent would have been infringed (had it been valid) given that the central part of the processing took place on a server in the United Kingdom, notwithstanding the fact that two functions took place abroad. This was on the basis that these features were subsidiary parts of the claim and that the substance of the method claimed was therefore performed in the United Kingdom.

Indirect (or contributory) infringement under subs.(2)

Scope of subs.(2)

After the eleventh paragraph (beginning "In Idenix v Gilead [2014] EWHC 3916 (Pat)"), add new paragraph:

60.09   In *Akebia v Fibrogen* [2020] EWHC 866 (Pat), the patentee argued contributory infringement of a medical use claim. Moreover infringement was put on a quia timet basis. The judge had held that the structural requirement of the claim had been met but as the drug was not yet on the market (and was unlikely to be on the market for some time) the court would need to consider both the defendants' state of mind and the state of mind of clinicians prescribing the drug (in terms of their intentions) at some indeterminate future point of time. The court considered the evidence in some detail (see §§595–638) concluding that neither aspect had been established.

Involving supply of a staple product (subs.(3))

To the end of the last paragraph, add:

60.10   In *IPcom v Vodafone* [2020] EWHC 132 (Pat), the court reached a similar conclusion in respect of SIM cards for mobile telephones.

Laches, acquiescence and estoppel

To the end of the second paragraph, add:

60.24   Similarly in *A Ward v Fabcon* [2021] EWHC 2145 (IPEC), the court concluded that not taking action following receipt of a letter responding to a letter before claim did not amount to acquiescence or provide the basis for an estoppel.

After the third paragraph, add new paragraph:

In *Optis v Apple* [2021] EWHC 1739 (Pat) the court found there was no proprietary estoppel where

Apple sought to rely on the behaviour of Ericsson, the former owner of the standards essential patent, and how it had behaved in relation to the adoption of the patented invention into a mobile telephone standard. It concluded there was neither reliance nor detriment and, accordingly, no unconscionability.

Joint tortfeasance by acting in a "common design"

After the last paragraph, add new paragraph:

In *Lufthansa v Astronics* [2020] EWHC 1968 (Pat), the court considered a claim to a system, hold-ing infringement on the basis of a common design between the defendants and its customers to con-nect the necessary components to that system. **60.28**

SECTION 61

Commentary on Section 61

Scope of the section

To the end of the fourth paragraph (beginning "The CPR, which almost entirely replaced"), add:

For commentary on recent changes to the CPR and IP litigation more generally, see Chris Ryan, **61.03**
"Procedure in IP litigation" [2020] 4 *CIPA* 22.

The forum for infringement proceedings

Replace the penultimate paragraph with:

In *Huawei v Conversant* [2019] EWCA Civ 38, the Court of Appeal confirmed that the courts of **61.04**
England and Wales were the correct forum for the determination of infringement of UK patents, notwithstanding the fact that several of the defendants were Chinese entities. The court noted that the Chinese courts could not determine the validity or otherwise of the UK patents. On appeal to the Supreme Court, [2020] UKSC 37, Conversant argued that China was a more appropriate forum for an infringement action, that therefore, jurisdiction should be declined as to the Chinese defendants and that the case permanently stayed as to English defendants. The issues before the court proceeded upon the assumption, with which the court agreed, that the English court had jurisdiction to settle a global licence on FRAND terms for a multinational SEP portfolio because issues as to a global licence needed to be determined so as to enable the court to adjudicate upon a contractual defence to the enforcement of an English patent by injunction. The court concluded [98]:

> "After hearing extensive expert evidence, the judge found that the Chinese courts do not, at present, have jurisdiction to determine the terms of a global FRAND licence, at least in the absence of agree-ment by all parties that they should do so. Even in the event of such an agreement, he described the prospect that the Chinese courts would embark on the exercise as no more than speculative. Notwithstanding the admission of fresh evidence on this issue, the Court of Appeal reached the same conclusion. In sharp contrast, we have decided, for the reasons set out above, that the English court does have such a jurisdiction, even in the absence of consent by the parties, and it has of course exercised that jurisdiction in the *Unwired* case. Directions have been given in the *Conversant* case (subject to the outcome of this appeal) for it to be done again. Furthermore, against the speculative possibility that the Chinese courts might accept jurisdiction to settle a global FRAND licence by consent, there is the judge's finding that Conversant had acted reasonably in refusing to give its consent, for reasons connected with the conditions which the appellants sought to impose, a conclu-sion which was not met with any persuasive challenge in this court."

Interim injunctions

The principles upon which pre-trial relief is granted

After the sixth paragraph (beginning "The difference between the American Cyanamid and Series 5 Software decisions"), add new paragraph:

For recent analysis of the *American Cyanamid* principles see the judgment of Floyd L.J. in *Neurim* **61.08**
v Mylan [2020] EWCA Civ 793 and the judgment of Roth J. in *Novartis v Teva* [2022] EWHC 959 (Ch).

The claimant's cross-undertaking

After the last paragraph, add new paragraph:

61.10   In *Dr Reddy's v Warner-Lambert* [2021] EWHC 2182 (Pat) the court addressed preliminary issues in respect of a series of parallel inquiry claims arising out of cross-undertakings given by a patentee to a number of potential infringers. The court found that the inquiry would have to proceed on the basis that the various threats, order and undertakings had not been made. Further, despite each inquiry being factually independent, the court ordered that any findings of fact on common issues in the inquiries should bind all parties as a matter of case management.

The requirement for the claimant to show a "serious issue to be tried"

After the last paragraph, add new paragraph:

61.11   In *Neurim v Mylan* [2020] EWHC 1362 (Pat) the patent had been revoked during opposition proceedings at the EPO. These were the subject of appeal (which is of suspensive effect). The argument that the revocation of the patent meant that there was no serious issue to be tried was rejected by the court. The case was appealed, but this line of argument was not pursued.

The adequacy of damages as a remedy

Replace the first paragraph with:

61.15   Under the *American Cyanamid* principles, each party will seek to satisfy the court that the balance of injustice is in its favour because, with or without an injunction, that party is likely to suffer damage that is unquantifiable. This is because, if damages are an adequate remedy and the defendant has the ability to pay them then, under the *American Cyanamid* principles, no injunction is normally granted (*Garden Cottage v Milk Marketing Board* [1984] A.C. 130 HL). It was on this basis that an interim injunction was refused in *Epoch v Character Options* [2015] EWHC 3436 (IPEC). Similarly, in *Evalve v Edwards* [2019] EWHC 1158 (Pat), an interim injunction was refused where an expedited trial had been ordered and an appropriate undertaking was offered by the defendant to limit its activities in the interim period. In *Neurim v Mylan* [2020] EWHC 1362 (Pat), again an expedited trial had been ordered (which would be possible in around 4 months) and so the court concluded that damages were an adequate remedy and refused the grant of an injunction. The Court of Appeal confirmed this on appeal ([2020] EWCA Civ 793) however, much of the first instance reasoning was criticised and should therefore not be relied upon. The judgment of the appeal court contains considerable factual analysis as to the circumstances in which damages may be adequate as a remedy.

Relief by post-trial injunction (subs.(1)(a))

Replace the fifth, sixth and seventh paragraphs (i.e., from "In Huawei v ZTE (C-170/13)" to "licensing offer prior to suing the defendant.") with:

61.21   In *Huawei v ZTE* (C-170/13) [2016] R.P.C. 4 the CJEU gave a preliminary ruling that it was not per se an abuse of a dominant position to seek injunctive relief on a "standard essential patent" (SEP) in respect of which there had been an agreement to grant licences on FRAND ("Fair, Reasonable and Non-Discriminatory") terms. The court set out guidance as to the criteria on which the question of alleged abuse should be assessed, as to which see Appendix D at D26.

        In *Unwired Planet v Huawei* [2020] UKSC 37 the ability of UK courts to grant injunctions and set global FRAND rates was considered, upholding the decision of the Court of Appeal at [2018] EWCA Civ 2344 and of the judge at first instance at [2017] EWHC 2988 (Pat) and [2017] EWHC 1304 (Pat). In summary, it was held that a court in the UK had jurisdiction to grant a "FRAND injunction" in respect of those patents that had been held to be valid and essential to the relevant standards but which injunction the defendants could avoid by taking the global FRAND licence as settled by such court. In so doing it interpreted *Huawei v ZTE* as requiring that the SEP holder give notice of the alleged infringement prior to issuing proceedings but as not otherwise establishing mandatory rules that if not adhered to would constitute abuse of a dominant position. It also discussed, and rejected, an argument advanced by the defendants, for the first time in the Supreme Court, based on s.50 of the Senior Courts Act 1981 (formerly under Lord Cairns's Act), that since the SEP holder's only interest was in obtaining reasonable royalties, and that interest can be fully recognised by an award of damages in lieu of an injunction, an award based on the royalties which would reasonably be agreed for a licence of each of the UK patents infringed, was the appropriate and proportionate remedy. An objection of forum non conveniens was raised, and the decision on that issue is summarised at §61.04.

        On the issue whether the English courts had jurisdiction and could properly exercise a power without the agreement of both parties to grant an injunction restraining the infringement of a UK SEP unless the defendant entered into a global licence on "FRAND" terms of a multinational patent portfolio, the court noted early in its opinion the position of the European Telecommunications Standards Institute ("ETSI"), a French association formed in 1988 and which has adopted an intellectual property rights ("IPR") policy and contractual framework governed by French law. When considering whether to include a technology in a standard, ETSI requires the patent owner to enter into an irrevocable undertaking or contract with it to allow implementers of the standard to obtain a licence to use the relevant patented technology on fair, reasonable and non-discriminatory ("FRAND") terms. The court also acknowledged industry practice in negotiating licence agreements, recognising [15] that no rational business would seek to license products country by country if it could be avoided. This was, as Birss J. said, in part because of the effort required to negotiate and agree so many different licences and thereafter to keep track of so many different royalty calculations and payments. It was also, as he recognised, because businesses and consumers would move mobile handsets across borders and an implementer would want to be able to bind the SEP owner into allowing the entry of otherwise unlicensed handsets into the jurisdictions in which the SEP owner had a valid SEP. The prohibitive cost of litigating the validity and essentiality of patents territory by territory was another obvious consideration that must have been part of the factual background of which the expert framers of the IPR Policy were aware when they devised that Policy. An argument was rejected [86] that it was disproportionate to exclude an implementer from the UK market unless it entered into a worldwide licence of untested patents solely because it has infringed a UK patent. This argument failed to acknowledge that what the implementer was purchasing in entering into such a licence with a SEP owner, which had a sufficiently large international portfolio of patents, was not solely access to the UK market but certainty that it had the ability legally to manufacture and sell products which complied with the standard on a worldwide basis.

The court rejected a submission [66] that in order to avoid the grant of an injunction for infringement of a national patent and in being prepared to determine the disputed terms of a global FRAND licence the English courts were uniquely setting themselves up as a de facto global licensing tribunal. It rejected a submission that Birss J. was out of line with the approach of courts in most significant jurisdictions. A number of US decisions were taken into account including *Apple v Motorola* 757 F.3d 1286 (Fed. Cir. 2014), *Microsoft v Motorola* 696 F.3d 872 (9th Cir. 2012), *Microsoft v Motorola* Case C10-1823JLR; 2013 US Dist. LEXIS 60233, *Apple v Qualcomm* Case No.3:17-cv-00108-GPC-MDD, September 7, 2017, and decisions of the German courts and the EU Commission. In summary [84] the US case law showed:

(i)   a recognition that the court in determining a FRAND licence in such cases is being asked to enforce a contractual obligation which limits the exercise of the patent owner's IP rights including its IP rights under foreign law;

(ii)   a willingness in principle to grant an injunction against the infringement of a national patent which is a SEP, if an implementer refuses a licence on FRAND terms;

(iii)   a willingness in principle to determine the FRAND terms of a worldwide licence;

(iv)   a practice of looking to examples of real life commercial negotiation of licences by parties engaged in the relevant industry when fixing the FRAND terms of a licence; and

(v)   a recognition that the determination of a FRAND licence by one national court does not prevent an implementer from challenging foreign patents on the grounds of invalidity or non-infringement in other relevant national courts.

Similarly, in Germany the developing case law showed:

(i)   a recognition that a worldwide licence might be FRAND and an implementer's counter-offer of a national licence confined to Germany might not be FRAND;

(ii)   a practice of having regard to the usual practices of parties in the relevant industry when the court determines the FRAND terms of a licence; and

(iii)   a willingness to grant an injunction against infringement of a national patent if the court holds that a SEP owner's offer of a licence is FRAND and the implementer refused to enter into it.

The courts in China had not rejected the proposition that a worldwide licence might be FRAND, nor had the courts ruled that they did not have jurisdiction to determine the FRAND terms of a worldwide licence with the consent of the parties, although it remained a matter of speculation whether they would or would not accept jurisdiction.

On the non-discriminatory aspect of FRAND, a licensee who was offered a "fair and reasonable" rate was not discriminated against merely because another licensee had been given lower rate, the court observing [113]:

"The choice between regarding the non-discrimination obligation as 'general' or 'hard-edged' is a matter of interpretation of the FRAND undertaking in clause 6.1 of the IPR Policy. The obligation set out in that provision is that licences should be available 'on fair, reasonable and non-discriminatory ... terms and conditions'. In our view, the undertaking imports a single unitary obligation. Licence terms should be made available which are 'fair, reasonable and non-discriminatory', reading that phrase as a composite whole. There are not two distinct obligations, that the licence terms should be fair and reasonable and also, separately, that they should be non-discriminatory. Still less are there three distinct obligations, that the licence terms should be fair and, separately, reasonable and, separately, non-discriminatory."

Nor was the launch of the present proceedings an abuse of a dominant position under art.103 TFEU following *Huawei v ZTE* because Unwired had not behaved abusively. Sufficient notice had been given before the injunction application had been made, there was no mandatory requirement that the patentee itself make an offer of terms which coincided with those that were ultimately determined by the court to be FRAND which was inconsistent with *Huawei* [68] which contemplated determination of the amount of the royalty by an independent third party. Unwired Planet had shown itself willing to license Huawei on whatever terms the court determined were FRAND, while Huawei had only been prepared to take a licence with a scope determined by itself [158].

The defendants further argued that an injunction would not be appropriate or proportionate since the claimants' interest was in obtaining reasonable royalties which could be recognised by an award of damages in lieu of an injunction, citing *Morris-Garner v One Step (Support)* [2018] UKSC 20; [2019] A.C. 649, *Co-operative Insurance Society v Argyll Stores (Holdings)* [1998] A.C. 1, *Coventry (t/a RDC Promotions) v Lawrence* [2014] UKSC 13; [2014] A.C. 822 and the US Supreme Court decision in *eBay v Mercexchange* 547 US 388 (2006) where it was noted that an injunction could be employed as a bargaining tool to charge exorbitant fees and that where the patented invention was only a small component of the product the defendant sought to produce, and the threat of an injunction was employed simply for undue leverage in negotiations, damages might well be sufficient to compensate for the infringement, and an injunction might not serve the public interest. In the present proceedings the eBay decision was distinguished on the grounds that the threat of an injunction here could not be employed by the claimants as a means of charging exorbitant fees, or for undue leverage in negotiations, since they could not enforce their rights unless they offered to license their patents on terms which the court was satisfied were fair, reasonable and non-discriminatory. Furthermore, an award of damages was unlikely to be an adequate substitute for what would be lost by the withholding an injunction because in the case of a SEP it might well be impractical for the patent-holder to bring proceedings to enforce its rights against an infringing implementer in every country where the patents had been infringed and if the patent-holder were confined to a monetary remedy, implementers who were infringing the patents would have an incentive to continue infringing until, patent by patent, and country by country, they were compelled to pay royalties. An injunction was likely to be a more effective remedy, since it did not merely add a small increment to the cost of products which infringed the UK patents, but prohibited infringement altogether.

Another issue [49] was whether the English courts have jurisdiction and may properly exercise a power without the agreement of both parties to determine royalty rates and other disputed items for a settled global licence and to declare that such terms are FRAND. In answer to this question, the court observed:

"63. We now turn to the submission (para 51 above) that the English courts have no jurisdiction to determine the terms of a licence involving disputed or potentially disputed foreign patents. We disagree. If the judgments of the English courts had purported to rule on the validity or infringement of a foreign patent, that would indeed be beyond their jurisdiction. But that is not what Birss J and the Court of Appeal have done. Instead, they looked to the commercial practice in the industry of agreeing to take a licence of a portfolio of patents, regardless of whether or not each patent was valid or was infringed by use of the relevant technology in the standard, and construed the IPR Policy as promoting that behaviour.

64. We agree with the parties that the FRAND obligation in the IPR Policy extends to the fairness of the process by which the parties negotiate a licence. If an implementer is concerned about the validity and infringement of particularly significant patents or a group of patents in a particular jurisdiction which might have a significant effect on the royalties which it would have to pay, it might in our view be fair and reasonable for the implementer to reserve the right to challenge those patents or a sample of those patents in the relevant foreign court and to require that the licence provide a mechanism to alter the royalty rates as a result. It might also be fair and reasonable for the implementer to seek to include in the licence an entitlement to recover sums paid as royalties attributable to those patents in the event that the relevant foreign court held them to be invalid or not infringed, although it appears that that has not been usual industry practice. Huawei suggests that it would serve no purpose for a UK court to fix the terms of a global licence but to provide for the altera-

tion of royalties in the event of successful challenges to declared SEPs overseas. This would, it suggests, reduce a licence to an interim licence. Again, we disagree. Under a FRAND process the implementer can identify patents which it wishes to challenge on reasonable grounds. For example, in the Conversant case, it might well be argued by Huawei or ZTE at trial that the obligation of fairness and reasonableness required any global licence granted by Conversant to include provision to allow for Huawei or ZTE to seek to test the validity and infringement of samples of Conversant's Chinese patents, with the possibility of consequential adjustment of royalty rates, given the importance of China as a market and a place of manufacture. In other cases, such challenges may make little sense unless, at a cost proportionate to what was likely to be achieved in terms of eliminating relevant uncertainty, they were likely significantly to alter the royalty burden on the implementer.

65. In the Unwired case, Huawei appears not to have sought any provision in the draft global licence to alter the royalties payable if Unwired's Chinese patents or a relevant sample of them were successfully challenged. As we have said (para 47 above) the only adjustment mechanism which the draft licence provided was to the royalties payable in relation to major markets. Huawei has not appealed the detailed terms of that draft licence but has focussed its attack on the principle of a national court determining that a global licence was FRAND without the consent of the parties to such an exercise. That notwithstanding, it would be open to Huawei in another case to seek to make such a reservation when negotiating or debating in court the terms of a licence and to seek to persuade the court at first instance that the reservation was appropriate in a FRAND process."

To the end of the penultimate paragraph, add:

In *Evalve v Edwards* [2020] EWHC 513 (Pat), however, the court granted a final injunction in respect of a catheter repair device: it rejected arguments that clinicians might prefer the infringing device noting that, had there been no alternative, it might have been minded to consider the public interest in refusing an injunction.

After the last paragraph, add new paragraphs:

In *Price v Flitcraft* [2019] EWHC 2476 (Pat), a director of the defendant was found to be in contempt of court for failing to comply with an injunction granted following a successful application for summary judgment.

In *Fiberweb v Geofabrics* [2021] EWHC 1996 (Pat), the court had previously found infringement and granted the general form of injunction "not to infringe the patent". Fiberweb sought to market a redesigned version of the product found previously to infringe and had launched proceedings for a declaration of non-infringement. The question was whether the general injunction on the first case bound them in the interim. The court held that in general the overall issue as to infringement by the redesign ought to be determined in the DNI proceedings with no injunction in the meantime. Whether there should be a variation from the general rule would depend on principles akin to those in a conventional interim injunction situation.

In *Autostore v Ocado* [2021] EWCA Civ 1003, the court refused a final injunction to prevent the contents of without prejudice material being used by the claimant in proceedings in other jurisdictions.

Euro-defences

Replace the last paragraph with:

In *Unwired Planet v Huawei* [2020] UKSC 37 the UK Supreme Court, upholding the decision of the Court of Appeal at [2018] EWCA Civ 2344, confirmed that the judge at first instance ([2017] EWHC 711 (Pat)) had been right to find that although the claimant standard essential patent (SEP) holder was in a dominant position, within the meaning of art.102 TFEU, its behaviour, in failing to provide its FRAND licence terms before suing the defendant was not abusive, since, on the facts, the claimant had shown itself to be willing to grant a licence to the defendants on whatever terms the court decided were FRAND. In doing so, it concluded that *Huawei v ZTE* (C-170/13) [2016] R.P.C. 4 did not, other than requiring notice of, or prior consultation as to the alleged infringement, set out mandatory steps that a patent licensor had to undertake prior to issuing proceedings but merely gave guidance as to the sort of subsequent behaviour that would not be abusive. **61.33**

Costs

The principles for award and assessment of costs

After the eighteenth paragraph (beginning "In my view, this apparent dichotomy may be resolved"), add new paragraphs:

In *Conversant v Huawei* [2019] EWHC 3130 (Pat), the court ordered the successful defendant to pay **61.34**

70% of the costs of the unsuccessful claimant. This was because the court found that, whilst the defendants had won, they had lost 19 out of 20 issues and had taken an unsatisfactory approach even on the single issue which they had won.

The issue-based approach remains the norm before the Patents Court. In *Coloplast v Salts* [2021] EWHC 107 (Pat), the court undertook an issue-based approach and made a number of deductions. A similar approach was adopted in *Edwards v Meril* [2020] EWHC 2938 (Pat).

In *Coloplast v Salts* the court adopted the guidance from *Pigot v Environment Agency* [2020] EWHC 144 (Ch) as to the application of issue based costs before adding its own additional observations:

> "'(1) The mere fact that the successful party was not successful on every issue does not, of itself, justify an issue-based cost order. In any litigation, there are likely to be issues which involve reviewing the same, or overlapping, sets of facts, and where it is therefore difficult to disentangle the costs of one issue from another. The mere fact that the successful party has lost on one or more issues does not by itself normally make it appropriate to deprive them of their costs.
> (2) Such an order may be appropriate if there is a discrete or distinct issue, the raising of which caused additional costs to be incurred. Such an order may also be appropriate if the overall costs were materially increased by the unreasonable raising of one or more issues on which the successful party failed.
> (3) Where there is a discrete issue which caused additional costs to be incurred, if the issue was raised reasonably, the successful party is likely to be deprived of its costs of the issue. If the issue was raised unreasonably, the successful party is likely also to be ordered to pay the costs of the issue incurred by the unsuccessful party. An issue may be treated as having been raised unreasonably if it is hopeless and ought never to have been pursued.
> (4) Where an issue-based costs order is appropriate, the court should attempt to reflect it by ordering payment of a proportion of the receiving party's costs if that is practicable.
> (5) An issue-based costs order should reflect the extent to which the costs were increased by the raising of the issue; costs which would have been incurred even if the issue had not been raised should be paid by the unsuccessful party.
> (6) Before making an issue-based costs order, it is important to stand back and ask whether, applying the principles set out in CPR rule 44.2, it is in all the circumstances of the case the right result. The aim must always be to make an order that reflects the overall justice of the case.'

5. I found that passage from *Pigot* to be a helpful summary. However, I would make the following additional points:

a. The approach to issue-based costs orders in patent litigation does not differ from the approach in other types of litigation (see *Hospira UK Ltd v Cubist Pharmaceuticals, LLC* [2016] 5 Costs LR 1011, per Henry Carr J. at [9]). However, patent cases lend themselves to issue-based costs orders because they often involve a large number of issues and a party can (as in the present case) lose on a number of issues but still be the overall winner. See *SmithKline Beecham Plc v Apotex Europe Limited* [2004] EWCA Civ 1703, per Jacob LJ at [25]-[26]. Further, as Henry Carr J said in Cubist at [9]: *'Patent litigation is very expensive, and it is important that parties should be encouraged only to pursue their best points, and to be aware of the cost implications of failing to do so.'*

   A similar point was made by Birss J in *Unwired Planet International Limited v Huawei Technologies Co. Limited* [2016] EWHC 410 (Pat) at [13] although Birss J went on, (at [18]), to note that courts must be careful because: *'If the court unduly penalises a party for dropping issues before trial, that may encourage parties to continue to run up issues all the way to trial, which will in turn increase the costs even further.'*

b. What constitutes a discrete or distinct issue (or, as it is often called in patent cases, a 'suitably circumscribed' issue) will vary from case to case. In the patent context, it may involve the consideration of an individual piece of prior art but may equally be an issue arising within a broader issue, such as an issue as regards experiments arising in relation to the broader issue of infringement. See *Unwired Planet* at [6].

c. Where the overall winner has lost on a discrete issue, it is likely to be deprived of its costs of that issue even if it acted reasonably. However, that is not inevitable. It must still be appropriate to make such an order.

d. Where the overall winner has lost on a discrete issue, it may also be ordered to pay the losing party's costs of that issue. As appears from *Pigot*, such an order is likely to be made where the overall winner had acted unreasonably in relation to that issue. However, such an order can be made even where the overall winner had not acted unreasonably. It has been said that to make such an order requires 'suitably exceptional' circumstances. However, in reality, the test is simply whether it would be appropriate and just in all the circumstances to make such an order. It is not intended that such orders should be extremely rare. See *Unwired Planet* at [6]-[8] and *Cubist* at [6]-[10].

e. Where an issue-based costs order is appropriate, the proportion of the winning party's costs to be paid is often expressed in terms of a percentage of its total costs. This percentage reflects the deduction necessary to reflect the winning party's costs in relation to an issue on which it lost and also, where appropriate, the losing party's costs in relation to that issue. Such percentages orders *'can usually be made in patent cases and should be made if they can be'*. See *Unwired Planet* at [10].

f. In determining the level of reduction, the court is not expected to undertake a detailed assessment. Indeed, it is unlikely to have the benefit of a detailed bill of costs. See *Cubist* at [3]-[4]. In this regard, Pumfrey J in *Monsanto Technology LLC v Cargill International SA* [2008] FSR 417 at [5] commented that: *'This brings me to the next problem confronting the judge who has to make an order for costs of the kind the parties want in this case. That problem is the doubts which their respective solicitors entertain as to the accuracy of the other side's estimate of the costs expended on the client's behalf upon the various issues …. I wish it to be clearly understood that parties cannot have it both ways. Either the case goes to detailed assessment, in which case issues of this description will fall by the wayside, or it is dealt with by the trial judge, who cannot resolve them. If the parties wish to take advantage of the benefits flowing from a comparatively rough-and-ready assessment by the judge, they cannot expect a detailed assessment of the correctness of each of the sums which they specify. This is a matter for the parties and not for the court. If neither seeks a detailed assessment, then the court will do its best with the material which is made available, and can only adjust figures deposed to by the solicitors concerned if there is a really good reason for doing so.'*

Birss J, having quoted that passage in *Unwired Planet* (at [11]), went on (at [12]) to conclude that: *'In my judgment what the learned judge there said about the comparatively rough and ready assessment which these percentage orders represent remains true. It cannot be overemphasised that this exercise is very approximate.'*

After the nineteenth paragraph (beginning "Issue-based costs orders may not always be appropriate"), add new paragraph:

In *Neurim v Generics* [2022] EWCA Civ 359, the court allowed a partial appeal of a cost decision (a rarity) arising out of the highly unusual facts of the case.

After the last paragraph, add new paragraphs:

In *Optis v Apple* [2020] EWHC 3248 (Pat) the court dealt with ordering costs on a solicitor and own client basis consequent upon the previous grant of a Certificate of Contested Validity. The court held that this did not affect the overall principles to be applied in making an issue based costs award.

For a recent decision on the summary assessment of costs in the Shorter Trials Scheme, see *Insulet v Roche* [2021] EWHC 2047 (Pat). In this the court was highly critical of the proportionality of the winning party's costs and made various deductions finding that £1.7M was disproportionate for a "three day trial of this nature". It should be noted that the losing party "capped" its costs at £1M (although it had spent in the region of £1.1 to £1.2M).

Practice under Section 61

Representation

After the last paragraph, add new paragraph:

In *Glencairn v Product Specialities* [2020] EWCA Civ 609, the Court of Appeal upheld a first instance decision dismissing an application which sought to restrain the solicitors acting for the defendants from continuing to act. The solicitors had previously acted for a third party, which had compromised proceedings brought by the claimant by means of a mediation. The court was not satisfied that the appellant had demonstrated that the information barriers operated by those solicitors had been inadequate and accordingly concluded that there was no conflict.

61.43

Transfer between the Patents Court and the Intellectual Property Enterprise and referral to the Court of Justice (CJEU)

To the end of the third paragraph, add:

61.44   In *IoT IP v Haandle* [2019] EWHC 534 (Pat), transfer was refused for similar reasons but also because the court concluded that the defendant had not shown that it could not afford to proceed in the Patents Court.

To the end of the sixth paragraph (beginning "In 77M v Ordnance Survey [2017] EWHC 1501 (IPEC)"), add:

      Similarly, in *Kwikbolt v Airbus* [2019] EWHC 2450 (IPEC), an application by the defendant to transfer the case to the Patents Court was refused given the small size of the claimant company and the relatively straightforward matters to be determined.

Conduct of an action

To the end of the third paragraph, add:

61.45   In *Akebia v Fibrogen* [2020] EWHC 866 (Pat) the court suggested that a technical primer should be regarded as mandatory in category 4 and 5 cases unless there are good reasons to the contrary. In *Fisher v Flexicare* [2020] EWHC 3282 (Pat) the court reiterated this point, noting that, even in simple cases, at least an agreed summary of the common general knowledge should be provided.

Before commencing an action

After the second paragraph, add new paragraph:

61.52   In *Optis v Apple* [2019] EWHC 3538 (Pat), the court found that there was no failure to comply with the practice direction (pre-action conduct), where the claimant had negotiated for some years with the third defendant on the reasonable assumption that the third defendant was negotiating on behalf of all three defendants.

Commencing a claim

After the fourth paragraph (beginning "Depending on the country in question"), add new paragraph:

61.53   In *Godo Kaisha v Huawei* [2021] EWHC 1261 (Pat) the court set-aside an order granting the claimant permission to serve the claim form by alternative means: the factors relied upon by the claimant were not found to amount to exceptional circumstances, as required for such an order.

Particulars of Claim

To the end of the third paragraph, add:

61.54   In *Facebook v Voxer* [2021] EWHC 657 (Pat), however, the court stated that Particulars of Infringement should contain, as a minimum, a statement by reference to each relevant claim feature that equivalence is relied upon.

After the last paragraph, add new paragraph:

      It is to be noted that, as of April 6, 2020, the statement of truth in the Particulars of Claim, other statements of case and witness statements has been updated with a requirement to include the following statement: *"I understand that proceedings for contempt of court may be brought against anyone who makes, or causes to be made, a false statement in a document verified by a statement of truth without an honest belief in its truth"*. Whilst the consequences of a false statement of truth have not changed, this requirement obliges whoever is signing the statement of truth to acknowledge the prospect of an action for contempt of court at the point of signature.

Further statements of case, amendments to statements, further information

After the penultimate paragraph, add new paragraph:

61.57   In *Lufthansa v Astronics* [2020] EWHC 83 (Pat), the defendant sought permission to retract an admission. Permission was, however, refused as the admission had been freely given by the defendant and permitting it to withdraw it at a late stage would unfairly prejudice the claimant. The question turned on transfer of title and the limitation period would have prevented the claimant from recovering damages from third parties if, having been allowed to withdraw its admission, the defendant was able to show that title had indeed passed and it was not responsible for any acts of infringement.

Case management: the case management conference

After the last paragraph, add new paragraphs:

In *Nicoventures v Philip Morris* [2020] EWHC 1594 (Pat) the court refused expedition, despite hearing extensive oral arguments regarding the requirement for the same.   **61.59**

In *Cabo Concepts v MGA* [2021] EWHC 491 (Pat) the court refused to transfer a case involving unjustified threats of patent litigation out of the Patents List into the general Chancery Division but also ordered a joint trial of liability and quantum on case management grounds.

In *Sandoz v Bristol-Meyers Squibb* [2021] EWHC 1123 the court ordered the patentee to identify no more than ten independently valid claims within 28 days of service of product and process descriptions, noting that it was likely that the number of claims would be further limited by the time of trial in any event.

Case management: summary judgment pursuant to CPR 12/strike-out pursuant to CPR 3.4(2)(a)

After the last paragraph, add new paragraphs:

In *ViiV Healthcare v Gilead* [2020] EWHC 615 (Pat), the court refused to strike out a plea referring   **61.62** to the intention of several scientists who had developed the allegedly infringing product. Whilst intention is not relevant to the first question posed in *Actavis*, regarding the doctrine of equivalence (i.e. does it operate in the same way), it was relevant to the second question (i.e. would it have been obvious that it so operated; this being on the basis that the product had been designed to operate in the same way).

In *Philips v Asustek* [2020] EWHC 29 (Ch) the court refused to grant summary judgment on a licensing point to enable some defendants to avoid participating in a liability trial. The court found that the interpretation of the licence was a question of fact that needed to be determined before any questions of quantum could be considered. In *Philips v Tinno* [2020] EWHC 2533 (Ch) the court followed the *Asustek* decision and refused to strike out an argument based on a global FRAND licence.

In *IPCom v HTC Europe* [2020] EWHC 2941 (Pat) the court struck out the aspects of a damages inquiry that were focused on sales of infringing products overseas. The court noted that damages in respect of those sales could only arise if the sales themselves were caused by acts of infringement in the United Kingdom, which they were not.

Case management: hearing of a preliminary issue

After the last paragraph, add new paragraph:

In *Neurim v Generics* [2021] EWHC 2198 (Pat) the court allowed an expedited trial ([2022] EWHC   **61.65** 109 (Pat)) of preliminary issues to enable the claimant to attempt to obtain injunctive relief prior to the expiry of a patent.

Case management: application to stay proceedings

To the end of the fourth paragraph (beginning "In Coloplast v Salts [2019] EWHC 1979 (Pat)"), add:

For similar reasons, a stay of an expedited trial of preliminary issues was refused in *Neurim v Generics* [2021] EWHC 2897 (Pat).   **61.66**

To the end of the penultimate paragraph, add:

In *Ablynx v VHsquared* [2019] EWCA Civ 2192, however, the court stayed proceedings in relation to UK designations of European patents where the overarching licence agreement conferred exclusive jurisdiction to the courts of Belgium.

After the penultimate paragraph, add new paragraphs:

In *Heineken v Anheuser-Busch* [2020] EWHC 892 (Pat), the court refused to adjourn the start date of the trial because of the coronavirus pandemic. Instead, the court ordered a short extension to the period for providing reply evidence and a modest extension to the time for preparing written closing submissions following completion of the evidence.

In *Teva v Chiesi* [2020] EWHC 1311 (Pat) the court refused a stay in any event (having refused to strike out a claim) on the basis that an offer to give 14 days' notice of launch was not a satisfactory alternative to proceeding to trial.

In *Amgen v Sanofi-Aventis* [2020] EWHC 2818 (Pat) the court lifted a stay in accordance with the agreed terms of a confidential schedule to a quasi-Tomlin order. It did so on the basis that the parties had agreed certain bases for a stay being lifted and, where one of those had arisen, it was open to the court to order that the stay be lifted.

In *Nokia v OnePlus* [2021] EWHC 2952 (Pat), the court refused to stay proceedings in favour of proceedings in China which were focussed on FRAND terms. The court noted that such proceedings would have no determinative effect over the infringement, essentiality or validity decision of the courts in the UK.

Disclosure: general rules

After the second paragraph, add new paragraph:

61.67   In *McParland v Whitehead* [2020] EWHC 298 (Ch), the court took the opportunity, at a disclosure guidance hearing, to remind the parties that issues for disclosure are not all issues that need to be determined at trial, not legal issues and not those issues where initial disclosure has revealed all relevant documents. They are only issues where further documents are needed to enable the court to resolve some issue within the case.

After the fifth paragraph (beginning "Documents in a party's "control" are defined to be"), add new paragraph:

In *Conversant v Huawei* [2020] EWHC 256 (Pat) an application by the claimant for disclosure of third-party licence agreements which the defendants had in place was refused where it would require an adjournment of the trial to determine fair, reasonable and non-discriminatory licence terms for standard-essential patents.

After the last paragraph, add new paragraphs:

In *Add2 Research v Dspace* [2020] EWHC 912 (Pat) an application for specific disclosure was refused on the basis that a product and process description should address the points that the information sought in the application sought to identify.

In *OnePlus v Mitsubishi* [2020] EWCA Civ 1562 the Court of Appeal considered the question of 'external eyes only' disclosure and provided guidance as to how this should be operated, with a particular focus on FRAND licensing.

In *Optis v Apple* [2021] EWHC 2080 (Pat) the court refused to allow the defendant to disclose a confidential agreement between it and a third party where the agreement had been entered into after the start of the litigation and its terms prohibited its disclosure. This was partly because the defendant could not explain why the particular licence would assist the court in establishing what would be a FRAND licence.

Breadth of disclosure in patent litigation

After the last paragraph, add new paragraph:

61.70   In *Teva v Janssen* [2020] EWHC 3157 (Pat) the court was persuaded to order extended disclosure but only under model B.

Evidence

After the last paragraph, add new paragraph:

61.76   In *L'Oréal v Liqwd* [2019] EWCA Civ 1943, the Court of Appeal upheld the decision of the judge at first instance who had refused permission to adduce new evidence after the judgment had been handed down but before the order had been sealed.

Expert evidence

After the eighth paragraph (beginning "Likewise, "any pressure, and any act which may have the effect of placing pressure"), add new paragraph:

61.77   In *Akebia v Fibrogen* [2020] EWHC 866 (Pat), Arnold L.J., sitting in the High Court reiterated *MedImmune* and made further complaints about the interference of instructing solicitors on both sides in the preparation of expert reports. He stated, at [13]: "If practitioners continue not to observe the standards required of them, the Patents Court will have to take steps to enforce those standards."

After the fifteenth paragraph (beginning "CPR 35 and CPR 35.10 require"), add new paragraph:
In *Neurim v Mylan* [2020] EWHC 3270 (Pat) the court criticised an expert who was not sufficiently familiar with patents and had failed to understand the "nuts and bolts" of patent law when drafting his reports.

Trial

To the end of the fifth paragraph (beginning "An expedited trial may be ordered"), add:
Expedition has recently been considered and allowed in *Advanced Bionics v Med-El* [2021] EWHC 2415 (Pat) and but refused in *Abbot v Dexcom* [2021] EWHC 2246 (Pat). In *Neurim v Generics* [2022] EWCA Civ 370, the Court of Appeal ordered an expedited appeal. **61.79**

To the end of the seventh paragraph (beginning "In all but the simplest cases"), add:
and now *http://caselaw.nationalarchives.gov.uk*. *Optis v Apple* [2021] EWHC 2694 (Pat) emphasises the need to limit those who see a draft judgment.

Appeal

To the end of the fourth paragraph (beginning "An appeal is by way of review rather than rehearing."), add:
In *Rockwool v Knauf* [2020] EWHC 1068 (Pat), an appeal from the Comptroller, the judge reiterated that for an appeal on non-obviousness to succeed, there must be an error of principle. He went on to note that, whilst the parties had dispensed with the need for cross-examination at first instance, that did not entitle him to substitute his view for that of the Hearing Officer. Finally, he noted that he should not be unduly critical of the way the decision was expressed, the Hearing Officer being an experienced tribunal. Finally, he observed that an appeal based on matters which had not been properly pleaded (if at all) at first instance was doomed to fail. **61.80**

After the fourth paragraph, add new paragraph:
In *Claydon v Mzuri* [2021] EWHC 1322 (IPEC) the original judgment was handed down without attendance. No "holding" order was sought to extend the time for making requesting leave to appeal. Accordingly, when such a request was made out of time, the court had no jurisdiction to retrospectively grant an extension of time enabling it to consider such a request.

Intellectual Property Enterprise Court: costs

To the end of the penultimate paragraph, add:
In *Response Clothing v Edinburgh Woollen Mill* [2020] EWHC 721 (IPEC), the court confirmed that, where VAT is recoverable, it is to be awarded within the overall caps (i.e. £50,000 or £25,000). **61.87**

Section 62

Notes

Delete item "5." from the list. **62.01**

Commentary on Section 62

Damages after amendment (subs. (3))

After the first paragraph, add new paragraph:
Nokia Oyj (Nokia Corp) v IPCom GmbH & Co KG [2011] EWHC 2719 (Pat); [2012] Bus L.R. 1311; [2012] R.P.C. 21 was decided under s.63(2), a provision equivalent to s.62(3). Floyd J. (as he then was) observed that, prior to amendment, the policy behind "framed in good faith and with reasonable skill and knowledge" was to ensure that patents were so drafted [28]. "The sin of failing to deploy GFRSK was to be visited with the punishment of withholding relief."[29] However, the amended section "is not **62.05**

intended to act as a sanction against careless drafting or lack of good faith when these matters have no bearing on the damages or other remedy sought by the patentee." The phrase "take into account" gives a wider discretion than the former prohibition on granting relief.

Replace the second paragraph with:

How the courts might "take into account" the circumstances set out in s.62(3) was considered by Meade J. in *Add2 Research And Development Ltd v DSpace Digital Signal Processing & Control Engineering GmBH* [2021] EWHC 1630 (Pat) at [189]–[202]. As the patent in suit was held invalid, his remarks and findings of fact were made in case of a successful appeal on validity.

Replace the third paragraph with:

On the test under subs.(3)(a), Meade J. noted at [195] that it "is particularly connected with the amendment to deal with the Enforcement Directive and is there to ensure that Defendants who know or have reason to believe that there is infringement do have to pay compensation". It would seem that it requires a threefold enquiry as to whether the defendant knew of the patent, of the infringement situation and of the validity situation. The first of these sets a test considerably less stringent than that of innocent infringement (s.62(1)) which does not seem easily justifiable on the mere basis that there has been a post-grant amendment. The second would appear to be difficult for a defendant to justify in practice as an amended patent will, by definition, be narrower than that granted. In *Add2*, it was clear that the defendants had been aware of all the facts that made the claims infringed. They therefore focused on validity, which in a previous edition of this work was suggested as the criterion that would in practice be that taken into account by the court. However, Meade J. held that in a normal case, mere belief the patent was invalid would not of itself engage s.62(3).

Replace the fourth paragraph with:

In relation to subs.(3)(b), namely "whether the specification of the patent as published was framed in good faith and with reasonable skill and knowledge" case law as to the same expression in s.63(2), which has been similarly amended, is relevant (see §63.03). In *Nokia*, Floyd J. observed at [19(iii)] that relief could be granted even where the specification was not so framed. One may also consider case law on the pre-amendment s.62(3), and its predecessor, s.59 of the 1949 Act. Relief under s.59 was denied in *Rediffusion Simulation v Link-Miles* [1993] F.S.R. 369 because amendment had been carried out carelessly so that the specification "as published" (albeit after amendment) had not been "framed with reasonable skill". In *Mabuchi Motor's Patents* [1996] R.P.C. 387, amendment was allowed on the basis that the Japanese attorney responsible, while knowing of the relevant prior art, accepted the view of the United Kingdom patent agent (who was unaware of that art) that broader claims than requested appeared to be allowable. However, this meant that the original claims had not been drafted with reasonable skill and knowledge, and therefore subs.(3) precluded the award of damages for infringement of the amended claim prior to the date of amendment. In *Add2*, this point was not pursued, but Meade J. saw nothing to suggest that the specification was not drafted in good faith and with reasonable skill and knowledge.

To the end of the fifth paragraph (beginning "Under s.62(3)(c) a further factor is whether"), add:

In *Add2*, the defendant's argument on good faith was based on the notion of "covetous claiming". Though not mentioned in s.62(3), Meade J. did not hold this unarguable, rather that it was not made out on the facts.

SECTION 63

Notes

Replace list with:

63.01   1.   An amendment to subs.(2) was prospectively made by the Patents Act 2004 (c.16) s.2(3), but this amendment was not brought into effect and it was repealed by SI 2006/1028 (reg.2(4) and Sch.4) with effect from April 29, 2006. However, by the same SI (reg.2(2) and Sch.2 para.3), and with the same date of effect, the subsection was again amended to insert the wording shown above in bold type. This was done to bring the section into compliance with art.13(1) of the European "Enforcement Directive" (No.2004/48/EC, OJ EC L157, April 30, 2004, p.45, with corrigendum OJ EC L195, June 2, 2004, p.16): see *Nokia Oyj (Nokia Corp) v IPCom GmbH & Co Kg* [2011]

EWHC 2719 (Pat); [2012] Bus L.R. 1311; [2012] R.P.C. 21 at [17]–[18]. SI 2006/1028 is "retained EU law" under s.2 of the European Union (Withdrawal) Act 2018.

2.   Subsection (4) was prospectively added by the Patents Act 2004 and came into effect on December 17, 2007, when EPC 2000 was brought into force.

Commentary on Section 63

Scope of the section

To the end of the fourth paragraph (beginning "While subs.(1) is silent as to the type of "relief""), add:
For considerations on damages in lieu of an injunction, and public interest factors, see *Evalve Inc v Edwards Life Sciences* [2020] EWHC 513 (Pat).   **63.02**

Requirement for good faith, skill and knowledge in patent draftsmanship (subs.(2))

To the end of the first paragraph, add:
These are now factors to be taken into account; relief may be still be awarded if lack of good faith   **63.03**
or careless drafting have no bearing on the remedy sought: *Nokia Oyj (Nokia Corp) v IPCom GmbH & Co Kg* [2011] EWHC 2719 (Pat); [2012] Bus L.R. 1311; [2012] R.P.C. 21 at [29].

After the penultimate paragraph, add new paragraph:
The effects of equivalent provisions in s.62(3) were considered in *Add2 Research And Development Ltd v DSpace Digital Signal Processing & Control Engineering GmBH* [2021] EWHC 1630 (Pat) at [189]–[202], see §62.05.

SECTION 65

Commentary on Section 65

Effect of certificate of contested validity (subs.(2))

Replace the first paragraph with:
Subsection (2) provides that, if a proprietor successfully relies upon the finding of validity made in   **65.04**
earlier proceedings in which a certificate of contested validity was granted, he shall (unless it is specifically directed otherwise) be entitled to his costs (expenses in Scotland) "as between solicitor and own client" on final order at first instance in the subsequent proceedings, though not on any appeal therefrom. Although this has previously been interpreted as effectively an order for "costs on the indemnity basis", as compared to the normal "costs on the standard basis", in *Optis v Apple* [2020] EWHC 3248 (Pat) the court made clear that the provisions are different and observed that it was generally the case that those under s.65 would be more favourable to the receiving party than assessment on an indemnity basis.

SECTION 67

Delete paragraph "Note.".   **67.01**

Commentary on Section 67

Definition of "exclusive licence"

After the first paragraph, add new paragraph:
Even if an exclusive licence agreement within the meaning of s.130(1) takes away the licensee's full   **67.03**
autonomy to litigate, for example by requiring that the patentee must be involved and in the driving seat of proceedings, it will be regarded as exclusive for the purposes of s.67: *Neurim Pharmaceutical (1991) Ltd v Generics UK Ltd (t/a Mylan)* [2022] EWCA Civ 359, reversing [2020] EWHC 3270 (Pat) at [120]–[147]. "The purpose of section 67 is to enable an exclusive licensee to recover its own losses (or its share of the infringer's profits) in the event of infringement" (at [22] per Arnold L.J., Newey and Birss L.JJ. concurring). Here, the second claimant Flynn had certain exclusive rights to exploit the invention, but Neurim retained the right to bring proceedings for infringement. (Note, Mylan had become Viatris by the time of the Court of Appeal's decision, but the court refers to Mylan.)

Replace the second paragraph with:
    Courtauld's Application [1956] R.P.C. 208 and *Dendron v Regents of the University of California*
[2004] F.S.R. 43 were discussed in a comparative article by Johnathon Liddicoat, "Standing on the
edge—what type of 'exclusive licensees' should be able to initiate patent infringement actions?" [2017]
IIC 626. The author concluded that, although obiter dicta, the judges' conclusions supporting the possibility of "partitioned" exclusive licences—partitioned by right, territory, etc—were correct.
Furthermore, on the basis of legal and economic arguments, the author recommends that Australia
recognize the standing to sue of partial or "partitioned" exclusive licensees. In *Neurim v Generics* [2020]
EWHC 3270 (Pat), the defendants failed to persuade the court that such "salami-slicing" was fatal to
exclusivity. Marcus Smith J. cited David Stone's characterisation of an exclusive licence in *Oxford
Nanopore v Pacific Biosciences* [2017] EWHC 3190 (Pat) at [44]. The Court of Appeal in *Neurim* (at
[29]) agreed on this point, though acknowledging that there might be "a limit as to how far one can
salami-slice the monopoly in a claim for this purpose". There was nothing in s.130(1) or case law to
support Mylan's contention that exclusivity had to be coextensive with a claim of the patent; the converse
was supported by s.67(2) and Pumfrey J.'s judgment in *Spring Form Inc v Toy Brokers Ltd* [2002] F.S.R.
17.

Right of exclusive licensee to sue for infringement

After the first paragraph, add new paragraph:
67.04   As illustrated in *Neurim Pharmaceutical (1991) Ltd v Generics UK Ltd* [2022] EWCA Civ 359 at
[22], citing the Swan Committee (Cmd 7206, September 1947), the right of an exclusive licensee to
recover damages for infringement or a share of the infringer's profits is the purpose of s.67.

SECTION 69

Commentary on Section 69

Rights conferred by the section (subs.(1))

After the last paragraph, add new paragraph:
69.06   In *Novartis AG v Teva UK Ltd* [2022] EWHC 959 (Ch), the claimant had been informed that its application for a dosage patent on its drug (for treatment of multiple sclerosis) was proceeding to grant,
but administrative formalities were not yet accomplished. The claimant applied for an interim injunction to restrain defendant generic companies from entering the market (for which they had authorisation).
Roth J. held that, despite s.69 referring only to damages, it did not act as a bar to the grant of an injunction under s.37 of the Senior Courts Act 1981. That jurisdiction was broad and flexible: *Broad Idea
International Ltd v Convoy Collateral Ltd* [2021] UKPC 24. In these exceptional circumstances, where
grant of the patent and the scope of its claims were certain, the court could contemplate grant of an
injunction. However, the Patents Court would be wary of attempts to seek interim relief prior to grant
of patent, given the "legislative policy underlying s. 69 PA that a remedy should not be given until the
scope of the claimant's patent has been determined" [39]. In the present instance, the injunction would
be refused, applying *American Cyanamid* principles. Damages should be adequate to protect the claimant; a downward price spiral upon market entry of the generics seemed unlikely.

SECTION 70—UNJUSTIFIED THREATS

Commentary on Section 70 – 70F

Scope of the section

Replace the second paragraph with:
70.02   Section 3 of the Intellectual Property (Unjustified Threats) Act 2017 (Commencement and
Transitional Provisions) Regulations 2017 (SI 2017/771) provides that where proceedings are brought
in respect of an alleged threat made before the appointed day the proceedings in respect of that alleged
threat are to be determined in accordance with the law in force at the time the alleged threat was made.
Section 70 before amendment, and the case law interpreting it, therefore continues to apply to communications made before that date.

Replace the third paragraph with:
    The 2017 Act also contains provisions in relation to threats of infringement of registered trade marks,

registered designs, and unregistered design rights. There is, however, no corresponding provision in respect of threats for infringement of other intellectual property rights, e.g. infringement of a copyright or in respect of a common law tort, such as an alleged "passing off". The absence of similar provisions in other statutes has been held to be deliberate so that threats of litigation of other unregistered intellectual property rights are not actionable, even if presented as an action for wrongful interference with contractual relations (*Granby v Interlego* [1984] R.P.C. 209). Threats of litigation in respect of other intellectual property rights which can be made with impunity may nevertheless become actionable if coupled with notification of the existence of an intellectual property right to which these provisions apply, such as a patent. This is despite such notification by itself being a permitted communication, see the design case of *Jaybeam v Abru Aluminium* [1976] R.P.C. 308 discussed in §70.06.

Replace the fourth paragraph with:

The revised provisions were introduced following a review requested in 2012 by the Department for Business, Innovation and Skills (BIS) and the Intellectual Property Office (IPO) which resulted in a report of the *Patents Trade Marks and Design Rights: Groundless Threats* (HMSO, 2014), Law Com. No.346, Cm.8851. One aim of the legislation was to limit the grounds for bringing a successful action in respect of threats of infringement, and the dearth of case law as to the provisions introduced by the 2017 Act suggests that the Act has been successful in achieving that aim.

At the beginning of the fifth paragraph, replace "A classic case of misuse of threats identified in that Report" with:

A classic case of misuse of threats identified in the Law Commission Report

In the last paragraph, after "The court considered the relevant provisions of the Brussels Convention (now Regulation 44/2001", add:

, but no longer, since the UK withdrawal from the EU, applicable in the UK

Threats of infringement proceedings

At the beginning of the fourth paragraph, after "The definition", add:

of "threat"   **70.03**

After the fourth paragraph, add new paragraph:

It was confirmed in *Shenzhen Carku Technology Co Ltd v Noco Co* [2022] EWHC 2034 (Pat), the first decision in which a detailed analysis of s.70 has been undertaken since its amendment, that the old law as to what constitutes a threat, as articulated in *Best Buy v Worldwide Sales Corp Espana* [2011] EWCA Civ 618, *Generics (t/a Mylan) v Warner-Lambert* [2015] EWHC 2548 (Pat) and *Zeno v BSM-Bionic Solutions* [2009] EWHC 1829 (Pat) and in particular the breadth of what constitutes a threat and the objective nature of the test, still applies. Having reviewed the decisions in *Quads 4 Kids v Campbell* [2006] EWHC 2482 (Ch), and *Cassie Creations Ltd v Blackmore* [2014] EWHC 2941 (Ch) concerning notifications to eBay under its VeRO Programme it was held, on the facts, that the nature of the patentee's communications with Amazon under the Amazon Intellectual Property Policy in *Shenzhen Carku* constituted threats under s.70 as amended.

Replace the seventh paragraph with:

To be actionable, the new section now specifically provides that the threat should be one made within, or reaching, the United Kingdom: otherwise the Act would have extra-territorial effect contrary to general jurisprudence. Threats of litigation in relation to EP patents may have no connection to the UK and are not intended to be globally caught by the UK threats provisions. In *Samsung v Apple* [2012] EWHC 889 (Ch), the court found that although parallel proceedings in the Netherlands and Germany indicated an intention to sue throughout the European Union, there had been no specific threat in the United Kingdom. A failure by the defendant to respond to a letter seeking agreement that there was no infringement could not be construed, in and of itself, as a threat. See also the Community trade mark decision in *Best Buy Co Inc v Worldwide Sales Corp España SL* [2011] EWCA Civ 618.

Professional advisers (s.70D)

In the first paragraph, after "this is specifically not limited to UK", delete "or even   **70.08**
to EU-based".

SECTION 71

Commentary on Section 71

Scope of the section

To the end of the third paragraph, add:

71.03   In *IPCom v Vodafone* [2020] EWHC 910 (Pat), the court made various declarations, including one as to the essentiality of various patent claims and another regarding non-infringement.

Requirements for seeking a declaration (subs.(1))

After the last paragraph, add new paragraph:

71.05   In *Pfizer v Roche* [2019] EWHC 1520 (Pat), the court refused to grant an Arrow declaration in the circumstances where the defendant had "de-designated" the United Kingdom from all relevant pending patent applications, such that the declaration would serve no purpose in the United Kingdom. In *Mexichem v Honeywell* [2020] EWCA Civ 473, the Court of Appeal upheld the first instance decision refusing to strike out a claim for an Arrow declaration. The judge at first instance ([2019] EWHC 3377 (Pat)) had concluded that it was not necessary to specify a specific product or process when seeking such a declaration.

REVOCATION OF PATENTS [SECTIONS 72–73]

SECTION 72

Notes

72.01   *Delete item "7." from the list.*

Commentary on Section 72

Grounds of revocation

Insufficient description (subs.(1)(c))

Replace the fifth paragraph with:

72.14   Because a specification cannot be validly amended after its filing date in a manner which would result in it disclosing additional matter, a specification must be "sufficient", in regard to the subject-matter covered by the scope of its claims as of its filing date, or as of its priority date if priority is to be accorded to the invention in issue. In *Regeneron Pharmaceuticals Inc v Kymab Ltd* [2020] UKSC 27, it was not in issue that sufficiency should be assessed at the priority date. Lord Briggs at [48] noted that this was the effect of *Biogen v Medeva* [1997] R.P.C. 1 HL. The relevant passage in *Biogen* is at [53]–[54], where the House of Lords rejected an argument that sufficiency should be measured at the date of publication of the application (May 28, 1986), as Aldous J. had held at first instance. Lord Hoffmann stated that, under the 1977 Act, it should be the date of the application for the patent. In this, he agreed with the Court of Appeal, who had held that for sufficiency purposes, the date of application for the European patent in suit was the relevant one (December 21, 1979). However, the European patent had claimed priority from an earlier UK patent, filed on December 22, 1978. It had been conceded (*Biogen* at [38]) that by the 1979 filing date of the EPO application, the claimed method was obvious over material published 6 months after the priority date. In his introduction to the sufficiency/dates issue, at [53], Lord Hoffmann pointed out that his previous finding, that the priority filing did not support the later application [as required by s.5(2)], would also lead to a conclusion of insufficiency.

After the fifth paragraph, add new paragraph:

One might imagine instances where similar reasoning would not apply to be vanishingly rare. However, one such instance may be *Eli Lilly and Co v Genentech Inc* [2020] EWHC 261 (Pat). In that case, a parent patent ('822') had been held invalid by Arnold J. at [2019] EWHC 3260 (Pat). One ground was that a second medical use claimed, for treatment of psoriasis, was insufficient for lack of plausibility at the priority date. At a very late stage, the patentee Genentech had sought to amend its defence, to allege that the claims were plausible at the date of filing. Arnold J. had refused the applications to amend in relation to 822 on case management grounds. In the later decision at [2020] EWHC 261 (Pat), Roger Wyand QC (sitting as a Deputy High Court Judge), was considering Eli Lilly's striking-out/summary judgment application, in their action for invalidity of the divisional patent ('084') Genentech had counterclaimed for infringement. Eli Lilly argued that the matters were res judicata given Arnold J.'s findings. The one issue on which Genentech was held not to be estopped, on which its pleadings were not struck out, was the contention that the patent was plausible/sufficient at the date of filing. Roger Wyand did not consider the merits of this, res judicata having been set down for decision as the preliminary issue.

At the start of the sixth paragraph, replace "However, later evidence" with:
Evidence later than the relevant filing date

At the end of the tenth paragraph (beginning "So-called "Biogen insufficiency" (excessive claim breadth) accepts"), replace "See, also, Regeneron Pharmaceuticals Inc v Genentech Inc [2013] EWCA Civ 93; [2013] R.P.C. 28 [100]–[101]." with:
See also, *Regeneron Pharmaceuticals Inc v Kymab Ltd* [2020] UKSC 27, allowing appeal from [2018] EWCA Civ 671. Despite the Court of Appeal's view that the ground-breaking nature of the invention disclosed a "general principle", the patent was not enabling over the most valuable part of the claim's scope. "The sufficiency requirement, namely that the disclosure in the patent should enable substantially all products within the scope of a product claim to be made by the skilled person as at the priority date, is part of the bedrock of the law, worked out over time both in the UK and by the EPO, which is essential to prevent patentees obtaining a monopoly which exceeds their contribution to the art" (Lord Briggs at [59]).

After the tenth paragraph, add new paragraph:
In *Saint-Gobain Adfors SAS v 3M Innovative Properties Co* [2022] EWHC 1018 (Pat), the patent claimed abrasive particles across a size range. It did not enable the skilled addressee, without due burden, to make particles at the upper end of the range, and was revoked.

To the end of the twelfth paragraph (beginning "Whether the higher Warner-Lambert standard of plausibility"), add:
The patent in this case has been revoked in EPO opposition proceedings and the Opposition Division's decision upheld by the Technical Board of Appeal on January 10, 2020: see [2020] EWHC 261 (Pat) and T 304/17.

To the end of the last paragraph, add:
The kind of insufficiency caused by inadequate definition, has also been described as "ambiguity" or, better, "uncertainty": *Anan Kasei Co Ltd v Neo Chemicals and Oxides Ltd* [2019] EWCA Civ 1646; [2020] F.S.R. 8 at [24].

Impermissible amendments (subs.(1)(d) and (e))

After the second paragraph, add new paragraph:
The touchstone of the skilled addressee learning something new has been applied in two recent decisions, *Philip Morris Products SA v RAI Strategic Holdings Inc* [2021] EWHC 537 (Pat) and *Insulet Corp v Roche Diabetes Care Ltd* [2021] EWHC 1933 (Pat). **72.15**

SECTION 73

Replace subss.(1A)–(1B) with:

(1A)   Where the comptroller issues an opinion under section 74A that section 1(1)(a) or (b) is not satisfied in relation to an invention for which there is a patent, the comptroller may revoke the patent. **73.01**

(1B)   The power under subsection (1A) may not be exercised before—
    (a)   the end of the period in which the proprietor of the patent may apply under the rules (by virtue of section 74B) for a review of the opinion, or
    (b)   if the proprietor applies for a review, the decision on the review is

made (or, if there is an appeal against that decision, the appeal is determined).

(1C)   The comptroller shall not exercise the power under subsection (1A) without giving the proprietor of the patent an opportunity to make any observations and to amend the specification of the patent without contravening section 76.

Note.

Replace paragraph with:
Subsections (2)–(4) were substituted for the original subss.(2) and (3) by Sch.5 para.19 to the CDPA 1988, effective from January 7, 1991 (SI 1990/2168). Subsections (1A), (1B) and (1C) were inserted by the Intellectual Property Act 2014, effective from October 1, 2014 (SI 2014/2330). Section 1C was omitted in error from some earlier versions of this work. The section text has been corrected in the 9th edition of this book on WestlawUK.

73.02   *Change title:*

Relevant Rule—Rule 35(6)

Replace paragraph with:

This rule appears at §27.02.

Commentary on Section 73

Add new paragraph §73.06A:

Avoiding effect of subsections (1A)–(1C)

73.06A   If the Comptroller initiates revocation proceedings under subs.(1A) following an Opinion finding a lack of novelty or inventive step, the proprietor is given an opportunity to respond. The proprietor may contest the finding and may submit amendments under s.27 or, in the case of an EP(UK) patent, via central limitation under EPC art.105a, to limit the scope of the patent. If, following further consideration, the invalidity is no longer considered "clear cut" or if the patent has been amended to adequately distinguish the invention, the Comptroller may decide not to proceed with revocation.

In *Merck Sharp & Dohme Corp's Patent* BL O/580/18, Opinions 9 & 10/16 found an EP(UK) patent to lack novelty. The Comptroller then initiated revocation proceedings, even though the patent had already expired. The patent did, however, serve as a basic patent for an SPC, so it was considered relevant for the Comptroller to consider whether revocation was necessary. The patent was limited to claims that were found to be valid in the Opinion, and the revocation proceedings were consequently terminated.

In *Fraunhofer-Gesellschaft zur Förderung der Angewandten Forschung E.V.'s Patent* BL O/740/19, Opinion 02/17 found an EP(UK) patent to lack novelty. The proprietor then requested a review of the Opinion. Although the examiner's opinion was found not to be wrong and the Opinion was not set aside, the Hearing Officer found that the patent was not clearly invalid and no action under s.73(1A) would be taken.

Practice under Section 73

Replace the third paragraph with:

73.08   Around 160 patents were revoked in 2019 under s.73, all but one under s.73(2). The provisions of subss.(1A) and (1B) provide for a limited extension of the Comptroller's existing powers to initiate revocation under s.73(1) and (2), and have so far been used sparingly. Around half of the opinions on validity issued under s.74A since the introduction of subss.(1A) and (1B) in 2014 have found the patent to be invalid, but only six have so far resulted in revocation (see §74A.10), and in each case the proprietor did not contest the examiner's finding. In other cases a decision was made either not to initiate or not to proceed with revocation proceedings, in some cases following amendment (see §73.07). The reasons behind the Office's decisions not to initiate revocation proceedings are unclear, as none are provided in the public decision. Based on the limited sample to date, however, these could include: relevant prior art not being available in English (Opinion 23/14); a strong defence made following initiation of revocation proceedings (05/15); and issues surrounding invalidity being complex and multifaceted (10/15, which found a claim for a dosage regime to lack inventive step).

PUTTING VALIDITY IN ISSUE [SECTION 74]

SECTION 74

Commentary on Section 74

Proceedings in which validity may be put in issue (subss.(1)–(3) and (8))

After the last paragraph, add new paragraph:

Commscope Technologies LLC v SOLiD Technologies Inc [2022] EWHC 769 (Pat) involved an application to amend one of the claimant's patents, EP626. When infringement claims and validity counterclaims regarding that patent were settled, the amendment application was carried over to the trial on another patent. Mellor J. held that the court's jurisdiction to allow the amendment had been extinguished by the parties' notices of discontinuance on the other issues. Likewise validity, in the absence of a clear indication under CPR r.63.10(2)(b). That rule requires an applicant for amendment to state "whether the applicant will contend that the claims prior to the amendment are valid". Mellor J. noted that parties often did not meet this requirement, assuming that seeking amendments unconditionally implied the patentee was not contending that the claims in their unamended form were valid (see [287]–[290], citing *Ferag v Muller Martini* [2007] EWCA Civ 15). Mellor J. advised at [291]:   **74.03**

> "In future, if an application to amend is received which does not comply with CPR 63.10(2)(b), the recipient would be well advised to insist on compliance so the position is clear. In this case, if I had decided not to allow the amendments, I do not think it would have been right to revoke EP626 in the absence of a clear and considered concession to that effect from CommScope."

Estoppel against challenge to validity

After the seventh paragraph (beginning "As regards the need for issues to have been previously decided"), add new paragraph:

A question of estoppel on the issue of validity arose in the complex of litigation between Neurim   **74.04**
Pharmaceuticals and Generics (UK), particularly in the decision of Meade J. at [2022] EWHC 109 (Pat) on preliminary issues. In December 2020, Marcus Smith J. handed down a decision that the claimant's patent (EP702 relating to slow-release melatonin for the treatment of insomnia) was valid and infringed. The patent had already been held invalid by the EPO's Opposition division but revocation had been suspended pending appeal to the EPO's Technical Board of Appeal. A couple of days after Marcus Smith J.'s decision was handed down, the patentee withdrew its appeal, so that revocation *ab initio* became effective. Marcus Smith J. revoked his orders consequent on the previous decision in a judgment of March 12, 2021. A divisional application from EP702 was granted in June 2021, whereupon Neurim sued for infringement and applied to amend the patent for its claims to be "patently indistinct" from those of EP702. They went on to argue that the defendants were estopped from contesting validity by Marcus Smith J.'s earlier decision. However, that decision had been rendered unappealable by Marcus Smith J.'s finding that the EPO Opposition decision "trumped" his own, making the defendants winners in the infringement litigation. A particular issue was the so-called "lay patient" argument, which had been considered by the EPO in opposition proceedings. Meade J. held that a similar argument had been run, though not clearly articulated, before Marcus Smith J. This did not give rise to an issue estoppel. In reaching this conclusion, Meade J. held that the ability to appeal an issue was a useful test, although the ultimate test was whether the issue was fundamental to the earlier judgment. Case law supported the argument that inability to appeal an issue, because the party had effectively won, would negate estoppel. Appeals were against the courts' judgments or orders, rather than the reasoning behind them.

[101]

Section 74A

Relevant Rules—Rules 92–97

Note.

Replace the second paragraph with:

74A.06   Rule 95(1)(b) would have been amended by r.2(3) of the Patents (Amendment) Rules 2016 (SI 2016/517) to come into force on the date of entry into force of the Agreement on a Unified Patent Court. In particular, "or, in the case of a European patent with unitary effect, in the Register for unitary patent protection kept under the Unitary Patent Regulation" was to be inserted at the end of r.95(1)(b). Following withdrawal by the UK from the Agreement on a Unified Patent Court, the prospective change was revoked by The Patents (European Patent with Unitary Effect and Unified Patent Court) (Repeal and Revocation) Regulations 2021 (SI 2021/355).

Commentary on Section 74A

Scope of the section

Possible revocation of patent under s.73(1A)

After the last paragraph, add new paragraph:

74A.10   In BL O/417/20 the patentee asked for an opinion to be set aside (that the patent lacked novelty over alleged availability of a product before the priority date) since there was a risk that the Comptroller may initiate revocation proceedings under s.73(1A). As the evidence had not been properly tested by the opinions procedure, the Hearing Officer suggested that it could not be said that the patent was "clearly invalid". Absent such clear invalidity, it seems unlikely the Comptroller will commence any revocation proceedings under this section.

Effect of s.74A on a European patent with unitary effect ("Unitary Patent")

Replace the first paragraph with:

74A.11   The Order (SI 2016/388) that was made to implement the Agreement on a Unified Patent Court ("UPC Agreement") and the EU Regulations establishing the Unitary Patent has been revoked by The Patents (European Patent with Unitary Effect and Unified Patent Court) (Repeal and Revocation) Regulations 2021 (SI 2021/355).

Delete the second and third paragraphs.

Refusal of request

In the second paragraph, after "clear the hurdle of raising a new question or argument (see BL O/370/07)", add:

74A.21   In BL O/310/21 the requester sought an opinion on validity over a document referred to in the patent itself, and cited in the search report as an "X" category document, the Hearing Officer found that a mere difference in view between the pre-grant Examiner and the requester as to the relevance of the document was not sufficient to find that there was a new argument to be addressed. It was entirely appropriate to assume that an X-category document has been properly considered pre-grant unless there is some very obvious evidence to the contrary, and so the request was refused.

SECTION 74B

Commentary on Section 74B

Scope of the section

—Decisions under section 74B

After the last paragraph, add new paragraph:

In BL O/139/21 (review of Opinion 20/19) the patentee attempted to have set aside an opinion of lack **74B.18** of novelty with an argument that the Examiner had failed to read the prior art in a purposive manner. This led the Examiner to conclude that the prior art was suitable for the same purpose as claim 1 of the patent, even though that purpose was not disclosed by the prior art. Claim 1 related to an electrical earthing nut, whereas the prior art related to lock nuts. The Hearing Officer agreed with the Examiner that the "an electrical earthing nut" of claim 1 means any nut that provides a conductive path. Furthermore, it was reasonable for the Examiner to conclude that it was highly probably the prior art lock nut was made of metal, and therefore that this amounted to a disclosure of an electrical earthing nut. The patentee argued that it is not enough to prove that an apparatus described in an earlier specification could have been used to produce this or that result, it must also be shown that the specification contains clear and unmistakeable directions so to use it (as in *Flour Oxidizing Co v Carr* [1908] 25 R.P.C. 428). However, the Hearing Officer disagreed, noting that *Flour Oxidising* relates to a new method using a known apparatus, rather than to an apparatus itself. Accordingly the guidance in *Flour Oxidising* was not helpful in this case and the Opinion was not set aside.

GENERAL PROVISIONS AS TO AMENDMENT OF PATENTS AND APPLICATIONS [SECTIONS
75–76A]

SECTION 75

Commentary on Section 75

Applicability of section 75

After the third paragraph, add new paragraph:

As noted at §74.03, infringement and validity issues having been settled on one patent owned by **75.04** Commscope, the amendment application was held over to trial of claims under a related patent; the defendant had undertaken not to oppose amendment: *Commscope Technologies LLC v SOLiD Technologies Inc* [2022] EWHC 769 (Pat). However, at [272]–[284], Mellor J. considered the authorities and held that he lacked jurisdiction to hear the amendment claim. *Congoleum* was not cited. In *Lever Bros & Unilever's Patent (No.5)* (1955) 72 R.P.C. 198, jurisdiction to amend under s.30(1) of the 1949 Act was held to have been lost when revocation proceedings were settled; there was no infringement claim. Conversely, in *Lars Eric Norling v Eez-Away* [1997] R.P.C. 160, Jacob J. held that jurisdiction was retained when a counterclaim for revocation was withdrawn, but a claim for infringement continued. However, this was decided under the pre-2005 version of s.75(1); post-amendment, s.75(1) more resembles the old s.30(1). The patentee would be able to apply to the Comptroller to amend. Mellor J. rejected an argument that the patent should be revoked, as the application for amendment had not clarified whether the patentee applicant would contend that the claims prior to the amendment were valid as required by CPR r.63.10(2)(b). Absent such consent, the patent would not have been revoked, even though the application to amend had been made on an "unconditional" basis: *Ferag v Muller Martini* [2007] EWCA Civ 15.

To the end of the last paragraph, add:

However, in *Commscope Technologies LLC v SOLiD Technlogies Inc* [2022] EWHC 769 (Pat) it was held that if both the infringement and revocation aspects of proceedings in relation to a patent have been discontinued, so that there are no longer proceedings in progress in which validity may be put in issue, then the court no longer had jurisdiction to grant amendment under s.75 (*Industrial Self-Adhesives v Teknek* was not cited in the decision, and *Lars Norling* was distinguished). The court did however note that no prejudice was caused, since an application could instead be made to the Comptroller.

SECTION 76 [SUBSTITUTED]

Commentary on Section 76

Scope of the section

After the eighth paragraph (beginning "Subsection (3) is concerned with amendment of granted patents"), add new paragraphs:

76.04　　In T 1121/17 *COLGATE-PALMOLIVE/Oral care whitening compositions* which concerned an objection as to added subject-matter under EPC art.123(2) the examining division relied on a passage relevant to the requirements under art.122(3) which appears in the Guidelines for Examination at H IV 3.5 and reads:

> "A composition which is specified in a claim as comprising a component in an amount which is defined by a numerical range of values is subject to an implicit proviso excluding the presence of that component in an amount outside of that range. An amendment restricting the breadth of that component, for instance by narrowing down a generic class or a list of chemical compounds defining that component, has the consequence of limiting the scope of this implicit proviso. However, a composition which is defined as comprising the components indicated in the claim is open to the presence of any further components, unless otherwise specified. Therefore, in a claim directed to such an openly defined composition, the restriction of the breadth of a component present therein may have the effect of broadening the scope of protection of that claim,"

However, on appeal it was explained that this was inappropriate, and that:

> "The Board finds that the above criteria is (sic) inappropriate for the assessment of compliance with Article 123(2) EPC. The relevant question for the purposes of Article 123(2) EPC is whether the amendments remain within the limits of what a skilled person would derive directly and unambiguously, using common general knowledge, from the whole of the application as filed (according to the "gold standard" of G 2/10, OJ 2012, 376). An amendment having the effect of broadening the scope of protection of a claim as originally filed, for instance by generalising it so as to allow the presence of some materials in amounts which were originally excluded from the claim, does not infringe Article 123(2) EPC if the amended subject-matter derives directly and unambiguously from the application as filed as a whole."

In T 1937/17 *PROCTOR & GAMBLE/High capacity disposable absorbent inserts for reusable outer covers*, it was explained at 4.3.1 that:

> "this Board finds that, other than for the purposes envisaged in G 1/93, 'technical contribution' is of no relevance when deciding on the allowability of amendments under Article 123(2) EPC. Instead, the gold standard set out in G 2/10 is the only criterion which has to be applied."

Amendment in contravention of section 76

To the end of the second paragraph, add:

76.05　　Deletion of a disclaimer was held contrary to EPC art.123(2) in T 2327/18 *COVENTYA/Electroplating bath* following T 236/12 *JENTEC/Wound dressing.*

After the last paragraph, add new paragraph:

It was held in relation to the prohibition on extension of protection under EPC art.123(3) in G 2/88 *MOBIL OIL/Friction reducing additive*, Reasons 3.3 that there is a clear distinction between the protection which is conferred and the rights which are conferred by a European patent. What has to be considered and decided is whether the subject-matter protected by the claims, as defined by their categories in combination with their technical features, is extended. It is not necessary to consider the national laws of the Contracting States in relation to infringement when making such a decision. Following that decision, it was held in T 970/17 *C. R. BARD/ Infusion apparatuses and related methods* that possible differences under German patent law with regard to contributory infringement do not change the assessment.

The general test—explicit disclosure, implicit disclosure and obviousness

After the first paragraph, add new paragraph:

76.07　　The date as of which a patent specification was to be construed in an art that was evolving between the priority date or application date and the date of grant was an issue in *Interdigital Technology v Lenovo* [2021] EWHC 2152 (Pat), the possibilities being the priority date, the filing date and the publication date of the granted patent. In the outcome, it was held that on a correct view the relevant date was the priority date or, if none, the filing date, and in the case before the court the patent should be interpreted as of its priority date.

After the fourth paragraph (beginning "The test has also been said to be"), add new paragraph:

A detailed summary of established case law was provided in *Philip Morris Products v RAI Strategic Holdings* [2021] EWHC 537 (Pat) at [111]–[115]. It was further explained in *Insulet v Roche Diabetes Care* [2021] EWHC 1933 (Pat) with reference to the above decision that:

"the overall approach involves asking whether the claim as amended presents the skilled person with information about the invention which is not derivable directly and unambiguously from the original disclosure of the application as filed. As this is a question relating to the disclosure of the application as filed and the patent as granted/amended, it is a matter for the court, not the expert witnesses, although the court will carry out this task through the eyes of the skilled person."

After the last paragraph, add new paragraphs:

Problems arising from amendment based on originally filed claims with single dependency as in the US was considered in T 1362/15 *FAURECIA EMISSIONS/Catalytic converter*. The appellants argued that where an amended claim was a combination of features from originally filed dependent claims that did not respect the original dependency, the existence of an embodiment in the disclosure containing all the combined features (albeit with even more features) should be enough to fulfil the requirement of EPC art.123(2). They submitted that the following questions should be referred to the Enlarged Board:

(1)   Does it comply with EPC art.123(2) if the features of a plurality of dependent claims are incorporated into an independent claim in a situation in which the application as originally filed includes a claims set with a "US-style" dependency (with the relevant dependent claims referring back to the independent claim separately), and includes an embodiment in which the features of the independent claim and the dependent claims are shown in combination?

(2)   If the answer to question (1) is "yes", may the fact that the embodiment possibly shows additional features, result in a violation of art.123(2) because of an intermediate generalization despite the fact that the features added to the independent claim are disclosed separately in the US-style claims set?

However, reference was refused on the ground that there was no conflict between decisions T 1414/11 *SGL CARBON/Composite material resistant to high temperatures* and T 2619/11 *AGILENT/Plasma torch*. In T 1414/11 the description directly and unambiguously disclosed a binding agent that was applicable to all the carbon and graphite layers of the invention, including the layer materials of dependent claims 2 and 3 and thus provided basis for the combination of features of previous dependent claims 2 and 3 with the amended claim 1. In contrast, in T 2619/11 disclosure that the tapered portion of the tube with the features of Figure 3 could extend over "the entire length of the tube" was the same as "the whole length" defined in the original claims, and "substantially the whole length" was a more specific embodiment of "at least a substantial portion" and not an alternative thereto. The Examining Division had therefore made a mistake by focusing disproportionately on the claim structure of the original application and not on what the skilled person would clearly and unambiguously have derived from the application as a whole. Both decisions relied on the same criteria and they did not contradict one another. In the present case the subject-matter of the amended claim extended beyond the content of the application as originally filed and the requirement of EPC art.123(2) was therefore not fulfilled.

Restriction to an intermediate generalisation

Replace the second paragraph with:

Cases where such an objection succeeded in the UK include *Palmaz, LG Philips v Tatung* [2007] R.P.C. 21; *Vector v Glatt* [2008] R.P.C. 10 and *Datacard v Eagle Technologies* [2011] EWHC 244 (Pat), see also *Technetix v Teleste* [2019] EWHC 3106 (Pat) in which the court observed [118]:

76.14

"If the skilled person would have understood that the particular embodiment of the invention disclosed in the application as filed exemplifies a broader class, in the sense that the invention may be performed without this or that incidental feature of the particular embodiment, there will be no intermediate generalisation if the claims in the patent as granted are not limited by reference to those incidental features. On the other hand, if this would not have been the skilled person's understanding, there will be an intermediate generalisation should those features, not perceived as merely incidental, be excluded from a claim in the patent as granted (or as sought to be amended)."

An objection of this kind was rejected in *Nokia* and in *Philips v Nintendo* [2014] EWHC 1959 (Pat).

After the fourteenth paragraph (beginning "In T 783/08 NOVARTIS/Antidiabetic combinations"), add new paragraphs:
In T 1621/16 *PROCTOR & GAMBLE/Hand dishwashing* it was concluded that selections from lists of converging alternatives should not be treated in the same way as selections from lists of non-converging alternatives.

"1.7.2 On the one hand, when fall-back positions for a feature are described in terms of lists of non-converging alternatives (i.e. mutually exclusive or partially overlapping elements), at least part of the subject-matter of each individual element in the list is unique and different from those of the other elements. Thus, even though each individual element of the list constitutes a restricted version of the broader (amended) feature, within the context of the list itself each non-converging alternative represents a distinct feature. Therefore, selecting specific elements from such lists leads to a singling out of an invention from among several distinct alternatives, which might provide an unwarranted advantage if there is no way to anticipate which of the different inventions will eventually be protected.

On the other hand, when fall-back positions for a feature are described in terms of a list of converging alternatives, each of the narrower elements is fully encompassed by all the preceding less preferred and broader options. Consequently, unlike in the case of non-converging alternatives, the elements of such a list do not represent distinct features, but more or less restricted versions of one and the same feature. Thus, amending a claim by selecting one element from a list of converging alternatives does not lead to a singling out of an invention from among a plurality of distinct options, but simply to a subject-matter based on a more or less restricted version of said feature.

There is thus an analogy between selecting an element from a list of converging alternatives and deleting options from a list of non-converging alternatives, in the sense that both actions lead to a restriction of the scope of protection and not to a singling out of a specific invention from among different options. The selection of an element from a list of converging alternatives is nevertheless more restrictive than the deletion of options from a list of non-converging alternatives, because in the former case the amendment is restricted to deletions of the less preferred broader options whereas in the latter case the amendment can involve arbitrary deletions of any one (or more) of the non-converging elements. Thus, provided that certain conditions are met (see next point), regarding multiple selections from lists of converging alternatives as extending the subject-matter of the original application appears to be at odds with the well-established practice (see T 615/95 cited above) of considering multiple deletions from lists of converging alternatives as an allowable limitation of the scope of protection under Article 123(2) EPC.

1.7.3 This does, however, not allow the conclusion that amendments based on multiple selections from lists of converging alternatives necessarily meet the requirements of Article 123(2) EPC, because even when each individual selection used to amend the claim is as such regarded as a convergent restriction of the scope of protection, it needs to be assessed whether the specific combination resulting from the multiple selections is supported by the content of the application as filed. For the Board, at least the following two conditions should be met: (i) the combination should not be associated with an undisclosed technical contribution, that is, no unwarranted advantage should be derived from linking the specific combination of more and less preferred alternatives to an inventive selection which is not supported by the application as filed; and (ii) the combination should be supported by a pointer in the application as filed. Such pointers can be provided by the example(s) (as in decisions T 27/16; Reasons, point 13.10 and T 615/95; Reasons, point 6, last paragraph) or by specific embodiment(s) of the application, as this/these generally represent(s) the most detailed and preferred form(s) of the invention. Thus, if an amended claim falls within this/these example(s) or embodiment(s), this might be seen as an indication that the combination resulting from the multiple selections is not arbitrary but purposeful, in the sense that it converges towards the most preferred form(s) of the invention. This condition is particularly relevant when at least some of the amendments are based on the description as filed because, as respondent 2 argued, amending the claim on the basis of optional features selected from among multiple equally ranked alternatives in the description might lead to an arbitrary combination of features which is not supported by the application as filed."

The reasoning in T 1621/16 was followed in T 2368/16 *IONIQUA/Ionic liquid supported catalyst*, T 640/17 *INNOSPEC/Use of PIBSI as a fuel antioxidant* and T 1482/17 *HENKEL/Powder component*.

However, in T 2635/16 *4SC Ag/Acrylamide salts* discussed at §2.20 in relation to novelty the Board declined to apply the reasoning to lists of equally preferred embodiments, instead following the two-list principle in T 12/81 *BAYER/Distereoisomers* and applying the "gold standard" of G 2/88 *MOBIL III/Friction reducing additive* (Reasons, 8.4), G 3/89 *Correction under Rule 88* (Reasons, 3), G 1/03 *PPG/Disclaimer* (Reasons, 2.2.2) and G 2/10 *SCRIPPS RESEARCH INSTITUTE/Disclaimer*, confirmed in G 1/16 *OLED/Disclaimer III* (e.g. Reasons, 17). In T 347/17 *LUBRIZOL/Zinc-free farm tractor fluid* which also involved selection from multiple lists the word "preferably" in one list governed three narrower ranges of amount of a friction modifier which were equally preferred. One of them might have been allowed as a single selection but in combination with a further selection allowability depended on whether the application as originally filed contained a pointer to the combination that was ultimately claimed. Following a dictum in T 2635/16 there was no such pointer and no distinction in the level of preference of each of the three alternatives so that the main request was therefore not allowable. A similar combination of amendments was held in T 149/18 *NUTRICIA/ Enteral composition comprising globular proteins* not to be covered by the converging alternative principle in T 1621/16 because the original application contained no clear and unequivocal pointer to the claimed combination of features and the "gold standard" was not met. The proposed amendments in T 1731/18 *RUBICON/Novel dispersible tablet composition* were rejected for similar reasons, see also T 3035/19 *EURO-CELTIQUE/Pharmaceutical preparations containing oxycodone and naloxone*.

Disclaimers and added features making no technical contribution

After the last paragraph, add new paragraph:

For a recent decision where the relevant prior art was considered a non-accidental anticipation so that EPC art.123(2) was infringed by the disclaimer introduced, see T 1218/14 *DÖHLER/Prolamin-reduced beverages*.

76.15

Amendment to the description

To the end of the fifth paragraph (beginning "The EPO Guidelines warn that alteration or excision of text"), add:

In T 1360/13 *DCA DESIGN/Pen-type injector* it was held that that any change in the description or drawings may have an influence on the understanding of a claimed feature, in particular when it has to be considered ambiguous in view of a piece of prior art or an allegedly infringing product, and may thus lead to a broadening of the extent of the protection conferred [4.5].

76.16

After the fifth paragraph, add new paragraphs:

In T 131/15 *CRANE PAYMENT/Apparatus for sensing optical characteristics of a banknote* the requirements of art.123(3) were held to have been complied with. There was a reference in the relevant granted claim to "light travelling substantially in the opposite direction." The amended claim read "travelling in said sensing plane (P2) in substantially the same path, but in the opposite direction from the light emitted by the transmitter (4), the small path difference being as a result of the fact that the physical sizes of the transmitter and receivers cause a small angle to be subtended between the light paths at the banknote". The opponents argued for a narrow definition of "opposite direction" which would have the effect that none of the disclosed embodiments would fall within the scope of protection of the claim. However, the definition introduced was found in a paragraph in the description, and the Board held that in judging compliance with the requirements of EPC art.123(3) the protection conferred by claim 1 as granted must be considered to include at least embodiments which would fall within the terms of the claim as understood according to this definition. It explained that:

"Where an expression in a granted claim, taken literally and in isolation, would have the effect of excluding all of the disclosed embodiments from the scope of protection, but where a definition of the expression may be derived from the patent itself which would locate (at least some of) the disclosed embodiments within the ambit of the claim, and provided this definition is not manifestly unreasonable, having regard to the normal meaning of the words used in the expression, then in judging compliance with the requirements of Article 123(3) EPC, the scope of protection should normally be considered to include at least that which would fall within the terms of the claim understood according to this definition."

In T 1127/16 *BOEING/Multi-network aircraft communication systems*, T 131/15 was held to be inapplicable because the described embodiment was not entirely excluded from the scope of protection.

SECTION 76A [ADDED]

Commentary on Section 76A

Scope of the section, TRIPS treaty and the European Biotechnology Directive 98/44/EC

76A.03
Replace the first paragraph with:
The arrangement of the various categories of topic is as follows:

> Preliminary and general considerations §§74A.04–74A.11
> Available protection §§76A.12–76A.17
> Exclusions §76A.18
> Disclosure requirements §§76A.19–76A.20

To the end of the seventh paragraph (beginning "In the EPO, the date from which"), add:
It will be interesting to see the impact of Brexit on the UK position regarding the Directive.

At the start of the eleventh paragraph, replace "It affirms the patent eligibility" with:
The Directive affirms the patent eligibility

Delete the tenth paragraph (beginning "The Directive has extensive recitals").

Preliminary and general considerations

Biodiversity and traditional knowledge

76A.05
At the end of the first paragraph, replace "still continue." with:
continues.

Delete the second paragraph.

Replace the third paragraph with:
The Convention on Biological Diversity (CBD–1993) agreed a Protocol in Nagoya in 2010 which gives Member States rights to control research on genetic resources originating in their countries. The Nagoya Protocol came into force on October 12, 2014, and at the date of writing has been ratified by 126 parties.

At the end of the last paragraph, replace "So far, apart from complicating research on genetic resources, there seem to be no direct effects on biotechnological patenting." with:
In addition to issues for patent applicants, non-commercial biodiversity researchers and institutions fear maintaining biological reference collections and exchanging material between institutions will become difficult.

After the last paragraph, add new paragraph:
In March 2020, CIPA submitted to the UK-IPO a response resisting a WIPO proposal for the requirement to disclose in the patent application process the country of origin of genetic resources and the details of the indigenous people or local community that provided traditional knowledge (see [2020] 4 *CIPA* 6-7).

Entitlement to priority

76A.06
After the last paragraph, add new paragraphs:
In T 205/14 *TEVA PHARMACEUTICAL INDUSTRIES Ltd/Ibandronate Sodium* the Board distinguished between entitlement issues (explicitly outside the EPO's powers as a result of EPC art.60(1) and (3)) and the ability of the EPO to apply national law of a contracting state e.g. in determining whether a transfer of a right to claim priority had taken place effectively and in a timely manner. The Board then proceeded to assess whether an assignment complied with national law, to determine entitlement to claim priority.

T 844/18, discussed in detail in the commentary at §5.20, addressed the right to claim priority where the applicant(s) named on the later application differ from those named on the first application. Absent a transfer of the right to claim priority a later application in the name of applicant A cannot validly claim priority from an application in the name of B, or from one in the name of A + B. At the same time, pending at the EPO are a number of Oppositions and Appeals in which multiple applicants are named on a PCT application, taking advantage of the option to name different applicants for different contracting states. In some cases the applicant at the EPO is not the same as the applicant for the priority application(s) and there has been no relevant transfer of the right to claim priority. In some of these cases, priority has been provisionally held validly claimed on the basis of the so-called "joint applicants" approach, relying inter alia on OJ EPO, 2014, A33, Notice from the President, section 9:

> "In the case of joint applicants filing the international application with the EPO as receiving Office and claiming priority from an earlier application, it is sufficient that one of the applicants is the applicant for that earlier application, or his successor in title. Since the international application has been filed jointly, thereby showing the consent of the applicant for the earlier application, there is no need for a special transfer of priority right to the other (additional) applicant(s). Likewise, no transfer of priority right is needed where the earlier application was filed by joint applicants, provided that all of them, or their successor(s) in title, are amongst the joint applicants for the international application."

Relevant EPO proceedings relate to EP1965823 and EP2215124 but no final EPO Board of Appeal decisions are available on this aspect of the right to claim priority.

Available protection

Plants and animals

Methods of culture of plants and of breeding animals and products obtained thereby

To the end of the second paragraph, add:
However, the decision in *Tomato II* and *Broccoli II* was later overruled by the EPO Enlarged Board itself—see G3/19 *Pepper* below.   **76A.17**

Replace the third paragraph with:
The principle that the process exclusion contained in art.53(b) EPC has no negative impact on the allowability of product claims was reaffirmed in T 83/05 *PLANT BIOSCIENCE/Broccoli III*, although again in view of G3/19 *Pepper* the reaffirmation is no longer relevant. The claim in issue was directed to an edible *Brassica* plant elevated in anticarcinogenic glucosinolates and produced by a defined method. The Board was satisfied, following the earlier ruling in G 2/13 that art.53(b) had no negative impact on the allowability of product claims in this form, and the case was remitted to the opposition division with an order to maintain the patent. Similarly, in T 1242/06 *STATE OF ISRAEL/Tomatoes III*. The main claim before the Board was directed to "A tomato fruit of the species *Lycopersicon esculentum* which is naturally dehydrated, wherein natural dehydration is defined as wrinkling of skin of the tomato fruit when the fruit is allowed to remain on the plant after a normal ripe harvest stage, said natural dehydration being generally unaccompanied by microbial spoilage." The Board was satisfied that the subject-matter of this claim was not excluded from patentability and the case was also remitted to the opposition division with an order to maintain the patent. Following recent changes to the EPC Implementing Regulations the applicability of these decisions is now in doubt, although the matter is still being decided by the EPO (see §76A.03).

At the end of the fourth paragraph, after "the claims presented", add:
(although this was decided prior to G3/19 *Pepper* discussed below)

Replace the thirteenth paragraph (beginning "It is uncertain whether or not the referral is admissible") with:
By way of background T 1063/18 *SYNGENTIA* concerned EP-A- 2567811 in which the alleged technical problem was to provide pepper plants that produced pepper fruits with enhanced deep and intense green colour, associated with enhanced nutritional value thanks to enhanced antioxidants, carotenoids and other healthy compound content as well as a green colour appearance that would render them attractive to the consumer, with enhanced perception of freshness and quality. The main claim in issue read as follows:

"A cultivated blocky fruit type pepper plant, bearing extreme dark green colour fruit at immature harvestable stage, said plant comprising two genetic determinants directing or controlling expression of said extreme dark green colour in the pepper fruit of the pepper plant wherein said two genetic determinants are represented by two QTL,

wherein the said genetic determinants are obtainable from *Capsicum annuum* 8728C, seed of which has been deposited under Deposit Number NCIMB 41858 on July 29th, 2011; and

wherein the first QTL, QTL1, is genetically linked to markers loci SP436 and SP626, and the second QTL, QTL2, is linked to markers loci SP693 and SP694; and

wherein the extreme "dark green colour" is associated with the following physicochemical characteristics of the pepper fruits at immature harvestable stage:

- a content in Chlorophyll B greater than 6, particularly greater than 7, more particularly greater than 8 and even more particularly greater than 9 myg/g of fresh weight,
- a content in Chlorophyll A greater than 20, particularly greater than 25, more particularly greater than 30 myg/g of fresh weight,
- a content in lutein greater than 5, particularly greater than 6, more particularly greater than about 7 myg/g of fresh weight,
- a content in violaxanthin greater than 2, particularly greater than 2,5, more particularly greater than 3, even more particularly greater than 3,5 myg/g of fresh weight."

It is notable that the objection that the claimed pepper plant had been produced by an exclusively biological process was contested neither before the Examining Division nor before the EPO Appeal Board. In the US, the pepper plant is the subject of patents 9,493,784 and 10,104,859.

The referral in G 3/19 was considered admissible (surprisingly for some) with the EBA rephrasing the questions and deciding (see also §1.08) that art.53(b) should be interpreted as excluding from patentability, animals, plants or plant materials exclusively obtained by means of an essentially biological process. The EBA thus abandoned the previous interpretation of art.53(b) given in the G2/12 *Tomato II* and G2/13 *Broccoli II* decisions. The EBA clarified that this new interpretation would not have retroactive effect on European patents granted before July 1, 2017, or pending European applications that were filed before this date.

At the beginning of the fourteenth paragraph, after "It", delete "will be noted that it".

Disclosure requirements

Insufficiency issues in relation to biotechnology

Replace the penultimate paragraph with:

76A.20   In *Regeneron Pharmaceuticals Inc v Kymab* [2016] EWHC 87 (Pat) the patents related to the production of human antibodies using transgenic mice. In the High Court, Mr Justice Carr found that the claims were insufficient on the basis that the method provided in the patent would not have worked in the hands of the skilled person. In the Court of Appeal, in contrast, it was found that the skilled person would have adjusted the teaching in the example, without undue burden, in order to perform the invention. The Court of Appeal pointed out that *"a patent does not cease to be sufficient simply because the specification promises too much"*. The Court of Appeal noted their judgment was consistent with the EPO approach on sufficiency of disclosure. In May 2020, the Supreme Court in the UK handed down their judgment on the matter [2020] UKSC 27, in which they agreed with the insufficiency of the claims, as found at the High Court (thus disagreeing with the Court of Appeal). The Supreme Court held that the contribution to the art was not commensurate with the scope of protection of the claims and the claims were insufficient. As explained in §14.29 a decision in T 2220/14 *REGENERON/VelocImmune* issued in relation to a parent patent EP-B-1360287 after the UK Court of Appeal decision but before that of the Supreme Court to which it now expresses a contrary view. In the case of a divisional patent EP-B-2264163 a decision of the Opposition Division maintaining the patent issued in April 2018, but appeal T 1043/18 against that decision remains pending at the time of writing and there is a significant possibility that the contrary view of the EPO will be again expressed.

PATENTS ACT 1977 (C.37) - PART II [SECTIONS 77-95]—PROVISIONS ABOUT INTERNATIONAL CONVENTIONS

EUROPEAN PATENTS AND PATENT APPLICATIONS [SECTIONS 77—85]

SECTION 83A—EUROPEAN PATENT WITH UNITARY EFFECT AND UNIFIED PATENT COURT

Add new paragraph §83A.04:

Developments in 2020

The German Federal Constitutional Court declared the law for German accession to the Unified Pat- **83A.04**
ent Court to be unconstitutional, see 2 BvR 739/17. It held that the Second Chamber of the German
Bundestag did not pass the Act of Approval to the UPC with the two-thirds majority required for amendments to the German constitution. Accordingly plans for the unitary patent and the unitary patent court
will need to be reassessed. But on July 9, 2021 that court in effect reversed its earlier decision, clearing
the way to the implementation of the Unitary Patent and the UPC: *https://www.epo.org/news-events/
news*, article dated 13.07.2021.

In any event, it now appears that that the UK will be participating in neither the unitary patent nor
in the unified patent court, see a statement by Amanda Solloway (Parliamentary Under Secretary of State,
Minister for Science, Research and Innovation) before the House of Lords on July 20, 2020 with the
title "Unified Patent Court":

"I am tabling this statement for the benefit of Honourable and Right Honourable Members to bring
to their attention the UK's withdrawal from the Unified Patent Court system.

Today, by means of a Note Verbale, the United Kingdom of Great Britain and Northern Ireland
has withdrawn its ratification of the Agreement on a Unified Patent Court and the Protocol on
Privileges and Immunities of the Unified Patent Court (dated 23 April 2018) in respect of the United
Kingdom of Great Britain and Northern Ireland and the Isle of Man, and its consent to be bound by
the Protocol to the Agreement on a Unified Patent Court on provisional application (dated on 6 July
2017) (collectively "the Agreements").

In view of the United Kingdom's withdrawal from the European Union, the United Kingdom no
longer wishes to be a party to the Unified Patent Court system. Participating in a court that applies
EU law and is bound by the CJEU would be inconsistent with the Government's aims of becoming
an independent self-governing nation.

The Agreements have not yet entered into force. However, in order to ensure clarity regarding the
United Kingdom's status in respect of the Agreements and to facilitate their orderly entry into force
for other States without the participation of the United Kingdom, the United Kingdom has chosen
to withdraw its ratification of the Agreements at this time. The United Kingdom considers that its
withdrawals shall take effect immediately and that it will be for the remaining participating states to
decide the future of the Unified Patent Court system."

The implications including continuing rights for UK representatives for both the unitary patent and
in the UPC are discussed by Leythem Wall, "The UK says goodbye, Germany decides, the UPC says…
?" [2020] 4 *CIPA* 17–21.

Add new paragraph §83A.05:

Developments since 2020

The Unitary Patent System is intended to start in the first half of 2023, at present on April 1, 2023. **83A.05**
The Unitary Patent Guide, second edition was published in April 2002 and is available on the EPO
website. It explains that in order to be eligible for registration as a unitary patent, a European patent must
have been granted with the same set of claims in respect of all the 25 participating Member States. This
condition must be met irrespective of the number of participating Member States in which the UPCA
will have taken effect at the date of registration of unitary effect by the EPO. It is therefore important
not to withdraw the designation of any of the 25 participating Member States because this would rule
out obtaining a unitary patent. Moreover, a European patent should not contain a different set of claims

for any of the participating Member States, as this too would also prevent the EPO from registering a unitary patent.

In order to obtain a unitary patent, the proprietor of a European patent must file a formal "request for unitary effect" in writing with the EPO, conveniently using the dedicated EPO Form 7000. The request must be filed no later than one month after the mention of the grant of the European patent is published in the European Patent Bulletin. Eligible applicants who have received a r.71(3) communication can request a decision to delay in issuing the decision to grant until April 5, 2023, the first publication day after the start of the unitary patent system, after which a request for unitary effect can be filed within one month after the publication of the grant. Alternatively, an early request for unitary effect is expected to be available as of December 20, 2022, which is the expected date of the deposit of Germany's ratification instrument, until the end of the period of provisional application on March 31, 2023.

The start date of the Unified Patent Court is also expected to be April 1, 2023. Details on UPC website— available since November 7, 2022.

COMMUNITY PATENTS [SECTIONS 86–88]

SECTION 88A

Note.

After the first paragraph, add new paragraph:

88A.01   Repealed by Patents (European Patent with Unitary Effect and Unified Patent Court) (Repeal and Revocation) Regulations 2021 (SI 2021/355) Sch.1 para.1 (April 12, 2021: repeal has effect on April 12, 2021 as SI 2021/355 reg.1(2) immediately after the other provisions of SI 2021/355 come into force in accordance with SI 2021/355 reg.1(2) as specified in SI 2021/355 reg.1(3)).

Commentary on Section 88A

Scope of the section

Replace the third paragraph with:

88A.02   As at September 2019 there have been 16 ratifications of the UPC Agreement including France and (rather extraordinarily) the UK. However, the UPC cannot enter into effect until ratification by Germany.

After the third paragraph, add new paragraphs:

Following the House of Lords EU Justice Sub-Committee's evidence session concerning the Unified Patent Court held on March 10, the Minister for Science, Research and Innovation (Amanda Solloway MP) wrote to the sub-committee chairman ruling out any continuing participation in the UPC. Letter of March 24, 2020: *https://d1pvkxkakgv4jo.cloudfront.net/app/uploads/2020/04/14131805/AStoLM-UPC-240320.pdf.*

A Parliamentary statement was issued in similar tone in July 2020 in which it was indicated that ratification was withdrawn with immediate effect, see §83A.04.

The revocation of this section has now been effected.

At present the future of the UPC, albeit without the UK, remains unclear.

SECTION 88B

Note.

After the first paragraph, add new paragraph:

88B.01   Repealed by Patents (European Patent with Unitary Effect and Unified Patent Court) (Repeal and Revocation) Regulations 2021 (SI 2021/355) Sch.1 para.1 (April 12, 2021: repeal has effect on April 12, 2021 as SI 2021/355 reg.1(2) immediately after the other provisions of SI 2021/355 come into force in accordance with SI 2021/355 reg.1(2) as specified in SI 2021/355 reg.1(3)).

Section 89 [Substituted]

Commentary on Section 89

The international phase

—International filing

In the eighth paragraph (beginning "Further, PCD r.418 provides that"), after "should be automatically made when this form", add:
(or online equivalent)   **89.11**

—International search and amendments to the claims and optional supplementary international search; third party observations

To the end of the third paragraph (beginning "It is also now possible to request"), add:
The relevant deadline is 22 months from the earliest priority date (PCT r.45bis.1(a)).   **89.12**

—International publication

In the ninth paragraph (beginning "In the case of international applications"), replace "(other than any document relating to international preliminary examination)" with:
(other than any document relating to international preliminary examination received or established   **89.13**
before July 1, 2020)

—International preliminary examination

To the end of the penultimate paragraph, add:
However, for documents received or established on or after July 1, 2020 the international preliminary   **89.16**
examining authority is now required to copy many other documents from its file to the International
Bureau, which would then make these available to the public on behalf of the elected office (PCT rr.71
and 94).

United Kingdom Intellectual Property Office as an international authority

—Excuse of delay in meeting time limits due to "force majeure" (PCT r.82quater)

Replace the first paragraph with:
Any interested party may offer evidence that a time limit fixed in the PCT Regulations for perform-   **89.23**
ing an action before the receiving Office, the International Searching Authority, the Authority specified
for supplementary search, the International Preliminary Examining Authority or the International Bureau
was not met due to war, revolution, civil disorder, strike, natural calamity, epidemic, a general unavailability of electronic communications services or other like reason in the locality where the interested
party resides, has his/her place of business or is staying, and that the relevant action was taken as soon
as reasonably possible (PCT r.82*quater*.1 (a)). PCT r.82*quater*.2 further specifically permits any national
Office or intergovernmental organization to provide that, where a time limit fixed in the PCT Regulations for performing an action before that Office or organization is not met due to the unavailability of
any of the permitted electronic means of communication at that Office or organization, delay in meeting that time limit may be excused, provided that the relevant action was performed on the next working day on which electronic means of communication were available.

In the second paragraph, replace "PCT r.82quater (b)" with:
PCT r.82quater.1.(b)

After the last paragraph, add new paragraphs:

In its Interpretative Statement of April 9, 2020 ("Interpretative Statement and Recommended Patent Cooperation Treaty (PCT) Practice Changes in light of the COVID-19 Pandemic"), it was stated that in the view of the International Bureau PCT r.82*quater*.1 applies in the circumstance of global COVID-19 disruption, and the International Bureau urged all PCT Offices and Authorities to adopt this interpretation also.

In addition, under PCT r.82*quater*.3 any receiving Office, International Searching Authority, Authority specified for supplementary search, International Preliminary Examining Authority or the International Bureau may itself establish a period of extension such that time limits fixed in the Regulations within which a party has to perform an action before that Office, Authority or the International Bureau may be extended when the state in which it is located is experiencing a general disruption caused by an event listed in PCT r.82*quater*.1(a) as discussed above, which affects its operations (thereby interfering with the ability of parties to perform actions before that Office, Authority or International Bureau within the time limits fixed in the Regulations). The Office, Authority or the International Bureau publishes the commencement and the end date of any such period of extension as applicable. The period of extension may not be longer than two months from the date of commencement and the Office or Authority notifies the International Bureau accordingly (PCT r.82*quater*.3 (a)). However the Office, Authority or the International Bureau concerned may establish additional, subsequent periods of extension, if necessary (PCT r.82*quater*.3 (b)).

Where the relevant Office, Authority or the International Bureau establishes a period of extension or additional period of extension under PCT r.82*quater*.3, any time limit fixed in the Regulations for performing a particular action before that specific Office, Authority or the International Bureau which would expire during that period expires instead on the first day after the expiration of that period, subject to PCT r.80.5 (expiration on a non-working day or official holiday).

The extension of a time limit under Rule 82*quater*.3 (a) or (b) PCT need not be taken into account by any designated or elected Office if, at the time the information referred to it in PCT r.82*quater*.3 (a) or (b) is published, national processing before that Office has already started (PCT r.82*quater*.3 (c)).

It should be noted also that the provisions under PCT r.82*quater* do not apply to time limits which are not fixed by the PCT Regulations, such as the priority period or time limits for entry to the national phase.

Practice under Section 89

International phase

Replace the second paragraph with:

89.31 Users of the PCT are also strongly recommended to consult the *PatentScope* portal of the WIPO website which can be accessed at the web address stated in §89.08. In particular, the section "PCT Resources" provides a great many very useful documents and resources, including, for example: current PCT Forms; information on current fees; the full online *PCT Applicant's Guide* (updated regularly); copies of the *PCT Newsletter* (since 2000); current copies of the Patent Co-operation Treaty, Regulations and Administrative Instructions; *Guidelines for Authorities and Offices*; details of IP Offices' closing dates; information on electronic filing; details of reservations and incompatibilities; details of time limits for entering national/regional phases; details of power of attorney waivers; a current list of PCT contracting states; ISA and IPEA agreements; a history of the PCT Regulations; Washington Diplomatic Conference on the PCT; and information on PCT seminars, meetings and documents, PCT presentations and forthcoming PCT Reform. Copies of the *PCT Gazette* (from 1998) are available. There is also a useful "Time Limit Calculator" which allows due dates to be automatically calculated and checked when the relevant priority dates and other dates are entered.

Delete the sixth paragraph (beginning "It is possible to file an international application at the UK-IPO by fax").

Replace the seventh paragraph with:

Although the e-mail addresses of the UK-IPO and other international authorities are well publicised and are included in the *PCT Applicant's Guide*, Vol.I (International Phase), Annex B1 (GB), it was not normally possible to file international applications by simple e-mail. Also, e-mail should not be used for correspondence in connection with the processing of international applications, particularly when time limits are important, as there is no guarantee as to how e-mail will be handled by the recipient. When possible, fax transmission was previously recommended for urgent correspondence. However, during the COVID-19 pandemic the UK-IPO stated that its fax service had been turned off so it could no longer receive documents through this channel. A new e-mail address was created for services that are not available online called "*paperformcontingency@ipo.gov.uk*". It was indicated that this can be used instead of faxing or posting documents. In the case there is more than one form to send, it is requested to file these in separate e-mails, with an accompanying fee-sheet if the form is fee-bearing. The UK-IPO has also indicated that it is able to accept electronic signatures on forms and other documents. It should be noted that as far as the International Bureau is concerned, only informal enquiries which are not related to specific international applications may be sent by e-mail by the applicants or their agents. E-mail cannot be validly used by an applicant or agent to perform any procedural act before the International Bureau (*PCT Newsletter*, 04/2009, p.10). The International Bureau strongly recommends use of the ePCT system for urgent communications as discussed under §89.33. The UK-IPO also now accepts the filing of international applications in electronic form using the ePCT filing system (see Official Notices (PCT Gazette), April 28, 2022, pp.103 et seq).

Replace the tenth paragraph with:

The UK-IPO, in its capacity as a receiving office, has notified the International Bureau under PCT r.89bis.1(d) that it is prepared to receive and process international applications in electronic (online) form (*PCT Gazette* 32/2004, p.18092) using EPO software or now also the web-browser based ePCT system (Official Notices (PCT Gazette) dated April 28, 2022, pp.103 et seq). Online filing attracts a reduction in the international filing fee and a further reduction if the application is in character-coded format. So-called "mixed-mode" filings of nucleotide and/or amino acid sequence listings are no longer normally allowed, so that international applications including sequence listings must be filed either entirely electronically (in which case there will normally be a cost saving in page fees) or in paper form (in which latter case full page fees will be payable and a data carrier will also need to be provided).

To the end of the eleventh paragraph (beginning "The UK-IPO no longer accepts PCT applications"), add:

PCT-SAFE itself is also being phased out by the International Bureau of WIPO and the latter has strongly advised applicants, as from July 1, 2022, not to prepare and file PCT applications using any existing versions of the PCT-SAFE software, even if a receiving Office has not yet formally notified the International Bureau that it will no longer accept PCT-SAFE filings (see the PCT Newsletter, July-August 2021, No. 07-08/2021).

Replace the twelfth paragraph with:

Subject to security considerations (for which see the commentary on s.23) it may also be possible to file an international application at the International Bureau online (and in any case also to review and upload subsequent documents at or to the International Bureau) using the ePCT system as discussed below under §89.33. Fax services are still available at the International Bureau (IB) in emergency situation but use of fax is now strongly discouraged. A "Contingency Upload Service" for uploading PDF files has been made available for use in the event that online filing such as ePCT is unavailable for technical reasons.

Replace the thirteenth paragraph with:

An international application which discloses one or more nucleotide and/or amino acid sequences should be prepared accordance with WIPO Standard ST.26 (which is identical to the PCT sequence listing standard at Annex C to the *PCT Administrative Instructions*). Filing software is available for download from the WIPO Sequence Suite on the WIPO website (*https://www.wipo.int/standards/en/sequence*). WIPO Sequence is a desktop tool that supports applicants in authoring and validating sequence listing information in order to generate a WIPO ST.26-compliant sequence listing.

After the thirteenth paragraph, add new paragraphs:

For international applications filed on or after July 1, 2022, nucleotide and amino acid sequences should therefore be disclosed in conformity with WIPO Standard ST.26 ("ST.26") in accordance with Annex C of the PCT Administrative Instructions. WIPO has warned that the submission of a sequence listing using the wrong standard is a formality defect which may be difficult or impossible to correct without adding subject matter (at least in some territories). WIPO therefore strongly advises that applicants should ensure that they use the ST.26 standard applicable at the time of filing (see the PCT Newsletter, 06/2022, p.1).

Applicants are advised to download the WIPO Sequence software from *https://www.wipo.int/standards/en/sequence/index.html* to convert any ST.25 sequence listing to ST.26 format well in advance of the proposed filing date. For further information on migration to ST.26, please also refer to the "Practical Advice" in the PCT Newsletter 02/2022.

Additional information on the implementation of ST.26 can also be found in the ST.26 FAQs at *https ://www.wipo.int/standards/en/sequence/faq.html*.

For further discussion of sequence listing requirements see the PCTH, para 22.9 and the further references provided therein.

ePCT system

After the last paragraph, add new paragraph:

89.33   During the COVID-19 pandemic the International Bureau suspended the transmittal of PCT documents and notifications on paper, and indicated that until further notice it would only transmit documents and notifications electronically. Due to the reduction of scanning operations at the International Bureau, all PCT users were advised to communicate with the International Bureau exclusively by electronic means, preferably through ePCT. This seems likely to be the preferred means of communication in future.

SECTION 89A [ADDED]

Commentary on Section 89A

Valid entry into the UK phase (subss.(2) and (3)(a))

—General

After the penultimate paragraph, add new paragraph:

89A.12   In *Nanjing University's Application* BL O/063/20 an international application was filed 14 months after the priority date claimed. A request was then made to enter the regional phase at the European Patent Office. However, after rejection of the priority claim, the European application was withdrawn and a late attempt was made to enter the national phase in the UK instead, apparently so that the UK-IPO (which applies the "unintentional" rather than "all due care" standard in this respect) might accept the priority claim where the European Patent Office had not. As it was too late for a valid extension under r.108 (which was requested but refused) a request was made for restoration of the UK application under s.20A. This request for restoration was also refused however, as it was held that the applicant had intended to proceed at the European Patent Office at the relevant time and had not had the necessary intention to enter the national phase in the UK, so that the failure to comply with the requirements in the UK could not be considered "unintentional".

—Filing of translation of the international application

Replace the sixth paragraph with:

89A.14   Although any listing of a nucleotide or amino acid sequence filed with the international application forms part of the application, when the sequence listing is in accordance with the PCT sequence listing standard prescribed in Annex C to the *PCT Administrative Instructions* (available on the WIPO website under the link "Treaty, Regulations and Administrative Instructions" and reprinted in the PCTH at Appendix III), the "Sequence Listing" part of the description does not require translation so long as it complies with the relevant requirements (described in WIPO Standard ST.26) of the PCT Administrative Instructions, Annex C (see also the discussion under §89.31). Any later filed sequence listing does not form part of the international application (PCT r.13 ter.1(e)) and does not need to be translated (unless it is in the form of an amendment annexed to the international preliminary examination report), though note also the warning on added matter issues as discussed under §89.31.

Practice under Section 89A

Translation of the international application

In the penultimate paragraph, replace "(WIPO Standard ST.25)" with:

89A.23   (WIPO Standard ST.26)

Section 89B [Added]

Commentary on Section 89B

The designation of the inventor for the United Kingdom (subs.(1)(c))

To the end of the last paragraph, add:

In *Thaler's Application* BL O/447/22, a case relating to the naming of an AI system as inventor, the **89B.07** UK-IPO held that s.89B(1)(c) did not preclude it from undertaking an examination of the indication of an inventor in an international application upon entry into the national phase. In this case the requirements of s.13(2) were not met and so the application was taken to be withdrawn.

CONVENTION COUNTRIES [SECTION 90]

SECTION 90

Commentary on Section 90

Scope of the section

Replace the first paragraph with:

Section 90 provides for countries, by Order in Council, to be declared "convention countries" for the **90.02** purposes of the claiming of priority under s.5. As of writing, the most recent Orders are SI 2007/276, the Patents (Convention Countries) Order 2007, which took effect on April 6, 2007, repealing all previous such orders, and consolidating the list of countries designated as "convention countries", the Patents (Convention Countries) (Amendment) Order 2009 (SI 2009/2746) which came into force on November 12, 2009 and inserted "Cape Verde", and the Patents (Convention Countries) (Amendment) Order 2013 (SI 2013/538) which came into force on April 6, 2013 and inserted "Samoa" and "Vanuatu" into the list of countries in the Schedule to the 2007 Order.

MISCELLANEOUS [SECTIONS 91–95]

SECTION 91

Note.

Replace the first paragraph with:

Subsection (1) was amended by the Patents Act 2004 (c.16) Sch.2 para.20. Subsections (1)(a) and **91.01** (6) would have been amended by the Patents (European Patent with Unitary Effect and Unified Patent Court) Order 2016 (SI 2016/388). However, these proposed changes have been revoked by the Patents (European Patent with Unitary Effect and Unified Patent Court) (Repeal and Revocation) Regulations 2021 (SI 2921/355).

Delete the second paragraph.

SECTION 92

Note.

Replace the first paragraph with:

Subsection (5) was amended by SI 1979/1714. Subsections (1) and (5) would have been amended **92.01** Patents (European Patent with Unitary Effect and Unified Patent Court) Order 2016 (SI 2016/388). However, these proposed changes have been revoked by the Patents (European Patent with Unitary Effect and Unified Patent Court) (Repeal and Revocation) Regulations 2021 (SI 2921/355).

Delete the second paragraph.

LEGAL PROCEEDINGS [SECTIONS 96–108]

SENIOR COURTS ACT 1981 (C.54)

Commentary on Section 96 [Repealed]

Territorial jurisdiction of the Patents Court

—*Extra-territorial jurisdiction*

After the last paragraph, add new paragraph:
    In *Otsuka Pharmaceutical v GW Pharma* [2022] EWHC 1012 (Pat) the court deemed that it had   **96.11**
jurisdiction to determine royalties notwithstanding the grant of a United States patent.

SECTION 97

Commentary on Section 97

Further appeals from the Patents Court after appeal from the Comptroller (subs.(3))

To the end of the sixth paragraph (beginning "In Ladney's and Hendry's International Application BL C/103/96"), add:
    In *Master Data Center v Comptroller* [2020] EWHC 572 (Pat) permission to appeal was refused   **97.06**
because the Patents Court had reached the same conclusions for substantially the same reasons as the
Hearing Officer at first instance, and because both the Hearing Officer and the Patents Court had relied
on a Court of Appeal decision to do so. Permission to appeal was subsequently granted by the Court of
Appeal however.

Practice under Section 97

Further appeals from the Patents Court to the Court of Appeal

—*Costs on appeal*

After the second paragraph, add new paragraph:
    In *Master Data Center Inc v Comptroller (Costs)* [2020] EWHC 601 (Ch) an appeal by the Appel-   **97.32**
lant (MDC) was unsuccessful against the UK-IPO's decision in relation to the term of an SPC. As there
was a possibility of further appeal by MDC, the Comptroller pursued his earlier application that recoverable costs of the appeal would be limited pursuant to CPR r.52.19. It was decided that proceedings in
the UK-IPO are proceedings in which costs recovery is normally limited or excluded, and therefore it
was open to the judge to make an order relating to recoverable costs pursuant to CPR r.52.19(1). In making the order the factors in r.52.19(2) and (3) were considered and it was decided that the implications
of UK-IPO's status as a public body, including access to justice, outweighed factors refusing a costs cap-
ping order.

SECTION 98

Commentary on Section 98

Jurisdiction of the Court in Scotland

—CJJA Schedule 8 and forum non conveniens

In the second paragraph, after "common law doctrine of forum non conveniens, as per", replace "Cook v Virgin Media Ltd; McNeil v Tesco Plc (2015) EWCA CIV 128." with:

98.11   Cook v Virgin Media Ltd; McNeil v Tesco Plc (2015) EWCA CIV 1287.

Interdict effective UK-wide: defender domiciled in Scotland

To the end of the first paragraph, add:

98.14   A recent example of this, albeit in a trade mark context, arose in *William Grant v Lidl* [2021] CSIH 38. The court allowed an appeal on jurisdiction, holding that since the defender was a Scottish company, the interdict applied to acts committed by it throughout the UK. See [31]–[35].

Types of patent proceedings competent in Scotland

After the last paragraph, add new paragraph:

98.17   In the case of *Reactec Ltd v Curotec Team Ltd* [2020] CSOH 77, the pursuer sought interdict on the ground that two of the defender's products had infringed their patent. The defender counterclaimed seeking revocation of the patent on the ground that that it lacked an inventive step as it was obvious from the prior art and the common general knowledge of the skilled person. The case was heard in the Outer House of the Court of Session. The court considered the *Windsurfing/Pozzoli* test for identifying whether the inventive step was obvious. In identifying the relevant skilled person, the judge accepted the skilled team comprised of a mechanical engineer/psychiatrist and an electronic engineer who were knowledgeable about vibration monitoring. On the inventive step part of the claim, the court rejected the defender's argument that these "were distinct and unrelated". It was held that there was an interaction between the features of the device. The information on the vibration and the duration of the vibration are both essential "in order for the apparatus taught by the claim to arrive at vibration dosage for the operator". The court concluded that the inventive idea was to combine steps that would not have been obvious to the skilled person to produce an "improved and more efficient monitoring apparatus". As such, the patent was valid and the devices manufactured by the defender infringed the pursuer's patent.

Practice Under Section 98

Proceedings before the Court

At the end of the last paragraph, replace "Lady Wolffe, Lord Doherty, Lord Ericht and Lord Bannatyne." with:

98.19   Lord Clark, Lord Ericht, Lord Harrower and Lord Braid.

SECTION 102A [REPEALED WITH EFFECT JANUARY 1, 2010]

Commentary on Section 102A

Replace the second paragraph with:

102A.02   However, this is now academic as all rights under this section have been superseded by rights granted under the Legal Services Act regime through the "Rights to Conduct Litigation and Rights of Audience and Other Reserved Legal Activities Certification Rules 2012", copies of which can be downloaded from *https://ipreg.org.uk/sites/default/files/IPReg_Regulations_Website_amended_July_20161.pdf.*

Section 107

Commentary on Section 107

The general rule for exercising the Comptroller's powers

—Departures from the standard scale of costs

Replace the first paragraph with:

As an exception rather than the norm, the Comptroller may depart from the standard (contributory) **107.04** scale of costs considered above. Guidance is set out in TPN 2/2000 and TPN 4/2007, the object being to give the tribunal power to deal with breaches of rules, delaying tactics or other unreasonable behaviour. As explained by TPN 2/2000, para.9 and TPN 4/2007 para.5, there is no exhaustive list of circumstances when the Comptroller may make an off-the-scale award partly because of the difficulties of drafting such a list, and partly because an exhaustive list may fetter the Comptroller's discretion. However, the Tribunal Practice Notices give some examples of behaviour that can warrant an off-the-scale award, namely: making an application to amend a statement of case which, if granted, would cause the other side to have to amend its statement or would lead to the filing of further evidence, where such an amendment could have been avoided; filing evidence in respect of grounds which are not pursued at the main or substantive hearing; rejecting efforts to settle a dispute; unreasonably declining the opportunity of Alternative Dispute Resolution; and failing to attend a hearing without informing the other side. TPN 3/2009 provides another example: acting unreasonably in the light of a Preliminary Evaluation.

In the second paragraph, after "without a genuine belief that there is an issue to be tried.", add:

This was the basis for award of costs off-scale in *AutoStore v Ocado* BL O/348/22.

After the last paragraph, add new paragraphs:

Close Brewery Rentals Ltd v Geco Holdings Ltd BL O/264/21 involved a successful entitlement claim (ss.12, 13, 37 and r.10). After finding in favour of the claimants in the main proceedings, the Hearing Officer (Huw Jones) invited submissions on costs, while stating that he did not expect to depart from the standard scale in Annex A of Tribunal Practice Notice 2/2016. Immediately after the decision was issued, the defendant invited the Hearing Officer to correct an alleged error in relation to entitlement to claims 2–9 of the patent (GB2571465). After receiving submissions from both sides, Huw Jones issued further decision BL O/458/21. He rejected the defendant's arguments on correction. On costs, the claimant pointed out that the defendant had put in expert evidence, having previously agreed not to do so (necessitating cross-examination of the expert and a report on the claimant's side). It also suggested that some of the defendant's evidence was on the "bounds of credibility". It requested full costs or a reduced proportion, relying on principles outlined in *Statoil ASA v University of Southampton* BL O/268/05 and comment in *Statoil*:

> "It is, though, right to depart from the scale if the behaviour of a party was such that it unreasonably caused the other side to incur costs, because without that sanction it gives a party a carte blanche to be as unreasonable as they like safe in the knowledge that they cannot be clobbered for the extra costs the other side has to incur."

However, in *Close Brewery*, the Hearing Officer held that, apart from the expert issue, the defendant had not acted unreasonably nor had its witnesses been in bad faith. The complexity of the case did not merit maximum scale costs; £4,500 was awarded (compared with the range of £3,900 to £6,050 for a 2-day hearing). However, the defendant should pay the claimant's full costs (£1,900) on the application to correct.

In *AutoStore v Ocado* BL O/348/22, an entitlement application subject to an application to strike out was withdrawn, ostensibly because the European patent was invalid and would be opposed. The application had been characterised as a ruse to delay grant. The Hearing Officer (Mr P Thorpe) stressed the Office's normal practice of awarding costs to the other side when an application was withdrawn, and noted that neither side had referred to the IPO database of cases on the issue. As stated in para.5.47 of the Hearings Manual, off-scale costs were intended to recompense for unnecessary costs, but not to punish. As well as referring to *Statoil* and *Diamond*, Mr Thorpe cited as persuasive the non-patent case of *Kazakhstan Kagazy v Zhunus* [2015] EWHC 404 (Comm), where Leggatt J. had stated:

"The touchstone is not the amount of costs which it was in a party's best interests to incur but the lowest amount which it could reasonably have been expected to spend in order to have its case conducted and presented proficiently, having regard to all the relevant circumstances."

So, rather than the claimed figure of £131,354.31, which included the services of four counsel (three of them QCs), three partners, two senior associates, two associates and two paralegals, the Hearing Officer awarded off-scale costs of £46,000.

Administrative provisions [Section 117–121]

Section 117

Commentary on Section 117

Nature of permissible corrections to specifications (r.105(3))

After the last paragraph, add new paragraph:

117.05   Relevant law is summarised in *Gazel Investment Group's Application* BL O/782/19. The application had been filed by the inventors, and patent attorneys were not appointed until shortly before the hearing. The documents as filed included a description (2 pages), a single claims page and an abstract (21 pages), and the applicants requested incorporation of the abstract in its entirety into the description either under s.117 or as an irregularity of procedure. It was acknowledged that if a skilled person looked at the entirety of the documents that were originally filed including the abstract, then it would be clear to them that there had been an error and that the abstract could be taken into account when considering what was originally contended, citing *Dukhovskoi's Application* [1985] R.P.C. 8, *Abbott Laboratories Ltd v Medinol Ltd* [2010] EWHC 2865 (Pat) and G 11/91 *CELTRIX/Glu-Gln*. However, as the documents as originally filed included a two-page description it was simply not clear, even if it was accepted that the 21-page abstract was incorrectly labelled and submitted as an abstract, whether those 21 pages were intended to be the whole description or whether they were intended to supplement the two pages labelled as the description. On that basis alone, it was not clear that what was now offered was what had been originally intended and hence the request for a correction must fail. The possibility of withdrawing the application and refiling had been explained to the applicants in a covering letter sent with the examining opinion and they had been advised to seek professional advice, but they had chosen not to do so at the relevant time. Accordingly, no irregularity of procedure has occurred that would warrant allowing the application to now be corrected as requested by the applicants.

Section 117B [Added]

Commentary on Section 117B

Scope of the section

After the last paragraph, add new paragraph:

117B.04   Section 117B also applies to extending time limits relating to applications for Supplementary Protection Certificates (SPCs). In *Chiesi Farmaceutici S.P.A.* BL O/019/22, the question arose of whether the Comptroller's discretion could be used to extend the Article 10(3) deadline beyond the normal expiry date of the SPC to allow the applicant to provide missing documents relating to an application for a paediatric extension. The Hearing Officer considered that it was necessary to consider carefully whether it was appropriate to exceed this date but, if the circumstances merited, he was not prevented from doing so and granted a discretionary extension to accept documents filed by the applicant.

Commentary on Section 125

Normal construction

After the seventh paragraph (beginning "It should be noted that this arrangement"), add new paragraph:

For a consideration of the "disclosed but not claimed" scenario in the context of equivalents, see **125.06** *FaceBook v Voxer* [2021] EWHC 1377 (Pat) considered at §125.08.

After the last paragraph, add new paragraphs:

Although a normal construction, being the interpretation of a document, is primarily a matter of law, it is none the less an issue on which evidence of the skilled addressee could be relevant. For that reason the Court of Appeal refused to allow a construction to be advanced on appeal which had not been ventilated at first instance. See *Conversant v Huawei and ZTE* [2020] EWCA Civ 1292 [91]–[110].

In *Interdigital Technology Corp v Lenovo Group Ltd* [2021] EWHC 2152 (Pat) the court considered the relevant date for construing a claim. It held that it was bound by the approach in the Court of Appeal's approach in *Nokia Corp v IPCom GmbH & Co KG* [2012] EWCA Civ 567 that a patent must be construed as at the priority date, or if there is no priority claim, the filing date. It would seem to follow from the other cases cited that the filing date should also be used where the priority claim is invalid.

Equivalents: general approach

After the last paragraph, add new paragraphs:

In *Akebia Therapeutics Inc v Fibrogen Inc* [2020] EWHC 866 (Pat) Arnold L.J. (sitting as a High **125.07** Court judge) stated that these questions are guidelines and not strict rules observing that "the language of some or all of the questions may sometimes have to be adapted to apply more aptly to the specific facts of a particular case."

For an interesting analysis of some of the earlier post-*Actavis* cases see Nicholas Fox, "Sheep farming and the doctrine of equivalents" [2020] 4 *CIPA* 11.

Equivalents: first *Actavis* question—'inventive concept'

After the last paragraph, add new paragraphs:

A yet pithier exposition of "inventive concept" was adopted in *A Ward v Fabcon* [2021] EWHC 2145 **125.08** (IPEC), the court finding it instructive to consider what gave the expert in the field a "buzz". The case is perhaps a further example of inventive concept being very much a feel taken from all the surrounding circumstances and one on which the first instincts of an appropriately instructed expert can be persuasive.

In *Excel-Eucon Ltd v Source Vagabond Systems Ltd* [2019] EWHC 3175 (Pat) only infringement was before the court. The court relied on various statements of advantage throughout the specification as a basis for its identification of the inventive concept. The contrary may also be relevant: in *Akebia Therapeutics Inc v Fibrogen Inc* [2020] EWHC 866 (Pat) the court held the lack of any hint in the specification as what was now being put forwards as the inventive concept was relevant in dismissing the patentee's submission (see [433]).

In *Evalve Inc v Edwards Lifesciences Ltd* [2020] EWHC 514 (Pat), Birss J. (as he then was) summarised Kitchin L.J.'s criteria in *Icescape* as follows [315]: "In other words one should examine what is the problem underlying the invention and how does the patent solve that problem."

The fact that there is only a single embodiment described in the description does not of itself indicate a restricted inventive concept. Meade J. in *Add2 Research and Development Ltd v DSpace Digital Signal Processing & Control Engineering GmBH* [2021] EWHC 1630 (Pat) at [92] explained this as follows:

"Counsel for the Defendants submitted that given that there is only one preferred embodiment, it was more likely than if there had been multiple embodiments that the patentee had chosen claim terms to correspond to the preferred embodiment, rather than to have a more general meaning. I do not accept this. Even where there is only one preferred embodiment the patentee is likely to have had a generalised concept in mind, and it is necessary to work out from the language whether that is so, and what the concept is. Multiple preferred embodiments may, by their consistency, give further clues as to what the claims were intended to mean, but general claim language cannot be restricted to the preferred embodiment just because there is only one."

In *Facebook v Voxer* [2021] EWHC 1377 (Pat) Birss L.J. (sitting at first instance) considered a scenario he described as "disclosed but not claimed". He reasoned that where the specific description disclosed two alternatives but the claim was only addressed to one of these, then the first and third questions (considered together) suggested that there would be no infringement. If one concentrated on the similarities between the two disclosed alternatives, then whilst the answer to the first question would be that it made no material difference to the way the invention worked, the patentee knew this too and so presumably had a reason for only including one alternative in its claim. Hence the answer to the third question would be no infringement. Conversely if one concentrated on the differences, then the two alternatives would not work in the same way, leading to a conclusion of non-infringement on the first question.

Many of the aspects that go to the first question seem also applicable to the third question and the reader is referred to §125.11.

Equivalents: second *Actavis* question

After the last paragraph, add new paragraph:

125.09   In *Evalve Inc v Edwards Lifesciences Ltd* [2020] EWHC 514 (Pat) the court was considering a fairly simple mechanical device and observed that in such circumstances it was sufficient that the skilled person would easily understand how it works and from this it automatically followed that the second question was satisfied.

Replace paragraph §125.10 with:

Equivalents: third Actavis question

125.10   In *Icescape Ltd v Ice-World International BV* [2018] EWCA Civ 2219 Lord Kitchin (sitting in the Court of Appeal) summarised four points as being made in *Actavis* as the approach to be taken to the third question (§64):

"(i)   Although "the language of the claim is important", consideration of this question does not exclude the specification of the patent and all the knowledge and expertise which the notional addressee is assumed to have.

(ii)   The fact that the language of the claim does not on any sensible reading cover the variant is certainly not enough to justify holding that the patentee does not satisfy the third question.

(iii)   It is appropriate to ask whether the component at issue is an "essential" part of the invention, but that that is not the same thing as asking if it is an "essential" part of the overall product or process of which the inventive concept is part. Here regard must be had to the inventive concept or the inventive core of the patent.

(iv)   When one is considering a variant which would have been obvious at the date of infringement rather than at the priority date, it is necessary to imbue the notional addressee with rather more information than he might have had at the priority date. Here Lord Neuberger had in mind the assumption that the notional addressee knows that the variant works."

The burden here seems to be for the alleged infringer to show that strict compliance with the language of the claim would be required.

Hence the approach taken in *RegenLab v Estar Medical* [2019] EWHC 63 (Pat):

"252.   The evidence indicated that the molarity of the sodium citrate is not essential to the inventive concept and would not have been so regarded by the skilled person at the priority date. That being so, it seems to me that the third question would only be answered yes if there had been a sufficiently clear indication to the skilled person that strict compliance with the figure of 0.10M was intended. In the present case anyway, I think that could only have come from the patent specification or something in the skilled person's common general knowledge. There was no such indication."

The following from *Mishan v Hozelock* [2019] EWHC 991 (Pat) puts the burden a little (but not much) more neutrally ([92]):

"But apart from the language, how can one tell whether the patentee regarded strict compliance with an integer in the claim to be an essential requirement of the invention or not? Relevant considerations appear to include whether a plausible reason can be advanced why any rational patentee should want to place such a limitation on his invention (see *Actavis* at [73]), and whether the inventive core of the patent has anything to do with the particular way in which the variant differs from the claims (see *Icescape* at [74] per Lord Kitchin and at [98] per Floyd L.J.)."

Again in *Geofabrics Ltd v Fiberweb Geosynthetics Ltd* [2020] EWHC 444 (Pat), the burden was on the alleged infringer to give a reason why the skilled addressee would conclude that strict compliance was an essential requirement. The same was also the case in *Evalve Inc v Edwards Lifesciences Ltd* [2020] EWHC 514 (Pat).

In the Editors' view, it is hard to see why the evidential burden should be on the alleged infringer, and why this reflects the neutral stance required by the Protocol. Moreover, against this it might be said that it is the patentee who drafts his/her patent in terms of his/her own choosing and it should be the patentee having done so (rather than the infringer) who should make the running on any presumption of strict compliance with its terms.

Indeed the evidential burden may to some degree be an unintended consequence. In the original formulation of the criteria in *Catnic v Hill* [1982] R.P.C. 183 the question was formulated in the alleged infringer's favour whereas the restatement in *Improver* favoured the patentee. There was no indication in *Improver* that this reformulation was intentional. Having said the above, this shift in burden was referred to albeit more as shift in emphasis in *RegenLab v Estar Medical* [2019] EWHC 63 (Pat) at [221].

In *Freddy v Hugz* [2020] EWHC 3032 (IPEC) it was submitted that the third question "acted as a check on the first two and invites a defendant to point out any material in the patent which might drive the court to conclude that the patentee really wanted the claim to be strictly construed so as to exclude variants that were established by the first two questions to be immaterial." This again would seem to indicate that the burden is on the alleged infringer rather than the patentee. Since it is the patentee's patent to draft, the Editors still query whether this is the correct burden to be imposed. In that case, examples given as to why strict compliance should be mandate were avoidance of acknowledge prior art or of the CGK.

In *Mishan v Hozelock* [2019] EWHC 991 (Pat) it was argued that a particular feature of the claim was described as 'preferable' in the description. It was therefore said that by including what he has described as 'preferable' in the claim, the patentee must have been taken to intend that feature as essential to the now expressed invention. This argument was rejected as being as insufficient basis upon which to find essentiality (see [91]–[94]).

It appears arguable that even the additional feature introduced by a dependent claim could be alleged to be inessential. In *Mishan* the judge noted as follows:

"95.   … I would have thought that where the patentee has gone to the trouble of identifying a separate claim 2 which differs from the main claim 1 only by the addition of another integer, then it might be arguable that that by itself would lead the reader to regard the additional integer as an essential requirement of the invention claimed in claim 2. That is after all what the patentee has identified as the difference between the two claims (quite apart from the fact that in the present case the patentee has chosen to use quite emphatic language to express the point)."

Despite having stated the above (which appears to the Editors to be the correct approach), the judge noted that he had not received detailed submissions in this respect and so proceeded to find infringement of a dependent claim by virtue of an equivalent to the feature introduced by that claim (see §96).

In *Akebia Therapeutics Inc v Fibrogen Inc* [2020] EWHC 866 (Pat) the court considered a number of aspects that might go to strict compliance (albeit having already dismissed infringement by equivalents on the basis of the first question). Many of these are context specific but a number are capable of more general application.

First was the fact that the patentee sought unconditional amendment so as to narrow claim 1, the independent claim of the resultant amendment to be claim 17A. The judge reasoned as follows [452]–[454]:

"… it is common ground that the skilled team is to be taken to be aware that granted claim 1 has been amended down to claim 17A and that the other granted claims have been deleted. I do not understand it to be disputed that they are also to be taken to be aware that the reason for the amendment was that the broader claims were invalid (or at least that there was a substantial risk that they would be found to be invalid).

As counsel for the Defendants submitted, it is contradictory for the Claimants on the one hand to be amending the claim down to just Compound C, particularly in order to save its validity, and yet at the same time to be asserting that the scope of protection of the amended claim extends well beyond Compound C to a structurally rather different compound, and by implication to a large number of other compounds as well. By amending down to Compound C, the Claimants are disclaiming the other ways of achieving the same effect disclosed in the specification, and in particular everything covered by the broader granted claims.

This is an extreme instance of a principle which is well established in the jurisprudence of the *Bundesgerichtshof* (German Federal Court of Justice, BGH). As the BGH held in Case X ZR 16/09 – *Okklusionsvorrichtung (Occlusion Device)*:

'If the description discloses a plurality of possibilities for achieving a specific technical effect, but only one of those possibilities is catered for in the patent claim, the utilisation of any of the other possibilities properly does not constitute infringement of the patent with equivalent means.'"

Another aspect (the seventh expounded by the judge) was that infringement by equivalents would result in a claim of sufficient breadth that it would be obvious over a specific prior art reference. It should perhaps be noted that a full-scale obviousness attack had been mounted over that prior art (Epstein) and also that it was acknowledged art in the patent itself (see [130]). It does not however appear that it was common general knowledge. See the discussion at §125.09.

The judge also held the prosecution history to be a relevant factor since the claim was limited during prosecution with the expressly stated purpose of avoiding certain prior art by limiting the claim to the specific formulation now claimed. Hence the prosecution history was admissible in the public interest.

For a consideration of the "disclosed but not claimed" scenario, which may impact on both the first and third question, see *Facebook v Voxer* [2021] EWHC 1377 (Pat) considered at §125.08 above.

It is not a relevant consideration to the assessment of the third question (i.e. it does not suggest the exercise of strict compliance) that had the claim been drafted to include the claimed infringement on a normal construction, then it would have been bad for added matter. Birss L.J. (sitting at first instance) so held in *Facebook v Voxer* [2021] EWHC 1377 (Pat), see [205], [206]. The judge explained that added matter is nothing to do with scope and so the point is entirely neutral.

The situation contemplated in *Facebook* in fact arose in *A Ward v Fabcon* [2021] EWHC 2145 (IPEC). The feature of relevance had been introduced into a divisional patent but was lacking in the parent (which claimed an allegedly equivalent feature). The divisional was argued to be infringed on a normal construction but the court held that the introduced feature rendered it invalid for added matter. However, it held that feature to be equivalent to that claimed in the parent and so held the parent patent infringed under the doctrine of equivalents.

The reader should therefore be in no doubts that *Actavis* appears to have effected a major change in the law and statements such as that in *Société Technique de Pulverisation v Emson* [1993] R.P.C. 513, reproduced below, are unlikely any longer to be good law :"The well known principle that patent claims are to have a purposive construction does not mean that an integer can be treated as struck out if it does not appear to make any difference to the inventive concept. It may have some other purpose buried in the prior art and even if this is not discernible, the patentee may have had some reason of his own for introducing it" (see *RegenLab v Estar Medical* [2019] EWHC 63 (Pat) at [219]–[224]).

In *Actavis UK Ltd v Eli Lilly and Co* [2014] EWHC 1511 (Pat) Mr Justice Arnold set out some interesting comments as to the three circumstances in which patentees "resort to arguments about equivalents":

"The first is where, with the benefit of hindsight, it can be seen that the patent was unfortunately drafted, whether because of poor instructions from the inventor or poor drafting by his patent attorney or a combination of these things. *Improver* might perhaps be regarded as an example of this. The second class is where technology has moved on since the priority or filing date of the patent. *Kirin-Amgen* might perhaps be regarded as an example of this. The third class is where the patentee now regrets a decision taken during the course of prosecution of the patent application, whether by himself or by the examiner, and is trying to avoid the consequences of that decision ...

In the first class of case, the law recognises that drafting patent claims is a difficult and imprecise art and that third parties should not be allowed to exploit infelicities of drafting where it is reasonably clear that those infelicities should not affect the scope of the claim. This is in order to provide 'fair protection for the patent proprietor'. The law also recognises, however, the countervailing consideration that third parties are entitled to rely on the drafting of the claim when deciding on a commercial course of action. There is no tort of avoiding a patent claim. Thus it is also necessary to provide 'a reasonable degree of legal certainty for third parties'. The problem, of course, is that what is fair protection to one person is legal uncertainty to another. Conversely, what is reasonable legal certainty to the second person is a denial of protection to the first. The courts have to strike a balance. In striking that balance, it is important to bear in mind that, as Lord Hoffmann and Jacob L.J. have pointed out, both the patentee and the third party will generally rely on skilled professional advice (and may have a remedy if the advice is incompetent).

In the second class of case, the problem is more acute. It is difficult for an applicant for a patent to anticipate how technology may evolve during the 20 year life of the patent. The law is sympathetic to the proposition that third parties should not be able to avoid infringement merely by employing new technical means to implement the invention. But on the other hand, a claim may be drafted in a manner which is inescapably tied to the old technology. There is no easy answer to this conundrum.

In the third class of case, there is no reason why the law should be sympathetic to the patentee. Not only do applicants generally rely on skilled professional advice, but also they can appeal against adverse decisions of examiners during the course of prosecution if they consider that those decisions are wrong. If the courts allow decisions as to claim scope made by the examiner during the course of prosecution which have not been successfully appealed effectively to be overturned by decisions on claim construction, the courts undermine the important role of the examiner. This is still more so if the courts allow decisions as to claim scope made by the applicant during the course of prosecution effectively to be reversed by decisions on claim construction."

The observations of Mr Justice Arnold (from the first instance hearing of *Actavis*) remain interesting reading. It is the Editors' view that these scenarios may now become relevant to any consideration of whether the doctrine of equivalents can be invoked and still give fair protection to the patentee. It is the first of these categories (unfortunate drafting) where the biggest difficulties may arise. In the second class (technology moved on), as Arnold J. observed, the law is more sympathetic and the change in the expression of the second *Improver* question will likely extend that sympathy further. As for the third (patentee regrets decision taken during prosecution) the Editors agree with the observation of Arnold J. that "there is no reason why the law should be sympathetic". The decided cases, however, suggest otherwise.

The need for a uniform construction of the extent of protection: the *Formstein* defence

After the penultimate paragraph, add new paragraph:

The court looked again at the *Formstein* defence, but again obiter in *Facebook v Voxer* [2021] EWHC 1377 (Pat). Having considered the approaches under various different jurisdictions ([209]–[216]) Birss L.J. sitting at first instance concluded as follows (at [216]): **125.11**

"… if I did have to decide the matter, I would hold that the right approach is the *Formstein* approach so that the conclusion if the equivalent device lacks novelty or is obvious is that the claim scope must be confined to its normal construction in that respect. I would do so for two reasons. If the claim on its normal construction is valid, then it seems harsh to invalidate it on this ground. What else could the patentee do but write their claim in a way which, normally construed, did not cover the prior art? So that approach promotes certainty. Secondly, since it is clear that other EPC countries work that way, this is a reason in itself for this EPC state to take the same approach."

"File wrapper estoppel"

After the penultimate paragraph, add new paragraphs:

Similarly in *Excel-Eucan Ltd v Source Vagabond System Ltd* [2019] EWHC 3175 (Pat) the alleged infringer sought to rely on submissions made by the patentee in co-pending revocation proceedings before the UK-IPO. The proceedings before the court concerned infringement only. In the co-pending proceedings the UK-IPO had issued a non-binding preliminary opinion and the patentee had relied upon the feature now said to be of no relevance to the inventive concept as part of its submissions in response to that opinion. The court declined to consider this as relevant to the first *Actavis* question on the basis that neither of the circumstances for admission were satisfied. **125.12**

For an example of a rare case in which statements and amendments made in prosecution were held to be admissible see *Akebia Therapeutics Inc v Fibrogen Inc* [2020] EWHC 866 (Pat) at [459]. Although the prosecution history of this patent is voluminous and complex (indeed the opposition is ongoing) it does appear that limitation and the reason behind it (to achieve novelty by expressly limiting to a particular formulation) were clearly expressed. That said, this case should be seen as very much the exception and not the rule.

Relevance of the prior art

After the last paragraph, add new paragraph:

In *Lufthansa Technik AG v Astronics Advanced Electronic Systems* [2020] EWHC 1968 (Pat) the court **125.13** rejected an argument that the discussion of a particular piece of prior art in the introduction (and its commonality with the claimed invention) would mandate that the skilled person should obtain that art and construe the patent in suit with the more detailed knowledge that such a study would allow. It should be noted however that this case sets out no principle of law to such effect, and on the evidence before the court on that case, neither expert suggested that the skilled addressee would perform such an exercise. See [67]–[79]. The decision and its reasoning was upheld on appeal, [2022] EWCA Civ 20, [59]–[62].

Replace paragraph §125.14 with:

Matters of drafting practice

125.14   In *Minnesota Mining v Plastus Kreativ* [1997] R.P.C. 737 CA, the word "opaque" was construed according to the stated purpose and non-infringement was found because the defendant's device failed to meet the inventive criteria indicated by the use of that word. Another example is *Hoechst Celanese v BP Chemicals [Iodide Removal]* [1997] F.S.R. 547 and [1999] F.S.R. 319 CA.
     The distinction between "consisting of" and "comprising of" is both well established and defined. A recent explanation from Floyd L.J. appears in *Anan Kasei Co Ltd v Neo Chemicals and Oxides Ltd* [2019] EWCA Civ 1646 and reads as follows [13]:

"In patent jargon there is a distinction between a claim for a composition of matter which 'consists' of something and a claim for such a composition 'comprising' something. The first formulation will normally be taken to impose a requirement that nothing else is present, while the latter formulation is simply a minimum requirement, agnostic as to whether other things are present as well. So a claim to a cake mix 'consisting of sugar, eggs, butter and flour' is not infringed by one containing chocolate chips, but that would not be the case if the word 'comprising' was substituted for 'consisting of'."

The courts have had to consider what Floyd L.J. described in *Anan* as the hybrid phraseology of "consisting essentially of". The judge at first instance (*Anan Kasei Co Ltd v Molycorp Chemicals and Oxides (Europe) Ltd* [2018] EWHC 843 (Pat)) held that this created a penumbra to the claim, meaning that apart from the mandatory ingredient (in that case ceric oxide) no other ingredients should be present which materially affected the essential characteristics of the product. This approach was not subject to any appeal which went to the insufficiency ramifications of such phraseology.
     See also the MOPP at para.14.123.1.
     As discussed in the Case Law of the Boards of Appeal of the EPO, 9th edition (2019), II.A.6.2, referring to decisions T 759/91 and T 522/91, the wording "consisting essentially of" is to be interpreted as identical to "comprising substantially". However, in view of the unequivocal character of "consisting", the expression "consisting" is to be preferred. As for its interpretation, the cited decisions T 759/91 (point 2.2. of the Reasons) and T 522/91 (point 2.2. of the Reasons) both refer to the decision T 472/88, wherein it was decided that the term "consisting essentially of" was clear and allowed the presence of other components in a claimed composition in addition to the components mandatory in the claim, provided that the essential characteristics of the claimed composition are not materially affected by their presence (see point 3 of the Reasons).

"The Board agrees with these previous decisions. Therefore, even though the word 'essentially' does not identify precisely the amounts of additional components which could still be contained in the claimed viscoelastic fluid, the wording 'consisting essentially of' allows in the present case that the composition of claim 1, which must be viscoelastic, consists of the mandatory components listed in the claims and can contain additionally only other components which do not materially affect the essential viscoelastic characteristics of the composition, e.g. minor amounts of impurities as submitted by Appellant I during oral proceedings."

Such terms of degree may also give rise to added matter issues: see for example the Case Law Book (9th edition) II.E.1.15.

Reference numerals

Replace paragraph §125.15 (except for last two paragraphs) with:
125.15   In *Virgin Atlantic Airways Ltd v Premium Aircraft Interiors UK Ltd* [2009] EWCA Civ 1062; [2010] R.P.C. 8 the Court of Appeal held that the skilled reader is to be taken to know the purpose of (i) including reference numerals in patent claims, (ii) dividing claims into pre-characterising and characterising portions and (iii) filing of divisional applications, and to bring that knowledge to bear when he considers the scope of the claim. This was justified by various reference to Kirin-Amgen on which the court reach the conclusion that it would be "unrealistic, indeed perverse" to ignore such practices.

Birss J. (as he then was) drew attention to various drafting conventions, specifically those in transmit-receive systems in *Conversant Wireless Licensing v Huawei* [2020] EWHC 14 (Pat):

"93.   A common problem is that inventions do not always lend themselves to simple claim drafting. Aside from satisfying the laws relating to validity, in practice a good patent claim has to do two different things. It has to define the invention, but it also has to do that in a way which allows the inventor to have worthwhile rights. The patent system exists to provide temporary economic rights to inventors as the reward for disclosing the invention to the public. A perfect definition of the invention is no use if it would not be infringed by persons taking advantage of that invention. An example of this problem is the difficulties which have arisen in framing claims and defining infringement relating to inventions which are the second medical uses of known drugs (see *Warner Lambert v Generics* [2018] UKSC 56).

94.   Another situation in which difficulties can arise is with inventions concerning activity on networks like the internet and cellular systems. The problem is that these systems involve multiple distinct elements which have to interact in a particular way. A patent claim to the network as a whole can be a good way of defining the invention but be of little practical utility because no-one sells the whole thing. The law of "means essential" infringement under s60(2) of the Act may or may not help in a given case. That is why Conversant have focussed on claim 18. It is a claim to a handset (mobile station). These are items with significant economic value. One can define infringing acts relating to them, pay royalties based on their sales and so on.

95.   Nevertheless, just because these problems are real enough does not mean that the patentee is entitled to some special dispensation in terms of the legal approach. The defendants rightly drew attention to the structure of the claims as a whole and noted that they could be categorised into four groups – methods of transmission, methods of reception, elements of RAN infrastructure (such as a Node B) which transmit to mobiles, and mobile stations configured to receive signals (mobile stations). Claim 1 is in the first category and claim 18 is in the fourth category. The defendants put it this way in opening:

'147. The approach to claim drafting has been to mirror the features of the transmission or reception method claims in the claims to network elements and mobile stations. However, the consequence of that approach is that a process feature which is a positive requirement of one of the method claims may not actually be a limiting requirement of the product claims to a mobile station configured in a certain way. The skilled person would not strain to make every feature of the language of the product claims have a limiting effect, because they would appreciate that those claims were part of a set of claims also covering methods of transmission and reception, and the language of the product claims had been chosen simply to match that used in the corresponding method claims.'

96.   I agree with the first two sentences. The third sentence is advocacy but I do agree that the reader would appreciate the claims are part of a set, with matching language, and read them accordingly."

In *L'Oreal v RN Ventures* [2018] EWHC 173 (Pat) the infringer referred to drafting practice, specially referring to an arrangement as relating to an "aspect of the invention" rather than an "embodiment of the invention" as an indication that such an arrangement was intended to be excluded from the claims (both on a normal construction and under the doctrine of equivalents). The judge did not accept there to be any such established practice in the EPO (worthy of influencing claim construction).

In *Lufthansa Technik AG v Astronics* [2022] EWCA Civ 20 the appellant criticised the trial judge for over reliance upon reference numerals. The Court of Appeal found the criticism unfounded, he was merely using them to see how the claim read onto the embodiment. Having done so, he returned to the language of the claim to construe it.

Two-part form

After the penultimate paragraph, add new paragraph:
Additionally, our previous commentary is perhaps a little unfair in view of the explanation given by   **125.16**
Birss L.J. in *Lufthansa Technik AG v Astronics* [2022] EWCA Civ 20 at [9].

Geometric terms

—Construction is a question of law

After the last paragraph, add new paragraph:

125.21   *IPCom v Vodafone Group Plc* [2020] EWHC 132 (Pat) is a recent reminder that, other than terms of art, construction is for the court and not the expert witnesses. See [69].

After the fifth paragraph (beginning "An item of hardware will not generally be suitable"), add new paragraph:

Claims containing a statement of purpose

125.24   *Rovi* together with other cases concerning statements of purpose in the context of computers were considered in *IPCom v Vodafone Group Plc* [2020] EWHC 132 (Pat). The judge's review was not extensive as the principles said to be established in the caselaw were agreed by the parties. These were set out in the judgment and were as follows [88]:

"(a)   One must be cautious of any principle which is said to codify the meaning of words: see *Philips* at [102], citing *Qualcomm*.

(b)   The EPO generally takes claim language of the means plus function to be read as means suitable for carrying out the function, save where the function is to be carried out by a computer. In that case the features are interpreted as means 'adapted to' carry out the relevant function rather than merely being suitable. See EPO Guidelines, F-IV, paragraph 4.13.2, November 2018 edition, headed 'Interpretation of means-plus-function features'.

(c)   Mann J's approach in *Rovi* was different. He held that a computer was not "suitable for" the processes in question without appropriate programming: see *Rovi* at [132].

(d)   The EPO approach and Mann J's approach are slightly different in form but it is doubtful whether they differ in substance: see *Philips* at [103].

(e)   A claim will still be infringed if all that is required is to supply power. Thus an apparatus for toasting bread infringes whether connected to the mains or not: see *Qualcomm* at [73]–[74], *Philips* at [104]. However if the apparatus has to undergo physical modification before it can be used for the relevant purpose, rather than merely being supplied with power, then prima facie it is not suitable for such use and does not infringe: ibid."

SECTION 125A

Commentary on Section 125A

Comparison with EPC and PCT provisions

After the last paragraph, add new paragraph:

125A.20   In an EPO decision of March 8, 2021 is a reminder that established case law of the Board of Appeal is that the mention of biological material in a scientific publication does not establish that material is available to the public in the sense of EPC r.31(1) [T 1045/16 *MONSATO/Closterovirus-Resistant Melon Plants*].

Practice under Section 125A

Procedure for deposit of biological material

Replace the third paragraph with:

—Factors influencing choice of depositary institution

125A.25   There are at present six IDAs situated in the United Kingdom and each is authorised under the Budapest Treaty to accept certain defined types of biological material only. The location, telephone number and the broad outline of what they can accept are as follows:

(1)   National Collections of Industrial, Food and Marine Bacteria (NCIMB) at NCIMB Ltd., Ferguson Building, Craibstone Estate, Bucksburn, Aberdeen AB21 9YA (tel. 01224 009333; e-mail *enquiries@ncimb.com*; web *http://www.ncimb.com*), which accepts bacteria, yeasts, bacteriophages and plasmids, including recombinants, provided that their hazard rating and physical containment requirements are no greater than ACDP category 2 or ACGM class 1, and orthodox seeds (i.e. those which can be dried to a low moisture content and stored at –20°C (or lower) without damage; all arable crops and many small seeded tree species produce orthodox seeds).

(2)   The European Collection of Cell Cultures ("ECACC") and the National Collection of Type Cultures ("NCTC") are now both part of the Health Protection Agency ("HPA") Culture Collections at Health Protection Agency, Centre for Emergency Preparedness and Response, Porton Down, Salisbury SP4 0JG (General Enquiries tel. 01980 612512 Technical Support 01980   612684);   e-mail: *culturecollections@phe.gov.uk*   (Sales), *culturecollections.technical@phe.gov.uk* (technical support); web: *http://www.phe-culturecollections.org.uk*. NCTC accepts bacteria as patent deposits, including those of ACDP Hazard Group 3, that can be preserved without significant change to their properties by freeze-drying and which are pathogenic to man and/or animals; they should also be free-living and grow on ordinary laboratory media. ECACC accepts the following types of patent deposits: human and animal cell lines including genetically modified lines up to GMO2, hybridomas, viruses up to and including ACDP Hazard Group 3 pathogens and eukaryotic and viral recombinant DNA either as naked DNA or cloned into a host organism. Viruses are processed on behalf of ECACC by the National Collection of Pathogenic Viruses ("NCPV"). HPA Culture Collections laboratory operations remain at their original parent sites at Porton Down, Colindale and Bristol in order to exploit the particular scientific expertise of each site. However the sales, marketing, financial and quality management has been centralised at Porton Down, based on the original ECACC organisation.

(3)   CABI, Genetic Resource Collection at Bakeham Lane, Egham, Surrey TW20 9TY (web *http://www.cabi.org* and for centre in UK *cabieurope-uk@cabi.org*; contact is via an online form at the previously mentioned website), which accepts nematodes, fungal isolates (including yeasts) and bacteria (including actinomycetes), other than known human and animal pathogens that can be preserved without significant change to their properties by methods of preservation in use. Organisms up to and including ACDP* Category 2 deposits are accepted.

(4)   National Collection of Yeast Cultures (NCYC) at the Quadram Institute Bioscience, Norwich Research Park, Norwich NR4 7UQ (tel. 01603 255274; fax 01603 458414; e-mail *ncyc@ncyc.co.uk*; web *http://www.ncyc.co.uk*), which accepts yeasts, other than known pathogens.

(5)   Culture Collection of Algae and Protozoa (CCAP) at SAMS Research Services Ltd, Scottish Marine Institute, Oban, Argyll PA37 1QA (tel. 01631 559000 or 559268 (direct dial); fax 01631 559001; e-mail *ccap@sams.ac.uk*; web *http://www.ccap.ac.uk*), which accepts freshwater and terrestrial algae and cyanobacteria, non-pathogenic free-living protozoa and marine algae and cyanobacteria, other than large seaweeds.

(6)   The UK Stem Cell Bank, hosted by the National Institute for Biological Standards and Control (NIBSC) at Blanche Lane, South Mimms. Potters Bar, Herts., EN6 3QG (tel. 01707 641050; e-mail *enquiries@ukstemcellbank.org.uk* ; web: *https://www.nibsc.org/ukstemcellbank*). The UK Stem Cell Bank's deposits are not confined to human stem cells. As well as human embryonic and somatic stem cell lines it accepts other human cell lines, animal cell lines and genetically modified animal and human cell lines.

SECTION 128A [ADDED]

Replace s.128A with: 128A.01

Compulsory pharmaceutical [EU compulsory] licences

128A.—(1)   In this Act a "compulsory pharmaceutical *[an "EU compulsory]* **licence" means a compulsory licence granted under Regulation (EC) No 816/ 2006 of the European Parliament and of the Council of 17 May 2006 on compulsory licensing of patents relating to the manufacture of pharmaceuti-**

cal products for export to countries with public health problems[1] (referred to in this Act as "the Compulsory Licensing Regulation").

(2)   In the application to compulsory pharmaceutical *[EU compulsory]* licences of the provisions of this Act listed in subsection (3)—

    (a)   references to a licence under a patent,

    (b)   references to a right under a patent, and

    (c)   references to a proprietary interest under a patent,

include a compulsory pharmaceutical *[an EU compulsory]* licence.

(3)   The provisions referred to in subsection (2) are—

sections 32 and 33 (registration of patents etc);

section 37 (determination of right to patent after grant);

section 38 (effect of transfer etc of patent under section 37), apart from subsection (2) and subsections (3) to (5) so far as relating to subsection (2);

section 41 (amount of compensation);

section 46(2) (notice of application for entry that licences are available as of right);

section 57(1) and (2) (rights of third parties in respect of Crown use).

(4)   In the following provisions references to this Act include the Compulsory Licensing Regulation—

sections 97 to 99B, 101 to 103, 105 and 107 (legal proceedings);

section 119 (service by post);

section 120 (hours of business and excluded days);

section 121 (comptroller's annual report);

section 123 (rules);

section 124A (use of electronic communications);

section 130(8) (disapplication of Part 1 of Arbitration Act 1996).

(5)   In section 108 (licences granted by order of comptroller) the reference to a licence under section 11, 38, 48 or 49 includes an EU compulsory licence.

(6)   References in this Act to the Compulsory Licensing Regulation are to that Regulation as amended from time to time.

Replace paragraph "Notes." with:

Notes.

This section was inserted by the Patents (Compulsory Licensing and Supplementary Protection Certificates) Regulations 2007 (SI 2007/3293) reg.2, with effect from December 17, 2007. It was amended by the Patents (Amendment) (EU Exit) Regulations 2019 (SI 2019/801) with effect from January 1, 2021 following the withdrawal of the UK from the EU.

Regulation (EC) No.816/2006 as it had effect immediately before the end of December 31, 2020 will continue in force as to the UK by virtue of the European Union (Withdrawal) Act 2018 as amended, but was also amended by virtue of the Patents (Amendment) (EU Exit) Regulations 2019 (SI 2019/801) as from such date by limiting its application to the UK.

Commentary on Section 128A

Scope of the section

To the end of the first paragraph, add:

128A.02   Although Regulation (EC) No.816/2006 is retained EU law it was amended, as to the UK, by virtue

---

[1]   [2006] OJ L157/1.

of the Patents (Amendment) (EU Exit) Regulations 2019 (SI 2019/801) as from January 1, 2021 by limiting its application to the UK, and the amendments made by the Regulations to s.128A are consequential on this.

Change title of paragraph: **128A.03**

Definition of "Compulsory pharmaceutical licence" and "Compulsory Licensing Regulation"

Replace paragraph with:
    Subsection (1) as amended defines the term "Compulsory pharmaceutical licence" as a compulsory licence granted under Regulation (EC) No.816/2006 as amended and the term "Compulsory Licensing Regulation" is defined accordingly. Subsections (2) and (3) makes it clear that references to a licence, right or proprietary interest under a patent in certain provisions of the Act include a Compulsory licence and subs.(4) clarifies in which provisions references to the Act include the Compulsory Licensing Regulation. Similarly, subs.(5) makes it clear that in s.108 (licences granted by order of Comptroller) reference to a licence includes an EU compulsory licence. In sub.(6), references to the Compulsory Licensing Regulation are to that Regulation "as amended from time to time," thereby avoiding the need for the legislation to have to be amended in the future simply to reflect any amendment to the Compulsory Licensing Regulation.

Delete paragraph §128A.04.

Section 128B [Added]

Note.

Replace the second paragraph with:
    The Patents (Amendment) (EU Exit) Regulations 2019 (SI 2019/801), the Intellectual Property **128B.02** (Amendment etc.) (EU Exit) Regulations 2020 (SI 2020/1050) and the Supplementary Protection Certificates (Amendment) (EU Exit) Regulations 2020 (SI 2020/1471), all of which came into force on "IP completion day", contain amendments to provisions governing Supplementary Protection Certificates in the UK, including the Patent Rules and Regulations 1610/96, 469/2009 and 2019/933 (each as incorporated into UK law). The amendments are intended to "address failures of retained EU law to operate effectively and other deficiencies arising from the withdrawal of the United Kingdom from the European Union". As defined in s.39(1) of the European Union (Withdrawal Agreement) Act 2020, "IP completion day" means December 31, 2020 at 23:00.

Replace paragraphs §128B.10 and §128B.11 with:

Note.

    Regulation (EC) No.469/2009 represents "direct EU legislation" in the sense of s.3 of European **128B.10** Union (Withdrawal) Act 2018. Therefore, by operation of s.3(1) of that Act, it now forms part of domestic law, albeit in amended form. Amendments to Regulation 469/2009 are set out in three Statutory Instruments (SIs), namely the Patents (Amendment) (EU Exit) Regulations 2019 (SI 2019/801), the Intellectual Property (Amendment etc.) (EU Exit) Regulations 2020 (SI 2020/1050) and the Supplementary Protection Certificates (Amendment) (EU Exit) Regulations 2020 (SI 2020/1471). The purpose of the amendments in those SIs is to "address failures of retained EU law to operate effectively and other deficiencies arising from the withdrawal of the United Kingdom from the European Union".
    The provisions of SI 2019/801 entered into force on "IP completion day", namely at 23:00 on 31 December 2020. Whilst the same is true for certain provisions of SI 2020/1050 and SI 2020/1471, certain other provisions of those SIs entered into force immediately before IP completion day. The latter provisions are those of Pts 1 to 6 of SI 2020/1050 and regs 2 and 3 of SI 2020/1471.
    The amendments made by SI 2019/801 are subject to the following transitional provisions (which include amendments from reg.37 of SI 2020/1050):

   69.—(1)   This regulation applies to—
      (a)   An application for an extension of the duration of a certificate, filed in accordance with Article 7 but not determined before IP completion day; and
      (b)   An extension of the duration of a certificate granted—

          (i)   before IP completion day; or

          (ii)   after IP completion day, pursuant to an application falling within sub-paragraph (a);

(2)   Where this regulation applies, Articles 1(e), 8(1)(d), 13(3), and 16(1) of Regulation 469/2009 continue to apply without the amendments made by these Regulations.

(3)   Where paragraph (1) applies—

    (a)   Article 8(1)(d)(ii) is to be read as if, for the words "all other Member States", there were substituted "all Member States";

    (b)   Articles 13(3) and 16(1) are to be read as if, for the words "all Member States" in Article 36(3) of Regulation 1901/2006, there were substituted "the United Kingdom and all Member States".

The amendments made by SI 2020/1050 are subject to the following transitional provisions:

43.—(1) Paragraph (2) applies where, before IP completion day, a product or a medicinal product containing that product, as defined in Article 1 of Regulation EC (No) 469/2009, is marked in accordance with that Regulation with the logo set out in Annex -I of that Regulation.

(2)   That product or medicinal product containing that product so marked is not required, after these Regulations come into force, to have the words "UK export" affixed to it.

(3)   Paragraph (4) applies where, before IP completion day, a notification is made to the Comptroller-General of Patents, Designs and Trade Marks in the form set out in Annex -Ia of Regulation (EC) No 469/2009.

(4)   That notification is to be treated, on and after IP completion day, as a notification made—

    (a)   on Patents Form SP5; and

    (b)   on the same date as the notification made on the form set out in that Annex -Ia.

The amendments made by SI 2020/1471 are subject to the following transitional provisions:

7.—(1) Where an application for an authorisation is made before IP completion day under—

    (a)   Directive 2001/83/EC of the European Parliament and of the Council of 6 November 2001 on the Community code relating to medicinal products for human use,

    (a)   Directive 2001/82/EC of the European Parliament and of the Council of 6 November 2001 on the Community code relating to veterinary medicinal products, or

    (a)   Regulation (EC) No 1107/2009 of the European Parliament and of the Council of 21 October 2009 concerning the placing of plant protection products on the market,

    but the authorisation is not granted until on or after IP completion day, these Regulations apply to any application for a supplementary protection certificate made in respect of the authorisation.

(2)   These Regulations apply to an application for a supplementary protection certificate made on or after IP completion day in respect of a UK authorisation granted or having effect as if granted before IP completion day.

(3)   The former regulations continue to apply to an application for a supplementary protection certificate made, but not determined, before IP completion day in respect of a UK authorisation granted or having effect as if granted before IP completion day.

(4)   Where on or after IP completion day a UK authorisation granted or having effect before IP completion day is withdrawn and replaced with a GB authorisation and a NI authorisation, any certificate granted in respect of the UK authorisation does not lapse.

(5)   For the purposes of paragraphs (2), (3) and (4), "UK authorisation" means an authorisation granted or having effect as if granted under—

    (a)   Directive 2001/83/EC of the European Parliament and of the Council of 6 November 2001 on the Community code relating to medicinal products for human use,

    (b)   Directive 2001/82/EC of the European Parliament and of the Council of 6 November 2001 on the Community code relating to veterinary medicinal products, or

    (c)   Regulation (EC) No 1107/2009 of the European Parliament and of the Council of 21 October 2009 concerning the placing of plant protection products on the market, and references to a UK, GB or NI authorisation, where they occur in these Regulations (but not including this regulation) are to be treated as meaning a "UK authorisation" as defined in this paragraph.

(6)   For the purposes of paragraphs (4) and (7)—

    (a)   "GB authorisation" has the meaning ascribed to it in paragraph 15 of Article 1 of Regulation (EC) 1610/96, as amended by regulation 4 of, and paragraph 2 of the Schedule to, these Regulations, and paragraph (ja) of Article 1 of Regulation (EC) 469/2009 as amended by regulation 5 of, and paragraph 9 of the Schedule to, these Regulations; and

(b)   "NI authorisation" has the meaning ascribed to it in paragraph 16 of Article 1 of Regulation (EC) 1610/96, as amended by regulation 4 of, and paragraph 2 of the Schedule to, these Regulations and paragraph (jb) of Article 1 of Regulation (EC) 469/2009 as amended by regulation 5 of, and paragraph 9 of the Schedule to, these Regulations.

(7)   For the purposes of paragraph (4), where the former regulations apply to a "UK authorisation" as defined in paragraph (5), the UK authorisation includes a GB authorisation and NI authorisation in combination.

(8)   For the purposes of this regulation, "former regulations" means Regulation (EC) 1610/96 and Regulation (EC) 469/2009 without the amendments made by these Regulations but including the amendments made by the Patents (Amendment) (EU Exit) Regulations 2019 and the Intellectual Property (Amendment etc.) (EU Exit Regulations) 2020.

Regulation 469/2009 repealed and replaced Council Regulation (EEC) 1768/92, of June 18, 1992, which came into force on January 2, 1993. That Regulation had been amended by the Act of Accession of Austria, Sweden and Finland (adapted by Council Decision 95/1/EC, Euratom, ECSC) and by Regulation (EC) No.1901/2006 of the European Parliament and of the Council of December 12, 2006 on Medicinal Products for Paediatric Use and amending Regulation (EEC) No.1768/92, Directive 2001/20/EC, Directive 2001/83/EC and Regulation (EC) 726/2004. The Regulation was also amended by the Act concerning the conditions of accession of the Czech Republic, the Republic of Estonia, the Republic of Cyprus, the Republic of Latvia, the Republic of Lithuania, the Republic of Hungary, the Republic of Malta, the Republic of Poland, the Republic of Slovenia and the Slovak Republic and the adjustments to the Treaties on which the European Union is founded and the Act of accession of Bulgaria and Romania. These amendments, which concern transitional provisions relating to the enlargement of the Community are not relevant in the United Kingdom.

Regulation 469/2009 codified amendments made to the earlier regulation, with the intention being to fully preserve the content of the acts being codified and do no more than bring together the previous legislation with only such formal amendments as are required by the codification exercise itself.

The recitals were numbered for the first time. However, as the first recital relates to the need for codification, the numbering of the remaining recitals does not correspond to the informal numbering used in judgments and patent office decisions referring to the former regulation. For example, the reference to Recital 9 of Regulation 1768/92 in the Plant Protection Products Regulation (no.1610/96), at Recital 17, should now be to Recital 10 of Regulation 469/2009.

Recitals 10, 11 and 12 of the former regulation were deleted in the codification. These related to transitional provisions that had become redundant at the time of codification. The definition of "basic patent" at art.1(c) was amended from "a patent which protects a product as defined in (b) as such" to "a patent which protects a product as such". Given that no changes of substance may be made to the instruments affected by codification, this amendment would appear to be merely editorial. The second sentence of art.3(b), inserted into the former regulation following the Act of Accession of Austria, Sweden and Finland, which required that a marketing authorisation granted in accordance with national legislation of Austria, Finland or Sweden is to be treated as a corresponding community authorisation, was deleted.

For clarity, art.8(1)(a), (1)(b) and (2) in the former regulation, which relate to aspects of the content of an application for a certificate, were renumbered as art.8(2), (3) and (4). Former art.15(a), which relates to the revocation of a paediatric extension, was renumbered as art.16, and former arts 16, 17 and 18 renumbered accordingly. Former art.19, which related to transitional provisions, was deleted. Although of no consequence to UK practice, art.19(a), which related to transitional provisions following EU enlargements in 2004 and 2007 was renumbered as art.20. Former art.20, which relates to further transitional measures, was renumbered as art.21. Former art.21 related to now redundant transitional measures, and was deleted. The provision of former art.22, which related to the effect of patent extensions granted under national law before the coming into force of Regulation 1768/92, was moved to art.13(4).

The correlation between the numbering of recitals and articles between the former regulation and the new regulation, together with paragraph reference is as follows:

Regulation (EEC) No 1768/92	Regulation (EC) 469/2009
[*new*]	Recital 1
Recital 1	Recital 2
Recital 2	Recital 3
Recital 3	Recital 4
Recital 4	Recital 5
Recital 5	Recital 6

Regulation (EEC) No 1768/92	Regulation (EC) 469/2009
Recital 6	Recital 7
Recital 7	Recital 8
Recital 8	Recital 9
Recital 9	Recital 10
Recital 10	[deleted]
Recital 11	[deleted]
Recital 12	[deleted]
Recital 13	Recital 11
Article 1	Article 1
Article 2	Article 2
Article 3, introductory wording Article 3, (a) Article 3, (b), first sentence Article 3, (b), second sentence Article 3, (c) and (d)	Article 3, introductory wording Article 3, (a) Article 3, (b), first sentence [deleted] Article 3, (c) and (d)
Article 4 to 7	Article 4 to 7
Article 8(1) Article 8(1)(a) Article 8(1)(b) Article 8(2)	Article 8(1) Article 8(2) Article 8(3) Article 8(4)
Article 9 to 12	Article 9 to 12
Article 13(1), (2) and (3)	Article 13(1), (2) and (3)
Article 14 and 15	Article 14 and 15
Article 15a	Article 16
Article 16, 17 and 18	Article 17, 18 and 19
Article 19	[deleted]
Article 19a, introductory wording *Article 19a, (a) to (l) : Non UK transitional provisions*	Article 20, introductory wording *Article 19a, (a) to (l) : Non UK transitional provisions*
Article 20 Article 21 Article 22 [new]	Article 21 [deleted] Article 13(4) Article 22
Article 23	Article 23

Regulation (EC) No 469/2009 of the European Parliament and of the Council of 6 May 2009 concerning the supplementary protection certificate for medicinal products (codified version; as incorporated into UK law)

THE EUROPEAN PARLIAMENT AND THE COUNCIL OF THE EUROPEAN UNION,

Having regard to the Treaty establishing the European Community, and in particular Article 95 thereof,

Having regard to the proposal from the Commission,

Having regard to the opinion of the European Economic and Social Committee,

Acting in accordance with the procedure laid down in Article 251 of the Treaty,

Whereas:

(1)   Council Regulation (EEC) No 1768/92 of 18 June 1992 concerning the creation of a supplementary protection certificate for medicinal products has been substantially amended several times. In the interests of clarity and rationality the said Regulation should be codified.

(2)   Pharmaceutical research plays a decisive role in the continuing improvement in public health.

(3)   Medicinal products, especially those that are the result of long, costly research will not continue to be developed in the Community and in Europe unless they are covered by favourable rules that provide for sufficient protection to encourage such research.

(4)   At the moment, the period that elapses between the filing of an application for a patent for a new medicinal product and authorisation to place the medicinal product on the market makes the period of effective protection under the patent insufficient to cover the investment put into the research.

(5)   This situation leads to a lack of protection which penalises pharmaceutical research.

(6)   There exists a risk of research centres situated in the Member States relocating to countries that offer greater protection.

(7)   A uniform solution at Community level should be provided for, thereby preventing the heterogeneous development of national laws leading to further disparities which would be likely to create obstacles to the free movement of medicinal products within the Community and thus directly affect the functioning of the internal market.

(8)   Therefore, the provision of a supplementary protection certificate granted, under the same conditions, by each of the Member States at the request of the holder of a national or European patent relating to a medicinal product for which marketing authorisation has been granted is necessary. A regulation is therefore the most appropriate legal instrument.

(9)   The duration of the protection granted by the certificate should be such as to provide adequate effective protection. For this purpose, the holder of both a patent and a certificate should be able to enjoy an overall maximum of 15 years of exclusivity from the time the medicinal product in question first obtains authorisation to be placed on the market in the Community.

(10)   All the interests at stake, including those of public health, in a sector as complex and sensitive as the pharmaceutical sector should nevertheless be taken into account. For this purpose, the certificate cannot be granted for a period exceeding five years. The protection granted should furthermore be strictly confined to the product which obtained authorisation to be placed on the market as a medicinal product.

(11)   Provision should be made for appropriate limitation of the duration of the certificate in the special case where a patent term has already been extended under a specific national law,

HAVE ADOPTED THIS REGULATION:

Article 1—Definitions

For the purposes of this Regulation:

(a)   'medicinal product' means any substance or combination of substances   **128B.11** presented for treating or preventing disease in human beings or animals and any substance or combination of substances which may be administered to human beings or animals with a view to making a medical diagnosis or to restoring, correcting or modifying physiological functions in humans or in animals;

(b)   'product' means the active ingredient or combination of active ingredients of a medicinal product;

(c)   'basic patent' means a patent which protects a product as such, a process to obtain a product or an application of a product, and which is designated by its holder for the purpose of the procedure for grant of a certificate;

(d)   'certificate' means the supplementary protection certificate;

(e)   'application for an extension of the duration' means an application for an extension of the duration of the certificate pursuant to Article 13(3) of this Regulation and regulation 58A(3) of the Human Medicines Regulations 2012(a);

(f)   'comptroller' means the Comptroller-General of Patents, Designs and Trade Marks;

(g)   'court' means—
    (i)   as respects England and Wales, the High Court;
    (ii)   as respects Scotland, the Court of Session;
    (iii)   as respects Northern Ireland, the High Court in Northern Ireland;

(h)   EEA authorization' means an authorisation to place a medicinal product on the market which has effect in an EEA state in accordance with Directive 2001/83/EC or Directive 2001/82/EC;

(i)   'patent' means a patent which has effect in the United Kingdom;

(j)   'UK authorisation' means, in relation to a product, an authorisation to place that product on the market in the United Kingdom as a medicinal product granted or having effect as if granted in accordance with—
    (i)   Part 5 of the Human Medicines Regulations 2012; or
    (ii)   regulation 4(3) of, and Schedule 1 to, the Veterinary Medicines Regulations 2013(b);

(ja)   "GB authorisation" means, in relation to a product, an authorisation to place that product on the market in England and Wales and Scotland as a medicinal product granted or having effect as if granted in accordance with—
    (i)   Part 5 of the Human Medicines Regulations 2012(14); or
    (ii)   regulation 4(3) of, and Schedule 1 to, the Veterinary Medicines Regulations 2013(15) as they have effect in England and Wales and Scotland;

(jb)   "NI authorisation" means, in relation to a product, an authorisation to place that product on the market in Northern Ireland as a medicinal product granted or having effect as if granted in accordance with Directive 2001/83/EC or Directive 2001/82/EC as they have effect by virtue of the Protocol on Ireland/Northern Ireland in the EU withdrawal agreement;

(k)   "maker" means the person, established in the United Kingdom, on whose behalf the making of a product, or a medicinal product containing that product, for the purpose of export to third countries outside the United Kingdom, the Isle of Man and the Member States of the European Union or for the purpose of storing, is carried out;

(l)   "prescribed" means prescribed by rules under section 123 of the Patents Act 1977.

Add new Note after Article 1—Definitions:

Note.

Article 1(e) was amended by reg.52(2) of SI 2019/801. This replaced "Article 36 of Regulation (EC) No 1901/2006 of the European Parliament and of the Council of 12 December 2006 on medicinal products for paediatric use" with "regulation 58A(3) of the Human Medicines Regulations 2012". This amendment is subject to the transitional provisions of reg.69 of SI 2019/801 (see Note 1 to §128B.18).

Articles 1(f) to 1(j) were introduced by reg.52(3) of SI 2019/801. However, arts 1(g) and 1(j) in the form reproduced above include amendments from reg.34 of SI 2020/1050 and reg.3(3) of SI 2020/1471.

Article 1(k) derives from art.1(1) of Regulation 2019/933, as amended by para.1 of the Schedule to SI 2020/1050.

Articles 1(ja) to 1(jb) and 1(l) were introduced by para.11 of the Schedule to SI 2020/1471.

Replace Article 2—Scope with: **128B.12**

Article 2—Scope

A product may, under the terms and conditions provided for in this Regulation, be the subject of a certificate if it is:
(a) protected by a patent; and
(b) the subject of a UK, GB or NI authorization prior to being placed on the market as a medicinal product.

Add new Note after Article 2—Scope:

Note.

Article 2 was amended by reg.54 of SI 2019/801, and by reg.3(4) of SI 2020/1471.

Replace Article 3—Conditions for obtaining a certificate with: **128B.13**

Article 3—Conditions for obtaining a certificate

Where an application is submitted under Article 7 a certificate shall be granted if, at the date of submission of that application:
(a) the product is protected by a basic patent in force;
(b) there is a valid UK, GB or NI authorisation to place the product on the market;
(c) the product has not already been the subject of a certificate;
(d) the authorisation referred to in point (b) is the first UK, GB or NI authorisation to place the product on the market as a medicinal product in the territory of the United Kingdom, the territory of England and Wales and Scotland or the territory of Northern Ireland as the case may be.

Replace Note with:

Note.

Article 3 was amended by reg.54 of SI 2019/801, and by reg.3(5) of SI 2020/1471.

128B.14 *Replace Article 4—Subject matter of protection with:*

Article 4—Subject matter of protection

Within the limits of the protection conferred by the basic patent, the protection conferred by a certificate shall extend only to the product covered by the UK, GB or NI authorisation to place the corresponding medicinal product on the market and for any use of the product as a medicinal product that has been authorised in the United Kingdom before the expiry of the certificate.

Replace Note with:

Note.

Article 4 was amended by para.12 of the Schedule to SI 2020/1471.

128B.15 *Replace Article 5—Effects of the certificate with:*

Article 5—Effects of the certificate

1. Subject to the provisions of Article 4 and paragraphs 1a and 1b, the certificate shall confer the same rights as conferred by the basic patent and shall be subject to the same limitations and the same obligations.

1a. The protection conferred by a certificate in accordance with paragraph 1 shall extend only to the territory in respect of which a valid, UK, GB or NI authorisation has been issued and where the authorisation—

(a) is the first authorisation for the product in the territory in accordance with Article 3(b) and (d), and

(b) has been issued before the certificate takes effect in accordance with Article 13(1).

1b. Where after the submission of an application for a certificate in accordance with Article 7(1) or (2) and before the certificate takes effect in accordance with Article 13(1), a GB or NI authorisation is granted in respect of the same product and the authorisation would have met the requirements of Article 3(b) and (d) had it been granted on the date of submission of the application, the protection conferred by a certificate in accordance with paragraph 1 shall extend to the territory of England and Wales and Scotland or the territory of Northern Ireland as the case may be.

2. By way of derogation from paragraph 1, the certificate referred to in paragraph 1 shall not confer protection against certain acts which would otherwise require the consent of the holder of the certificate ("the certificate holder"), if the following conditions are met:

(a) the acts comprise:

(i) the making of a product, or a medicinal product containing that product, for the purpose of export to countries outside the United Kingdom, the Isle of Man and the Member States of the European Union; or

(ii) any related act that is strictly necessary for the making, in the United Kingdom, referred to in point (i), or for the actual export; or

(iii) the making, no earlier than six months before the expiry of the certificate, of a product, or a medicinal product containing that product, for the purpose of storing it in the United Kingdom, in order to place that product, or a medicinal product containing that product, on the market of the United Kingdom, the Isle of Man or one or more Member States of the European Union after the expiry of the corresponding certificate; or

  (iv) any related act that is strictly necessary for the making, in the United Kingdom, referred to in point (iii), or for the actual storing, provided that such related act is carried out no earlier than six months before the expiry of the certificate.

(b) the maker, through appropriate and documented means, notifies the comptroller, and informs the certificate holder, of the information listed in paragraph 5 of this Article no later than three months before the start date of the making in the United Kingdom, or no later than three months before the first related act, prior to that making, that would otherwise be prohibited by the protection conferred by that certificate, whichever is the earlier;

(c) if the information listed in paragraph 5 of this Article changes, the maker notifies the comptroller and informs the certificate holder, before those changes take effect;

(d) in the case of products, or medicinal products containing those products, made for the purpose of export to countries outside the United Kingdom, the Isle of Man and the Member States of the European Union, the maker ensures that the words 'UK export' are affixed so as to be sufficiently clear and visible to the naked eye to the outer packaging of the product, or the medicinal product containing that product, referred to in point (a)(i) of this paragraph, and, where feasible, to its immediate packaging;

(e) the maker complies with paragraph 9 of this Article.

3.   The exception referred to in paragraph 2 shall not apply to any act or activity carried out for the import of products, or medicinal products containing those products, into the United Kingdom merely for the purpose of repackaging, re-exporting or storing.

4.   The information provided to the certificate holder for the purposes of points (b) and (c) of paragraph 2 shall be used exclusively for the purposes of verifying whether the requirements of this Regulation have been met and, where applicable, initiating legal proceedings for non-compliance.

5.   The information to be provided by the maker for the purposes of point (b) of paragraph 2 shall be as follows:

(a) the name and address of the maker;

(b) an indication of whether the making is for the purpose of export, for the purpose of storing, or for the purpose of both export and storing;

(c) the number of the certificate granted; and

(d) for medicinal products to be exported to countries outside the United Kingdom, the Isle of Man and the Member States of the European Union, the reference number of the marketing authorisation, or the equivalent of such authorisation, in each country of export, as soon as it is publicly available.

6.   For the purposes of notification to the comptroller under points (b) and (c) of paragraph 2, the maker shall use the standard prescribed form.

7.   Failure to comply with the requirements of point (e) of paragraph 5 with regard to a country outside the United Kingdom, the Isle of Man and the Member States of the European Union shall only affect exports to that country, and those exports shall, therefore, not benefit from the exception.

9.   The maker shall ensure, through appropriate and documented means, that any person in a contractual relationship with the maker who performs acts falling under point (a) of paragraph 2 is fully informed and aware of the following:

(a)   that those acts are subject to paragraph 2;

(b)   that the placing on the market, import or re-import of the product, or the medicinal product containing that product, referred to in point (a)(i) of paragraph 2 or the placing on the market of the product, or the medicinal product containing that product, referred to in point (a)(iii) of paragraph 2 could infringe the certificate referred to in paragraph 2 where, and for as long as, that certificate applies.

10.   Paragraph 2 shall apply to certificates that are applied for on or after 1 July 2019.

Paragraph 2 shall also apply to certificates that have been applied for before 1 July 2019 and that take effect on or after that date. Paragraph 2 shall only apply to such certificates from 2 July 2022.

Paragraph 2 shall not apply to certificates that take effect before 1 July 2019.

11.   The Secretary of State may by regulations make further provision as to the manner and form (including design and colour) of affixing the words "UK export" to the outer packaging of the product, or the medicinal product containing that product, referred to in paragraph 2(a)(i) of this Article, and, where feasible, to its immediate packaging.

12.   Those regulations are to be made by statutory instrument which is subject to annulment pursuant to a resolution of either House of Parliament.

Replace Note with:

Note.

Prior to its incorporation into UK law, art.5 was amended by Regulation 2019/933, which entered into force on July 1, 2019. Annex-I and Annex-Ia to Regulation 2019/933 reproduce the logo and the form, respectively, that are required under EU law (as mentioned in art.5(2)(d) and art.5(6) as introduced into Reg.469/2009 by Reg.2019/933).

Article 5 was amended by para.3 of the Schedule to SI 2020/1050, and by reg.13 of SI 2020/1471. Annex-I and Annex-Ia of Reg.469/2009 were deleted by para.6 of the Schedule to SI 2020/1050.

SI 2020/1050 also introduced new r.116A (see §128B.60). The transitional provisions set out in reg.43 of SI 2020/1050:—waive the requirement for marking with the words "UK export" for those medicinal products marked, prior to IP completion day, with a logo set out in Annex-I of Reg.469/2009 (as introduced by Reg.2019/933); and—retain the effective date of a notification made prior to IP completion day and in accordance with Annex-Ia of Reg.469/2009 (as introduced by Reg.2019/933), and treats that notification as if it had been made on the prescribed form (Patents Form SP5).

128B.17   *Replace Article 7—Application for a certificate with:*

Article 7—Application for a certificate

—1.   The application for a certificate shall be lodged within six months of the date on which the UK, GB or NI authorisation referred to in Article 3(b) and (d) to place the product on the market as a medicinal product was granted. Where more than one such authorisation is granted before the application for a certificate is lodged, the application shall be lodged within six months of the date of grant of the earliest of such authorisations.

2.   Notwithstanding paragraph 1, where the authorisation to place the product on the market is granted before the basic patent is granted, the application for a

[142]

certificate shall be lodged within six months of the date on which the patent is granted.

3. The application for an extension of the duration may be made when lodging the application for a certificate or when the application for the certificate is pending and the appropriate requirements of Articles 8(1)(d) or 8(2), respectively, are fulfilled.

4. The application for an extension of the duration of a certificate already granted shall be lodged not later than two years before the expiry of the certificate.

5. Notwithstanding paragraph 4, for five years following the entry into force of Regulation (EC) No 1901/2006, the application for an extension of the duration of a certificate already granted shall be lodged not later than six months before the expiry of the certificate.

Replace Note with:

Note.

Article 7 was amended by reg.14 of SI 2020/1471.

Replace Article 8—Content of the application for a certificate with: **128B.18**

Article 8—Content of the application for a certificate

—**(1)**   The application for a certificate shall contain:
(a)   a request for the grant of a certificate, stating in particular:
  (i)   the name and address of the applicant;
  (ii)   if the applicant has appointed a representative, the name and address of the representative;
  (iii)   the number of the basic patent and the title of the invention;
  (iv)   the number and date of the UK, GB or NI authorisation, or where there is more than one such authorisation, of each authorisation as referred to in Article 3(b) and (d); and
  (v)   the number and date of the earliest EEA authorization, the granting of which predates the granting of the UK, GB or NI authorisation as referred to in Article 3(b) and (d);
(b)   a copy of the UK, GB or NI authorisation or, where there is more than one such authorisation, of each authorisation to place the product on the market, as referred to in Article 3(b) and (d), in which the product is identified, containing in particular the number and date of the authorisation and the summary of the product characteristics listed in Article 11 of Directive 2001/83/EC, Article 14 of Directive 2001/82/EC, Part 2 to Schedule 8 of the Human Medicines Regulations 2012 or Part 1 of Schedule 1 to the Veterinary Medicines Regulations 2013;
(c)   where the product is the subject of one or more EEA authorizations granted prior to the UK, GB or NI authorization referred to in Article 3(1)(b) and (d), the applicant must provide in relation to the earliest of any such EEA authorizations—
  (i)   information regarding the identity of the product thus authorised;
  (ii)   information regarding the legal provision under which the authorisation procedure took place; and

     (iii)   a copy of the notice publishing the authorisation in the appropriate official publication;

(d) where the application for a certificate includes a request for an extension of the duration:

     (i)   a copy of the statement indicating compliance with an agreed completed paediatric investigation plan as referred to in regulation 58A(2)(a) of the Human Medicines Regulations 2012;

     (ii)   details of the territory in respect of which the statement referred to in sub-paragraph (i) has been made.

(2)   Where an application for a certificate is pending, an application for an extended duration in accordance with Article 7(3) shall include the particulars referred to in paragraph 1(d) of this Article and a reference to the application for a certificate already filed.

(3)   The application for an extension of the duration of a certificate already granted shall contain the particulars referred to in paragraph 1(d) and a copy of the certificate already granted.

Replace Notes with:

Notes

1.   Article 8 was amended by reg.55 of SI 2019/801, and by paras 6 and 7 of reg.3 of SI 2020/1471. The amendment to para.(1)(d)(i) of art.8 is subject to the transitional provision of reg.69 of SI 2019/801 (as amended by reg.37 of SI 2020/1050). This essentially applies the former (i.e. pre-Brexit) regulations to SPC extension applications filed but not determined before IP completion day exit day, and to SPC extensions granted either pre-Brexit or pursuant to such applications. The amendments to art.8 made by SI 2020/1471 are subject to the transitional provisions of reg.7 of that SI (see §128B.10). Whilst those transitional provisions do not explicitly address the situation for an application for extension of an SPC, any such extension application will presumably (for the purposes of determining which provisions are to be applied) be treated as if it were "an application for a supplementary protection certificate" in the sense of paras 1 to 3 of the transitional provisions.

2.   Prior to amendment by SI 2019/801 and SI 2020/1471, art.8(1)(c) used the term "on the market as a medicinal product in the Community". This means (as from July 1, 1994) the then existing Member States of the European Community, together with the then EFTA countries, Austria, Finland, Iceland, Norway and Sweden (Decision No.7/94 of the EEA Joint Committee [1994] OJ EC L160/1), as modified by Council Decision of January 1, 1995, upon the accession to the European Community of Austria, Finland and Sweden [1995] OJ EC L1/1 and (from May 1, 1995) also Liechtenstein (Decision No.1/95 of the EEA Council [1995] OJ EC L86/58). Thus, at least for authorisations issued after May 1, 1995, the "Community" means the EEA. Although Switzerland did not become an EEA Member State, until July 1, 2005, marketing authorisations for Switzerland automatically extended to Liechtenstein with immediate effect and therefore are to be taken into account for SPC applications filed from May 1, 1995 to May 31, 2005. On June 1, 2005, a modification to the bilateral agreement between Switzerland and Liechtenstein relating to the recognition by Liechtenstein of authorisations delivered by Swissmedic, the Swiss regulatory body, came into force, according to which authorisations granted by Swissmedic would no longer be recognised immediately in Liechtenstein, but in principle only after 12 months. The Czech Republic, the Republic of Estonia, the Republic of Cyprus, the Republic of Latvia, the Republic of Lithuania, the Republic of Hungary, the Republic of Malta, the Republic of Poland, the Republic of Slovenia and the Slovak Republic acceded to the EU on May 1, 2004. Bulgaria and Romania acceded to the EU on January 1, 2007. Croatia acceded to the EU on 1 July 2013.

Replace Article 9—Lodging of an application for a certificate with: **128B.19**

Article 9—Lodging of an application for a certificate

—1. An application for a certificate (or an extension of the duration of a certificate) shall be lodged with the comptroller.

2. Notification of the application for a certificate shall be published by the comptroller. The notification shall contain at least the following information:

(a) the name and address of the applicant;

(b) the number of the basic patent;

(c) the title of the invention;

(d) the number and date of the UK, GB or NI authorisation or, where there is more than one such authorisation, each authorisation provided under Article 8(1)(b), the product identified in the authorisation or each authorisation and the territory in respect of which the authorisation has been granted or has effect as if granted;

(e) where there are authorizations granted in the EEA before any UK, GB or NI authorisation provided under Article 8(1)(b), the number and date of the earliest EEA authorisation;

(f) where applicable, an indication that the application includes an application for an extension of the duration;

(g) where an indication is given in accordance with sub-paragraph (f), details of the territory in respect of which an extension has been applied for.

3. Paragraph 2 shall apply to the notification of the application for an extension of the duration of a certificate already granted or where an application for a certificate is pending. The notification shall additionally contain an indication of the application for an extended duration of the certificate.

Replace Note with:

Note.

Article 9 was amended by reg.56 of SI 2019/801, and by reg.3(8) of SI 2020/1471. For the EU law meaning of the term "market in the Community" (as used in art.9(2)(e) of the original Reg.469/2009), see the Notes to §128B.18.

Replace Article 10—Grant of the certificate or rejection of the application with: **128B.20**

Article 10—Grant of the certificate or rejection of the application

—1. Where the application for a certificate and the product to which it relates meet the conditions laid down in this Regulation, the comptroller shall grant the certificate.

2. The comptroller shall, subject to paragraph 3, reject the application for a certificate if the application or the product to which it relates does not meet the conditions laid down in this Regulation or any prescribed fee is not paid.

3. Where the application for a certificate does not meet the conditions laid down in Article 8 or the prescribed fee relating to the application has not been paid, the comptroller shall ask the applicant to rectify the irregularity, or to settle the fee, within a stated time.

4. If the irregularity is not rectified or the fee is not settled under paragraph 3 within the stated time, the comptroller shall reject the application.

5. Paragraphs 1 to 4 shall apply mutatis mutandis to the application for an extension of the duration.

Add new Note after Article 10—Grant of the certificate or rejection of the application:

Note.

Article 10 was amended by reg.57 of SI 2019/801, and by reg.3(9) of SI 2020/1471.

128B.21 *Replace Article 11—Publication with:*

Article 11—Publication

—1. Notification of the fact that a certificate has been granted shall be published by the comptroller. The notification shall contain at least the following information:
(a) the name and address of the holder of the certificate;
(b) the number of the basic patent;
(c) the title of the invention;
(d) the number and date of the UK, GB or NI authorisation or, where there is more than one such authorisation, of each authorisation provided under Article 8(1)(b) or Article 13A(1), the product identified in the authorisation and the territory in respect of which the authorisation has been granted or has effect as if granted;
(e) where there are EEA authorizations granted before any UK, GB or NI authorisation provided under Article 8(1)(b), the number and date of the earliest EEA authorisation;
(f) the duration of the certificate.
2. Notification of the fact that the application for a certificate has been rejected shall be published by the comptroller. The notification shall contain at least the information listed in Article 9(2).
3. Paragraphs 1 and 2 shall apply to the notification of the fact that an extension of the duration of a certificate has been granted or of the fact that the application for an extension has been rejected.
3a. Where notification is made that an extension of the duration of a certificate has been granted, the notification shall specify the territory in respect of which the extension has been granted.
4. The comptroller shall publish, as soon as possible, the information listed in Article 5(5), together with the date of notification of that information. The comptroller shall also publish, as soon as possible, any changes to the information notified in accordance with point (c) of Article 5(2).

Replace Note with:

Note.

Paragraph 4 of art.11 was introduced by Reg.2019/933, which entered into force on July 1, 2019.
For the purposes of incorporation into UK law, art.11 was amended by reg.58 of SI 2019/801, para.4 of the Schedule to SI 2020/1050, and by reg.17 of SI 2020/1471.

Replace Article 12—Annual fees with: **128B.22**

Article 12—Annual fees

[Deleted]

Replace Note with:

Note.

Article 12 was amended (by introduction of para.2 of) by Regulation (EU) 2019/933. For the purposes of incorporation into UK law, art.12 was deleted (by reg.59 of SI 2019/801).

Replace Article 13—Duration of the certificate with: **128B.23**

Article 13—Duration of the certificate

—1. The certificate shall take effect at the end of the lawful term of the basic patent for a period equal to the period which elapsed between the date on which the application for a basic patent was lodged and the date of the first authorisation to place the product on the market in the area comprising the European Economic Area and the United Kingdom, reduced by a period of five years.
2. Notwithstanding paragraph 1, the duration of the certificate may not exceed five years from the date on which it takes effect.
3. The periods laid down in paragraphs 1 and 2 shall be extended by six months in the case where regulation 58A(2)(a) of the Human Medicines Regulations 2012 applies. In that case, the duration of the period laid down in paragraph 1 of this Article may be extended only once.
4. Where a certificate is granted for a product protected by a patent which, before 2 January 1993, had its term extended or for which such extension was applied for, under national law, the term of protection to be afforded under this certificate shall be reduced by the number of years by which the term of the patent exceeds 20 years.
5. An extension of the duration of a certificate in accordance with paragraph 3 in respect of—
    (a) a UK authorisation shall apply in the United Kingdom,
    (b) a GB authorisation shall apply in only England and Wales and Scotland, and
    (c) a NI authorisation shall apply in Northern Ireland only,
on condition that the territorial protection conferred by the extension does not exceed that conferred by the certificate.

Replace Note with:

Note.

Article 13 was amended by reg.60 of SI 2019/801, and by para.18 of the Schedule to SI 2020/1471. The amendment to art.13(3) is subject to the transitional provisions of reg.69 of SI 2019/801 (see Note 1 to §128B.18). Article 13(5) is subject to the transitional provisions of reg.7 of SI 2020/1471. Amongst other things, this means that the pre-Brexit version of art.13 (which excludes art.13(5)) applies to SPC applications "made, but not determined, before IP completion day in respect of a UK authorisation granted or having effect as if granted before IP completion day".
For the EU law meaning of the term "market in the Community" (as used in art.13(1) of the original Reg.469/2009), see Note 2 to §128B.18.

128B.23A *Add new paragraph §128B.23A:*

Article 13A—Authorisation granted after submission of an application for a certificate

—1. Where after the date of submission of an application under Article 7(1) or (2), but before the grant of a certificate under Article 10(1) in relation to a NI authorisation, a valid UK or GB authorisation is granted which, at its date of grant, is the first authorisation to place the product on the market as a medicinal product in the territory of the United Kingdom or the territory of England and Wales and Scotland as the case may be, the applicant shall notify the comptroller of the grant of the authorisation, within six months of its date of grant and before the certificate takes effect under Article 13(1), and provide the details set out in Article 8(1)(a)(iv) and (b) on the prescribed form.

2. Where after the submission of an application under Article 7(1) or (2), but before the grant of a certificate under Article 10(1) in relation to a UK or GB authorisation, a valid NI authorisation is granted which, at its date of grant, is the first authorisation to place the product on the market as a medicinal product in the territory of Northern Ireland, the applicant shall notify the comptroller of the grant of the authorisation, within six months of its date of grant and before the certificate takes effect under Article 13(1), and provide the details set out in Article 8(1)(a)(iv) and (b) on the prescribed form.

3. Where after the grant of a certificate under Article 10(1) in relation to a UK or GB authorisation, but before expiry of the basic patent, a valid NI authorisation is granted which, at its date of grant, is the first authorisation to place the product on the market as a medicinal product in the territory of Northern Ireland, the certificate holder shall notify the comptroller of the grant of the authorisation, within six months of its date of grant and before the certificate takes effect under Article 13(1), and provide the details set out in Article 8(1)(a)(iv) and (b) on the prescribed form.

4. Where after the grant of a certificate under Article 10(1) in relation to a NI authorisation, but before expiry of the basic patent, a valid UK or GB authorisation is granted which, at its date of grant, is the first authorisation to place the product on the market as a medicinal product in the territory of the United Kingdom or the territory of England and Wales and Scotland as the case may be, the certificate holder shall notify the comptroller of the grant of the NI authorisation, within six months of its date of grant and before the certificate takes effect under Article 13(1), and provide the details set out in Article 8(1)(a)(iv) and (b) on the prescribed form.

5. If the applicant or the certificate holder fails to notify the comptroller of the grant of an authorisation in accordance with paragraph 1, 2, 3 or 4 the protection conferred by a certificate granted under Article 10 shall not extend to any additional territory covered by that authorisation.

6. On receipt of a notification under any of paragraphs 1 to 4, the comptroller shall publish:
   (a) the number and date of the authorisation,
   (b) the product identified in that authorisation, and
   (c) the territory in respect of which the authorisation has been granted or has effect as if granted.

Note.

Article 13A was introduced by para.19 of the Schedule to SI 2020/1471. Article 13A is subject to the transitional provisions of reg.7 of SI 2020/1471. Amongst other things, this means that the pre-Brexit version of Reg.469/2009 (which excludes art.13A) applies to SPC applications "made, but not determined, before IP completion day in respect of a UK authorisation granted or having effect as if granted before IP completion day". The IPO has published some guidance that discusses this point (*https://www.gov.uk/guidance/spcs-and-the-northern-ireland-protocol*). However, it is understood that, for SPC applications filed before January 1, 2021, the IPO may ask for the GB product licence number for any product whose (EU) "centralised" Marketing Authorisation has been converted to a GB licence via a "grandfathering" process. (See also *https://www.gov.uk/guidance/converting-centrally-authorised-products-caps-to-uk-marketing-authorisations-mas-grandfathering-and-managing-lifecycle-changes*.)

Add new paragraph §128B.23B: 128B.23B

Article 13B—Extension of the duration of a certificate

—**1.** Where after an application for an extension of the duration of a certificate in accordance with Article 7(3) or (4) has been made in respect of a GB authorisation, but before the application is granted, an application is also made for an extension of the duration of the certificate in respect of a NI authorisation in accordance with Article 7(3) or (4), the duration of the certificate, if the extension is granted, shall be extended in accordance with Article 13(3) and (5) to include the territory of Northern Ireland.

2. Where after an application for an extension of the duration of a certificate in accordance with Article 7(3) or (4) has been made in respect of a NI authorisation, but before the application is granted, an application is also made for an extension of the duration of the certificate in respect of a GB authorisation in accordance with Article 7(3) or (4), the duration of the certificate shall be extended in accordance with Article 13(3) and (5) to include the territory of England and Wales and Scotland.

3. Where after the grant in accordance with Article 10(6) of an application for an extension of the duration of a certificate in respect of a GB authorisation, an application is made, in accordance with Article 7(4), for an extension of the certificate in respect of a NI authorisation, the duration of the certificate shall be extended in accordance with Article 13(3) and (5) to include the territory of Northern Ireland.

4. Where after the grant, in accordance with Article 10(6) of an application for an extension of the duration of a certificate in respect of a NI authorisation, an application is made, in accordance with Article 7(4), for an extension of the certificate in relation to a GB authorisation, the duration of the certificate shall be extended in accordance with Article13(3) and (5) to include the territory of England and Wales and Scotland.

Note.

Article 13B was introduced by para.19 of the Schedule to SI 2020/1471. Article 13B is subject to the transitional provisions of reg.7 of SI 2020/1471 (see the Notes to §128B.23 and §128B.23A). Whilst those transitional provisions do not explicitly address the situation for an application for extension of an SPC, any such extension application will presumably (for the purposes of determining which provisions are to be applied) be treated as if it were "an application for a supplementary protection certificate" in the sense of paras 1 to 3 of the transitional provisions.

128B.24   *Replace Article 14—Expiry of the certificate with:*

Article 14—Expiry of the certificate

—1.   The certificate shall lapse:

(a)   at the end of the period provided for in Article 13;

(b)   if the certificate-holder surrenders it;

(c)   if the prescribed annual fee is not paid in time;

(d)   if and as long as the product covered by the certificate may no longer be placed on the market following the withdrawal of all UK, GB and NI authorisations to place on the market. The comptroller referred to in Article 9(1) of this Regulation may decide on the lapse of the certificate either of the comptroller's own motion or at the request of a third party.

2.   Where a UK authorisation is withdrawn and replaced simultaneously with a GB authorisation and a NI authorisation, the certificate granted in respect of the UK authorisation shall not lapse.

3.   Where a UK, GB or NI authorisation is withdrawn, but one or more such authorisations remain valid, the protection conferred by the certificate shall, as from the date of withdrawal, no longer extend to the territory covered by the authorisation withdrawn but shall continue in respect of the territory covered by any remaining authorisation.

Replace Note with:

Note.

Article 14 was amended by reg.61 of SI 2019/801, and by reg.3(11) of, and para.20 of the Schedule to, SI 2020/1471. The transitional provisions of reg.7 of SI 2020/1471 do not explicitly address the situation for SPCs granted prior to IP completion day. However, the intention appears to have been for the provisions of art.14 as amended to be applied to such SPCs.

128B.25   *Replace Article 15—Invalidity of the certificate with:*

Article 15—Invalidity of the certificate

—1.   The certificate shall be invalid if:

(a)   it was granted contrary to the provisions of Article 3;

(b)   the basic patent has lapsed before its lawful term expires;

(c)   the basic patent is revoked or limited to the extent that the product for which the certificate was granted would no longer be protected by the claims of the basic patent or, after the basic patent has expired, grounds for revocation exist which would have justified such revocation or limitation.

2.   Any person may submit an application or bring an action for a declaration of invalidity of the certificate before the comptroller or the court.

Add new Note after Article 15—Invalidity of the certificate:

Note.

Article 15 was amended by reg.62 of SI 2019/801 and reg.36 of SI 2020/1050.

Replace Article 16—Revocation of an extension of the duration with: **128B.26**

Article 16—Revocation of an extension of the duration

—**1.**   The extension of the duration may be revoked if it was granted contrary to the provisions of regulation 58A(2)(a) of the Human Medicines Regulations 2012.
2.   Any person may submit an application for revocation of the extension of the duration to the comptroller or the court.

Add new Note after Article 16—Revocation of an extension of the duration:

Note.

    Article 16 was amended by reg.63 of SI 2019/801. The amendment to art.16(1) is subject to the transitional provision of reg.69 of SI 2019/801 (as amended by reg.37 of SI 2020/1050). This essentially applies the former (i.e. pre-Brexit) regulations to SPC extension applications filed but not determined before IP completion day exit day, and to SPC extensions granted either pre-Brexit or pursuant to such applications.

Replace Article 17—Notification of lapse or invalidity with: **128B.27**

Article 17—Notification of lapse or invalidity

—**1.**   If the certificate lapses in accordance with point (b), (c) or (d) of Article 14, or is invalid in accordance with Article 15, or if the territorial extent of the certificate is limited in accordance with Article 14(3), notification thereof shall be published by the comptroller.
2.   If the extension of the duration is revoked in accordance with Article 16, notification thereof shall be published by the comptroller.

Add new Note after Article 17—Notification of lapse or invalidity:

Note.

    Article 17 was amended by reg.64 of SI 2019/801, and by para.21 of the Schedule to SI 2020/1471.

Replace Article 18—Appeals with: **128B.28**

Article 18—Appeals

[Deleted]

Add new Note after Article 18—Appeals::

Note.

    For the purposes of incorporation into UK law, art.18 was deleted (by reg.65 of SI 2019/801).

Replace Article 19—Procedure with: **128B.29**

Article 19—Procedure

—**1.**   In the absence of procedural provisions in this Regulation, the procedural provisions applicable to the corresponding basic patent (as modified by section 128B of, and Schedule 4A to, the Patents Act 1977) shall apply to the certificate.

2. Notwithstanding paragraph 1, the procedure for opposition to the granting of a certificate shall be excluded.

Add new Note after Article 19—Procedure:

Note.

Article 19 was amended by reg.66 of SI 2019/801.

128B.30 *Replace Article 20—Additional provisions relating to the enlargement of the Community with:*

Article 20—Additional provisions relating to the enlargement of the Community

[This Article is not relevant in the UK. For the purposes of incorporation into UK law, art.20 was deleted (by reg.67 of SI 2019/801).]

128B.31 *Replace Article 21—Transitional provisions with:*

Article 21—Transitional provisions

[Deleted]

Replace Note with:

Note.

For the purposes of incorporation into UK law, art.21 was deleted (by reg.67 of SI 2019/801).

128B.31A *Add new paragraph §128B.31A:*

Article 21a Evaluation

[Deleted]

Add new Note:

Note.

Article 21a was introduced by Reg.2019/933. For the purposes of incorporation into UK law, art.21a was deleted (by para.5 of the Schedule to SI 2020/1050).

128B.33 *Replace Article 23—Entry into force with:*

Article 23—Entry into force

This Regulation shall enter into force on the 20th day following its publication in the Official *Journal of the European Communities*.

Replace Note with:

Note.

Article 23 was amended by reg.68 of SI 2019/801.

Replace paragraphs §§128B.34 and 128B.35 with:

Regulation (EC) No. 1610/96 of the European Parliament and of the Council of 23 July 1996 concerning the creation of a supplementary protection certificate for plant protection products (as incorporated into UK law)

THE EUROPEAN PARLIAMENT AND THE COUNCIL OF THE EURO-   **128B.34**
PEAN UNION

Having regard to the Treaty establishing the European Community, and in particular Article 100a thereof,

Having regard to the proposal from the Commission [[1994] OJ EC, C390/21],

Having regard to the opinion of the Economic and Social Committee [[1995] OJ EC, C155/14],

Acting in accordance with the procedure referred to in Article 189b of the Treaty[Opinion of the European Parliament, [1995] OJ EC C166/89; common position of the Council, [1995] OJ EC C353/36; and decision of the European Parliament, [1996] OJ EC C96/30],

(1) Whereas research into plant protection products contributes to the continuing improvement in the production and procurement of plentiful food of good quality at affordable prices;

(2) Whereas plant protection research contributes to the continuing improvement in crop production;

(3) Whereas plant protection products, especially those that are the result of long, costly research, will continue to be developed in the Community and in Europe if they are covered by favourable rules that provide for sufficient protection to encourage such research;

(4) Whereas the competitiveness of the plant protection sector, by the very nature of that industry, requires a level of protection for innovation which is equivalent to that granted to medicinal products by Council Regulation (EEC) No 1768/92 of 18 June 1992 concerning the creation of a supplementary protection certificate for medicinal products [[1992] OJ EC L182/1];

(5) Whereas, at the moment, the period that elapses between the filing of an application for a patent for a new plant protection product and authorisation to place the said plant protection product on the market makes the period of effective protection under the patent insufficient to cover the investment put into the research and to generate the resources needed to maintain a high level of research;

(6) Whereas this situation leads to a lack of protection which penalizes plant protection research and the competitiveness of the sector;

(7) Whereas one of the main objectives of the supplementary protection certificate is to place European industry on the same competitive footing as its North American and Japanese counterparts;

(8) Whereas, in its Resolution of 1 February 1993 [[1993] OJ EC C138/1] on a Community programme of policy and action in relation to the environment and sustainable development, the Council adopted the general approach and strategy of the programme presented by the Commission, which stressed the interdependence of economic growth and environmental quality; whereas improved protection of the environment means maintaining the economic competitiveness of industry;

[153]

whereas, accordingly, the issue of a supplementary protection certificate can be regarded as a positive measure in favour of environmental protection;

(9) Whereas a uniform solution at Community level should be provided for, thereby preventing the heterogeneous development of national laws leading to further disparities which would be likely to hinder the free movement of plant protection products within the Community and thus directly affect the functioning of the internal market; whereas this is in accordance with the principle of subsidiarity as defined by Article 3b of the Treaty;

(10) Whereas, therefore, there is a need to create a supplementary protection certificate granted, under the same conditions, by each of the Member States at the request of the holder of a national or European patent relating to a plant protection product for which marketing authorisation has been granted is necessary; whereas a Regulation is therefore the most appropriate legal instrument;

(11) Whereas the duration of the protection granted by the certificate should be such as to provide adequate, effective protection; whereas, for this purpose, the holder of both a patent and a certificate should be able to enjoy an overall maximum of fifteen years of exclusivity from the time the plant protection product in question first obtains authorisation to be placed on the market in the Community;

(12) Whereas all the interests at stake in a sector as complex and sensitive as plant protection must nevertheless be taken into account; whereas, for this purpose, the certificate cannot be granted for a period exceeding five years;

(13) Whereas the certificate confers the same rights as those conferred by the basic patent; whereas, consequently, where the basic patent covers an active substance and its various derivatives (salts and esters), the certificate confers the same protection;

(14) Whereas the issue of a certificate for a product consisting of an active substance does not prejudice the issue of other certificates for derivatives (salts and esters) of the substance, provided that the derivatives are the subject of patents specifically covering them;

(15) Whereas a fair balance should also be struck with regard to the determination of the transitional arrangements; whereas such arrangements should enable the Community plant protection industry to catch up to some extent with its main competitors, while making sure that the arrangements do not compromise the achievement of other legitimate objectives concerning the agricultural policy and environment protection policy pursued at both national and Community level;

(16) Whereas only action at Community level will enable the objective, which consists in ensuring adequate protection for innovation in the field of plant protection, while guaranteeing the proper functioning of the internal market for plant protection products, to be attained effectively;

(17) Whereas the detailed rules in recitals 12, 13 and 14 and in Articles 3(2), 4, 8(1)(c) and 17(2) of this Regulation are also valid, mutatis mutandis, for the interpretation in particular of recital 9 and Articles 3, 4, 8(1)(c) and 17 of Council Regulation (EEC) No 1768/92.

HAVE ADOPTED THIS REGULATION

Article 1—Definitions

128B.35   For the purposes of this Regulation, the following definitions shall apply:

1. "plant protection products": active substances and preparations containing one or more active substances, put up in the form in which they are supplied to the user, intended to:

(a) protect plants or plant products against all harmful organisms or prevent the action of such organisms, in so far as such substances or preparations are not otherwise defined below;

(b) influence the life processes of plants, other than as a nutrient (e.g. plant growth regulators);

(c) preserve plant products, in so far as such substances or products are not subject to special provisions on preservations;

(d) destroy undesirable plants; or

(e) destroy parts of plants, check or prevent undesirable growth of plants;

2. "substances": chemical elements and their compounds, as they occur naturally or by manufacture, including any impurity inevitably resulting from the manufacturing process;

3. "active substances": substances or micro-organisms including viruses, having general or specific action;

(a) against harmful organisms; or

(b) on plants, parts of plants or plant products;

4. "preparations": mixtures or solutions composed of two or more substances, of which at least one is an active substance, intended for use as plant protection products;

5. "plants": live plants and live parts of plants, including fresh fruit and seeds;

6. "plant products": products in the unprocessed state or having undergone only simple preparation such as milling, drying or pressing, derived from plants, but excluding plants themselves as defined in point 5;

7. "harmful organisms": pests of plants or plant products belonging to the animal or plant kingdom, and also viruses, bacteria and mycoplasmas and other pathogens;

8. "product": the active substance as defined in point 3 or combination of active substances of a plant protection product;

9. "basic patent": a patent which protects a product as defined in point 8 as such, a preparation as defined in point 4, a process to obtain a product or an application of a product, and which is designated by its holder for the purpose of the procedure for grant of a certificate;

10. "certificate": the supplementary protection certificate.

11. 'comptroller' means the Comptroller-General of Patents, Designs and Trade Marks;

12. 'court' means— :

(i) as respects England and Wales, the High Court;

(ii) as respects Scotland, the Court of Session; and

(iii) as respects Northern Ireland, the High Court in Northern Ireland.

13. 'EEA authorization' means an authorization to place a plant protection product on the market which has effect in an EEA state in accordance with Regulation (EC) No 1107/2009;

14. 'patent' means a patent which has effect in the United Kingdom;

15. "GB authorisation" means an authorisation, to place a plant protection product on the market in England and Wales and Scotland, granted or having effect as if granted under Regulation (EC) 1107/2009;

16. "NI authorisation" means an authorisation, to place a plant protection product on the market in Northern Ireland, granted or having effect as if granted in accordance with Regulation (EC) 1107/2009 as it has effect by virtue of the Protocol on Ireland/Northern Ireland in the EU withdrawal agreement;

17. "prescribed" means prescribed by rules under section 123 of the Patents Act 1977.

Note.

Article 1 was amended by reg.20 of SI 2019/801, by reg.31 of SI 2020/1050, and by reg.2(3) of, and para.2 of the Schedule to, SI 2020/1471.

128B.36 *Replace Article 2—Scope with:*

Article 2—Scope

A plant protection product may, under the terms and conditions provided for in this Regulation, be the subject of a certificate if it is:
  (a)   protected by a patent; and
  (b)   the subject of a GB or NI authorization prior to being placed on the market as a plant protection product.

Add new Note after Article 2—Scope:

Note.

Article 2 was amended by reg.22 of SI 2019/801 and by reg.2(4) of SI 2020/1471.

128B.37 *Replace Article 3—Conditions for obtaining a certificate with:*

Article 3—Conditions for obtaining a certificate

—1.   Where an application is submitted under Article 7, a certificate shall be granted if, at the date of submission of the application—
  (a)   the product is protected by a basic patent in force;
  (b)   there is a valid GB or NI authorisation to place the product on the market;
  (c)   the product has not already been the subject of a certificate;
  (d)   the authorisation referred to in (b) is the first authorisation to place the product on the market as a plant protection product in the territory of England and Wales and Scotland or the territory of Northern Ireland as the case may be.

2.   The holder of more than one patent for the same product shall not be granted more than one certificate for that product. However, where two or more applications concerning the same product and emanating from two or more holders of different patents are pending, one certificate for this product may be issued to each of these holders.

Add new Note after Article 3—Conditions for obtaining a certificate:

Note.

Article 3 was amended by reg.23 of SI 2019/801, and by reg.2(5) of SI 2020/1471.

Replace Article 4—Subject-matter of protection with: **128B.38**

Article 4—Subject-matter of protection

Within the limits of the protection conferred by the basic patent, the protection conferred by a certificate shall extend only to the product covered by the GB or NI authorisation or both GB and NI authorisations to place the corresponding plant protection product on the market and for any use of the product as a plant protection product that has been authorised in the United Kingdom before the expiry of the certificate.

Add new Note after Article 4—Subject-matter of protection:

Note.

Article 4 was amended by para.3 of the Schedule to SI 2020/1471.

Replace Article 5—Effects of the certificate with: **128B.39**

Article 5—Effects of the certificate

—**1.** Subject to Article 4, the certificate shall confer the same rights as conferred by the basic patent and shall be subject to the same limitations and the same obligations.

2. The protection conferred by a certificate in accordance with paragraph 1 shall extend only to the territory in respect of which a valid GB or NI authorisation has been issued and the authorisation—

(a) is the first authorisation for the product in the territory in accordance with Article 3(1)(b) and (d), and

(b) has been issued before the certificate takes effect in accordance with Article 13(1).

3. Where after the submission of an application for a certificate in accordance with Article 7 and before the certificate takes effect in accordance with Article 13(1), a GB or NI authorisation is granted in respect of the same product and the authorisation would have met the requirements of Article 3(b) and (d) had it been granted on the date of submission of the application, the protection conferred by a certificate in accordance with paragraph 1 shall extend to the territory of England and Wales and Scotland or the territory of Northern Ireland as the case may be.

Add new Note after Article 5—Effects of the certificate:

Note.

Article 5 was amended by para.4 of the Schedule to SI 2020/1471.

Replace Article 7—Application for a certificate with: **128B.41**

Article 7—Application for a certificate

—**1.** The application for a certificate shall be lodged within six months of the date on which the GB or NI authorisation referred to in Article 3(1)(b) and (d) to place the product on the market as a plant protection product was granted. Where more than one such authorisation is granted before the application for a certificate is lodged, the application shall be lodged within six months of the date of grant of the earliest of such authorisations.

2. Notwithstanding paragraph 1, where the authorisation to place the product on the market is granted before the basic patent is granted, the application for a certificate shall be lodged within six months of the date on which the patent is granted.

Add new Note after Article 7—Application for a certificate:

Note.

Article 7 was amended by para.5 of the Schedule to SI 2020/1471.

128B.42 *Replace Article 8—Content of the application for a certificate with:*

Article 8—Content of the application for a certificate

—1. The application for a certificate shall contain:
(a) a request for the grant of a certificate, stating in particular:
  (i) the name and address of the applicant;
  (ii) the name and address of the representative, if any;
  (iii) the number of the basic patent and the title of the invention;
  (iv) the number and date of the GB or NI authorisation or both GB and NI authorisations, as referred to in Article 3(1)(b) and (d); and
  (v) the number and date of the earliest EEA authorization, the granting of which predates the granting of the GB or NI authorization as referred to in Article 3(1)(b) and (d);
(b) a copy of the GB or NI authorisation or both GB and NI authorisations to place the product on the market, as referred to in Article 3(1)(b) and (d), in which the product is identified, containing in particular the number and date of the authorisation and the summary of the product characteristics listed in Commission Regulation 283/2013, Part A section 1, points 1.1 to 1.7 or Part B, Section 1 points 1.1 to 1.4.3;
(c) where the product is the subject of one or more EEA authorizations granted prior to the GB or NI authorization referred to in Article 3(1)(b) and (d), the applicant must provide in relation to the earliest of any such EEA authorizations—
  (i) information regarding the identity of the product thus authorised;
  (ii) information regarding the legal provision under which the authorisation procedure took place; and
  (iii) a copy of the notice publishing the authorisation in the appropriate official publication or, failing such a notice, any other document proving that the authorisation has been issued, the date on which it was issued and the identity of the product authorised.

Add new Note after Article 8—Content of the application for a certificate:

Note.

Article 8 was amended by reg.24 of SI 2019/801, by reg.33 of SI 2020/1050, and by regs 2(6) and 2(7) of SI 2020/1471.

Replace Article 9—Lodging of an application for a certificate with: **128B.43**

Article 9—Lodging of an application for a certificate

—1.   The application for a certificate shall be lodged with the comptroller.
2.   Notification of the application for a certificate shall be published by the comptroller. The notification shall contain at least the following information:
(a)   the name and address of the applicant;
(b)   the number of the basic patent;
(c)   the title of the invention;
(d)   the number and date of the GB or NI authorisation or both a GB and a NI authorisation provided under Article 8(1)(b), the product identified in the authorisation and the territory in respect of which the authorisation has been granted or has effect as if granted;
(e)   where there are EEA authorizations granted before any GB or NI authorisation provided under Article 8(1)(b), the number and date of the earliest EEA authorisation.

Add new Note after Article 9—Lodging of an application for a certificate:

Note.

Article 9 was amended by reg.25 of SI 2019/801, and by reg.2(8) of SI 2020/1471.

Replace Article 10—Grant of the certificate or rejection of the application with: **128B.44**

Article 10—Grant of the certificate or rejection of the application

—1.   Where the application for a certificate and the product to which it relates meet the conditions laid down in this Regulation, the comptroller shall grant the certificate.
2.   The comptroller shall, subject to paragraph 3, reject the application for a certificate if the application or the product to which it relates does not meet the conditions laid down in this Regulation or any prescribed fee is not paid.
3.   Where the application for a certificate does not meet the conditions laid down in Article 8 or the prescribed fee relating to the application has not been paid, the comptroller shall ask the applicant to rectify the irregularity, or to settle the fee, within a stated time.
4.   If the irregularity is not rectified or the fee is not settled under paragraph 3 within the stated time, the authority shall reject the application.

Add new Note after Article 10—Grant of the certificate or rejection of the application:

Note.

Article 10 was amended by reg.26 of SI 2019/801, and by reg.2(9) of SI 2020/1471.

128B.45   *Replace Article 11—Publication with:*

Article 11—Publication

—1.   Notification of the fact that a certificate has been granted shall be published by the comptroller. The notification shall contain at least the following information:

(a)   the name and address of the holder of the certificate;

(b)   the number of the basic patent;

(c)   the title of the invention;

(d)   the number and date of the UK, GB or NI authorisation or, where there is more than one such authorisation, of each authorisation provided under Article 8(1)(b) the product identified in that authorisation and the territory in respect of which the authorisation has been granted or has effect as if granted;

(e)   where there are EEA authorizations granted before any authorisation provided under Article 8(1)(b), the number and date of the earliest EEA authorisation;

(f)   the duration of the certificate;

2.   Notification of the fact that the application for a certificate has been rejected shall be published by the comptroller. The notification shall contain at least the information listed in Article 9(2).

Add new Note after Article 11—Publication:

Note.

Article 11 was amended by reg.27 of SI 2019/801, and by regs 2(10) and 2(11) of, and para.6 of the Schedule to, SI 2020/1471.

128B.46   *Replace Article 12—Annual fees with:*

Article 12—Annual fees

[Deleted]

Add new Note after Article 12—Annual fees:

Note.

For the purposes of incorporation into UK law, art.12 was deleted (by reg.28 of SI 2019/801).

128B.47   *Replace Article 13—Duration of the certificate with:*

Article 13—Duration of the certificate

—1.   The certificate shall take effect at the end of the lawful terms of the basic patent for a period equal to the period which elapsed between the date on which the application for a basic patent was lodged and the date of the first authorisation to place the product on the market in the area comprising the European Economic Area and the United Kingdom reduced by a period of five years.

2.   Notwithstanding paragraph 1, the duration of the certificate may not exceed five years from the date on which it takes effect.

3.   For the purposes of calculating the duration of the certificate, account shall be taken of a provisional first marketing authorisation only if it is directly followed by a definitive authorisation concerning the same product.

Add new Note after Article 13—Duration of the certificate:

Note.

Article 13 was amended by reg.29 of SI 2019/801.

Add new paragraph §128B.47A:

Article 13A—Authorisation granted after submission of an application for a certificate

—1. Where after the submission of an application under Article 7(1), but before **128B.47A** the grant of a certificate under Article 10(1) in relation to a GB authorisation, a valid NI authorisation is granted which, at its date of grant, is the first authorisation to place the product on the market as a plant protection product in the territory of Northern Ireland, the applicant shall notify the comptroller of the grant of the NI authorisation, within six months of its date of grant and before the certificate takes effect under Article 13(1), and provide the details set out in Article 8(1)(a)(iv) and (b) on the prescribed form.

2. Where after the submission of an application under Article 7(1), but before the grant of a certificate under Article 10(1) in relation to a NI authorisation, a valid GB authorisation is granted which, at its date of grant, is the first authorisation to place the product on the market as a plant protection product in the territory of England and Wales and Scotland, the applicant shall notify the comptroller of the grant of the GB authorisation, within six months of its date of grant and before the certificate takes effect under Article 13(1), and provide the details set out in Article 8(1)(a)(iv) and (b) on the prescribed form.

3. Where after the grant of a certificate under Article 10(1) in relation to a GB authorisation, but before expiry of the basic patent, a valid NI authorisation is granted which, at its date of grant, is the first authorisation to place the product on the market as a plant protection product in the territory of Northern Ireland, the certificate holder shall notify the comptroller of the NI authorisation, within six months of its date of grant and before the certificate takes effect under Article 13(1), and provide the details set out in Article 8(1)(a)(iv) and (b) on the prescribed form.

4. Where after the grant of a certificate under Article 10(1) in relation to a NI authorisation, but before expiry of the basic patent, a valid GB authorisation is granted which, at its date of grant, is the first authorisation to place the product on the market as a plant protection product in the territory of England and Wales and Scotland, the certificate holder shall notify the comptroller of the grant of the GB authorisation, within six months of its date of grant and before the certificate takes effect under Article 13(1), and provide the details set out in Article 8(1)(a)(iv) and (b) on the prescribed form.

5. If the applicant or certificate holder fails to notify the comptroller of the grant of an authorisation in accordance with any of paragraphs 1 to 4, the protection conferred by a certificate granted under Article 10(1) shall not extend to any additional territory covered by that authorisation.

6. On receipt of a notification under any of paragraphs 1 to 4, the comptroller shall publish:
(a) the number and date of the authorisation,
(b) the product identified in that authorisation, and

(c) the territory in respect of which the authorisation has been granted or has effect as if granted.

Note.

Article 13A was introduced by para.7 of the Schedule to SI 2020/1471. Article 13A is subject to the transitional provisions of reg.7 of SI 2020/1471. Amongst other things, this means that the pre-Brexit version of Reg.469/2009 (which excludes art.13A) applies to SPC applications "made, but not determined, before IP completion day in respect of a UK authorisation granted or having effect as if granted before IP completion day". The IPO has published some guidance that discusses this point (*https ://www.gov.uk/guidance/spcs-and-the-northern-ireland-protocol*).

128B.48   *Replace Article 14—Expiry of the certificate with:*

Article 14—Expiry of the certificate

—**1.**   The certificate shall lapse:
(a)   at the end of the period provided for in Article 13;
(b)   if the certificate-holder surrenders it;
(c)   if the prescribed annual fee is not paid in time;
(d)   if and as long as the product covered by the certificate may no longer be placed on the market following the withdrawal of all authorisations to place on the market in accordance with Article 28 of Regulation 1107/2009. The comptroller may decide on the lapse of the certificate either of the comptroller's own motion or at the request of a third party.
2.   Where a UK authorisation is withdrawn and replaced simultaneously with a GB authorisation and a NI authorisation, the certificate granted in respect of the UK authorisation shall not lapse.
3.   Where a UK, GB or NI authorisation is withdrawn, but one or more such authorisations remain valid, the protection conferred by the certificate shall, as from the date of withdrawal, no longer extend to the territory covered by the authorisation withdrawn but shall continue in respect of the territory covered by any remaining authorisation.
4.   For the purposes of paragraphs 2 and 3, "UK authorisation" means an authorisation to place a plant protection product on the market in the United Kingdom, granted or having effect as if granted, prior to IP completion day, under Regulation (EC) 1107/2009 of the European Parliament and of the Council of 21 October 2009 concerning the placing of plant protection products on the market.

Add new Note after Article 14—Expiry of the certificate:

Note.

Article 14 was amended by reg.30 of SI 2019/801, and by regs 2(12) and 2(13) of, and para.8 of the Schedule to, SI 2020/1471.

128B.49   *Replace Article 15—Invalidity of the certificate with:*

Article 15—Invalidity of the certificate

—**1.**   The certificate shall be invalid if:
(a)   it was granted contrary to the provisions of Article 3;
(b)   the basic patent has lapsed before its lawful term expires;

(c) the basic patent is revoked or limited to the extent that the product for which the certificate was granted would no longer be protected by the claims of the basic patent or, after the basic patent has expired, grounds for revocation exist which would have justified such revocation or limitation.

2. Any person may submit an application or bring an action for a declaration of invalidity of the certificate before the comptroller or the court.

Add new Note after Article 15—Invalidity of the certificate:

Note.

Article 15 was amended by reg.31 of SI 2019/801.

Replace Article 16—Notification of lapse or invalidity with: **128B.50**

Article 16—Notification of lapse or invalidity

If the certificate lapses in accordance with Article 14(1) (b), (c) or (d) or is invalid in accordance with Article 15, or if the territorial extent of the certificate is limited in accordance with Article 14(3), notification thereof shall be published by the comptroller.

Add new Note after Article 16—Notification of lapse or invalidity:

Note.

Article 16 was amended by reg.32 of SI 2019/801, and by para.9 of the Schedule to SI 2020/1471.

Replace Article 17—Appeals with: **128B.51**

Article 17—Appeals

—1. The decision to grant the certificate shall be open to an appeal aimed at rectifying the duration of the certificate where the date of first authorisation to place the product on the market in the Community, contained in the application for a certificate as provided for in Article 8, is incorrect.

Add new Note after Article 17—Appeals:

Note.

For the purposes of incorporation into UK law, para.(1) of art.17 was deleted (by reg.33 of SI 2019/801)

Replace Article 18—Procedure with: **128B.52**

Article 18—Procedure

—1. In the absence of procedural provisions in this Regulation, the procedural provisions applicable to the corresponding basic patent (as modified by section 128B of, and Schedule 4A to, the Patents Act 1977) shall apply to the certificate.

2. Notwithstanding paragraph 1, the procedure for opposition to the granting of a certificate shall be excluded.

Add new Note after Article 18—Procedure:

Note.

Article 18 was amended by reg.34 of SI 2019/801.

128B.53   *Replace Article 19 with:*

Article 19

[Deleted]

Add new Note after Article 19:

Note.

For the purposes of incorporation into UK law, art.19 was deleted (by reg.35 of SI 2019/801).

128B.54   *Replace Article 20 with:*

Article 20

[Deleted]

Add new Note after Article 20:

Note.

For the purposes of incorporation into UK law, art.20 was deleted (by reg.35 of SI 2019/801).

128B.55   *Replace Article 21—Entry into force with:*

Article 21—Entry into force

This Regulation shall enter into force six months after its publication in the *Official Journal of the European Communities*[that is, on 8 February 1997].

Add new Note after Article 21—Entry into force:

Note.

Article 21 was amended by reg.36 of SI 2019/801.

128B.56   *Replace heading "Relevant Rule—Rule 116" and paragraph §128B.56 with:*

Relevant Rules—Rules 116 and 116A

Rule 116—Supplementary protection certificates
116.—(1)   An application for—
    (a)   a supplementary protection certificate shall be made on Patents Form SP1; and
    (b)   an extension of the duration of a supplementary protection certificate under Article 8 of the Medicinal Products Regulation shall be made on Patents Form SP4.

(2)   The period prescribed for the purposes of paragraph 5(a) of Schedule 4A to the Act is—

(a)   three months ending with the start date; or

(b)   where the certificate is granted after the beginning of that period, three months beginning with the date the supplementary protection certificate is granted.

(3)   The comptroller must send a notice to the applicant for the certificate—

(a)   before the beginning of the period of two months immediately preceding the start date; or

(b)   where the certificate is granted as mentioned in paragraph (2)(b), on the date the certificate is granted.

(4)   The notice must notify the applicant for the certificate of—

(a)   the fact that payment is required for the certificate to take effect;

(b)   the prescribed fee due;

(c)   the date before which payment must be made; and

(d)   the start date.

(5)   The prescribed fee must be accompanied by Patents Form SP2; and once the certificate has taken effect no further fee may be paid to extend the term of the certificate unless an application for an extension of the duration of the certificate is made under the Medicinal Products Regulation.

(6)   Where the prescribed fee is not paid before the end of the period prescribed for the purposes of paragraph 5(a) of Schedule 4A to the Act, the comptroller shall, before the end of the period of six weeks beginning immediately after the end of that prescribed period, and if the fee remains unpaid, send a notice to the applicant for the certificate.

(7)   The notice shall remind the applicant for the certificate—

(a)   that payment is overdue; and

(b)   of the consequences of non-payment.

(8)   The comptroller must send the notices under this rule to—

(a)   the applicant's address for service; and

(b)   the address to which a renewal notice would be sent to the proprietor of the basic patent under rule 39(3).

116A.— Notifications relating to supplementary protection certificates

(1) Notifications under Article 5(2)(b) and (c) of the Medicinal Products Regulation must be made on Patents Form SP5;

(2) Notifications under Article 13A of Regulation (EC) 1610/96 and Article 13A of Regulation (EC) 469/2009 must be made on Patents Form SP6.

Note.

The first and second paragraphs of r.116A were introduced by different Statutory Instruments, namely SI 2020/1050 and SI 2020/1471, respectively. Both of those Statutory Instruments entered into force on "IP completion day" (namely at 23:00 on 31 December 2020).

For a discussion of the transitional provisions applicable to the above-mentioned changes, see:

-   §128B.10 and the Note to §128B.15 in respect of Notifications under para.(1) of r.116A; and

-   §128B.10 and the Notes to §128B.23A and §128B.47A in respect of Notifications under para.(2) of r.116A.

Replace paragraph §128B.57 with:

Extension to the Isle of Man

128B.57   The Patents (Compulsory Licensing and Supplementary Protection Certificates) Regulation 2007 (SI 2007/3293) revoked both the Patents (Supplementary Protection Certificates for Medicinal Products) Regulations 1992 (SI 1992/3091) (the "1992 Regulations") and the Patents (Supplementary Protection Certificate for Plant Protection Products) Regulations 1996 (SI 1996/3120) (the "1996 Regulations"). The 1992 SPC Regulations were replicated in the Isle of Man by virtue of the Patents (Medicinal Products) Regulations [Act of Tynwald], Statutory Document No.447/93. Similarly, the 1996 SPC Regulations (SI 1996/3120, relating to plant protection products) were replicated in the Isle of Man by virtue of the Patents (Plant Protection Products) Order (Statutory Document No.698/99 and the Patents (Plant Protection Products) Regulations (Statutory Document No.746/99).
    The Patents Act 1977 as applied to the Isle of Man has not been amended to reflect the changes made by SI 2007/3293. It appears that it was not possible to extend SI 2007/3293 to the Isle of Man because it was an instrument under the European Communities Act 1972.
    The Patents (Medicinal Products) Order 2014 (SI 2014/0088), which came into operation on March 31, 2014, directly applied to the Isle of Man the provisions of Reg.1901/2006 that relate to the extensions of protection provided by way of art.36. It also indicated that Reg.469/2009 shall apply to the Isle of Man with the omission of arts 7–12, 14–21 and 23, and as if the Island were part of the United Kingdom.
    The European Union and Trade Act 2019 (Deficiencies) (Patents) Regulations 2019 (Statutory Document No.2019/0121) amended SD 698/99 and SI 2014/0088 "in order to address deficiencies arising from the withdrawal of the United Kingdom from the European Union in relation to patents and connected areas including supplementary protection certificates".
    Certain provisions of Reg.2019/933 were (subject to various amendments, including replacing references to "1 July 2019" with references to "1 November 2019") replicated in the Isle of Man by virtue of the Patents (Supplementary Protection Certificate Waiver) Order 2019, Statutory Document No.2019/0379.
    Finally, the European Union and Trade Act 2019 (Withdrawal Agreement) Regulations 2020 (Statutory Document No.2020/0058) indicates, amongst other things, that references to "exit day" in Statutory Documents (such as No.2019/0121) are to be read instead as references to "IP completion day".

Commentary on Section 128B and Supplementary Protection Certificates Generally

Scope of the section

Replace the first paragraph with:

128B.58   This is the second of two new sections (the other being s.128A) inserted into the Patents Act 1977 by the Patents (Compulsory Licensing and Supplementary Protection Certificates) Regulations 2007 (SI 2007/3293). Together with Sch.4A, which is also inserted into the 1977 Act by the same instrument, this section sets out how certain provisions of the Act apply to supplementary protection certificates ("SPCs") and applications for SPCs. SPCs were originally made available in the UK under two Community Regulations, Regulation (EC) No 469/2009 of May 6, 2009 which repealed and replaced Council Regulation (EEC) No.1768/92 of June 18, 1992 which created SPCs for medicinal products (referred to at para.7 of the Schedule as "the Medicinal Product Regulation") and Regulation (EC) No.1610/96 of the European Parliament and of the Council of July 23, 1996 which created SPCs for plant protection products (referred to at para.7 of the Schedule as "the Plant Protection Products Regulation"). Regulation 469/2009 was subsequently amended by Reg.2019/933, which introduced various exceptions to the protection provided by SPCs for medicinal products (see §128B.62 and §128B.75).

After the first paragraph, add new paragraph:

    In order to address deficiencies arising in view of Brexit, various amendments were made to both of Regs 469/2009 and 1610/96 for the purpose of their incorporation into UK law (as "retained EU law"). The versions of Regs 469/2009 and 1610/96 that have been incorporated into UK law are reprinted above. The original versions of Regs 469/2009, 2019/933 and 1610/96, which continue to define the law applicable in EU Member States, are published in EU Official Journals (see [2009] OJ EU L152/1, [2019] OJ EU L153/1 and [1996] OJ EC L198/30, respectively; see also *https://www.legislation.gov.uk/eur/2009/469/contents*, *https://www.legislation.gov.uk/eur/2019/933/contents* and *https://www.legislation.gov.uk/eur/1996/1610/contents*).

Replace the second paragraph with:

Under the UK law versions of Regs 469/2009 and 1610/96, it is possible to protect certain medicinal and plant protection products beyond the normal 20-year patent term by means of an SPC. According to the EU law versions of art.19 of the Medicinal Product Regulation and art.18 of the Plant Protection Product Regulation, in the absence of procedural provisions in the Regulations, the procedural provisions applicable under UK law to the patent which is the subject of the SPC shall apply to the certificate, unless that law lays down special procedural provisions for SPCs. Until the coming into force of s.128B, although certain rules had been enacted (notably SI 1992/3091 and SI 1996/3120, see below), the provisions of the Act could only be applied to SPCs in a rather general way, for example in relation to rights conferred by an SPC application pending at the time of expiry of the basic patent. The UK law versions of art.19 of the Medicinal Product Regulation and art.18 of the Plant Protection Product Regulation now explicitly refer to both s.128B and Schedule 4A.

Replace the third paragraph with:

The Medicinal Product Regulation provides for a six-month extension to the term of the SPC for medicinal products if the product in question has undergone approved testing for paediatric use (and has not received an alternative reward under Reg.1901/2006 (see §§128B.74 and 128B.77A).

Replace the last paragraph with:

Reviews of recent decisions can be found in Daniel Wise et al, [2016] 8–9 *CIPA* 14, [2016] 10 *CIPA* 40, [2017] 7–8 *CIPA* 27, [2017] 9 *CIPA* 19, [2018] 7–8 *CIPA* 10, [2018] 9 *CIPA* 17, [2019] 7–8 *CIPA* 12 and [2020] 7–8 *CIPA* 44. Discussions of amendments made in view of Brexit can be found in Michael Pears et al, [2020] 11 *CIPA* 11 and Joel Beevers et al, [2020] 12 *CIPA* 8.

References to patents, etc.

In the fourth paragraph (beginning "Curiously, in point 6 of an interpretative note"), replace the last sentence with:

At least when it was originally issued (at which point the UK was still an EU Member State and a **128B.59** Participating Member State of the UPC Agreement), this conclusion appears to have been unjustified in the light of para.4(2) of Sch.4A.

Replace paragraph 128B.62 with:

The legal basis for supplementary protection certificates

The object of creating supplementary protection certificates for certain types of products is to provide **128B.62** some compensatory monopoly protection for products the exploitation of which has suffered delays due to the requirement first to obtain an administrative regulatory marketing permission, as in the case of medical and veterinary medicines (defined as "medicinal products"), later extended also to agrochemical products (defined as "plant protection products"). The SPC scheme is, therefore, not one for the general protection of the fruits of research, but rather to provide some compensation for time lost in the exploitation of patented inventions due to delays in obtaining a marketing authorisation, see *Draco's SPC Application* [1996] R.P.C. 417.

Accordingly, supplementary protection certificates ("SPCs") have the effect of extending the term of certain aspects of certain patents after their expiry. They have resulted from an original Proposal for a Supplementary Protection Certificate for Medicinal Products dated April 19, 1990 [1990] OJ EC C114/10 which led eventually to two EC Regulations (the "Regulations" or "Regs"), the first in 1992 for medicinal products (Council Regulation (EEC) No.1768/92, the "Medicinal Products Regulation", effective from January 2, 1993 and published [1992] OJ EC L182/1; OJ EPO 12/1992, 812); and the second in 1997 for plant protection products (Regulation (EC) No.1610/96, the "Plant Protection Products Regulation", effective from February 8, 1997 and published [1996] OJ EC L198/30). These Regulations were originally implemented into UK law by the Patents (Supplementary Protection Certificate for Medicinal Products) Regulations 1992 (SI 1992/3091) and the Patents Supplementary Protection Certificates for Plant Protection Products) Regulations 1996 (SI 1996/3120) now revoked by the Patents (Compulsory Licensing and Supplementary Protection Certificates) Regulations 2007 (SI 2007/3293), which introduced s.128B and Sch.4A as discussed above.

Subsequent to being implemented into UK law, Reg.1768/92 was repealed and replaced by Reg.469/2009 ([2009] OJ EU L152/1), which latter Regulation was then amended by Reg.2019/933 ([2019] OJ EU L153/1). Both Reg.469/2009 (as amended) and Reg.1610/96 were amended by SIs 2019/801, 2020/1050 and 2020/1471 for the purposes of incorporation into UK law (as "retained EU law").

Although SPCs are created under Community Regulations, they take effect only under national law. Consequently, the Regulations may have differing effect in different States of the European Community. Only the application (as "retained EU law") to the United Kingdom is considered here, particularly by reference to the above-mentioned Compulsory Licensing and SPCs regulations. Here SPCs are granted on application to the UK-IPO. The MOPP contains an extensive commentary on SPCs.

An SPC may only be granted in respect of a particular product and in relation to a "basic patent". When granted, the SPC only takes effect from the end of the term of that patent and, in effect, regrants that patent for a period not exceeding five years, but only in respect of that "product", the definition of which is discussed in §128B.66. While SPCs are, formally, a sui generis intellectual property right, the applications, and the SPCs when granted, are treated mutatis mutandis with the provisions of the patent statutes and the rules (including rules of court) made in relation to them.

The validity of the Medicinal Product Regulation was challenged by the Kingdom of Spain on the basis of alleged lack of competence to make this form of regulation or that it was adopted on an incorrect legal basis, but that challenge failed (*Kingdom of Spain v EU Council* (C-350/92) [1996] F.S.R. 73; [1996] 1 C.M.L.R. 415 ECJ).

Both Regulations have been amended to take account of the enlargement of the Community from 12 Member States at the time of coming into force of Regulation 1768/92 to the present 28 Member States following the accession of Austria, Finland and Sweden in 1995, the 2004 act of enlargement bringing in 10 new Member States, the addition of Bulgaria and Hungary in 2007 and of Croatia in 2013. Further, both Regulations are included within the scope of the EEA Agreement, such that they each apply to Iceland and Norway (but not Liechtenstein, where by virtue of a treaty, Swiss SPCs take effect).

On two occasions (once in December 2015 and again June 2016), the European Commission called for tenders in connection with a "Study on the legal aspects of the supplementary protection certificates in the EU". After no qualifying bids were received in response to the first call, the breadth of the proposed study was narrowed significantly. This led to the Max Planck Institute for Innovation and Competition being awarded the contract for the second call. The resulting study was published on May 28, 2018. Also published on May 28, 2018 was a study (on the economic impact of supplementary protection certificates (SPCs), pharmaceutical incentives and rewards in Europe) conducted by Copenhagen Economics.

Simultaneously with the publication of the two studies on May 28, 2018, the Commission proposed an amendment to Regulation 469/2009 (COM(2018) 317 final) aimed at introducing an exemption from SPC infringement in respect of the manufacture of medicines for export and, in the six months prior to SPC expiry, in respect of the manufacture of medicines for stockpiling in advance of post-expiry marketing in the EU. These manufacturing waivers entered into force (in revised form, as set out in Regulation 2019/933) on July 1, 2019.

In July 2020, the Commission followed up this point by producing a Roadmap (Ares(2020)3662148) indicating that, as part of an objective of upgrading the system for IP protection in Europe, the Commission will "consider ways to make the SPC system less fragmented". The Roadmap points to art.118 TFEU as a legal basis for a possible unitary SPC.

On October 17, 2019, the UK and EU27 concluded an "Agreement on the withdrawal of the United Kingdom of Great Britain and Northern Ireland from the European Union and the European Atomic Energy Community" (the so-called 2019 Withdrawal Agreement). Of particular relevance to SPCs is art.60 of the 2019 Withdrawal Agreement, which specifies that: (i) the EU's SPC Regulations continue to apply to all SPC (extension) applications filed in the UK throughout the transitional period which ran from February 1, 2020 to December 31, 2020, and also subsequently to any such applications that were ongoing at the end of that period; and (ii) SPCs granted subject to such applications should provide for "the same level of protection" as that provided for in the EU's SPC Regulations. The UK's obligation to honour art.60 of the 2019 Withdrawal Agreement is reflected in the transitional provisions to SIs 2019/801, 2020/1050 and 2020/1471 (which, where relevant, specify the end of the transitional period as the cut-off point for applying the EU law versions of Regs 469/2009 and 1610/96 to SPCs and SPC applications in the UK).

Also of relevance to SPCs is art.89(1) of the 2019 Withdrawal Agreement, which provides that "Judgments and orders of the Court of Justice of the European Union handed down before the end of the transition period, as well as such judgments and orders handed down after the end of the transition period in proceedings referred to in Articles 86 and 87, shall have binding force in their entirety on and in the United Kingdom".

The obligation of art.89(1) of the 2019 Withdrawal Agreement was originally reflected by the provisions of s.6 of the European Union (Withdrawal) Act 2018, which indicated that all courts other than the Supreme Court (or, in Scotland, the High Court of Justiciary) should interpret any retained EU law, so far as that law is unmodified on or after the end of the transitional period, in accordance with any retained case law and any retained general principles of EU law. However, s.26 of the European Union (Withdrawal Agreement) Act 2020 modified s.6 of the 2018 Act by introducing para.5A. This provided

Ministers of the Crown with the power to designate additional courts as "relevant courts" that, to an extent to be determined by the Minister, are not bound by retained EU case law.

The power provided by s.6(5A) of the EU (Withdrawal) Act was exercised by the Lord Chancellor, and resulted in the European Union (Withdrawal) Act 2018 (Relevant Court) (Retained EU Case Law) Regulations 2020 (SI 2020/1525). This designates a number of "relevant courts", which include the Court of Appeal in England and Wales, the Inner House of the Court of Session (in Scotland) and the Court of Appeal in Northern Ireland. In reg.4, it also details the extent to which such a relevant court is not bound by retained EU case law:

4.—(1) A relevant court is not bound by any retained EU case law except as provided in paragraph (2).

(2) A relevant court is bound by retained EU case law so far as there is post-transition case law which modifies or applies that retained EU case law and which is binding on the relevant court.

The reference to "post-transition case law" in para.2 of reg.4 is to case law of a UK court or tribunal. Thus, provided that there is no such post-transition case law, a relevant court (such as the Court of Appeal in England and Wales) would be free to depart from retained EU case law. However, reg.5 of SI 2020/1525 outlines a test that should be applied by a relevant court before departing from retained EU case law:

5. In deciding whether to depart from any retained EU case law by virtue of section 6(4)(ba) of the 2018 Act and these Regulations, a relevant court must apply the same test as the Supreme Court would apply in deciding whether to depart from the case law of the Supreme Court.

There is perhaps a question mark over whether the ability of the Court of Appeal to depart from retained EU case law fully complies with the UK's obligations under art.89(1) of the 2019 Withdrawal Agreement. Nevertheless, it will be interesting to see whether, and to what extent the Court of Appeal exercises this power. This is not least because, for SPCs, a significant proportion of the retained EU case law consists of rulings of the Court of Justice of the EU (CJEU, formerly known as the ECJ) that provide interpretations of the legislation that are unclear, inconsistent (with other CJEU rulings) and/or difficult to apply to cases having different underlying facts.

The Interpretation of the Regulations—Role of the Recitals

In the second paragraph, replace "Court of Justice of the EU (CJEU, formerly known as the ECJ)" with:
CJEU   128B.63

Replace paragraph §128B.64 with:

Scope of, and adaptations to, the Community Regulations under United Kingdom law and practice

As incorporated into UK law, the Community SPC Regulations provide for the grant of a SPC for a   128B.64
"product" which is: (1) either a "medicinal product" or a "plant protection product" (each as respectively defined in the Regulations, see §128B.11 and §128B.35); (2) protected by a patent which is in force; and (3) which is subject, prior to its being placed on the market (in the UK, GB or NI), to an administrative procedure.

The administrative procedures giving rise to a marketing authorisation permitting the holder to sell a medicinal product or a plant protection product have been harmonised under EU law. Prior to Brexit, marketing authorisations in respect of the whole of the UK could, for human medicinal products may be granted either by the United Kingdom's Medicines and Healthcare Products Regulatory Agency (EMA, previously known as MHRA), in accordance with Directive 2004/24, e.g. using the mutual recognition procedure, or at the Community level, by the European Commission, subsequent to a positive opinion from the European Medicines Agency (EMEA), in accordance with Reg.726/2004 (which replaced Reg.2309/93). A "centralised" Community authorisation allows a medicinal product to be sold throughout the Community (but not the EEA states of Norway, Iceland and Liechtenstein) and the single authorisation may be used to initiate applications for SPCs in each Member State of the EU in which there is a basic patent.

A consequence of the Northern Ireland Protocol is that "centralised" MAs issued by the European Commission will continue to extend to the territory of Northern Ireland (though not to the territory of Great Britain). Further, it remains possible to designate NI as a Concerned Member State in connection with either the mutual recognition procedure or the decentralised procedure under EU law. In this respect, art.1(jb) of Reg.469/2009 formally recognises (as a "NI authorisation") a MA for a human or veterinary medicinal product that is granted, or having effect as if granted, under EU legislation (Directive 2001/83/EC or Directive 2001/82/EC) and that extends to NI.

The MHRA and the Veterinary Medicines Directorate (VMD) have established "grandfathering" processes for issuing UK product licence numbers to products that were centrally authorised by the European Commission prior to January 1, 2021 (see *https://www.gov.uk/guidance/converting-centrally-authorised-products-caps-to-uk-marketing-authorisations-mas-grandfathering-and-managing-lifecycle-changes* and *https://www.gov.uk/guidance/application-and-authorisation-information-hub-explainer*).

For centralised applications that were still pending on January 1, 2021, the MHRA has established two options for "fast-track" processing in the UK, namely an "in-flight" assessment in parallel with the EMA's assessment, or reliance on a positive opinion from the CHMP, which is a sub-committee of the EMA (see *https://www.gov.uk/guidance/guidance-on-the-handling-of-applications-for-centrally-authorised-products-caps*). The MHRA has also established the EC Decision Reliance Procedure (ECDRP), which, at least until January 1, 2023, enables the MHRA to issue a UK MA by relying upon a decision taken by the European Commission (EC) on the approval of a new MA in the centralised procedure.

For plant protection products, the administrative procedure is governed by regulations made under the Food and Environmental Protection Act 1985 (c.48), namely the Control of Pesticides Regulations 1986 (SI 1986/1510, as amended) and the Plant Protection Products (Sustainable Use) Regulations 2012 (SI 2012/1657), but subject to the terms and conditions of the plant protection product Directive 91/414/EEC (now replaced by Regulation (EC) No. 1107/2009). The 2012 Regulations came into force on July 18, 2012 and replaced the Plant Protection Products Regulations 1995 (SI 1995/887). For the purpose of incorporation into UK law, amendments to Reg.1107/2009 are outlined in the Plant Protection Products (Miscellaneous Amendments) (EU Exit) Regulations 2019 (SI 2019/556), the Pesticides (Maximum Residue Levels) (Amendment etc.) (EU Exit) Regulations 2019 (SI 2019/557), the Environment (Miscellaneous Amendments and Revocations) (EU Exit) Regulations 2019 (SI 2019/559), the Pesticides (Amendment) (EU Exit) Regulations 2019 (SI 2019/1410) and the Pesticides (Amendment) (EU Exit) Regulations 2020 (SI 2020/1376).

Article 19(1) of the original Medicinal Products Regulation (Regulation 1768/92), as well as art.19(1) of the Plant Protection Products Regulation provides that SPCs are available only where the first authorisation to place the product on the market anywhere within the European Community (which, in effect, generally means the EEA and, in certain circumstances, Switzerland, see §128B.73), and in the form of such a product, was obtained after January 1, 1985 (Regs, art.19(1)). However, there is no corresponding provision in the current Medicinal Products Regulation (Regulation 469/2009). Article 19 of Reg.1610/96 has been deleted for the purposes of incorporation into UK law (see the Note to §128B.54). Nevertheless, at least for those (pre-Brexit) SPCs to which the amendments of reg.35 of SI 2019/801 do not apply, it is thought that the Comptroller should interpret the art.19(1) provisions as requiring him to ignore any marketing authorisation granted in a country which, at the date of the grant of the SPC, was not then a Member State of the European Community, even if that state had become one by the date of application for the SPC. However, as explained in §128B.73, from July 1, 1994, the Medicinal Products Regulation was extended to cover all Member States of the EEA with this being extended to Liechtenstein from January 1, 1995 when that country joined the EEA; and, likewise, for the Plant Protection Products Regulation from August 1, 1997 for Liechtenstein and from January 2, 1998 for Iceland and Norway. This therefore opens up the possibility of a first marketing authorisation in an EFTA country being taken into account even if this was granted at a date before the relevant Regulation came into effect for that country, except where this occurred before the entry into force of the EEA Agreement on July 1, 1994, see MOPP paras SP0.08 and SP0.09. For example, the UK SPC for toremifine, granted on a basic patent with a normal expiry of May 2003, therefore expired in December 2003, because the product was first authorised in Finland in December 1988, even though an EC authorisation was not granted until February 1996. For the effect of a first marketing authorisation in Switzerland, see §128B.73.

The legal significance of pre-accession marketing authorisations in EEA countries to SPCs in EU Member States is determined in part by the fact that the EEA Agreement effectively treats such authorisations as if they were authorisations granted in accordance with EU law. By way of contrast, the 2003, 2005 and 2011 EU accession treaties do not contain any provisions that afford such equivalence to pre-accession marketing authorisations in the EU accession states. It therefore seems that the legal significance (for SPCs in EU Member States) of pre-accession marketing authorisations in the Czech Republic, Estonia, Cyprus, Latvia, Lithuania, Hungary, Malta, Poland, Slovenia, Slovakia, Bulgaria, Romania and Croatia may well be different from that of pre-accession authorisations in EEA Member States, such as Switzerland.

In its rulings in *Synthon v Merz Pharma and Generics v Synaptech* (C-195/09 and C-427/09, respectively, which decisions are discussed further in §128B.73), the CJEU held that, for human medicinal products, the administrative procedure to which the product is subjected must be in accordance with Council Directive 65/65/EEC (now replaced by Directive 2001/83/EC). In particular, the product defined in respect of an SPC application must have undergone safety and efficacy testing before being "placed on the market in the European Community as a medicinal product for human use", as otherwise that product is not within the scope of the SPC Regulation, and may not be the subject of a certificate.

In *Leibniz-Institut für Neue Materialien Gemeinnützige GmbH*, BL O/328/14, the Hearing Officer at the IPO ruled upon the eligibility for SPC protection for a product that was described as an "Aqueous dispersion of iron oxide nanoparticles", and that was authorised by way of an EC Design Examination Certificate under Directive 93/42/EEC. The Hearing Officer found that the SPC application failed to comply with art.2, and that the product defined in the application was outside of the scope of Regulation 469/2009. A reason for finding *Leibniz-Institut's SPC application* non-compliant with art.2 (instead of art.3(b), as for *Cerus' SPC application* discussed in §128B.73) was that the device in the *Leibniz-Institut* case did not include "a substance which, if used separately, may be considered to be a medicinal product". Instead, it was held that the device exercised its activity by physical means alone. Similar reasoning, as supported by the CJEU's commentary on art.1(b) in *Forsgren* (C-631/13, discussed in more detail in §128B.66), was relied upon by the German Federal Patent Court (*Bundespatentgericht*, case 14 W (Pat) 45/12) to uphold the rejection of Leibniz's corresponding German SPC application. Non-compliance with art.2 was also found by the IPO in *Angiotech Pharmaceuticals and University of British Columbia* BL O/466/15, on the grounds that the products in question had not been "subject to an administrative procedure as laid down in Directive 2001/83/EC" (instead being "authorised" by way of an EC Design Examination Certificate, which was held to not be equivalent to an authorisation under Directive 2001/83/EC).

The question of whether an authorisation for a drug/device combination falls within the scope of the SPC Regulation was referred to the CJEU by the German Federal Patent Court (decision no.14 W (pat) 13/16, relating to an SPC application for a drug-eluting stent). In response to the question in that case (C-527/17 *(Boston Scientific)*), the CJEU essentially confirmed the IPO's stance in the *Angiotech* case by ruling that:

"Article 2 of Regulation (EC) No 469/2009 of the European Parliament and of the Council of 6 May 2009 concerning the supplementary protection certificate for medicinal products must be interpreted as meaning that a prior authorisation procedure, under Council Directive 93/42/EEC of 14 June 1993 concerning medical devices, as amended by Directive 2007/47/EC of the European Parliament and of the Council of 5 September 2007, for a device incorporating as an integral part a substance, within the meaning of Article 1(4) of that directive as amended, cannot be treated in the same way, for the purposes of applying that regulation, as a marketing authorisation procedure for that substance under Directive 2001/83/EC of the European Parliament and of the Council of 6 November 2001 on the Community code relating to medicinal products for human use, as amended by Directive 2004/27/EC of the European Parliament and of the Council of 31 March 2004, even if that substance was the subject of the assessment provided for in the first and second paragraphs of section 7.4 of Annex I to Directive 93/42, as amended by Directive 2007/47."

Thus, even medical devices incorporating an active ingredient fall outside of the scope of art.2 of the Medicinal Products Regulation, and are therefore not entitled to SPC protection.

As confirmed by the decision of the Hearing Officer in BL O/610/20 (*Erber Aktiengesellschaft*), the situation is similar for microorganisms authorised for use as animal feed additives. This is on the grounds that, in the view of the Hearing Officer, the aims and objectives of the EU legislation relating to feed additive (Reg.1831/2003) were not the same as those of the veterinary medicines Directive (2001/82/EC), with the consequence that MAs under those two laws could not be considered as equivalent for the purposes of the SPC regulation. In addition, and following the CJEU's decision in C-527/17, the Hearing Officer was essentially of the view that a microorganism authorised for use as a feed additive could not be considered to be a "medicinal product" because it had not been assessed as such.

Replace paragraph §128B.65 with:

Conditions for obtaining an SPC

Article 3 in both Regulations (as amended for the purposes of incorporation into UK law) sets out **128B.65** the conditions to be fulfilled at the date of making the application for a certificate in the United Kingdom. To obtain a valid certificate at the date of making application, there must be:

(a) a patent in force in the United Kingdom protecting "the product", being either a "medicinal product" as defined in art.1 of the Medicinal Products Regulation or a "plant protection product" as defined in art.1 of the Plant Protection Products Regulation;

(b)   a valid UK, GB or NI authorisation for marketing the product as a "medicinal product" , or a valid GB or NI for marketing the product as a "plant protection product";

(c)   the product must not already have been the subject of a certificate; and

(d)   the authorisation referred to in (b) must be the first UK (or GB or NI) authorisation to place the product on the UK (or GB or NI) market as a medicinal or plant protection product as the case may be (Regs, art.3, §§128B.13 and 128B.37).

The Comptroller, in interpreting art.3 (*BASF's SPC Application* [2000] R.P.C. 1), was guided by the original Proposal for a Supplementary Protection Certificate for Medicinal Products dated April 19, 1990 ([1990] OJ EC C114/10).

At the date of submission of the SPC application, the basic patent protecting the product must be in force in the United Kingdom, the product must not previously have been the subject of a certificate in the United Kingdom, there must be a valid UK (or GB or NI) marketing authorisation to place the product, as a medicinal product or plant protection product, as appropriate, on the market and the marketing authorisation must be the first authorisation to place the product on the market as a medicinal/plant protection product in the UK (or GB or NI), though there may have been an earlier authorisation in the EEA. Although the basic patent may expire before the certificate is granted, it is not possible to apply for an SPC after patent expiry.

The ninth recital of the Medicinal Products Regulation and the eighth recital of the Plant Protection Products Regulation each state that the duration of protection granted by the certificate should be such as to provide adequate effective protection. The proprietor of a patent and an SPC subsequently granted in relation to it will enjoy an overall maximum of 15 years of exclusivity from the time the medicinal product in question first obtains authorisation to be placed on the market in the community. Nonetheless, the Regulations do not define what is meant by "protected". As the European Court pointed out in *Farmitalia Carlo Erba S.r.L's SPC* (C-392/97) [2000] R.P.C. 580, the provisions concerning patents have not yet been made the subject of harmonisation at Community level or of an approximation of laws. The extent of protection of the basic patent is therefore a question for national law, which, however, will be interpreted in accordance with the normal canons of claim construction. The MOPP further indicates that, in *Takeda's SPC Application* No. SPC/GB93/017 (unreported oral decision, noted in MOPP para.SPM3.02), a patent claiming a peptide was regarded as protecting an acetate salt of that peptide applying the usual canons of construction for patent claims, it perhaps being significant that the specification referred to this salt although it did not fall within the literal wording of the patent claims.

On one view this might imply that the test for whether or not a product is protected by the basic patent is whether or not the product, if sold by a third party, would infringe that basic patent. However, even before the CJEU's judgments in 2011 (discussed below) that revisited the meaning of "protected" in art.3(a), such a test was repeatedly rejected, for example in *Takeda Chemical Industries' SPC Applications (No.3)* [2004] R.P.C. 37 and similar rulings elsewhere in the Community: Sweden, *AB Hässle*, January 2, 2000, Supreme Administrative Court Case Number 3248-1996; Denmark, *Merck and Co Inc v The Patent Board of Appeal*, December 12, 2003, Eastern Division of the High Court, B-2667-01; and France, *Abbott Laboratories v M. le Directeur de l'INPI*, January 19, 2005, Cours d'Appel, 04/14435.

In *Gilead Sciences, Inc's SPC Application* [2008] EWHC 1902 (Pat), a claim directed to a composition comprising tenofovir (amongst other compounds) together with a carrier and optionally other active ingredients was held to protect a product comprising the combination of tenofovir and emtricitabine, though this finding was effectively reversed in Arnold J.'s 2018 judgment in *Teva v Gilead* (discussed below).

In *Astellas Pharma Inc v Comptroller General of Patents* [2009] EWHC 1916 (Pat), the basic patent disclosed emodepside, but not prazaquantel or a combination of emodepside and praziquantel, for the treatment of cats with roundworm. A marketing authorisation had been obtained for a veterinary medical product comprising both emodepside and praziquantel. Astellas sought an SPC for the combination, which was refused on the ground that the patent did not protect the combination. Arnold J. referred to *Farmitalia* (C-392/97) [1999] E.C.R. I-5553; *Takeda No.3* [2004] R.P.C. 37, [2003] EWHC 649 (Pat); and *Gilead* [2008] EWHC 1902 (Pat), but was not convinced that *Takeda* was wrong and so left the question of a reference to the CJEU for any appeal.

In *Medeva's SPC Applications* [2010] EWCA Civ 700, on appeal from the High Court [2010] EWHC 68 (Pat), in turn on appeal from BL O/357/09, in both instances the applications having been rejected, the Court of Appeal referred several matters relating to the interpretation of art.3(a) and art.3(b) in relation to combination products, in particular multi-disease vaccines, to the CJEU for a preliminary ruling under *Medeva v Comptroller General of Patents* (C-322/10), summarised as follows:

1.   What is meant in art.3(a) of the Regulation by "the product is protected by a basic patent in force" and what are the criteria for deciding this?

2.   In a case involving a medicinal product comprising more than one active ingredient, are there further or different criteria for determining whether or not "the product is protected by a basic

patent" according to art.3(a) of the Regulation and, if so, what are those further or different criteria?

3. In a case involving a multi-disease vaccine, are there further or different criteria for determining whether or not "the product is protected by a basic patent" according to art.3(a) of the Regulation and, if so, what are those further or different criteria?

4. For the purposes of art.3(a), is a multi-disease vaccine comprising multiple antigens "protected by a basic patent" if one antigen of the vaccine is "protected by the basic patent in force"?

5. For the purposes of art.3(a), is a multi-disease vaccine comprising multiple antigens "protected by a basic patent" if all antigens directed against one disease are "protected by the basic patent in force"?

6. Does the SPC Regulation and, in particular, art.3(b), permit the grant of a Supplementary Protection Certificate for a single active ingredient or combination of active ingredients where:

    (a) a basic patent in force protects the single active ingredient or combination of active ingredients within the meaning of art.3(a) of the SPC Regulation; and

    (b) a medicinal product containing the single active ingredient or combination of active ingredients together with one or more other active ingredients is the subject of a valid authorisation granted in accordance with Directive 2001/83/EC or 2001/82/EC which is the first marketing authorisation that places the single active ingredient or combination of active ingredients on the market?

In *Georgetown University, Loyola University of Chicago, and University of Rochester's SPC applications* BL O/401/09, which involved multi-ingredient vaccines, the Hearing Officer rejected the SPC applications on the grounds that they did not satisfy the requirements of art.3(b) of the Regulation as the marketing authorisations related to products with multiple active ingredients. The marketing authorisations comprised further active ingredients in addition to the active ingredient listed in the product definition of the SPC application. Thus a valid authorisation to place the product (for which an SPC had been applied) on the market as a medicinal product had not been supplied. On appeal, the Patents Court referred to the CJEU, as C-422/10, a question identical to the sixth question in *Medeva*.

By order of January 12, 2011, *Medeva* and *Georgetown University et al.* were joined for the purposes of the oral procedure and the judgment. In its judgment issued on November 24, 2011, the CJEU held that art.3(a) of the SPC Regulation precludes the grant of an SPC relating to active ingredients not specified in the claims of the basic patent relied on in support of the application for the SPC, but art.3(b) does not preclude the grant of an SPC for a combination of two active ingredients specified in the wording of the claims of the basic patent, where the medicinal product for which the marketing authorisation is submitted in support of the application for the SPC contains not only that combination of the two active ingredients but also other active ingredients. In other words the SPC had to be granted for active ingredients "*specified in the wording of the claims*" of the patent, but the product the subject of the marketing authorisation could be one containing other active ingredients as well as those specified in the patent.

Another case relating to combination products was *Daiichi Sankyo Company* (C-6/11). In a judgment issued by way of reasoned order on November 25, 2011, the CJEU effectively reiterated the first points of its rulings in *Medeva and Georgetown University et al.*, with the exception that the phrase "identified in the wording of the claims" was used instead of "specified in the wording of the claims".

A second case decided by the CJEU on November 25, 2011 was *Yeda Research and Development Company Ltd* (C-518/10, discussed in more detail in §128B.67). In that case, claims relating to a combination of two active ingredients were held not to protect one of those active ingredients on its own. Thus, mere "naming" (or identifying in some form) of an active ingredient is a claim of a basic patent is not sufficient to satisfy art.3(a) if the patent does not contain claims directed towards that active ingredient alone.

The conclusion on art.3(a) reached by the CJEU in *Medeva* and *Georgetown University et al.* differs from that reached by AG Trstenjak in her earlier Opinion on the same cases. That is, whereas the CJEU ruled that the product must be "specified in the wording of the claims", AG Trstenjak had opined that regard is always to be had to the *subject-matter* of the patent in question, and not to its protective effects. However, the CJEU and AG Trstenjak used very similar reasoning to reach these apparently different conclusions. That is, both emphasised that, whilst art.3(a) had to be assessed according to non-European Union (i.e. national) laws governing the extent of patent protection, the "uniform solution" provided by Regulation (EC) No.469/2009 meant that the absence of harmonisation of national patent laws could not be allowed to affect the conditions under which an SPC can be obtained (which must be the same in each Member State of the EU).

Thus, unless and until the national laws of all EU Member States become fully harmonised, the CJEU's rulings in *Medeva* and *Georgetown University et al.* clearly rule out use of the "infringement" test under art.3(a). However, the alternative test proposed by the CJEU ("specified in the wording of the claims") only clarified matters to a limited extent (see the articles: "Supplementary Protection Certificates: the CJEU issues its decision in two seminal cases" by M. Snodin, J. Miles and M. Pears [2012] B.S.L.R. Vol. 12(2); and "Recent European developments regarding patent extensions (SPCs and Paediatric Extensions)" by G.J. Kuipers, T.J. Douma and M. Kokke [2012] B.S.L.R. Vol. 12(4)). It therefore did not take long before, in *Eli Lilly v Human Genome Sciences* (C-493/12) the High Court of England and Wales referred the following questions to the CJEU:

1.   What are the criteria for deciding whether "the product is protected by a basic patent in force" in art.3(a) of Regulation [No 469/2009]?
2.   Are the criteria different where the product is not a combination product, and if so, what are the criteria?
3.   In the case of a claim to an antibody or a class of antibodies, is it sufficient that the antibody or antibodies are defined in terms of their binding characteristics to a target protein, or is it necessary to provide a structural definition for the antibody or antibodies, and if so, how much?

The ruling of the CJEU in C-493/12, issued on December 12, 2013, clarified that, in order to satisfy art.3(a), it is not necessary for the active ingredient to be identified in the claims of the patent by way of a structural formula. Indeed, the CJEU also made it clear that defining an active ingredient by way of a *functional* formula may satisfy the requirements of art.3(a), but only on the condition that:

"it is possible to reach the conclusion on the basis of those claims, interpreted inter alia in the light of the description of the invention, as required by Article 69 of the Convention on the Grant of European Patents and the Protocol on the interpretation of that provision, that the claims relate, implicitly but necessarily and specifically, to the active ingredient in question".

Whilst the judgment of the CJEU in C-493/12 provided a degree of clarity, it still left the UK High Court with a the difficult task of applying the judgment to the facts of the dispute between Eli Lilly and Human Genome Sciences. In a judgment tackling this task (*Eli Lilly and Company v Human Genome Sciences Inc* [2014] EWHC 2404 (Pat)), Warren J. expressed his disappointment that the CJEU had not given express guidance about what it meant by "specified" in *Medeva* (or "identified" in subsequent cases). However, he concluded that this must be because the CJEU considered the guidance in *Medeva* to be sufficient once it had identified (in para.32 of the judgment in C-493/12), the applicable rules for determining what is protected by a basic patent. The rules identified by the CJEU were those relating to the *extent of the invention* covered by a patent (e.g. s.125 of the UK Patents Act 1977 and/or, for a patent granted by the EPO, the rules laid down in the EPC and the Protocol on the Interpretation of Article 69 EPC). Applying those rules, Warren J. concluded that, subject to one important proviso, the criterion for determining protection under art.3(a) is "If the product falls within the claims, it will be protected within Article 3(a)". The proviso to this criterion is discussed at [66] of Warren J.'s judgment:

"The proviso relates to products which are combinations of active ingredients and is necessary to reflect the *Medeva* approach where the claims contain some general word or words extending their extent beyond the principal scope of the claims, typically by the use of a word such as 'comprises'. In the absence of such an extending word, the claims have a focused scope and the question is simply whether the product falls within the scope of the claims. In the language of *Medeva*, the question is whether the product (ie the combination of active ingredients) is 'specified' in the claims, a question which is answered by a close examination of the claims. If general words are included, the position is different. The product does not fall within the focus of the claims and is not within its scope apart from the general words. In such a case, the product is not 'specified' any more than it is 'specified' where the general words are absent".

Thus, Warren J. appeared to suggest that a product is "protected" within the meaning of art.3(a) if it both falls within and represents the focus of a patent claim.

With regard to what appeared at first sight to represent an additional condition imposed by the CJEU on claims defining active ingredients by way of a functional formula, Warren J. concluded that:

"the Court was saying that an active ingredient is 'identified' so as to fall within the protection of a basic patent if the active ingredient is within the claims of the basic patent provided the claims relate, implicitly but necessarily and specifically, to the active ingredients. Those words reflect, in the context of a functional definition, no more and no less than the word 'specified' in *Medeva* and 'identified' in subsequent cases."

This suggested a relatively straightforward approach, wherein art.3(a) is satisfied where both the product for the SPC and the claims of the basic patent relate to a single active ingredient, and where the active ingredient also falls within the extent of protection conferred by the claims (as determined under s.125 and Article 69 EPC and the Protocol thereto).

However, in his judgment in *Teva UK Ltd v Gilead Sciences Inc* [2017] EWHC 13 (Pat), Arnold J. took issue with certain aspects of Warren J.'s reasoning in *Eli Lilly*. Having done so he also decided to seek further guidance from the CJEU, by referring (yet again) the question "What are the criteria for deciding whether 'the product is protected by a basic patent in force' in Article 3(a) of the SPC Regulation?" On July 25, 2018, that question was answered by the CJEU in *Teva UK* (C-121/17) as follows:

"Article 3(a) of Regulation No.469/2009 of the European Parliament and of the Council of 6 May 2009, concerning the supplementary protection certificate for medicinal products, must be interpreted as meaning that a product composed of several active ingredients with a combined effect is 'protected by a basic patent in force' within the meaning of that provision where, even if the combination of active ingredients of which that product is composed is not expressly mentioned in the claims of the basic patent, those claims relate necessarily and specifically to that combination. For that purpose, from the point of view of a person skilled in the art and on the basis of the prior art at the filing date or priority date of the basic patent:

— the combination of those active ingredients must necessarily, in the light of the description and drawings of that patent, fall under the invention covered by that patent, and
— each of those active ingredients must be specifically identifiable, in the light of all the information disclosed by that patent."

In reaching this decision, the CJEU effectively confirmed Arnold J.'s view that, for satisfying art.3(a), it is necessary but not sufficient that the product falls within at least one claim of the basic patent applying the "extent of protection" test. However, the CJEU's decision clearly rejects the additional ("inventive advance") test that was proposed by Arnold J., and that was supported in one form or another in the majority of submissions to the CJEU in case C-121/17 (including those from the governments of the UK, the Netherlands, Greece and Latvia). Instead, at least for products "composed of several active ingredients with a combined effect", the CJEU has established an additional test that focuses upon the question of whether each active ingredient is "specifically identifiable" in the light of all the information disclosed by the basic patent.

The case again came before Arnold J. in *Teva v Gilead* [2018] EWHC 2416 (Pat) where he observed at [10] that in a nutshell, what the court is saying is that the purpose of the SPC Regulation is to enable the holder of the basic patent to obtain supplementary protection for what the patentee actually invented and not for what the patentee did not invent. The first test was whether the combination was one that the skilled person would understand, on the basis of the description and drawings and their common general knowledge, to embody the technical contribution made by the patent. Here, there was no disclosure in the patent that the ingredients TD and emtricitabine could be combined to treat HIV but merely that the claimed compounds could be administered with other ingredients. TD embodied the technical contribution of the patent, but that was a different matter. The second test was that, from the point of view of a person skilled in the art and on the basis of the prior art at the priority date, each of the active ingredients must be specifically identifiable, in the light of all the information disclosed by the patent. Emtricitabine was not mentioned in the patent and was not even a member of a specific class of compounds mentioned in the patent, whether by reference to their structure or activity, as being suitable for combination with the compounds of the invention.

In an appeal against Arnold J.'s judgment, the Court of Appeal (in *Teva v Gilead* [2019] EWCA Civ 2272) disagreed with Arnold J.'s assessment of the first part of the *Teva* test. In this regard, Lord Justice Floyd observed that "I do not think that by using the term 'fall under the invention covered by the patent' the court is intending to refer to the inventive advance or technical contribution of the patent. The court has definitely set its face against the introduction of such a test". He also stated that:

"In my judgment, the first limb is simply a more elaborate exposition of the 'necessarily' part of the test first advanced in *Eli Lilly*, namely that 'the claims relate ... necessarily ... to the active ingredient in question'. I agree with Mr Mitcheson that this limb means that a claim to 'a formulation comprising compound A' does not protect a combination of A and B. That is because the presence of B is not a necessary part of the invention claimed. It follows that, to protect a combination product, a claim must require the presence of two compounds, not just one."

However, despite interpreting it in a different manner from Arnold J., the Court of Appeal nevertheless held that the first part of the *Teva* test was not satisfied, on the grounds that "it is not possible to understand claim 27 as requiring the presence of another therapeutic ingredient when it expressly states that it is optional".

The CJEU's ruling in *Teva* did not set out the precise requirements of the art.3(a) test, not least because it did not indicate which degree of specificity is required to satisfy the "specifically identifiable" criterion. Unsurprisingly, this resulted in different national courts reaching different conclusions with regard to the meaning of the art.3(a) test set out in C-121/17. For example, despite dealing with SPCs deriving from the same (European) patent, courts in the Netherlands (decision of the District Court of The Hague dated January 8, 2019, see ECLI:NL:RBDHA:2019:72) and France (High Court of Paris (*Tribunal de Grande Instance de Paris*) decision dated January 11, 2019, see *http://thespcblog.blogspot.com/ 2019/02/no-more-launch-at-risk-in-france.html*) arrived at divergent conclusions on the question of whether art.3(a) was satisfied for the product darunavir. Also, compared to Lord Justice Floyd in *Teva v Gilead* [2019] EWCA Civ 2272, the Irish Court of Appeal (in *Merck Sharp & Dohme Corp and Clonmel Healthcare Ltd* [2021] IECA 54), reached a completely different conclusion regarding interpretation of the requirement for the product to "fall under the invention". That is, the Irish Court of Appeal confirmed the conclusion of the Irish High Court that express mention (in the claims of the basic patent) of the active ingredients of a combination product was not enough to satisfy this requirement. This is on the grounds that "the addition of an existing compound to a novel compound cannot, without more, make the combination an invention in itself".

Whilst issued prior to the CJEU's judgment in C-121/17, another judgment from Arnold J. (*Teva UK Ltd v Merck Sharp & Dohme Corp* [2017] EWHC 539 (Pat)) reached a conclusion that was arguably compatible with the CJEU's art.3(a) test. This is because Arnold J. found an SPC to a triple combination to be invalid under art.3(a) on the grounds that a claim to a combination of one active ingredient with "a nucleoside analog" could not be construed to "protect" (in the art.3(a) sense) a combination of that active ingredient with two such nucleoside analogs.

In *Eli Lilly v Genentech* [2019] EWHC 388 (Pat), Arnold J. applied the test from C-121/17 to claims in two different categories (claim 1, directed to a product per se, and claim 12, directed towards a "Swiss" format medical use) and arrived at a different conclusion for each claim. For claim 1, which defined an antibody in functional terms, Arnold J. held that art.3(a) was satisfied on the grounds that the skilled team would understand that the antibody in question (ixekizumab, which was not created until after the priority date of the patent) "embodies the technical contribution" of that claim. He also considered that "ixekizumab would be specifically identifiable by the skilled team because it is identifiable by reference to the functions specified in claim 1".

By way of contrast, Arnold J. held that claim 12 of Genentech's patent failed both limbs of the CJEU's art.3(a) test, for reasons based upon his finding that "the skilled team reading the Patent in the light of their common general knowledge as at the priority date would not have considered it plausible that an anti-IL-17A/F would have a discernible therapeutic effect on psoriasis", as required by Claim 12.

Arnold J.'s conclusion with respect to claim 12 is based upon the CJEU's finding in C-121/17 at [50] that account cannot be taken of "results from research which took place after the filing date or priority date of the basic patent". Nevertheless, a controversial aspect of that conclusion was that it relied upon evidence that was not adduced in the manner specified in C-121/17. That is, the evidence in question addressed the issue of whether the medical use specified in claim 12 was sufficiently disclosed in the basic patent, whereas C-121/17 indicates that the relevant evidence should instead address "the point of view of a person skilled in the art and on the basis of the prior art at the filing date or priority date of the basic patent" with respect to whether the product for the SPC necessarily falls "under the invention" of the basic patent and is "specifically identifiable" in the light of the information disclosed by the patent.

It remains to be seen whether, and to what extent, evidence relating to sufficiency of disclosure can substitute for the evidence specified in C-121/17. In the meantime, Arnold J.'s judgment in *Eli Lilly v Genentech* perhaps suggests that, at least for claims in medical use format, satisfying the sufficiency of disclosure requirement may have a bearing on the chances of art.3(a) also being satisfied.

In *Royalty Pharma Collection Trust* (C-650/17) EU:C:2019:704 the German Federal Patent Court (by way of decision 14W(pat) 12/17) sought clarification of the art.3(a) test by referring the following questions to the CJEU:

1.   Is a product protected by a basic patent in force pursuant to Article 3(a) of Regulation (EC) No.469/2009 only if it forms part of the subject-matter of protection defined by the claims and is thus provided to the expert as a specific embodiment?

2.   Is it not therefore sufficient for the requirements of Article 3(a) of Regulation (EC) No.469/ 2009 if the product in question satisfies the general functional definition of a class of active ingredients in the claims, but is not otherwise indicated in individualised form as a specific embodiment of the method protected by the basic patent?

3.   Is a product not protected by a basic patent in force under Article 3(a) of Regulation (EC)

No.469/2009 if it is covered by the functional definition in the claims, but was developed only after the filing date of the basic patent as a result of an independent inventive step?

In *Sandoz and Hexal* (C-114/18), the English Court of Appeal (by way of the decision in *Sandoz Ltd v GD Searle LLC* [2018] EWCA Civ 49) sought clarification with regard to how the art.3(a) test is to be applied to claims defined by reference to a generic (Markush) structure. The question referred to the CJEU in C-114/18 was as follows:

"Where the sole active ingredient the subject of a supplementary protection certificate issued under [the SPC Regulation] is a member of a class of compounds which fall within a Markush definition in a claim of the patent, all of which class members embody the core inventive technical advance of the patent, is it sufficient for the purposes of Article 3(a) of the SPC Regulation that the compound would, upon examination of its structure, immediately be recognised as one which falls within the class (and therefore would be protected by the patent as a matter of national patent law) or must the specific substituents necessary to form the active ingredient be amongst those which the skilled person could derive, based on their common general knowledge, from a reading of the patent claims?"

After issuance of Advocate-General Hogan's opinion on joined cases C-650/17 and C-114/18, but before the CJEU's ruling in those cases, the UK Court of Appeal withdrew its request for a preliminary ruling in case C-114/18. Thus, the ruling issued by the CJEU on April 30, 2020 only addressed the questions posed in C-650/17. In response to those questions, the CJEU ruled as follows:

1. Article 3(a) of Regulation (EC) No 469/2009 of the European Parliament and of the Council of 6 May 2009 concerning the supplementary protection certificate for medicinal products must be interpreted as meaning that a product is protected by a basic patent in force, within the meaning of that provision, if it corresponds to a general functional definition used by one of the claims of the basic patent and necessarily comes within the scope of the invention covered by that patent, but is not otherwise indicated in individualised form as a specific embodiment of the method of that patent, provided that it is specifically identifiable, in the light of all the information disclosed by that patent, by a person skilled in the art, based on that person's general knowledge in the relevant field at the filing date or priority date of the basic patent and on the prior art at that date.

2. Article 3(a) of Regulation No 469/2009 must be interpreted as meaning that a product is not protected by a basic patent in force, within the meaning of that provision, if, although it is covered by the functional definition given in the claims of that patent, it was developed after the filing date of the application for the basic patent, following an independent inventive step.

In paragraphs 31 and 32 of its ruling, the CJEU also confirmed that the concept of the "core inventive advance" of the patent is not relevant to the interpretation of art.3(a).

The ruling in C-650/17 raises at least as many questions as it answers. Thus, whilst it may now be more straightforward to determine art.3(a) compliance in some cases, difficulties are likely to remain in other cases. If the remaining difficulties lead to continued disharmony with regard to the interpretation of art.3(a), national courts in EU Member States may well have little choice but to seek yet further guidance from the CJEU. In particular, there may be a need to clarify the meaning and significance of "an independent inventive step" in the context of a product developed after the filing date of a basic patent. Of course, the situation will be different in the UK, as UK courts will now have the option of reaching their own conclusions on how to interpret the CJEU's rulings on art.3(a). Moreover, at least the Court of Appeal and the Supreme Court will have the additional option of diverging from those rulings of the CJEU.

Following an appeal from the Hearing Officer's decision in *University of Queensland & CSL Ltd* BL O/335/10, a case which again involved multi-disease vaccines, in addition to referring the first, second, fourth and sixth questions of *Medeva* to the CJEU (as questions 1, 2, 4 and 7 respectively), the Patents Court referred the following further questions, C-630/10:

3. Is one of these further or different criteria [for deciding whether a product is protected by a basic patent in force] whether the active ingredients are admixed together rather than being delivered in separate formulations but at the same time?

5. In a case like the present one involving a medicinal product comprising more than one active ingredient, is it relevant to the assessment of whether or not 'the product is protected by a basic patent' according to art.3(a) that the basic patent is one of a family of patents based on the same

original patent application and comprising a parent patent and two divisional patents which between them protect all the active ingredients in the medicinal product?

8. Does the answer to Question [6 in *Medeva*] differ depending on whether the authorisation is for the single active ingredient admixed with the one or more other active ingredients rather than being delivered in separate formulations but at the same time?

In *University of Queensland* (C-630/10), the CJEU answered these questions by reference to the answers it had already given in *Medeva* (above). In relation to the further question whether "in a case like the present one involving a basic patent with claims to "a process to obtain a product" in the sense of art.1(c) [of the SPC Regulation], does the "product" of art.3(a) [of the Regulation] have to be obtained directly by means of that process" the court answered that art.3(a) precludes an SPC being granted for a product "other than that identified in the wording of the claims of that patent as the product deriving from the process in question. Whether it is possible to obtain the product directly as a result of that process is irrelevant in that regard."

The ruling in *University of Queensland* was used by Arnold J. in *Novartis v MedImmune* ([2012] EWHC 181 (Pat)) to reject an SPC application based upon a patent to a process that defined the product of the process merely as "a molecule with binding specificity for a particular target". Whilst emphasising that he had his doubts about the meaning of "specified (or identified) in the wording of the claims" in *Medeva* and its progeny, Arnold J. nevertheless held that the ruling in *University of Queensland* imposed a stricter test for claims in process format. In this respect, he observed that "even if *Medeva* can be interpreted as leaving open the possibility that it is sufficient for the product to be within the scope of the claim where the claim is a product claim, it seems to me that *Queensland* lays down a narrower rule in the case of process claims". With this in mind, he concluded that art.3(a) was not satisfied, on the grounds that there was nothing at all in the wording of the claim (or the specification of the patent), to identify the product for the SPC application (ranibizumab) as being the product of the patented process.

The ruling in *University of Queensland* was also relied upon by the IPO in *Icahn School of Medicine at Mount Sinai* BL O/552/14. In that decision, the Hearing Officer concluded that by explicitly stating that it is irrelevant whether or not it is possible to obtain the product for which the SPC is being sought directly as a result of the process, the CJEU has effectively excluded any alternative interpretation which could require evidence of whether the product has been or can be produced by the claimed process. However, as the Hearing Officer did not analyse the extent of protection conferred by the claims, it is unclear whether the approach to assessing art.3(a) adopted in *Icahn School of Medicine at Mount Sinai* is compatible with the requirement (from C-650/17) for the product to necessarily come "within the scope of the invention" covered by the basic patent. By way of contrast, extent of protection appears to have been a key issue in a later, contrary decision from the Dutch patent office. In that decision, the examiner rejected Mount Sinai's corresponding Dutch SPC application for failure to comply with art.3(a), on the grounds that all claim limitations must be taken into account when determining what is "protected" by the basic patent. Withdrawal of an appeal against the Dutch decision means that the CJEU is unlikely to be provided with an early opportunity to provide a ruling that will harmonise national patent office practices in connection with the assessment of art.3(a) for claims in process format. In this regard, it is currently far from clear how, or even whether, the art.3(a) test established by the CJEU in C-121/17 and C-650/17 (see above) should be applied to claims directed to processes.

The IPO has indicated that a product is specified/identified in the wording of the claims of the basic patent in the sense of art.3(a) if "having regard to the normal cannons of claim interpretation it is: (i) indicated in a claim; (ii) encompassed by a Markush formula; (iii) shown to result from the process protected by the basic patent; or (iv) encompassed by a functional definition" (see the MOPP, para.SPM3.02.6.3). Evidence, for example in the form of a statutory declaration, may be required if either of options (iii) and (iv) is relied upon. The IPO has also indicated that "in relation to Markush formulae (ii) or functional definition claims (iv), it is necessary to consider whether the product was identifiable at the priority date of the basic patent, using the test set out in *Teva* (C-121/17) as informed by *Royalty Pharma* (C-650/17)".

The IPO has indicated that post-grant amendment of a patent (under the provisions of s.27 of the 1977 Act) may be used in order to meet the requirements of art.3(a). However, it is at present uncertain whether this practice is correct. This is because questions relating to that practice were referred to the CJEU in *Actavis Group PTC EHF, Actavis UK Ltd v Boehringer Ingelheim Pharma GmbH & Co KG* (C-577/13), but were not answered by the court.

At the date of submission of the SPC application, the United Kingdom marketing authorisation must already have been granted (*Yamanouchi's SPC Application*, BL O/112/93, noted I.P.D. 17136; and BL C/67/94, noted I.P.D. 18007, upheld on appeal to the CJEU: *Yamanouchi Pharmaceuticals Co Ltd v Comptroller-General of Patents, Designs and Trade Marks* (C-110/95) [1997] R.P.C. 844), and discussed by Natalie Young [1997] B.S.L.R. 81; see also *Sumitomo Chemical Co Ltd* (C-210/12)). A (pre-Brexit) marketing authorisation for the same product in another Member State, or granted later in the same Member State after patent expiry, will not suffice. An authorisation must, inter alia, include a summary of product characteristics ("SmPC") as required by art.8(1)(b) see §§128B.18 and 128B.42 above. This appears to rule out the granting of permission by a regulatory authority for a product to be supplied for a clinical trial to be considered as an appropriate marketing authorisation, as the required summary SmPC will not be available.

As regards (b) above, a full "marketing authorisation" is required, a letter granting permission to carry out a clinical trial not being sufficient (*British Technology's SPC Application* [1997] R.P.C. 118). A conditional marketing authorisation, granted in accordance with Regulation 507/2006, which are valid for one year on a renewable basis would appear to constitute a valid authorisation for marketing a product as a medicinal product, as it granted under a procedure falling within the scope of Regulation 726/2004. According to the Plant Protection Products Regulation (see art.13(3), reprinted at §128B.47) a provisional marketing authorisation (granted under art.8.1 of Directive 91/414 or art.30 of Regulation 1107/2009) may suffice if it is "directly followed by a definitive authorisation concerning the same product" and this position has been confirmed by the CJEU in *Hogan Lovells International LLP v Bayer CropScience AG* (C-229/09). However, an "emergency" authorisation under art.8(4) of Directive 91/414 has been held by the CJEU in *Sumitomo Chemical Co Ltd* (C-210/12, issued on October 17, 2013) to be insufficient to support the grant of an SPC. This conclusion presumably also applies to "emergency" authorisations granted under art.53 of Regulation 1107/2009. Also, the EFTA Court (in *Pharmaq AS v Intervet International BV* (E-16/14)) has opined that permissions granted on the basis of the first paragraph of art.8 of Directive 2001/82 do not constitute a marketing authorisation within the meaning of reg.1768/92.

In *Merck Sharp & Dohme Corp* BL O/117/16, the Hearing Officer at the IPO considered whether the date of authorisation in the UK could be taken as the date of an "End of Procedure Communication of Approval" issued by the Reference Member State in connection with a "decentralised" approval procedure. Compliance with art.3(b) for the product in question hinged upon this issue, as the basic patent had expired in the period between the date of the "End of Procedure Communication of Approval" and the date of the formal authorisation granted by the MHRA. In rejecting the SPC application for failing to satisfy art.3(b), the Hearing Officer noted that considerations relating to determining the duration of the SPC ruled out accepting either that the date of a valid authorisation in the UK was that of End of Procedure Communication or that the absence of a valid UK authorisation prior to patent expiry was an "irregularity" that could be cured under art.10(3). In view of different national offices reaching divergent conclusions in connection with corresponding SPCs, an appeal against the Hearing Officer's conclusions led to the Patents Court referring the following questions to the CJEU ([2016] EWHC 1896 (Pat)), in C-567/16:

1. Is an end of procedure notice issued by the reference member state under art.28(4) of the Medicinal Products Directive equivalent to a granted marketing authorisation for the purposes of art.3(b) of the SPC Regulation?

2. If the answer to question (1) is no, is the absence of a granted marketing authorisation at the date of the application for a certificate an irregularity which can be cured under art.10(3) of the SPC Regulation once the marketing authorisation has been granted?

On December 7, 2017, the CJEU essentially answered "no" to both of these questions. Whilst this decision from the CJEU is refreshingly clear, it can lead to disharmonious results. That is, with respect to the availability of SPC protection, the CJEU's decision effectively confirms that two EU legal regimes (Directive 2001/83 and Regulation 469/2009) can combine to provide different results in different EU Member States.

The Medicinal Products Regulation does not explicitly extend to medical devices. However, in *Genzyme Biosurgery Corp v Industrial Property Office*, BIE 70 (2002) 360-362 (Netherlands), the District Court in the Hague was asked to consider whether in respect of a medical device, authorised in accordance with the Medical Device Directive 93/42, which incorporates as an integral part a substance which if used separately can be considered to be a medicinal product within the meaning of Directive 65/65, an SPC could be obtained for that substance. The court was of the opinion that although art.2 of the Regulation does not refer to Directive 93/42, that need not be a bar to the application of the Regulation if the safety, quality and usefulness of the substance for which an SPC was being sought was verified as part of the authorisation procedure, being a procedure analogous to that for a medicinal product. Similar arguments may apply to the other device Directives, namely Directive 90/385 on active implantable medical devices and Directive 98/79 on in vitro diagnostic medical devices.

Following an appeal from the German Patent Office rejecting an application for an SPC for Yttrium-90 Glass Microspheres, based on an authorisation under Council Directive 90/385, rather than Directive 65/65, the German Federal Patent Court in 14W (pat) 12/07 ruled that authorisations granted under the device Directives 93/42 and 90//385 are to be considered as analogous to those granted under

Directive 65/65 (now replaced by Directive 2001/83) and so the applicant was entitled to the grant of an SPC for the product in question. The German court specifically referred to the similar practice of the Dutch court in *Genzyme Biosurgery Corp.*

Nevertheless, in a case before the IPO relating a medical device (*Cerus Corporation*, BL O/141/14), the Hearing Officer, who was fully aware of the above-mentioned decisions from the Netherlands and Germany, rejected the SPC application. The grounds for rejection were that art.3(b) of the SPC regulation makes it clear that a valid marketing authorisation is one that is granted "in accordance with Directive 2001/83/EC". In this respect, the Hearing Officer held that the assessment (under Directive 93/42/EEC) of the quality, safety and usefulness of a substance incorporated into a medical device and having an action ancillary to that of the device is not the same as or equivalent to the assessment of quality safety and efficacy of a medicinal product under Directive 2001/83/EC. That same conclusion was used by the Hearing Officer in *Angiotech Pharmaceuticals Inc* (BL O/466/15) to reject SPC applications based upon an authorisation for a drug/device combination (a taxol-eluting stent). The conclusion reached by the Hearing Officer was essentially confirmed by the CJEU in *Boston Scientific* (C-527/17, discussed in §128B.64).

In *Arne Forsgren* (C-631/13), the CJEU issued a decision on January 15, 2015 which held that the grant of an SPC for an active ingredient is precluded when the effects of that active ingredient do not fall within the therapeutic indications covered by the wording of the marketing authorisation. Relying in part upon the wording of art.4 for reaching this conclusion, the CJEU argued that the use of a product which has not been authorised, as a medicinal product, by the marketing authorisation may not be covered by an SPC. This conclusion is hard to rationalise, given that the CJEU had previously decided in *Yissum* (C-202/05), discussed in §128B.67) that that use of an active ingredient does not form an integral part of the definition of the "product" for the SPC. Thus, the decision in *Forsgren* may well be inconsistent with the CJEU's prior case law, to the extent that *Forsgren* requires an analysis under art.3(b) that involves anything other than determining whether the relevant active ingredient(s) is (are) present in the authorised medicinal product.

A literal interpretation of art.3(c) in the Medicinal Product Regulation seems to rule out the grant, in one EU Member State, of a certificate for a product which is already the subject of a certificate in that State. The Explanatory Memorandum accompanying the Commission Proposal for the Regulation suggests that the intention of this provision was to prevent a new SPC being granted each time that there was a minor change in the medicinal product, e.g. a new formulation, leading to a new marketing authorisation. This in turn would lead to extension of the duration of the term of the SPC protection for the product. However, in *Takeda's SPC Applications (No.2)* [2004] R.P.C. 2 it was held that under art.3(c) of the SPC Regulation, which states that an SPC can only be granted where "the product has not already been the subject of a certificate", applications for SPCs based on different marketing authorisations for combinations containing the patented active ingredient were refused as the relevant "product" was the same in each case, namely the active ingredient which was the subject of the patent.

In *Chiron and Novo-Nordisk's SPC Application* [2005] R.P.C. 24 two other companies had already obtained SPCs relating to a particular product under different patents, and the present applicants sought a further SPC under their own patent which had been granted subsequently. Article 3(c) was here given a "teleological" (object-based) interpretation as limited to the situation where multiple SPCs would be granted to the same applicant, but not where different applicants were involved. The application was therefore allowable, and could be distinguished from *Takeda*, above. The practice established by the UK-IPO in *Chiron* has now been confirmed following the CJEU's ruling in *AHP Manufacturing BV v BIE* (C-482/07) [2009] E.C.R. I-7295.

Recital 17 of reg.1610/96 (the Plant Protection Regulation) suggests that art.3 of the Medicinal Products Regulation is to be interpreted in accordance with art.3(2) of reg.1610/96 which states:

"2. The holder of more than one patent for the same product shall not be granted more than one certificate for that product. However, where two or more applications concerning the same product and emanating from two or more holders of different patents are pending, one certificate for this product may be issued to each of these holders."

The second sentence of this provision is consistent with the ruling of the European Court in *Biogen Inc v SmithKline Beecham Biologicals* (C-181/95) [1997] R.P.C. 833, which stated that where a medicinal product is covered by a basic patent, the Regulation does not preclude the grant of an SPC to each holder of a basic patent. The European Court has not explicitly considered the situation in which two or more applications for the same product emanate from one patent holder, but the practice of many patent offices is to allow only one SPC from such applications, see for example *Takeda Chemical Industries Ltd's Applications* [2004] R.P.C. 2. The same reasoning was applied in *Knoll AG's Application* BL O/138/05, where the applicant filed two co-pending applications relating to the same product based upon common marketing authorisations, but different basic patents. The applicant's argument that under a literal interpretation of art.3(c) of the Medicinal Products Regulation no objection could be made was rejected, as was the argument that art.3(2) of the Plant Protection Regulation No.1610/96 could not be used in the interpretation of art.3 of the Medicinal Products Regulation. In particular, the Hearing Officer found that it was not inequitable to deny a patent holder more than one certificate for a product whilst allowing other patent holders one certificate for that product. This decision is consistent with that of the same Hearing Officer in *Takeda No.2* (above).

Note: It appears that relationships between companies will be disregarded in determining whether SPCs should be granted to multiple applicants. Thus the UK-IPO has granted SPCs relating to the same product where the basic patents are in the name of different companies apparently belonging to the same group. As noted in §12.1.3 of the Study on the Legal Aspects of Supplementary Protection Certificates in the EU conducted by the Max Planck Institute for Innovation and Competition, it appears that the practices of different national offices are not entirely harmonised on this point.

For many years, patent offices and national courts had interpreted art.3(c) as only preventing the grant of more than one SPC to the same proprietor for the same product. Thus, there were many instances in which multiple SPCs (for different products) were granted upon the basis of a single patent protecting more than product. However, doubts over whether this practice was correct surfaced when, in her opinion in *Neurim* (C-130/11), discussed in §128B.66), Advocate-General Trstenjak stated that:

"according to the Court's case-law, Article 3(c) must be interpreted to the effect that only one certificate may be granted for each basic patent which protects an active ingredient or a combination of active ingredients" (see point 36 of the Opinion) and;

"Having regard to the case-law on Article 3(c) of Regulation No 1768/92, according to which that provision prohibits the grant of more than one certificate *for each basic patent*" (see point 54 of the opinion).

In the light of A-G Trstenjak's comments, questions were referred to the CJEU in both *Georgetown University* (C-484/12), a reference from the Court of the Hague) and *Actavis Group PTC EHF, Actavis UK Ltd v Sanofi* (C-443/12, a reference from the High Court of England and Wales). The questions relating to art.3(c) that were referred to the CJEU in these two cases are typified by the second question in *Actavis v Sanofi*, which was:

2. In a situation in which multiple products are protected by a basic patent in force, does Regulation [No 469/2009], and in particular Article 3(c), preclude the proprietor of the patent being issued a certificate for each of the products protected?

In *Georgetown University*, the CJEU ruled (on December 12, 2013) that, where an SPC for a combination of active ingredients has already been granted on the basis of a patent protecting that combination, art.3(c) does *not* preclude the grant (to the same proprietor) of an SPC to a single active which, individually, is also protected by the same patent.

However, in *Actavis v Sanofi*, the CJEU held (also on December 12, 2013) that, where an SPC for an "innovative" active ingredient has been granted on the basis of a patent protecting that active ingredient, then art.3(c) *precludes* the grant (to same proprietor and on the basis of the same patent) of a further SPC for the combination of that active ingredient with another active ingredient, where that other active ingredient is not protected "as such" by the patent.

The different answers that the CJEU provided in *Georgetown University* and *Actavis v Sanofi* left room for uncertainty regarding the interpretation of art.3(c). This is not least because, although it was a point that was arguably accepted by the CJEU, it was unclear whether the claims of Sanofi's basic patent satisfied art.3(a) with respect to the (combination) product of Sanofi's second SPC. However, although not stated in either of the CJEU's rulings, a difference between the two cases was that Georgetown's basic patent arguably provided "as such" protection for each individual ingredient in each of Georgetown's two combination products (combinations of HPV-6, HPV-11, HPV-16 and HPV-18, or of HPV-16 and HPV-18), whereas Sanofi's basic patent provided "as such" protection for only one ingredient (irbesartan) of a combination product that also contained hydrochlorothiazide.

The relevance of "as such" patent protection for a product was a theme that was picked up again by the CJEU in the judgment in *Actavis v Boehringer* (C-577/13). In that judgment, the CJEU observed that:

"It should be recalled in that regard, first, that it is possible, in principle, on the basis of a patent which protects several different 'products', to obtain several SPCs in relation to each of those different products, provided, inter alia, that each of those products is 'protected' as such by that 'basic patent' within the meaning of Article 3(a) of Regulation No 469/2009, in conjunction with Article 1(b) and (c) of that regulation".

The CJEU also made the important observation that the objective of reg.469/2009 was not to compensate the patentee for delay in connection with the marketing of his/her invention in all its possible commercial forms, including in the form of combinations based on the same active ingredient. In the light of these observations, the CJEU concluded that the grant of an SPC for an active ingredient which constitutes "the sole subject-matter of the invention" of the basic patent precludes the grant of a second SPC based upon a claim in the same patent to a product comprising combination of that active ingredient with another substance.

The CJEU did not provide any guidance upon the law(s), rules or principles that should be used when assessing whether a particular active ingredient represents "the sole subject-matter of the invention" of a basic patent. Thus, for example, it is currently unclear whether two SPCs can be granted upon the basis of a patent that includes claims to an innovative active ingredient, as well as claims to an independently innovative combination of that active ingredient with another (known) substance. Guidance of a sort upon this point is provided *Actavis v Sanofi*, where the CJEU indicated that "a new patent" covering "a totally separate innovation" could enable the grant of a second SPC (see the article "Three CJEU decisions that answer some questions but pose many more" by Snodin (M.) [2014] JIPLP 9(7), 599-604). However, it remains to be seen whether such requirements are decisive and, if so, how they are to be interpreted. Indeed, in *Merck Sharp & Dohme Corp* (discussed above) the Hearing Officer at the IPO, relying upon commentary in *Actavis v Boehringer*, effectively concluded that it was not necessary to have "a new patent", and that a second SPC based upon the same patent could be granted if the product for the first SPC did not represent the "sole subject-matter of the invention" of that patent. The current practice of the IPO is to grant SPCs to combinations that include an active ingredient for which an SPC has already been obtained "if the combinations are themselves the subjects of separate patents are specifically identifiable from the patent as viewed by the person skilled in the art at the priority or filing date using the test set out in *Teva* (C-121/17)" (see MOPP para.SPM2.03).

In *Teva UK Ltd v Merck Sharp & Dohme Corp* [2017] EWHC 539 (Pat) discussed above, Arnold J. also considered whether the SPC in question, directed to a combination of three active ingredients, satisfied the provisions of art.3(c) in the light of the prior grant of an SPC based upon the same patent and directed to one of the three active ingredients (efavirenz). In order to answer the question of whether the triple combination qualified for further SPC protection, Arnold J. held that it was necessary to decide whether that combination represented "a distinct invention protected by the patent", for which purpose it could be assumed that the subject-matter of the earlier SPC (efavirenz and its biological activity) was known to the skilled person at the priority date. Arnold J. justified adopting such an unusual approach to assessing validity of a patent claim on the grounds that the relevant question under art.3(c) was "whether, given the invention of efavirenz, claim 16 represents a distinct invention such that it could in principle form the subject-matter of a separate patent". Using this approach, Arnold J. concluded that there was nothing in the basic patent to suggest that the triple combination represented a distinct invention. He also considered that the expert evidence supported a lack of independent validity for the claim protecting the triple combination.

It is evident that national courts have experienced difficulties in arriving at a coherent and consistent interpretation of the case law of the CJEU on art.3(c). This can be illustrated by reference to divergent conclusions reached by different courts in connection with the validity of SPCs directed towards that combination of ezetimibe and simvastatin. Thus, whilst overturned by the Paris Court of Appeal, decisions of the Paris First Instance Court and the High Court of Paris (dated October 25, 2018 and March 7, 2019) found the SPC to comply with art.3(c), the Hague Court of Appeal and the Higher Regional Court Düsseldorf (in decisions dated October 23, 2018 and March 15, 2019, respectively) reached the opposite conclusion, as did the High Court of Paris in an earlier judgment (dated June 26, 2018). Moreover, the German and Dutch courts expressed divergent views on the question of whether the CJEU's ruling in *Teva* (C-121/17) contained principles that were relevant to the assessment of compliance with art.3(c). Such divergence is perhaps not surprising given the lack of clarity regarding the principles underpinning the CJEU's decisions on art.3(c). Thus, at least in EU Member States, one or more further references to the CJEU will be required in order to establish a truly harmonised approach to the assessment of art.3(c).

A further reference that could have helped to shed more light on the interpretation of art.3(c) was that made to the CJEU by the Swedish Patent and Market Court of Appeal (PMAC) in *Novartis* (C-354/19). The question referred to the CJEU in that case was as follows:

In view of the fundamental purpose which the supplementary protection certificate for medicinal products is intended to fulfil, namely that of stimulating pharmaceutical research in the European Union, does Article 3(c) of Regulation No 469/2009, having regard to Article 3(2) of Regulation No 1610/96, preclude an applicant who has previously been granted a supplementary protection certificate in respect of a product protected by a basic patent, in force in respect of the product per se, from being granted a supplementary protection certificate for a new use of the product in a case

[182]

such as that at issue in the main proceedings in which the new use constitutes a new therapeutic indication which is specifically protected by a new basic patent?

However, the CJEU did not provide a ruling on this question, as the reference in C-354/19 was withdrawn by the Swedish court.

Definition of "product" for which a supplementary protection certificate can be granted

Replace the tenth paragraph with:

In *Arne Forsgren* (C-631/13), the CJEU was asked to clarify whether an SPC may be granted for an   **128B.66**
active ingredient that is protected by a basic patent, where that active ingredient is present in a medicinal product as part of a covalent (molecular) bond with other active ingredients but nonetheless retains an effect of its own. The CJEU ruled that art.1(b) and art.3(a) do not preclude the grant of an SPC in such circumstances. Thus, it appears that, in principle, the term "active ingredient" in art.1(b) encompasses "active" portions of larger active ingredients, such as the "drug" portion of an antibody-drug conjugate. Nevertheless, the CJEU also ruled in *Forsgren* that an SPC for the active ingredient can only be granted if "it is established that it produces a pharmacological, immunological or metabolic action of its own which is covered by the therapeutic indications of the marketing authorisation". The *Forsgren* case was remitted to the national courts in Austria to determine whether this criterion has been satisfied with respect to Protein D (which is present in the medicinal product Synflorix, but only in conjugation with various different polysachharide antigens). Subsequently, the Austrian Supreme Court, in decision 4 Ob 20/15t, concluded that whilst it was necessary for the applicant to demonstrate that Protein D had a "pharmacological, immunological or metabolic action of its own" that was covered by the indications in the MA, it was not necessary for Protein D to be explicitly mentioned in the MA.

Replace the fourteenth paragraph with:

A related problem is when separate authorisations have been granted by the different authorities for marketing the same active ingredient as a human and a veterinary medicine. However, it has been held that the term "first marketing authorisation", as used in art.3(d) of Reg.1768/92 (and art.3(d) of the EU law version of Reg.469/2009), means an authorisation for either type of medicine (*Farmitalia Carlo Erba's SPC Application* [1996] R.P.C. 111).

Replace the eighteenth paragraph with:

On its own, the common name or INN given to a biological active ingredient might not provide a clear distinction over a similar but structurally distinct active ingredient. The MOPP does not contain any comments upon which (if any) objections under art.3(c) or (d) the IPO might raise in cases where this issue arises. However, objections have been raised in certain cases in other jurisdictions. For example, the Paris Court of Appeal confirmed the rejection of an SPC directed towards HPV Type 16 L1 protein and based upon the authorisation for Cervarix® (Paris Court of Appeal, Section 5, Chamber 1, April 12, 2016, case 15/12234, *The Government of the United States of America v General Director of the French IP Office ("INPI")*). The SPC application in question (FR08C0003) had been rejected by INPI for non-compliance with art.3(c), on the grounds that the applicant had already obtained an SPC (FR07C0020) for a product having the same definition, but based upon a different marketing authorisation (that for Gardasil®). Attempts by the applicant to amend the definition of the product and to rely upon differences in glycosylation and primary structure (due to production in insect cells as opposed to yeast cells) were unsuccessful, as it was held that the definition of the product for the earlier SPC encompassed all such variants of HPV Type 16 L1 protein. For comparison, the IPO simultaneously granted UK equivalents of both SPCs (SPC/GB07/030 and SPC/GB08/001, though only after the product definition for the latter was amended to specify that the protein was "made in insect cells"). At least in certain cases, the IPO therefore appears to acknowledge that structurally distinct variants of single protein can be recognised as different products for the purposes of the SPC legislation. In the absence of a pre-Brexit ruling from the CJEU on this point, it appears likely that the IPO will continue this practice. However, it may be that a ruling from the CJEU will be required to harmonise practice across the Member States of the EU.

Replace the twenty-first paragraph with:

The CJEU's decision in *Neurim* (which is now seemingly obsolete; see the discussion of *Santen* below) was interpreted and applied in variety of different ways by national patent offices and courts. For example, the IPO appeared to interpret it as permitting the grant of a new SPC in circumstances where there is both a new indication (or "application" in the words of the CJEU) and a new patent that has claims directed towards that indication. However, the IPO now accepts that *Neurim* has been overturned by *Santen*, (see the MOPP at para.SPM3.05.2).

Replace from "Thus, the judgment in Abraxis essentially upholds" to "may already be pending before the CJEU, namely Novartis (C-354/19; see §128B.65)." with:

The judgment in *Abraxis* therefore essentially upheld the judgment in *Neurim*, in as far as it applied to new therapeutic applications of old active ingredients, but ruled out SPCs being based upon authorisations for reformulations of old active ingredients.

In view of still unresolved questions regarding the true meaning and breadth of the ruling in *Neurim*, such as the criteria for assessing whether a new indication for an old active ingredient represents a "different application" whose authorisation can support the grant of a (further) SPC for that ingredient, the Paris Court of Appeal (in C-673/18, *Santen*) referred questions to the CJEU that were answered as follows.

"Article 3(d) of Regulation (EC) No 469/2009 of the European Parliament and of the Council of 6 May 2009 concerning the supplementary protection certificate for medicinal products must be interpreted as meaning that a marketing authorisation cannot be considered to be the first marketing authorisation, for the purpose of that provision, where it covers a new therapeutic application of an active ingredient, or of a combination of active ingredients, and that active ingredient or combination has already been the subject of a marketing authorisation for a different therapeutic application."

In essence, the CJEU's ruling in *Santen* overturns *Neurim*. This is made clear by paragraphs [44] and [53] of the CJEU's ruling, which respectively state that:

"It follows that the term 'product' within the meaning of Regulation 469/2009 is not dependent on the manner in which that product is used and that the intended use of the medicinal product does not constitute a decisive factor for the grant of an SPC"; and

"It follows that, contrary to what the Court held in paragraph 27 of the judgment in *Neurim*, to define the concept of 'first [MA for the product] as a medicinal product' for the purpose of Article 3(d) of Regulation No 469/2009, there is no need to take into account the limits of the protection of the basic patent".

To the end of the last paragraph, add:

The IPO's commentary on this point is non-committal (see the MOPP at para.SPM6.03). However, it is understood that the IPO will not raise an objection on the grounds that an SPC application relies upon a MA that is issued to a party that has no connection with the holder of the basic patent.

Definition of "basic patent" upon which a supplementary protection certificate can be granted

Replace the fifth paragraph (beginning "In view of the CJEU's ruling in Neurim") with:

128B.67   The CJEU's ruling in *Neurim* cast doubt upon whether there are circumstances under which it is possible for the same applicant to be awarded two (or more) SPCs for the same product. However, the CJEU's ruling in *Santen* appears to have eliminated that doubt, by making it impossible to obtain a further SPC for a product upon the basis of an authorisation for a new medical indication of that product.

Replace the third paragraph with:

Subject-matter of protection

128B.68   As the CJEU noted in *Pharmacia Italia v Deutsches Patentamt* (C-31/03) [2005] R.P.C. 27, the protection conferred by the certificate relates to any use of the product as a medicinal product without any distinction between use of the product as a medicinal product for human use and as a veterinary medicinal product. Thus a product first authorised as a veterinary medicinal product could not be granted an SPC following its authorisation as a human medicinal product. On the other hand, medicinal products are frequently authorised for further uses before the expiry of the certificate. For example, the SPC for a product first authorised for the treatment of stress incontinence in women, and then later, for the treatment of severe depression, will cover both uses, provided that the relevant basic patent protects both uses.

After the last paragraph, add new paragraphs:

For SPC applications filed on or after January 1, 2021, SI 2020/1471 amends art.4 of Regs 469/2009 and 1610/96 by changing:

• "the product covered by the authorisation" to read "the product covered by the UK, GB or NI authorisation" (for Reg.469/2009) or "the product covered by the GB or NI authorisation or both GB and NI authorisations" (for Reg.1610/96); and
• "any use of the product ... authorised before the expiry of the certificate" to read "any use of the product ... authorised in the United Kingdom before the expiry of the certificate".

These amendments are to be read in conjunction with those made by SI 2020/1471 to art.5 of the two regulations (see §128B.75 below), which essentially limit the protection conferred by a certificate to the nation(s) of the UK (i.e. GB or NI, or both GB and NI) in which there is a valid authorisation to place the product on the market. Nevertheless, it is not entirely clear how art.4 as amended by SI 2020/1471 is to be understood in the situation where a product has separate GB and NI authorisations, but those authorisations differ with respect to the definition of the product and/or the indications authorised. In particular, in situations where the authorised indications differ between GB and NI, it is unclear whether art.4 as amended is to be read as conferring protection in both GB and NI for any indication that is authorised in either territory.

Entitlement to the certificate

To the end of the first paragraph, add:
(see §128B.66)   **128B.69**

Replace paragraph §128B.70 with:

Deadline for filing the application for a certificate, or for an extension of a certificate

Usually the patent will be granted before grant of the marketing authorisation, in which case the ap-   **128B.70**
plication for the certificate must be filed within six months of the date of grant of the marketing authorisation. For SPC applications filed on or after 1 January 2021, SI 2020/1471 amends art.7 of Regs 469/2009 and 1610/96 by specifying that where more than one authorisation is granted in respect of the UK (or nation(s) thereof, namely, GB or NI), the application for a certificate must be lodged within six months of the date of grant of the earliest of such authorisations.
Where the marketing authorisation is granted before the patent, the application for the certificate must be filed within six months of patent grant. Where the basic patent is a European patent validated in the UK which has been opposed, the patent may still be designated under the SPC Regulation, although if the patent is revoked, then any certificate granted to the patent will also be treated as being revoked.
Care needs to be taken with establishing the date of grant of the marketing authorisation, used to calculate the six-month period for lodging an application. For MAs granted under the centralised procedure according to Reg.726/2004 (which MAs continue to take effect in NI), the date of the MA is not, as was mistakenly assumed by many national patent offices, the date of grant of the marketing authorisation, but merely inform the applicant for the authorisation, in a letter, that the medicinal product has been authorised. The usual practice is to take the date of the grant of the authorisation in such circumstances to be the date of the letter. The UK-IPO in *Abbott Laboratories' SPC Application* [2004] R.P.C. 20 at 391 took the view that the relevant date is the actual date of grant of the of the authorisation, but other patent offices, e.g. the Italian, have taken the view that the date is the date of publication in the relevant Official Gazette. In *Health Research Inc (C-452/07)*, the German Supreme Court referred the question of whether the "date on which the authorisation referred to in art.3(b) to place the product on the market as a medicinal product was granted", referred to in art.7(1) is determined according to Community law or whether it refers to the date on which authorisation takes effect under national law to the CJEU for a preliminary ruling. Whilst that case was abandoned in September 2008, identical questions were referred (albeit in a different context) in the *Seattle Genetics* case. In *Seattle Genetics* C-471/14; ECLI:EU:C:2015:659 the CJEU held that art.13(1) of Regulation (EC) No 469/2009 must be interpreted as meaning that the "date of the first authorisation to place the product on the market in the [European Union]" is determined by EU law and is the date on which notification of the decision granting marketing authorisation was given to the addressee of the decision.
There have been occasions when the applicant has missed the six-month deadline for filing the SPC

the application. Prior to their amendment by SI 2019/801, art.9 of the Medicinal Product Regulation and art.18 of the Plant Protection Regulation each provided that in the absence of procedural provisions in the Regulation, the procedural provisions under national law to the corresponding basic patent shall apply to the certificate, unless that law lays down special procedural provisions for certificates. As amended by SI 2019/801, both articles now specifically refer to the procedural provisions applicable to UK patents, as modified by s.128B of, and Sch.4A to, the Patents Act 1977. In *Abbott* the period for applying for an SPC in the UK was extended by six days, the application having been late filed because of genuine misunderstandings (occasioned by a transfer of rights) and prompt action having been taken once the position had been revealed. It was therefore decided that the relevant period (which was held to run from the actual date of grant of the marketing authorisation, and not from the (later) date of publication of the authorisation in the London Gazette) could be extended at the Comptroller's discretion under r.110(1) of the Patents Rules 1995, now r.108(1) of the Patents Rules 2007.

The CJEU's decision in *Seattle Genetics* (C-471/14), discussed in more detail in §128B.73, ought to also affect the calculation of the deadline for filing an SPC application based upon a "centralised" marketing authorisation. That is, the deadline ought to be set as six months from the date of notification of that authorisation, as opposed to the (typically two to four days earlier) deadline of six months from the date of the European Commission's decision to issue the authorisation. However, as the CJEU did not comment on this specific point there is perhaps some (small) room for doubt that this is indeed the correct interpretation of the filing deadline. The practice of the IPO is to admit evidence showing a different (later) "date of legal effect" than the date of grant of an authorisation, and (where relevant) to base the duration of the SPC upon that later date (see MOPP paras SPM8.03.1 and SPM13.05.1). Frustratingly, however, the MOPP is silent upon whether the same practice applies to calculation of the deadline for filing SPC applications under art.9.

Article 7(3) and (4) of Reg.469/2009 indicate that an application for extension of the duration of a certificate can be filed together with the application for a certificate, but cannot be filed any later than two years before the expiry of the certificate. (The later deadline specified in art.7(5) is no longer applicable, as more than five years have passed since the entry into force of Reg.1901/2006.)

Replace paragraph §128B.71 with:

Application for, and grant of, a supplementary protection certificate in the United Kingdom

128B.71   Applications for an SPC in the United Kingdom are made to the UK-IPO (Regs art.9, §§128B.19 and 128B.43). The procedure is governed by r.116. It requires the filing of PF SP1 (see r.116(1)) and a fee (£250 at the time of printing), see SPC Rules Sch.4. The application is given a number in the form "SPC/GB93/001". Notice of the application is published in the *Patents Journal* (2007 Rules r.44(7)). This notice includes: the name and address of the applicant; the number of the basic patent; the title of the invention; the number and date of the UK marketing authorisation upon which the SPC is requested; and, if different, the number and date of the first marketing authorisation for the product within the EEA (Regs art.9(2)).

For SPC applications filed on or after January 1, 2021, art.13A of the Regulations is relevant. Article 13A(1) and (2) indicate that information (under art.8(1)(a)(iv) as amended by SI 2020/1471) regarding the UK, GB or NI authorisations upon which the SPC application is based can be supplied after filing but before grant of an SPC application, provided that the information is submitted:

(a)   within 6 months of the date of grant of the additional authorisation(s); and

(b)   before the certificate takes effect under art.13(1).

Article 13A(3) and (4) indicate that such additional information can also be supplied after the grant of an SPC but before expiry of the basic patent, again provided that the information is submitted in by the deadlines mentioned in (a) and (b) above.

Notifications to the comptroller under art.13A of the regulations must be made on Patents Form SP6 (para.2 of r.116A). It is important to ensure that the IPO is provided, in a timely manner, with information regarding any authorisations of a product in additional nation(s) of the UK. This is not only because that information will determine the nation(s) of the UK to which the protection conferred by the SPC extends but also because art.13A(5) indicates that the territorial scope of protection of an SPC will not be extended if notification of the additional authorisations is not provided to the comptroller in accordance with art.13A(1)–(4).

All of art.13A(1)–(4) specify an identical deadline for notifying the comptroller of additional authorisations, namely the deadline defined by (a) and (b) above. However, art.13A(1) and (2) differ from art.13A(3) and (4) with respect to the definition of the date by which the additional authorisation(s) must be granted. That is, art.13A(1) and (2) both refer to "after the submission of an application under Article 7(1) or (2), but before the grant of a certificate under Article 10(1)", whereas art.13A(3) and (4) instead refer to "before expiry of the basic patent". This means that the paragraph of art.13A that is relevant to the submission of information regarding additional authorisations is determined by the date of grant of the additional authorisation(s) in question (together with the status of the SPC (application) in question), and not the date upon which the comptroller is notified of those authorisations.

Because art.13(1) specifies that "The certificate shall take effect at the end of the lawful term of the basic patent", it appears that the deadline for notifying the comptroller of additional authorisations may, in some circumstances (i.e. where the deadline is that specified in (b) above), be identical to the date by which, under art.13A(3) and (4), those additional authorisation must be granted ("before expiry of the basic patent").

However, there may be some difficulty in determining how the notification deadline specified in art.13A(1) and (2) should be interpreted with respect to SPC applications that are still pending after expiry of the basic patent. This is because it could be argued that a pending application does not qualify as a "certificate" in the sense of art.13(1) and/or that a pending application cannot "take effect" unless and until it is granted. The latter argument would be consistent with the IPO's view that even a granted certificate will not "take effect" if the prescribed annual fees are not paid in due time (see the MOPP para.12.14, though it may also be relevant to consider the s.69-type rights that arise in respect of SPC applications and SPC extension applications, as discussed in §128B.59). As a consequence, it may be possible to argue that art.13A(1) and (2) permit the notification of additional authorisations that are granted after expiry of the basic patent (provided that such notifications are made within the deadline specified in (a) above). The same difficulties of interpretation apply to a deadline in art.5(1b) of Reg.469/ 2009 and art.5(3) of Reg.1610/96, which is defined in essentially identical terms ("after the submission of an application for a certificate ... and before the certificate takes effect in accordance with Article 13(1)") and which relates to the territorial scope in which a certificate takes effect (see §128B.75).

Once filed, the SPC application is subjected to examination in a manner similar to the examination of patent applications, although there is no overall time limit by which that examination must be concluded. Reasonable individual periods for response to each letter outlining an objection to the SPC grant will be set and the Comptroller will not reject an application without having given the applicant an opportunity of being heard, as s.101 of the 1977 Act applies. Any such rejection may be made the subject of an appeal under s.97 of the 1977 Act initially to the Patents Court and thereafter, with leave, to the Court of Appeal and possibly the Supreme Court (Medicinal Product Reg art.18, Plant Protection Reg art.17, §§128B.28 and 128B.51). Before Brexit, there was also the possibility of reference to the CJEU for an interpretation of the Regulation under what is now art.234 EC and this has happened, see for example, §128B.63. The rejection of an application has to be advertised in the *Patents Journal* (2007 Rules r.44(7), implementing Regs, art.11(2)). As art.3(c) and 3(1)(c) of the Regulations stipulate only that an application must be one where "the product has not already been the subject of a certificate", refusal of an SPC application does not preclude a later application (*British Technology's SPC Application* [1997] R.P.C. 118).

If the requirements of the appropriate Regulation appear to be met, the Comptroller must grant the certificate (Regs, art.10(1)). Grant of the SPC is then made and the certificate indicates the date of expiry of its maximum period and that its entry is subject to the payment of the prescribed fees, for which see §128B.78. Under the 1997 SPC Rules, the form of a certificate was set out in Sch.3 to those rules, but no such provisions are included in the 2007 Rules. However, essentially the same format is used as before, which identified the SPC number, the grantee, the product, the basic patent number and its title, as well as the date on which the certificate will take effect (subject to the payment of fees) and the maximum expiry date of the SPC. Notice of the grant is published in the *Patents Journal* (r.44(7), implementing Regs, art.11), and the published information reflects that published for the application (for which see above), together with the duration of the SPC (Regs, arts.11(1)). An entry is also made in the register of patents, but in the case of SPCs granted on "existing patents" that register is maintained manually and for information on this a special application has to be made, see §118.18, There is no publication of an SPC as such, nor of an application for one (see MOPP paras SPM9.02 and SPM11.03). The granted SPC retains the same number as its application, for which see above (and see MOPP para.SPM10.19). Opposition to the grant of an SPC is precluded (Regs, art.18(2)), but third parties may submit observations under s.21, for which see §§21.06 and 128B.03.

In view of amendments to art.11 made by SI 2020/1471, notification must also be published of the number(s) and date(s) of the or each UK, GB or NI authorisation upon which the SPC relies. This includes any authorisation(s) for which the applicant has notified the comptroller after submission of an SPC application but prior to its grant. Such notifications are important for determining the nation(s) of the UK to which the protection conferred by the SPC extends.

Article 11 as amended by SI 2020/1471 also requires publication of the number and date of the earliest EEA authorisation, if such an authorisation has been granted in the EEA before (the earliest of) any UK, GB or NI authorisation upon which the SPC relies. This information is important on the grounds that the duration of SPCs under UK law (i.e. under art.13(1) as amended by SI 2019/801) is determined by reference to the date of the first authorisation to place the product on the market in the area comprising the EEA and the UK (see §128B.73).

The *Patents Journal* also gives notice when an SPC comes into force.

In practice, it is not easy for industrial property offices to verify whether or not the authorisation referred to in the application is the first authorisation to place the product on the market as a medicinal product. In Case COMP/A. 37.507/F3 *AstraZeneca*, the European Commission fined AstraZeneca €60 million relating to abuse of art.82 of the EC Treaty (now art.102 TFEU), a key aspect of which was the finding that in applying for SPCs, AstraZeneca made misleading representations to patent offices, including the UK-IPO, about the dates of marketing authorisations which the national industrial property offices concerned were under no obligation to verify. In *AstraZeneca v the Commission* (T–321/05), the General Court confirmed the majority of the findings of the European Commission that AstraZeneca's practices in relation to SPC filings were an abuse of art.82 of the EC Treaty (now art.102 TFEU), but reduced the fine to take account of a different date for the start of the abuse.

Applications for an SPC extension in the United Kingdom are also made to the UK-IPO (Reg.469/2009 art.9(1), §128B.19). The procedure is governed by r.116. It requires the filing of PF SP4 (see r.116(1)(b)) and a fee (£200 at the time of printing).

For SPC extension applications, art.8(1)(d)(ii) of the EU law version of Reg.469/2009 requires submission of "proof of possession of authorisations to place the product on the market of all other Member States, as referred to in Article 36(3) of Regulation (EC) No 1901/2006". This requirement is no longer relevant to SPC extension applications that do not fall under the transitional provisions of reg.69 of SI 2019/801 (as amended by SI 2020/1050). Thus, for SPC extension applications filed on or after January 1, 2021, applicants need only provide:

- a copy of the statement indicating compliance with an agreed completed paediatric investigation plan as referred to in reg.58A(2)(a) of the Human Medicines Regulations 2012 (see art.8(1)(d)(i) as amended); and
- details of the territory in respect of which that statement has been made (see art.8(1)(d)(ii) as amended).

Information under art.8(1)(d)(i) and (ii) can be supplemented (with respect to one or more additional nation(s) of the UK) after filing of an SPC extension application, or after grant of an SPC extension (provided that the deadline specified in art.7(4) has not passed). This can determine the nations of the UK in which the SPC extension confers protection. Article 11(3a) of Reg.469/2009 as amended by SI 2020/1471 requires publication, together with the notification of grant of an SPC extension, of the territory (or territories) in respect of which the extension has been granted.

The documentary requirements for an application for an extension of the duration of a granted certificate have been clarified in *E I du Pont Nemours & Co v UK Intellectual Property Office* [2009] EWCA Civ 966; [2010] R.P.C. 6, allowing an appeal against a decision of the Patents Court [2009] EWHC 1112 (Ch); [2010] R.P.C. 5, which in turn was an appeal from a decision of the Hearing Officer in BL O/096/09; [2010] R.P.C. 4. The Hearing Officer held that any deficiency in the documentary requirements for making the extension application could not be rectified afterwards. However, construing art.10(3) (which requires that the patent office asks the applicant to rectify any irregularity in art.8 broadly), Jacob L.J. held that the Comptroller should take into account all relevant factors, including the reason for the failure to include all the art.8(1) materials in the application, the extent to which the applicant was guilty of unreasonable conduct or delay, and how close to the date of the expiry of the SPC full compliance was expected. Unless the applicant had behaved unreasonably, time should be extended so that it got its reward.

In *Otsuka Pharmaceuticals Co Ltd* BL O/98/15, an application for an SPC extension was filed at a time before the relevant Paediatric Investigation Plan (PIP) had been completed. In refusing the extension application, the Hearing Officer held that the absence of a compliance statement under art.28(3) of reg.1901/2006 (confirming completion of the agreed PIP) was an "irregularity" in the application, and that it must be determined whether the materials provided by the applicant after the deadline for filing the SPC extension cured that "irregularity". At the time of the hearing, the applicant had provided neither the crucial compliance statement nor any of the materials demanded by art.8(1)(d)(ii). Also, the Hearing Officer held that it was unlikely that the missing statement would be available before expiry of the normal term of the SPC. Relying upon obiter comments of the Court of Appeal in *E I Du Pont Nemours & Co* (relating to third parties being entitled to enter the market once the normal term of the SPC had expired) the Hearing Officer found that the "irregularity" in the application could only be corrected before expiry of the SPC. However, as discussed in §128B.59, it is perhaps questionable whether the obiter comments of the Court of Appeal are correct, in the light of s.69-type rights afforded to SPC extension applications by para.1 (1)(b)(ii) of Sch.4A.

Fees and the time for their payment

Replace the first two paragraphs with:

Prior to their incorporation into UK law, the Regulations provided for the possibility of both application and annual fees (Regs, arts 8(2) and 12). The United Kingdom has exercised both these options. For the purpose of incorporation into UK law, arts 8(2) and 12 have been deleted. However, art.10(2) and (4) as amended now provide the comptroller with the authority to reject an application for which the "prescribed fee" has not been paid in due time. Further, art.14(1)(c) as amended indicates that a certificate shall lapse if the "prescribed annual fee" has not been paid in time. The "annual fees" must be paid cumulatively in a single payment. Rule 116(4) makes it clear that, besides a fee payable with the application, the SPC becomes effective only when the "prescribed fee" has been paid in accordance with r.116(5) (i.e. using Patents Form SP2).

128B.72

After the fourth paragraph, add new paragraphs:

In *Genentech Inc v Comptroller General of Patents* [2020] EWCA Civ 475, the Court of Appeal were faced with a situation where some, but not all, annual fees for an SPC were paid in due time. The Court of Appeal's ruling dismissed the appeals before it and thereby upheld the earlier decisions of the Hearing Officer (BL O/111/20, February 21, 2020) and the High Court (*Master Data Center Inc v Comptroller General Of Patents* [2020] EWHC 572 (Pat)). In essence, the Court of Appeal held that:

- it not possible to correct the underpayment of annual fees for a granted SPC after the latest date stipulated in UK law for the payment of those fees (6 months after expiry of the full 20-year term of the patent upon which the SPC is based);
- the filing of a request for a 6-month (paediatric) extension of the term of an SPC does not provide an opportunity to correct an earlier underpayment of annual fees for an SPC; and
- a request for a 6-month (paediatric) term extension cannot be granted in respect of an SPC for which some, but not all, annual fees have been paid.

The failure to address (in a timely manner) an inadvertent underpayment of the annual fees for an SPC can therefore lead not only to a shortened "normal" term for that SPC but also to that SPC becoming ineligible for a 6-month extension of its term.

Replace paragraph §128B.73 with:

Duration of the certificate and meaning of "Community"

While an application for an SPC must be filed before patent expiry, a granted certificate does not take effect until the expiry of the lawful term of "the basic patent". Thus, since the basic patent expires the day before the 20th anniversary of its filing date, the SPC in the United Kingdom will, provided that prescribed annual fees have been paid, take effect from the 20th anniversary. Thereafter, art.13(1) of the original (EU law) versions of the regulations both specify that SPC has a duration of a period not exceeding five years which is a period "equal to the period which elapsed between the date on which the application for the basic patent was lodged and the date of the first authorisation to place the product on the market in the Community, reduced by a period of five years".

128B.73

For the purposes of incorporation of the regulations into UK law, regs 29 and 60(2) of SI 2019/801 replace "the Community" in art.13(1) with "the area comprising the European Economic Area and the United Kingdom" (§§128B.23 and 128B.50). This change effectively means that the determination of the MAs that are relevant to the calculation of SPC duration in the UK has been completely unaffected by Brexit. Thus, references to "the Community" in discussions below of pre-Brexit case law relating to art.13(1) can, for the purposes of post-Brexit SPC law in the UK, be understood as being synonymous with "the area comprising the European Economic Area and the United Kingdom".

Whilst outside of the scope of this text, it is important to note that Brexit may affect the determination of the MAs that are relevant to the calculation of the duration of SPCs in EU Member States. This is because, in a Notice to Stakeholders dated June 15, 2020, the European Commission stated that:

"An authorisation to place the product on the market granted by a United Kingdom competent authority after the end of the transition period will not be considered a first authorisation to place the product on the market in the European Union for the purposes of Article 13 of Regulation (EC) No 469/2009 and Article 13 of Regulation (EC) No 1610/96."

However, this statement may not take account of the possibility for UK regulatory authorities (such as the MHRA or VMD) to issue MAs that have effect in Northern Ireland, whether alone or as part of the UK. This possibility is significant because NI effectively remains within the EU single market for the movement of goods, and MAs in NI must comply with the EU pharmaceutical acquis. Such factors could conceivably make MAs in NI relevant to the calculation of SPC duration in EU Member States (see also the discussion below regarding the relevance of Swiss MAs, due to their effect in Liechtenstein, an EEA Member State).

Where a basic patent has a duration of longer than 20 years from filing, such as those filed under a pre-TRIPS law in Portugal, the CJEU's ruling in *Merck Canada* (C-555/13, issued on February 13, 2014) means that art.13(1) of the Medicinal Products Regulation must, in the light of Recital 9, be interpreted as limiting the duration of the SPC to no more than 15 years from the date of the first marketing authorisation in the Community.

The marketing authorisation is deemed to be that provided for any purpose under the product licence regulations. Thus, where there had been a prior authorisation of a veterinary formulation, in a UK application, the Hearing Officer held that the SPC was to have effect from that date and not from the much later date when the active ingredient was first approved for human use (*Farmitalia Carlo Erba's SPC Application* [1996] R.P.C. 111). This practice of the UK-IPO has subsequently been confirmed by the European Court in *Pharmacia Italia SpA* (C-31/03) [2004] E.C.R. I–10001, where the CJEU ruled that the authorisation of a veterinary product was the first authorisation in the Community for an SPC application for a human medicinal product, therefore precluding the grant of a certificate for the human medicinal product.

The maximum duration of an SPC will be 15 years from the date of the first marketing authorisation in the Community (or, under UK law, in the area comprising the EEA and the UK) or five years from the date of normal patent expiry, whichever is the shorter. The patent must have run its full term for the SPC to take effect, so must not have been revoked or lapsed prior to normal patent expiry. The duration of the SPC will be less than the period under art.13 if the holder of the certificate fails to pay all the required annuity fees, either deliberately or inadvertently.

As incorporated into UK law, art.3(3) of Reg.469/2009 provides for the possibility of a (single) 6-month extension of the term of an SPC to which reg.58A of the Human Medicines Regulations 2012 applies. This requirement mirrors that under art.13(3) of the EU law version of Reg.469/2009 (which version is still relevant to cases falling under the transitional provisions of reg.69 of SI 2019/801), and relates to human medicinal products for which an agreed paediatric investigation plan has been confirmed as completed (see §128B.71). The maximum duration of an extended SPC will be 15½ years from the date of the first marketing authorisation in the Community (or, under UK law, in the area comprising the EEA and the UK) or 5½ years from the date of normal patent expiry, whichever is the shorter.

In the context of art.13 of the two Regulations, the word "Community" has been effectively replaced by "the EEA" (for the Medicinal Products Regulation as from July 1, 1994, see *Patents Journal* November 30, 1994, although for Liechtenstein only from January 1, 1995 when that country joined the EEA; and for the Plant Protection Products Regulation from August 1, 1997 for Liechtenstein, and from January 2, 1998 for Iceland and Norway). Thus, since July 1, 1994 (or January 1, 1995 for Liechtenstein), the first marketing authorisation (for a medicinal product) within the EEA (that is within the European Community as it then was, together with Austria, Finland, Iceland, Norway and Sweden) has been the controlling date for the duration of a medicinal product SPC, see note on PF SP1; and, since August 1, 1997 (or January 2, 1998 as regards Iceland and Norway), the first marketing authorisation for a plant product SPC within the present EEA (that is within the present European Community, together with Iceland, Liechtenstein and Norway) has been that controlling date, as indicated in §128B.64. Since Liechtenstein is a member of the EEA, and since marketing authorisations granted in Switzerland until June 1, 2005 automatically extended to Liechtenstein, Switzerland was also considered to be a country to be taken into account in determining the country for which the "first marketing authorisation" was issued: *Patents Journal* January 3, 1996. The effect of a Swiss marketing authorisation, granted before the June 1, 2005, on the duration of an SPC under the Regulation was addressed by the European Court in *Novartis AG, University College London, Institute of Microbiology and Epidemiology v Comptroller-General of Patents, Designs and Trade Marks for the United Kingdom and Ministre de l'Economie v Millennium Pharmaceuticals Inc* (C-207/03 and C-252/03) [2005] E.C.R. I–3209 ECJ, April 21, 2005, where the court ruled that as Swiss marketing authorisation was automatically recognised by Liechtenstein, it constituted the first authorisation in the Community. In coming to this conclusion, the court noted that if Swiss marketing authorisations were precluded from constituting a first marketing authorisation for the purposes of art.13, the duration of SPCs would have to be calculated by reference to a marketing authorisation issued subsequently in the EEA. In *Millennium*, the Swiss authorisation for the relevant medicinal product was granted two years before the Community authorisation under the centralised procedure. From June 1, 2005, the Swiss–Liechtenstein union was modified so that Swiss marketing authorisations no longer automatically extend to Liechtenstein, but instead are be subject to a minimum of a year's delay before taking effect, see press release, "*Secrétariat d'Etat à l'Economie SECO, Confédération Suisse*", April 21, 2005, *http://www.seco.admin.ch*.

As a consequence of the EEA Agreement, an authorisation to place a product on the market granted in accordance with national legislation of an EFTA State may be treated as an authorisation granted in accordance with EU legislation (e.g. Directive 65/65 and its successors). Thus, where the first authorisation in the Community (e.g. in Portugal, Spain or Greece) was not in accordance with Directive 65/65, because at the time of granting the authorisation the Member State in question had not yet implemented the Directive, the marketing authorisation is still treated as the first authorisation in the Community. In the UK, Netherlands, Italy and Sweden, SPCs were granted for aceclofenac, expiring in March 2005, based on a Portuguese marketing authorisation granted in March 1990, even though the first authorisation in the Community in accordance with Directive 65/65 was not granted (in the UK) until April 1995. In Germany, in 14 W (pat) 42/04 *Aceclofenac*, July 18, 2006, the Federal Patent Court took a different view, basing the duration of the SPC on the UK marketing authorisation, relying on the reasoning set out in *Hässle AB and Ratiopharm GmbH* (C-127/00) [2003] E.C.R. I–14781 ECJ. However, in a later nullity action in Belgium, the court of first instance in *NV Merck v Almirall Prodesfarma*, Docket Nr 06/10.756/A, Register Nr. 07/26125, June 15, 2007 found that the duration of the aceclofenac SPC should be determined by the Portuguese marketing authorisation and allowed correction of the SPC to change the date of expiry from March 2009 to March 2005, relying in part in the reasoning set out by the Advocate General in *Novartis*.

The question of whether an earlier marketing authorisation not in accordance with EU legislation can determine the duration of an SPC was referred to the CJEU in two separate and unrelated proceedings, *Synthon v Merz Pharma* [2009] EWHC 656 (Pat) and *Generics v Synaptech* [2009] EWCA Civ 1119 (on appeal from [2009] EWHC 659 (Ch)), as C-195/09 and C-427/09 respectively. In *Synthon*, the active ingredient memantine was placed on the German market before 1976, under legislation which predated Directive 65/65/EEC (the precursor of Directive 2001/83/EC). In 1983, a marketing authorisation was granted in Luxembourg, but this relied on the German authorisation, and no safety or efficacy studies were carried out. Both these marketing authorisations concerned memantine in the treatment of Parkinson's disease. However, in 2002, following safety and efficacy studies a community authorisation (under Regulation 2309/93) was granted for the use of memantine as a medicinal product in the treatment of Alzheimer's disease, and the earlier authorisations withdrawn. In the UK, an SPC was granted, identifying a basic patent which related to use of memantine in the treatment of Alzheimer's disease and citing the 2002 marketing authorisation as the first authorisation in the Community, for the purpose of determining the duration of the SPC under art.13. Four questions were referred to the CJEU following an action to invalidate the SPC or to fix its term at zero:

"1.   For the purposes of art.13 and 19 of [Reg. 1768/92], is an authorisation a 'first authorisation to place … on the market in the Community' if it is granted in pursuance of a national law which is compliant with [Directive 65/65], or is it necessary that it be established in addition that, in granting the authorisation in question, the national authority followed an assessment of data as required by the administrative procedure laid down in that directive?

2.   For the purposes of art.13 and 19 of [Regulation No 1768/92], does the expression 'first authorisation to place … on the market in the Community' include authorisations which had been permitted by national law to co-exist with an authorisation regime which complies with [Directive 65/65]?

3.   Is a product which is authorised to be placed on the market for the first time in the EEC without going through the administrative procedure laid down in [Directive 65/65] within the scope of [Reg. 1768/92] as defined by art.2?

4.   If not, is an SPC granted in respect of such a product invalid?"

Taking the third question first, and answering it in the negative, the court reasoned that it would be contrary to the objective of offsetting the time taken to obtain a marketing authorisation—which requires long and demanding testing of the safety and efficacy of the medicinal product concerned—if an SPC, which amounts to an extension of exclusivity, could be granted for a product which has already been sold on the Community market as a medicinal product before being subject to an administrative authorisation procedure as laid down in Directive 65/65, including safety and efficacy testing. In answering the fourth question, the court, following the reasoning in *Hässle*, held that because of the connection between art.19 and art.3, the SPC was invalid, irrespective of whether or not art.15.1 was an exhaustive list of the grounds of validity of an SPC. In view of the answers to the third and the fourth questions, the first and second questions were not answered. In *Generics v Synaptech*, which concerned an active ingredient, galantamine, which had been on sale as a medicinal product in various European countries for over 40 years, the court came to an essentially similar conclusion.

In *AstraZeneca v Comptroller-General* [2012] EWHC 2840 (Pat) the facts were that AstraZeneca had submitted an application for a marketing authorisation (MA) for Switzerland which was initially granted in 2004 but later suspended because of the need to submit further data. By virtue of the customs and patent union between Switzerland and Liechtenstein, the Swiss MA was automatically recognised in

Liechtenstein. An application for a European MA based on the same studies as in Switzerland was initially refused. A later application to the European authorities with data from further studies led to the grant of a European MA in 2009 and the suspension of the Swiss MA was lifted on submission of the same data. The IPO granted AstraZeneca an SPC calculated by reference to the Swiss MA. This meant that the expiry date was in 2019. AstraZeneca appealed that decision contending that the duration of the SPC should be calculated by reference to the European MA giving an expiry date in 2021. Article 13(1) of the SPC Regulation says that the duration is calculated based on the date of the first authorisation to place the product on the market "in the Community". The EEA agreement, of which Liechtenstein is a contracting party, says that references to the "Community" shall be understood to be references to the "territories of the Contracting Parties" as defined in the EEA agreement. Arnold J. noted that there was a divergence of interpretation between the different national authorities on this point. The patent offices in the Czech Republic, Latvia, Portugal, Spain, Sweden and the UK had all granted AstraZeneca SPCs on the basis that the Swiss MA was the "first authorisation" for the purposes of art.13(1) whereas Bulgaria, Denmark, Estonia, Greece, Italy, Lithuania, Luxembourg, Norway, Slovenia, Romania and Slovakia had proceeded on the basis that the European MA was the "first authorisation". Accordingly he referred the following questions to the CJEU:

1. Is a Swiss marketing authorisation not granted pursuant to the administrative authorisation procedure laid down in Directive 2001/83/EC, but automatically recognised by Liechtenstein, capable of constituting the "first authorisation to place the product on the market" for the purposes of art.13(1) of Regulation 469/2009/EC?

2. Does it make a difference to the answer to the first question if:
   (a) the set of clinical data upon which the Swiss authority granted the marketing authorisation was considered by the European Medicines Agency as not satisfying the conditions for the grant of a marketing authorisation pursuant to Regulation 726/2004/EC; and/or
   (b) the Swiss marketing authorisation was suspended after grant and was only reinstated following the submission of additional data?

3. If art.13(1) of Regulation 469/2009 refers solely to marketing authorisations granted pursuant to the administrative authorisation procedure laid down in Directive 2001/83/EC, does the fact that a medicinal product was first placed on the market within the EEA pursuant to a Swiss marketing authorisation automatically recognised in Liechtenstein which was not granted pursuant to Directive 2001/83/EC render that product ineligible for the grant of a supplementary protection certificate pursuant to art.2 of Regulation 469/2009?

In a judgment issued by reasoned order, the CJEU merely referred to its ruling in joined cases C-207/03 and C-252/03 and held that a marketing authorisation issued by SwissMedic that predates any other authorisations for the same product in the Community must (if it is automatically recognised in Liechtenstein) be regarded as the first authorisation to place that medicinal product on the market within the meaning of art.13(1). Factors such as refusal of a corresponding authorisation application by the European Medicines Agency, or the suspension of the Swiss authorisation were held to be irrelevant.

For the reasons discussed in §128B.64, the legal significance (for SPCs in EU Member States) of pre-accession marketing authorisations in the Czech Republic, Estonia, Cyprus, Hungary, Latvia, Lithuania, Hungary, Malta, Poland, Slovenia, Slovakia, Bulgaria, Romania and Croatia may well be different to that of pre-accession authorisations in EEA Member States, such as Switzerland.

In the light of the CJEU's decisions, the date of the first (relevant) marketing Authorisation in the Community is clearly determinative for the duration of SPCs filed and granted under the provisions of Community law. However, the situation was less clear for SPCs filed and/or granted at a time when a Community law did not apply in the country in question. If taken at face value, the transitional provisions of art.21 apply different standards to pre-accession SPCs in Austria and Finland (art.21(1)) and those in the Czech Republic, Estonia, Cyprus, Hungary, Latvia, Lithuania, Malta, Poland, Slovenia, Slovakia and Romania (art.21(2)). That is, whilst art.21(2) purports to apply Community law retroactively to pre-accession SPCs in the 2004 and 2007 accession countries, art.21(1) adopts the opposite approach for Austria and Finland. These divergent approaches reflect differences between the relevant Treaties of Accession to the EU. However, because the approach adopted in art.21(2) could have the effect of retroactively curtailing the duration of pre-accession SPCs, the Supreme Court (*Riigikohus*) of Estonia referred the following questions to the CJEU in *F. Hoffmann-La Roche* (C-572/15):

1. Must art.21(2) of Regulation No 469/2009 of the European Parliament and of the Council of 6 May 2009 concerning the supplementary protection certificate for medicinal products (codified version) be interpreted as shortening the duration of a supplementary protection certificate issued in a Member State which was issued under national law before the accession of the State in question to the European Union and whose duration in relation to an active substance, as

stated in the supplementary protection certificate, would be longer than 15 years from the time when the first marketing authorisation in the Union was granted for a medicinal product consisting of the active substance or containing it?

2. If the answer to the first question is in the affirmative, is art.21(2) of Regulation No 469/2009 of the European Parliament and of the Council of 6 May 2009 concerning the supplementary protection certificate for medicinal products (codified version) compatible with European Union law, in particular the general principles of European Union law on the protection of acquired rights, the principle of the prohibition of retroactive effect of law, and the Charter of Fundamental Rights of the European Union.

Whilst the CJEU answered question 1 in the affirmative, it declined to answer question 2 (on the grounds of lack of jurisdiction to rule on the validity of a provision deriving from a Treaty of Accession). At this point, it is unclear whether the retroactive curtailment of SPC duration that can result from applying the CJEU's answer to question 1 is consistent with the right to peaceful enjoyment of property enshrined in art.1 of Protocol 1 to the European Convention of Human Rights (in relation to which see the discussion in the article by Mike Snodin in *Bio-Science Law Review* 15(6), 248).

Where the certificate is granted with an incorrect duration because the first marketing authorisation within the Community (EEA or Switzerland) set out in the SPC application was incorrect, an appeal is possible (see art.17(2) of the Plant Protection Regulation, as well as §128B.63 and MOPP para.SPM18.02). In *Novartis*, the European Court was asked whether the authorities of the EEA Member States were obliged to rectify certificates, the duration of which had been erroneously calculated. As a result of finding that the duration had been correctly calculated, the court did not address this question. However, in his opinion in the case, Advocate General Ruiz-Jarabo Colomer expressed the view that national authorities are obliged to rectify the dates used to determine the duration of the certificate if, when they were set, a mistake had been made. In the absence of Community legislation, he continued, it is for the domestic legal systems of the Member States to make provision about the detailed procedural rules for obtaining rectification.

The issue of whether the appeal under art.17(2) of the Plant Protection Regulation is time-limited arose in the case of *Syngenta v Octrooicentrum Nederland*. In a judgment issued on February 18, 2015 (no. 201406096/1/A3, see *http://thespcblog.blogspot.co.uk/2015/02/dutch-council-of-state-upholds.html*), the Dutch Council of State agreed with the applicant that the rectification possibility provided by the second paragraph of art.17 would become pointless if it were subject to the same time limits as the appeals under national law specifically mentioned in the first paragraph of art.17 (which paragraph has been deleted for the purposes of incorporation into UK law). Thus, the view of the Council of State was that art.17(2) must be interpreted such that the appeal aimed at rectifying the duration of the certificate is not subject to a time limit. Nevertheless, patent offices of other EU Member States remained reluctant to accept the reasoning of the Dutch Council of State. As a result, a court in Hungary (*Fővárosi Törvényszék*) referred questions to the CJEU in *Incyte Corporation* (C-492/16) which were answered as follows:

1. Article 18 of Regulation (EC) No 469/2009 of the European Parliament and of the Council of May 6, 2009 concerning the supplementary protection certificate for medicinal products, read in the light of art.17(2) of Regulation (EC) No 1610/96 of the European Parliament and of the Council of July 23, 1996 concerning the creation of a supplementary protection certificate for plant protection products, must be interpreted as meaning that the date of the first authorisation to place the product on the market, as stated in an application for a supplementary protection certificate, on the basis of which the national authority competent for granting such a certificate calculated the duration of the certificate, is incorrect in a situation, such as that at issue in the main proceedings, where the date led to a method for calculating the duration of the certificate which does not comply with the requirements of art.13(1) of Regulation No.469/2009, as interpreted by a subsequent judgment of the court.

2. Article 18 of Regulation No 469/2009, read in the light of recital 17 and of art.17(2) of Regulation No.1610/96, must be interpreted as meaning that, in a situation such as that set out in point 1 of this operative part, the holder of a supplementary protection certificate may, under art.18 of Regulation No 469/2009, bring an appeal for rectification of the duration stated in the certificate, provided that that certificate has not expired.

In addition to clarifying that art.18 of the Medicinal Products Regulation (which article has been deleted for the purposes of incorporation into UK law) must be interpreted in the light of art.17(2) of the Plant Protection Products Regulation, the judgment in C-492/16 confirms that appeals aimed at rectifying the duration of granted certificates are not subject to any time limit other than expiry of the certificate (presumably by the earlier, incorrect expiry date). Nevertheless, not all national patent offices have established formal procedures for such appeals. In some countries, this could lead to such appeals being handled under (national) procedures that are not fully in line with C-492/16.

Prior to the CJEU's decision in C-492/16, appeals (PMÖÄ case nos. 9632-16, 9824-16, 9828-16, 9836-16, 9838-16, 9845-16, 9847-16 and 9848-16) aimed at correcting the duration of granted SPCs were filed were filed in Sweden under the only procedure available at the time, namely a national administrative law procedure (for requesting reconsideration of a Patent Office decision). The Patent and Market Court of Appeal (PMAC) denied appeals where the SPC had entered into force but allowed those where this was not the case. On 19 February 2018, and presumably despite the 20 December 2017 ruling in C-492/16 having been brought to its attention, the Swedish Supreme Court declined to hear appeals in the cases where correction of SPC term had been denied by the PMAC. Other than through the filing of new appeals in accordance with C-492/16 (for those SPCs that have not yet expired), it is not clear how the disharmony between the decisions of the Swedish courts and the CJEU's case law can be eliminated.

In general, UK practice before the *Novartis* referral was to take account of an earlier Swiss authorisation in determining the duration of an SPC, and whilst the reference was pending before the European Court, all pending UK SPC applications whose duration would have been effected by a change in practice were stayed, so no rectification of the duration of SPCs was necessary. Subsequent to the decision in *Genzyme Corporation* BL O/418/13 the IPO issued a practice note setting out the procedures for requesting correction of the date of a "centralised" marketing authorisation specified on an SPC application, and for requesting rectification of the term of a granted SPC, including when filing a simultaneous request for an SPC extension (see *http://webarchive.nationalarchives.gov.uk/20140603093549/http://www.ipo.gov.uk/p-pn-spcduration.htm*). The procedures all include the step of writing to the IPO to request rectification, and providing evidence for the correct date for the "centralised" marketing authorisation.

Until the coming into force of the amendments to the Medicinal Product Regulation made by the Paediatric Regulation (EC) 1901/2006, which amendments are now incorporated into Reg.469/2009, the maximum combined effective protection of patent and an SPC was 15 years. Accordingly, where the first marketing authorisation in the Community was granted less than five years after the filing date of the basic patent, an SPC would have no duration. However, the situation changed after the coming into force of the Paediatric Regulation, which permits the term of an SPC to be extended by six months where an application for a marketing authorisation includes the results of all studies conducted in accordance with an agreed paediatric investigation plan as set out in art.36 of that Regulation (see the article "Making the most of paediatric SPC extensions" by M. Snodin and J. Miles [2007] *RAJ Pharma*, July, 459–463). Upon the basis of arguments that even an SPC with a negative term might, if extended by six months, provide a useful additional period of exclusivity beyond patent expiry, the UK-IPO in *Merck and Co Inc's SPC Application* BL O/108/08 granted a negative term SPC, i.e. an SPC whose duration extends beyond that of the basic patent only if extended by 6 months.

Practice developed unevenly in the Community in relation to the grant of "negative term" SPCs under the Medicinal Products Regulation, with the Netherlands and Bulgaria following the UK practice, but the German and Estonian patent offices rejecting corresponding SPC applications. Following an appeal to the German Federal Patent Court, 15W (pat) 36/08, the case parallel to that decided in *Merck and Co Inc's SPC Application*, BL O/108/08, was referred to the CJEU as *Merck and Co Inc v Deutsches Patent- und Markenamt* (C-125/10). The CJEU's ruling in C-125/10, which confirmed the prior opinion of AG Bot, essentially held that an SPC can be granted if the period between the date on which the application for the basic patent was lodged and the date of the first MA for the product in the Community is less than five years, in which case the six-month term provided for in art.13(3) starts from the date determined by subtracting from the date of the expiry of the patent the difference between five years and the period which has elapsed between the filing of the patent application and the grant of the first MA. The effect of this is that a "negative term" SPC can be conferred so that a paediatric extension is then possible.

For determining the date of a "centralised" marketing authorisation (i.e. an authorisation issued by the European Commission, following receipt of a positive opinion from the European Medicines Agency), the standard practice of almost all national patent offices was to rely upon the date specified on the authorisation document, which is the date that the European Commission issued its decision to grant a marketing authorisation. However, it was argued that this standard practice was incorrect, and that the relevant date for the purposes of art.13(1) was instead that upon which the Commission's decision is notified to the applicant for marketing authorisation (see the article "Every day counts: why pharmaceutical companies in the EU need to make sure they get the right SPC term" by M. Snodin [2011] *Scrip Regulatory Affairs*, September 23). The basis for preferring the notification date is that the authorisation only becomes valid upon that date (in the light of art.297(2) TFEU). Whilst not appearing on the authorisation document, the notification date for each authorised medicinal product is nevertheless published in the Official Journal of the EU. In BL O/418/13 (*Genzyme Corporation*), the IPO accepted arguments in favour of use of the notification date and subsequently changed its practice regarding calculation of the duration of SPCs for which a "centralised" authorisation was the first in the

Community (see the discussion of the IPO's practice note in §128B.73). Despite this development, patent offices in other jurisdictions resisted changing their standard practices, which ultimately led to the Appellate Court in Vienna (*Oberlandesgericht Wien*) referring the following questions to the CJEU in *Seattle Genetics* (C-471/14):

1. Is the date for the first authorisation to place the product on the market, pursuant to art.13(1) of Regulation No.469/2009 concerning the supplementary protection certificate for medicinal products determined according to Community law, or does that provision refer to the date on which the authorisation takes effect in the law of the member state in question?

2. If the court determines that the answer is that the date is determined by Community law, is this the date of authorisation or the date of notification?

In a decision that essentially followed the (more detailed) opinion of the Advocate-General, the CJEU ruled that the date of authorisation is determined by EU law, with the consequence that the "date of the first authorisation" in art.13(1) is the date of *notification* of the decision granting the authorisation to the addressee of that decision. As discussed in §128B.70, the practice of the IPO is to admit evidence showing a different (later) "date of legal effect" than the date of grant of an authorisation, and (where relevant) to base the duration of the SPC upon that later date (see MOPP paras SPM8.03.1 and SPM8.13.05.1).

Although not made clear by the wording of art.8 as amended, it can be implied from the wording of art.13B (which was inserted by SI 2020/1471) that the statement mentioned in art.8(1)(d)(i) as amended may, in respect of the territory of Northern Ireland, include a statement under EU law in accordance with art.36(1) and (2) (and art.28(3)) of Reg.1901/2006. The wording of art.13B also clarifies that:

- the information demanded by art.8(1)(d)(i) and (ii) as amended can, before grant but after filing of the SPC extension application, be supplemented with respect to one or more additional nations of the UK (see art.13B(1) and (2));
- if an extension is granted in respect of GB only (or NI only), an application for extension in respect of the remaining nation(s) of the UK can still be made, if filed within the deadline set by art.7(4) (see art.13B(3) and (4)); and
- the nation(s) of the UK to which the protection conferred by the SPC extension extends will be determined by the nation(s) for which the information demanded by art.8(1)(d)(i) and (ii) has been supplied (see also art.13B(5)).

In any event, art.13(5) makes it clear that whilst it is possible for the extension of an SPC to confer protection in fewer nation(s) of the UK than the unextended SPC upon which it is based, it is not possible for the territorial scope of protection conferred by the extension to exceed that conferred by the unextended SPC.

Replace paragraph §128B.74 with:

Lapse or invalidity of the supplementary protection certificate, or revocation of the extension of its duration

While an SPC (which has come into effect by the due payment of the appropriate fees, for which see §128B.72) will normally lapse at the end of the period for which it was granted, it can lapse prematurely if the SPC is surrendered by its holder (using s.29 of the 1977 Act) or if the product has been ordered to be withdrawn from the market (Regs, art.14, §§128B.24 and 128B.48). **128B.74**

Although a third party cannot oppose the grant of an SPC as such (art.19(2) of Reg.469/2009 and art.18(2) of Reg.1610/96), any person can seek a declaration, either from the Comptroller or the court (2007 Rules Pt 7, as well as art.15(2) of the Regs as incorporated into UK law), that the certificate is invalid on a ground that:

(a) it was granted contrary to the provisions of art.3 of the Community Regulations (for which see §128B.65);

(b) the basic patent had lapsed before its lawful term expired; or

(c) the basic patent is revoked or limited to the extent that the product for which the SPC was granted is no longer protected by its claims; or, after the basic patent expired, grounds for revocation exist which would have justified such revocation or limitation. (Regs, art.15(1))

Although this is on its face an exhaustive list, in *Hässle AB and Ratiopharm GmbH* (C-127/00) [2003] E.C.R. I-14781 ECJ, the European Court ruled that a certificate that has been delivered contrary to the requirements of the transitional provisions of art.19 is invalid pursuant to art.15 and remarked that this must be so even it is not possible to infer from the wording or origin of art.15(1) that the list of grounds of invalidity of a certificate set out there is not exhaustive.

An application may also be made by any person for a decision that the SPC has lapsed on the grounds that the authorisation referred to in art.14(1)(d) of the Regulations has been withdrawn so that the product may no longer be lawfully marketed. Such an application may be made only to the Comptroller, as the SPC grant authority (2007 Rules Pt 7, as well as art.14(1)(d) of the Regs as incorporated into UK law).

For proceedings to seek from the Comptroller a decision of lapsing or a declaration of invalidity, an application is made on PF SP3. The fee payable with this form is currently £50, and the form must be accompanied by a statement of case in duplicate. For the subsequent procedure, see §128B.79. Any decision of the Comptroller under these provisions must be published in the *Patents Journal* (Regs, art.16, §§128B.27 and 128B.50); and is recorded in the register of patents (MOPP paras SPM15.01 and SPM16.01). The Comptroller's decision is appealable in the normal manner (this point was confirmed by art.18 of Reg.469/2009 and art.17(1) of Reg.1610/96, both of which have been deleted for the purpose of incorporation into UK law, §§128B.28 and 128B.51), see §128B.71. Likewise, any decision of the court should also be appealable in the normal manner for appeals from a decision of the court in question.

A withdrawal of the underlying marketing authorisation only affects the SPC when the product is ordered to be withdrawn from the market. Often, a marketing authorisation is withdrawn and replaced by a modified one, perhaps in favour of a different entity, and such replacement has no effect upon the SPC. Also, an order for the product to be withdrawn from the market may be only a temporary one so that there is the possibility that the lapsing of the SPC under art.14(1)(d) of the Regulations may also only have temporary effect. Provision for this is made by the opening words to this article: "If and as long as the product may no longer be placed on the market". Consequently, unless the SPC holder surrenders his/her certificate, for example to obtain a remission of fees (for which see §128B.72), grant of a subsequent marketing authorisation, or rescission of the withdrawal thereof, has the automatic effect of the SPC once more being in force. In such a circumstance, the SPC holder should advise the UK-IPO so that appropriate notice of termination of lapse can be published in the *Patents Journal* (MOPP para.SPM14.07). It is also possible for any person to apply to the Comptroller for a declaration that the ground of lapse under art.14(1)(d) no longer exists. This procedure could be useful when the marketing authorisation is granted to a licensee under the basic patent who retains his licence under the SPC. No formal requirements govern such a procedure (MOPP para.SPM14.08).

Due to amendments made by SI 2020/1471, a prerequisite to lapse under art.14(1)(d) of Reg.469/2009 is now the withdrawal of all UK, GB and NI authorisations to place on the market. Similarly, art.14(1)(d) of Reg.1610/96 refers to the withdrawal of "all authorisations". These amendments reflect the possibility that, as a consequence of Brexit, there may be multiple MAs that have different territorial scope with respect to the nation(s) of the UK that they cover (i.e. MAs covering the whole of the UK, or just GB or NI). The amendments are also subject to the transitional provisions of reg.7 of SI 2020/1471 (see the Note to §128B.24, which also discusses the applicability of the amendments to SPCs granted prior to January 1, 2021).

Related amendments made by SI 2020/1471 include:

- art.13(2) of the Regulations, which clarify that a certificate granted in respect of a UK authorisation does not lapse if that authorisation is withdrawn and replaced simultaneously with a GB authorisation and a NI authorisation; and

- art.13(3) of the Regulations, which indicate that the withdrawal of one or more (but not all) of the MAs covering nations of the UK will have the effect that "the protection conferred by the certificate shall, as from the date of withdrawal, no longer extend to the territory covered by the authorisation withdrawn but shall continue in respect of the territory covered by any remaining authorisation".

If and when an SPC lapses, either at the end of the period for which the fees were paid, or because of loss of the UK marketing authorisation referred to in art.14(d) of the Regulations, or if the certificate is declared invalid, then the fact is published in the *Patents Journal* (SPC r.10(d) and (f), implementing Regs, art.16, §§128B.27 and 128B.50), and an entry is also made in the register of patents (MOPP para.SPM14.01).

Under art.16(2) of Reg.469/2009, any person can submit an application to either the comptroller or the court for revocation of an extension of the duration of an SPC. If the application is submitted to the Comptroller, it must be made on PF SP3. According to art.16(1), the sole ground for revoking an extension of term is if that extension was granted contrary to the provisions of reg.58A(3) of the Human Medicines Regulations 2012. Of course, revocation of the basic patent and/or of the underlying SPC would also have the effect of revoking the extension of term.

For the purposes of assessing compliance with reg.58A(3) of the Human Medicines Regulations 2012 (or its EU law predecessor, art.36 of Reg.1901/2006), it is relevant to consider not only requirements relating to completion of a Paediatric Investigation Plan but also whether the MA holder has benefited from an alternative reward mentioned in reg.58A(4) or (5) of the Human Medicines Regulations 2012 (which include provisions related to art.36(4) and (5) of Reg.1901/2006). For example, as confirmed by the decision of the Hearing Officer in *Chugai Seiyaku Kabushiki Gaisha and Tadamitsu Kishimoto* BL O/321/20, a product that is designated as an orphan medicinal product, and that has already received a 1-year extension to the period of (orphan) marketing protection for the medicinal product, is not eligible for a 6-month extension of SPC term (as specified in art.36(5) of Reg.1901/2006, the provisions of which are now reflected in reg.58A(5) of the Human Medicines Regulations 2012; see also §128B.77A).

Replace paragraph §128B.75 with:

Effect of a supplementary protection certificate

CPR 49E PD 1 has been replaced by CPR 63.1–63.3 (reprinted in Appendix F). **128B.75**
The SPC is not itself a "patent", nor an extension of the basic patent as such. Nevertheless, in the nation(s) of the UK in which it confers protection, the certificate has effect to extend (up to its expiry) the protection conferred by the basic patent on its proprietor for the further term of the SPC, though only in respect of the single "product" (or a preparation thereof in the case of a plant protection product, or of the production or application of any such product), for which the SPC was granted and for any use of the product as a medicinal or plant protection product that is authorised before and during the life of the SPC (Regs, arts 4 and 5, §§128B.14 and 128B.38 and 128B.15 and 128B.39), as discussed in §128B.66. Otherwise, with the exception of the acts covered by Regulation 2019/933 (discussed below), now incorporated into UK law by way of art.5(2) to (11) of Reg.469/2009 (§128B.15), the SPC confers the same rights as the basic patent and is subject to the same limitations and obligations.
A consequence of Brexit is the possibility for a single product to be the subject of multiple MAs that have different territorial scope with respect to the nation(s) of the UK that they cover (i.e. MAs covering the whole of the UK, or just GB or NI). Amendments to the regulations made by SI 2020/1471 account for this possibility, essentially by stipulating (in art.5(1a) of Reg.469/2009 and art.5(2) of Reg.1610/96) that the protection conferred by a certificate shall extend only to the nation(s) of the UK for which there is a valid authorisation that:

- is the first authorisation for the product in the territory in accordance with art.3(b) and (d), and
- has been issued before the certificate takes effect in accordance with art.13(1).

Both art.5(1b) of Reg.469/2009 and art.5(3) of Reg.1610/96 indicate that the territorial scope of an SPC can be extended to additional nation(s) of the UK in the circumstances where a MA is granted in respect of such additional nation(s):

- after submission of an SPC application; and
- before the certificate takes effect in accordance with art.13(1),

provided that the MA in question is granted in respect of the same product and would have met the requirements of art.3(b) and (d) had it been granted on the date of submission of the SPC application.
The procedure for notifying the comptroller of MAs in respect of additional nation(s) of the UK is discussed in §§128B.71 and 128B.77, as are difficulties of interpretation with regard to deadlines (such as those in in art.5(1b) of Reg.469/2009 and art.5(3) of Reg.1610/96) that are set by reference to "after the submission of an application for a certificate ... and before the certificate takes effect in accordance with Article 13(1)".
The grant of an SPC is dependent upon the basic patent being in force at the date of expiry of its lawful term (Regs, art.15(1)(b) and (c)), and the due payment of the prescribed fees, for which see §128B.72. Thus, if the basic patent is revoked with the consequence that it is deemed never to have had existence, the SPC is itself invalid (cf. Regs, art.15(1)(c)). The position is likewise if the basic patent is amended so as to exclude the "product" for which the SPC is granted, because such amendment is deemed to have had effect from the grant of the patent (ss.27(3), 75(3), 76(6) of the 1977 Act). The SPC can also be declared invalid after the expiry of the basic patent where grounds for revocation exist which would have justified such revocation or amendment of the basic patent (cf. Regs, art.15(1)(c)).
However, while the SPC can extend to further authorisations given in respect of the same product after the initial UK marketing authorisation, e.g. to enable the product to be marketed for a further medical indication, there is no provision for updating the information supplied to the UK-IPO. Nevertheless, presumably, an SPC holder can notify the UK-IPO of such further authorisations so that the information is available to interested persons via inspection of the SPC file at the UK-IPO. The SPC will, in any event, be given in respect of "the product", as specified on the certificate, and in practice marketing of that product, as a "medicinal (or plant protection) product" will be possible only where there is a marketing authorisation for the product.
It appears that the monopoly protection granted by an SPC may be enforced by action for infringement as if the SPC were a patent, and that the effect of the SPC Regulations art.5(1) is that proceedings

for infringement may be brought before any forum (before which proceedings for patent infringement may be brought, the term "court" having the same meaning as under the 1977 Act (Regs, art.2, §§128B.04 and 128B.36), and that such proceedings can lead to the same relief as is available against acts of patent infringement, i.e. as available under ss.61–68 of the 1977 Act. There should also be the possibility of action against unjustified threats of SPC infringement under the 1977 Act s.70, and for seeking a declaration of non-infringement under the 1977 Act s.71. However, a certificate of contested validity granted in respect of the "basic patent" may not have automatic effect as regards infringement of an SPC based on it, but an award of costs is always a question of judicial discretion so that it should not be assumed that costs on an indemnity basis will not be awarded in infringement proceedings on an SPC for which the basic patent had such a certificate.

Before the Medicinal Products Regulation was incorporated into UK law, it was amended by Reg.2019/933, which defines exemptions from SPC infringement that are intended to allow the EU-based manufacture of generic and biosimilar medicines either: (a) at any time during the term of an SPC, for the purpose of export to a "third country" (i.e. a country that is not an EU Member State); or (b) during the final six months of SPC term, for the purpose of stockpiling for "day-one" market entry in EU Member States.

Article 1(2) of Reg.2019/933 introduced new paragraphs (2) to (10) into art.5 of the Medicinal Products Regulation, which specified that, under EU law, the following acts are excluded from the protection conferred by an SPC:

(i)   the making of a product, or a medicinal product containing that product, for the purpose of export to third countries; or

(ii)   any related act that is strictly necessary for the making, in the Union, referred to in point (i), or for the actual export; or

(iii) the making, no earlier than six months before the expiry of the certificate, of a product, or a medicinal product containing that product, for the purpose of storing it in the Member State of making, in order to place that product, or a medicinal product containing that product, on the market of Member States after the expiry of the corresponding certificate; or

(iv)   any related act that is strictly necessary for the making, in the Union, referred to in point (iii), or for the actual storing, provided that such related act is carried out no earlier than six months before the expiry of the certificate.

For the purpose of incorporation into UK law, these provisions have been amended to read as follows (in art.5(2)(a) of Reg.469/2009):

(i)   the making of a product, or a medicinal product containing that product, for the purpose of export to countries outside the United Kingdom, the Isle of Man and the Member States of the European Union; or

(ii)   any related act that is strictly necessary for the making, in the United Kingdom, referred to in point (i), or for the actual export; or

(iii) the making, no earlier than six months before the expiry of the certificate, of a product, or a medicinal product containing that product, for the purpose of storing it in the United Kingdom, in order to place that product, or a medicinal product containing that product, on the market of the United Kingdom, the Isle of Man or one or more Member States of the European Union after the expiry of the corresponding certificate; or

(iv)   any related act that is strictly necessary for the making, in the United Kingdom, referred to in point (iii), or for the actual storing, provided that such related act is carried out no earlier than six months before the expiry of the certificate.

Most significantly, "third countries" in art.5(1)(a)(i) has been replaced with "countries outside the United Kingdom, the Isle of Man and the Member States of the European Union". This has the effect of retaining as the "home" market (i.e. the countries to which export is not permitted whilst the SPC is in force) the territories that were covered by art.5(1)(a)(i) immediately prior to Brexit (though there is some doubt over the EEA Member States, which are not listed in art.5(1)(a)(i) as amended but which arguably formed part of the "home" market immediately prior to Brexit). A related amendment to art.5(1)(a)(iii) also effectively retains the pre-Brexit status quo by defining the UK, the Isle of Man and the EU Member States as collectively representing the "home" market for the purposes of the stockpiling waiver.

Regulation 2019/933 entered into force on July 1, 2019 and applies to SPCs that are applied for on or after July 1, 2019 and, from July 2, 2022 onwards, also to SPCs applied for prior to July 1, 2019 and that enter into force ("take effect") on or after that date. These dates of effect continue to apply to the UK, as they are included in art.5(10) of Reg.469/2009 as incorporated into UK law. Thus, the only SPCs to which the exemptions from infringement defined in art.5(2) of the Medicinal Products Regulation (as amended) will not be applied are those that entered into force prior to July 1, 2019, and those applied for prior to July 1, 2019 and that will expire prior to July 2, 2022.

The Medicinal Products Regulation as amended by Regulation 2019/933 also includes safeguards (such as marking and notification requirements) that are intended to prevent abuse of the exemptions from SPC infringement, such as diversion to the EU market of products manufactured for export (see, for example, art.5(3) to 5(9) of the Medicinal Products Regulation as amended, though note that, for the purpose of incorporation into UK law, arts.5(5) to 5(7) have been amended, art.5(8) has been deleted and arts 5(10) and (11) have been inserted).

Other consequences of the SPC Regulations art.5(1) and the effect of Sch.4A (see §128B.75) are, for example: that an SPC may be surrendered under art.14 of the Community Regulations in accordance with the provisions of s.29 of the 1977 Act, see §128B.75; that it may be assigned (under the 1977 Act s.30); that it is subject to employee-inventor compensation (s.40 of the 1977 Act); and that the provisions for Crown use and compensation apply (ss.55–59 of the 1977 Act). However, not only does an SPC confer upon its holder the same rights as it had under the basic patent, but that these rights are subject to the same limitations and obligations (Regs, art.5, §§128B.15 and 128B.39). While there may be a little doubt that this applies to limitations and obligations imposed by statute, the position is not so clear with regard to limitations and obligations which have their origin in inter partes contracts, such as those contained in an agreement which granted a licence under the "basic patent". This is because the term "patent" cannot, on the face of it, be read as including reference to an SPC, unless there is some indication in the contract which gives that effect.

However, it has been held that an SPC is subject to "licences of right" if the patent which is replaced was so subject (*Research Corp's SPC* [1994] R.P.C. 387 and [1994] R.P.C. 667 CA) and, by analogy, a licence agreement which grants a licence under a patent should be construed as extending to an SPC which becomes effective upon expiry of that patent, absent clear words in the contract to the contrary. If this were not so, then the licensee would become an infringer of the SPC upon expiry of the patent, and hence also expiry of his/her licence. A purposive construction of the terms of the contract would not lead to such an inequitable result. Indeed, on appeal in this case the Patents Court stated "A SPC gives no more nor less rights than those that existed under the basic patent". In the substantive decision settling the terms of the licence of right in this case (*Research Corp's SPC (No.2)* [1996] R.P.C. 320), the Comptroller followed this view by holding that, though the SPC was solely for the previously patented substance, importation of formulated compositions containing that product would fall under the protection of the SPC and should therefore be covered by the licence of right with royalties payable thereon.

Another consequence of the SPC being treated as if it were a patent, and an application for an SPC being treated as if it were an application, is that errors in the documents submitted are correctable under s.117. For an example of this, see *Patents Journal* March 8, 1995.

To give full effect to these provisions, general arrangements have been made to extend the law and practice of Great Britain and Northern Ireland to SPCs as if they were patents, see Sch.4A, §§128B.03–128B.09. Consequently, for proceedings in the UK-IPO involving SPCs or applications for them, the same Patents Forms are to be used, and the same fees (if any) are applicable, as if the proceedings involved a patent or application therefor, except where any of Forms SP1, SP2 or SP3 are required to be used (2007 Rules r.4). Also, CPR 63 (reprinted in Appendix F) embraces proceedings based on an SPC (see r.63.1(2)(e)). Consequently all proceedings in the High Court of England and Wales concerning such certificates must come before the Patents Court, as will appeals from the Comptroller relating to SPCs. Proceedings (other than appeals from the Comptroller) can also be brought before any other defined court, for which see §96.06.

Whilst now of uncertain relevance to the UK (in view of Brexit-related changes to the legal basis for the exhaustion of IP rights, see *https://www.gov.uk/guidance/exhaustion-of-ip-rights-and-parallel-trade*), close connections between SPCs and patents are also evident with respect to the so-called Specific Mechanism, which represents an exception under EU law to the doctrine of exhaustion of rights and is a feature of the 2003, 2005 and 2011 Acts of Accession to the EU. The Specific Mechanism provides a limited set of circumstances under which an IP right (a patent or an SPC) in an "old" EU Member State will not be exhausted by marketing (in certain "new" EU Member States, and by or with the consent of the IP right holder) of a pharmaceutical product protected by that IP right.

An important feature of the Specific Mechanism is that it can only be invoked if the IP right in the "old" EU Member State was filed at a time when such protection could not be obtained in the "new" Member State in question. The CJEU's judgment in C-681/16 (*Pfizer Ireland*) effectively confirms that the Specific Mechanism can be invoked: (i) if the legal system of the "new" Member State did not provide for equivalent protection at the time when the application for a basic patent was filed in the "old" Member State; and (ii) for as long as the (extended) SPC remains in force in the "old" Member State. Thus, whilst the ability to invoke the Specific Mechanism is tied to the (filing date of) the basic patent, the period during which it can be invoked is dictated by the term of supplementary protection (if any) awarded upon the basis of that patent.

Delete paragraph §128B.76, "Period within which application for a supplementary protection certificate in the United Kingdom must be filed".

Practice Concerning Supplementary Protection Certificates

Procedure for obtaining a supplementary protection certificate

Replace the fifth paragraph with:

128B.77   The applicant is required to identify the product for which protection is sought (s.6). Although art.8(1)(b) implies that the product should be described in the same manner that it is referred to in the marketing authorisation, e.g. dopexamine hydrochloride, the UK-IPO has long accepted formats such as X optionally in the form of the hydrochloride or X optionally in the form of a pharmaceutically acceptable salt such as the hydrochloride or X optionally in the form of a pharmaceutically acceptable salt (see the MOPP para.SPM2.04). However, this approach is not consistently followed across the EEA, the German patent office (and courts) preferring the format "X in all forms protected by the basic patent". It appears that the UK-IPO no longer accepts this format.

Replace the sixth paragraph with:

As the active ingredient of a medicinal product is usually identified by its international non-proprietary name (INN), but referred to by its systematic IUPAC name (for a chemical) or a code name (for a biological product, such as a monoclonal antibody), it is possible to set out what is meant by the INN, though it appears that the IPO may not encourage this approach. Proposed and accepted INN are published in "WHO Drug Information", which is a useful source of this information.

Replace the eighth paragraph with:

The first authorisation for placing the product on the market within the UK, GB or NI, as a medicinal product in accordance with either of Directives 2001/83/EC (for human medicines), 2001/82/EC (for veterinary medicines), or as a plant protection product in accordance with Directive 91/414/EEC, must be identified by number and date, for applications filed on or after January 1, 2021, the territory covered by that authorisation must be indicated. A copy of this authorisation must also be supplied. Corresponding information and documentation must be supplied in respect of any additional authorisations covering one or more nations of the UK.

After the eighth paragraph, add new paragraphs:

For SPC applications filed before January 1, 2021, the IPO may ask for the GB product licence number for any product whose (EU) "centralised" Marketing Authorisation has been converted to a GB licence via a "grandfathering" process.

The first authorisation to place the product on the market within the UK, GB or NI must be valid at the date of the application, and the copy must contain a summary of the product characteristics listed in art.11 of Directive 2001/83/EC or art.5A of Directive 81/851/EEC. For centrally authorised medicinal and veterinary products, a suitable excerpt from the OJEU should be provided in order to confirm the date of notification of the authorisation (see MOPP para.SPM8.03.1).

Replace the ninth paragraph with:

In the case of a human pharmaceutical product, it is necessary to file a complete copy of the Product Licence granted by the MHRA granted under the Medicines Act 1968 (c.67), together with a Marketing Authorisation issued under the Medicines for Human Use (Marketing Authorisation etc.) Regulations 1994 (SI 1994/3144). In the case of a veterinary product, there should be supplied a copy of the Veterinary Product Licence granted by the Veterinary Medicines Directorate of the Department for the Environment, Food and Rural Affairs, commonly referred to as DEFRA (including the accompanying Schedule) granted under the Medicines Act 1968 (c.67) and a Marketing Authorisation issued under the Veterinary Medicinal Products Regulations 1994 (SI 1994/3142), see the MOPP para.SPM2.01 and notes on PF SP1. Alternatively, at least in respect of NI and for either human or veterinary products, the marketing authorisation can be one issued by the central European Medicines Agency (the EMA) in the form of a Commission decision incorporating a grant document (bearing a number in the format "EU/1/23/4567" for a human product or "EU/2/34/567" for a veterinary product) issued under Council Regulation (EC) 726/2004, formerly Regulation (EEC) 2309/93. The copy of the authorisation filed should include the attached Schedule or authenticated copy of the licence application, commonly called the "product characteristics". This requirement can be satisfied by supply of information published on the Community register (*https://ec.europa.eu/health/documents/community-register/html/*) or on the electronic Medicines Compendium (*https://emc.medicines.org.uk*, replacing information previously available as a data sheet for the compendium of approved pharmaceutical products distributed by the Association of the British Pharmaceutical Industry).

Replace the thirteenth paragraph with:

Also to be provided are details of the first EEA authorisation (i.e. the first authorisation to place the product on the market within the European Community, EEA Member States or Switzerland, if appropriate, for which see §§128B.64 and 128B.71). For this, the State, the number and the date of such authorisation must be given as well as information identifying the product thus authorised and the legal provision under which this authorisation took place. A copy of the notice publishing such authorisation in the appropriate official publication should also be provided. In the case of the first authorisation having been obtained in GB or the United Kingdom, this official publication would appear to be the notice which appears in the *London Gazette* when a marketing authorisation is granted under the above-mentioned Directives. If no such notice is published in respect of the "first marketing authorisation", it is now permitted to file "any other document proving that the authorisation has been issued, the date on which it was issued and the identity of the product authorised", see the Plant Protection Products Regulation (art.8(1)(c)), probably also applicable to medicinal products, and see Recital 17 of that Regulation, discussed in §128B.63.

Replace the fifteenth paragraph with:

The application is then referred for formality and substantive examinations as with patent applications. The substantive examiner has to determine that: (a) the product is protected by the specified basic patent; (b) a valid authorisation exists for marketing the product in the UK, GB or NI as a medicinal product (or in GB or NI as a plant protection product); and (c) the product has not already been the subject of a United Kingdom SPC, all as required by art.3 of the Regulations (see, for example, MOPP para.SPM10.04). Article 10(5) of the EU law versions of the Regulations permit the examining authority to grant a certificate without verifying whether the conditions of art.3(c) and (d) (or, for plant protection products, art.3(1)(c) and (d)) are met. For the purposes of incorporation into UK law, art.10(5) of the Regulations has been deleted. However, the IPO's practice still relies upon this provision to the extent that no search is carried out (under art.3(d) and (1)(d) of the Regulations) to establish whether the authorisation specified was the first authorisation for marketing the product in the United Kingdom as a medicinal (or plant protection) product. However, the Office will raise an objection if such seems to arise, e.g. because of information supplied by an applicant, or by a third party informant (acting under the 1977 Act s.21) or information contained in a parallel application as in *Draco's SPC Application* [1996] R.P.C. 417, see MOPP para.SPM10.05.

Replace the sixteenth paragraph with:

If the examiner is of the view that there is a formality irregularity and/or that the requirements for the grant of an SPC are not met, an objection is raised in writing, and a time for response and rectification (usually two months) is then set, in accordance with art.10(3) and (4) of the Regulations. Where an application is deficient as regards the supply of required particulars or documents, the applicant is normally given an opportunity to rectify these deficiencies without loss of filing date (see MOPP para.SPM10.12.1). As confirmed by the CJEU's decision in C-567/16, the absence of information or documents establishing that the basic patent was in force and a marketing authorisation was granted by the date of submission of an SPC application is not "an irregularity" that can be cured in accordance with art.10(3) (see the MOPP para.SPM10.01). Extensions of the time set for response may also be requested and (as for patent applications) will be allowed at the Comptroller's discretion.

After the last paragraph, add new paragraph:

In accordance with art.13A of Reg.469/2009, it is possible to notify the IPO, after either filing or grant of an SPC application, with information and documents that demonstrate that the requirements for grant are met in one or more additional nations of the UK. The additional information should be provided on Patents Form SP6, for which there is no fee (see the MOPP at para.SPM8.06.1). The information on Form SP6 must be submitted to the IPO before the certificate takes effect under art.13(1), and within 6 months of the date of grant of (the earliest of) the additional authorisation(s) listed. As discussed in §128B.71, the territorial scope of the certificate will be limited to those nation(s) of the UK for which the comptroller is provided, in a timely manner, information and documents demonstrating compliance with the requirements for grant. After the filing (or the grant) of an SPC application, and before the certificate comes into effect, it is therefore particularly important to ensure that the IPO is notified promptly of additional (UK, GB or NI) authorisations relating to the product covered by the SPC (application). However, for SPC applications that are still pending after expiry of the basic patent, there may be some difficulty in interpreting the notification deadlines specified in art.13A(1) and (2) of Reg.469/2009 (for which see the discussion in §128B.71).

Add new paragraph §128B.77A:

Procedure for obtaining an extension to a supplementary protection certificate

128B.77A Application for an extension to an SPC, following is made on PF SP4 accompanied by the prescribed fee (currently £200, see the 2007 Fee Rules Sch.1). The request should specify a granted certificate number or certificate application number (s.2). If filing for an extension at the same time as making an application for a certificate, the UK-IPO will fill in this part. If the applicant already has a granted certificate, then its number and its expiry date should be given. Current practice requires that where the certificate is granted, a copy should be supplied. The applicant is required (s.5) to identify the active ingredient(s) or active substance(s), using, if possible, the chemical or generic names. If a certificate has already been granted, the applicant should use the definition of the product on the granted certificate. The number, title and expiry date of the basic patent (GB or EP(UK)) must be given (s.6), the number(s) and date(s) of the UK, GB or NI authorisation(s) containing the statement of compliance with an agreed completed paediatric investigation plan (as referred to in reg.58A(2)(a) of the Human Medicines Regulations 2012 which is the provision of UK law that corresponds to art.36(1) of Regulation (EC) No 1901/2006 (s.7)). For extension applications filed before January 1, 2021, the transition provisions of reg.69 of SI 2019/801 means that the requirements of art.8(1)(d) (and of art.13(3) and 16(1)) of Reg.469/2009 continue to apply, subject to the minor amendments of reg.69(3) of SI 2019/801. However, for applications filed on or after January 1, 2021, it is no longer necessary to provide an indication of whether the product has been authorised in all (other) EU Member States. Extension applications filed on or after January 1, 2021 are subject to the additional requirement to provide information on the nation(s) of the UK that are covered by the or each authorisation containing a compliance statement. The applicant is also required to state if a copy of the authorisation(s) required at s.7 is filed with the SP4. Following *E I Du Pont Nemours & Co v UK Intellectual Property Office* [2009] EWCA Civ 966, [2010] R.P.C. 6, failure to provide such documents at the time of submitting the application for an extension to a certificate is an irregularity which may be remedied after the date of application, during examination under art.10(3).

The MOPP at para.SPM8.12 notes that except where it is immediately apparent, the applicant should also provide whatever information is necessary to enable the Comptroller to confirm that the product in question satisfactorily completed the agreed paediatric investigation plan. For SPC extension applications filed before January 1, 2021, this can pose challenges where the medicinal product was not authorised through the centralised route, as evidence of authorisations will then, at least in principle, be required in each of the UK and the 27 Member States of the EU (but not the additional Member States of the EEA).

The MOPP at para.SPM10.09 indicates that the IPO will examine whether the product has already been the subject of the alternative reward set out in Regulation (EC) No 1901/2006. In this respect, it is understood that the IPO will check whether the product is designated as an orphan medicinal product. This is on the grounds that, in common with art.36(4) of Regulation (EC) No 1901/2006, reg.58A(5) of the Human Medicines Regulations 2012 (as amended, inter alia, by SI 2019/775 and SI 2020/1488), indicates that the reward of a six-month extension of SPC term will not apply if the medicinal product is designated (and authorised) as an orphan medicinal product. As discussed in §128B.74, this point is confirmed by the decision of the Hearing Officer in BL O/321/20 (*Chugai Seiyaku Kabushiki Gaisha and Tadamitsu Kishimoto*). Whilst the MOPP (at paras SPM8.13 and 16.01) has been updated to reference this decision, it is unclear whether the IPO's general practice has been updated to include a check on whether the product has benefited from any of the alternative rewards mentioned in reg.58A of the Human Medicines Regulations 2012 or art.36 of Reg.1901/2006.

In accordance with art.13(5) of Reg.469/2009, an SPC extension will only have effect in the nation(s) of the UK for which the requirements for the extension are met. However, in view of the provisions of art.13B of Reg.469/2009, it is possible to provide the IPO, after either filing or grant of an SPC extension application, with information and documents that demonstrate that the requirements for extension are met in one or more additional nations of the UK. Such additional information and documents must be submitted by way of a separate application for the paediatric extension to apply in the additional nation(s) of the UK, and may be made by filing another Form SP4 (see the MOPP at para.SPM8.17). All such separate applications for (territorial expansion of) an SPC extension must be filed before the deadline set by art.7(4), namely no later than two years before the expiry of the (unextended) certificate. It is understood that no fee is payable in respect of such (separate) applications to expand the territorial scope of an SPC extension.

In any event, the territorial protection conferred by the extension cannot exceed that conferred by the certificate (art.13(5) of Reg.469/2009).

Payment of fees to make a supplementary protection certificate effective

Replace the first paragraph with:

The onus is upon the certificate holder to pay the appropriate fees to make the SPC effective within **128B.78**
the required period, which runs from three months before the lawful date of expiry of the basic patent
up to the 20th anniversary of the filing of this, but the Office has to send a reminder if the fees are not
paid by the due date, see r.116(6) of the 2007 Rules. If the fees are not paid within this time, they may
be paid within the following six months with a 50 per cent surcharge; and, again, the Office must send
a reminder if the fees have not been paid by the due date, see also §128B.72. However, the Office will
not send a reminder in the event that some, but not all, of the annual fees are paid by the due date. Thus,
great care must be taken to confirm, before expiry of the period during which the annual fees can be
paid, that the fees for the period of protection desired (which will almost always be the full period
awarded) have in fact all been paid. For the possible consequences of underpayment, see the discussion of *Genentech Inc v Comptroller General of Patents* in §128B.72. Also explained in §128B.72 is
how the fee required is to be calculated, with the possibility of paying for less than the maximum possible duration of the SPC, although without possibility of its extension after that.

Procedure for challenge of grant or refusal of a supplementary protection certificate

In the first paragraph, after "MOPP paras SPM14.03;", replace "SPM15.03"
with:
SPM15.05   **128B.79**

**Inspection of documents filed at the UK-IPO in connection with supplementary protection
certificates and applications therefor**

Replace the second paragraph with:

Data relating to an application for an SPC is usually made available on the UK-IPO website within **128B.80**
two weeks of the application being made. Besides publication of details of applications for, and grant
and revocation of, SPCs which are published in the *Patents Journal*, and the entries which are made in
the register, the documents filed or sent to the UK-IPO become open to public inspection 14 days after
it under the 2007 Rules r.51, unless a confidentiality direction is sought and granted under the 2007 Rules
r.53. Thus, as regards such documents, the position is the same as that applying to documents filed at,
or sent to, the UK-IPO in connection with patents and applications, and copies of such non-
confidential documents are obtainable on request under the 2007 Rules r.52. Applicants can request, and
be granted, confidentiality in respect of any marketing authorisation documents (and/or associated
schedules) for which public inspection is not permitted by the regulatory authorities. If confidentiality
is required, care should be taken to request it within the 14 days specified in the 2007 Rules r.53. For
medicinal products, the summary of product characteristics (SmPC) is now published shortly after the
authorisation of a medicinal product by either the MHRA or the EMA (formerly the EMEA). A request
for confidentiality of the SmPC is therefore not appropriate.

*Delete paragraph §128B.81, "Procedure for obtaining an extension to a sup-
plementary protection certificate".*

SECTION 132

Replace Notes with: **132.01**

Notes

1.   The current order under subs.(2) is the Patents (Isle of Man) Order 2013 (SI 2013/2602), as
      amended by the Patents (Isle of Man) (Amendment) Order 2016 (SI 2016/559).
2.   Subsection (4) was first amended by the Oil and Gas (Enterprise) Act 1982 (c.23) Sch.3 para.39
      and the references to it then updated by the Petroleum Act 1998 (c.17) Sch.4.

Relevant Statutory Instruments

To the end of the first paragraph, add:
; the Patents (Isle of Man) (Amendment) Order 2016 (SI 2016/559)   **132.02**

Commentary on Section 132

Extension of the Act beyond the United Kingdom

After the last paragraph, add new paragraph:

132.06   For territory-by-territory information, see *https://www.gov.uk/government/publications/extension-of-uk-intellectual-property-rights-abroad.*

—Extension of the Act to the Isle of Man (subs.(2))

Replace the second paragraph with:

132.07   However, although the Isle of Man was not part of the European Union, by the Act of Accession of the United Kingdom to the European Communities 1972, the Isle of Man became part of the customs union of the EEC as later expanded to the EEA. Consequently, the EU Regulations for supplementary protection certificates did not apply as such to the Isle of Man, but these were applied by separate Isle of Man legislation, as it appears at least partially to have been done by Isle of Man Statutory Documents SD 447/93 and 748/99 see the Manual, §SPD,005 and §128B.57.

Replace the fourth paragraph with:

Court procedure in the Isle of Man High Court is governed by its own rules of court. The Rules of Court for intellectual property litigation in the Isle of Man are now to be found in Pt 12, Ch.7 and Sch.13 of IoM SD 352.09, as shown on the revised website *https://www.courts.im/rules-of-court.* It is also noted that a list of Statutory Documents for secondary legislation in the Isle of Man can be found on the website: *https://www.tynwald.org.im/links/tls/SD/pages/default.aspx.*

Replace the fifth paragraph with:

Because, at least for some purposes, the Isle of Man was not part of the European Community, the application of the doctrine of "exhaustion of rights" in relation to products first, or subsequently, placed on the market in the Isle of Man could differ from that where that first marketing occurs within the European Economic Area as such. Since the end of 2020, when the UK's exit from the EU took full effect, the UK has applied "asymmetric" regional exhaustion—the UK recognises exhaustion of rights occurring within the EEA but not vice versa. So there is unlikely to be a distinct issue for the Isle of Man. For the extent to which the Court of Justice of the EU ("CJEU") considered itself competent to decide matters of the law of the Isle of Man, see the employment law case of *DHSS (Isle of Man) v Barr* (C-355/89) [1991] 3 C.M.L.R. 325 CJEU.

PART V [SECTIONS 274–281] PATENT AGENTS AND TRADE MARK AGENTS

PATENT AGENTS [SECTIONS 274–281]

SECTION 275A

Commentary on section 275A

Code of Conduct

In the third paragraph, replace "To date three decisions have been issued" with:
To date five decisions have been issued   275A.08

After the last paragraph, add new paragraphs:
Mr Y v Keith Boden and Fry Heath & Spence (January 28, 2020) was another case dealt with under the summary procedure. The case arose due to the second respondent's failure to report the issuance of an examination report in a timely manner and then attempting to conceal the delay and the fact that the respondent had already applied for an extension of time by forwarding an amended version of the examination report which was altered to represent the extended deadline as an original deadline for response. The delay in reporting and responding to the examination report arose due to the report being issued shortly before the first respondent went on long term sick leave and the second respondent making inadequate arrangements for dealing with the examination report in his absence. When matters came to light and a new representative was appointed, the respondents also failed to provide copies of the prosecution file to the new representative despite repeated requests to do so.

As part of the summary procedure provided for in the Disciplinary Rules, a Complaint Review Committee is required as a preliminary matter to assess whether the evidence before the committee establishes a "prima facie case" that breaches of the rules had occurred. In doing so the Complaint's Review Committee adopted the definition of "prima facie" as set out in *R. v Galbraith* [1981] 1 W.L.R. 1039 which in the context of the proceedings amounted to asking the question: "Is there sufficient evidence taken at its highest to amount to a case to answer?"

The Committee held that the actions of the respondents amounted to breaches of rr.5, 6, 8 and 9 of the Code of Conduct and issued the first respondent with a warning and the second respondent with reprimand and ordered the respondents collectively to pay costs of £1,675 to the complainant and £5,412 to IPReg.

In *The Trade Mark Regulation Board v Duncan Welch and Manish Joshi* (February 27, 2020), a Disciplinary Board had to consider the obligations of trade mark attorneys and by extension patent attorneys to maintain run-off cover when an IPReg regulated firm ceased trading. The respondents were directors in J&W Ltd which ceased trading on or around April 2015. On May 31, 2015, J&W Ltd's professional indemnity insurance came to an end because no application for renewal was made. In September 2015 J&W Ltd's insurers wrote to J&W Ltd offering to provide continuous cover with effect from June 1, 2015 but no application for insurance was made despite IPReg writing to the Respondents in November 2015 indicating that run-off cover was required under r.17 of the Code of Conduct.

In addition to failing to provide run-off cover for the firm, J&W Ltd was also subject to a complaint from a client to the Legal Services Ombudsman that J&W Ltd had failed to pay a foreign associate for services rendered despite the client having paid an invoice respect of the associates' fees. This resulted in the client having to incur additional costs in order to keep its trade mark application alive. Despite the Legal Ombudsman upholding the complaint and ordering J&W Ltd to cover the costs and release their files to the client no action was taken by J&W Ltd to comply with the Legal Ombudsman's order for 23 months.

Although the facts forming the background to the complaint were accepted by the respondents, the respondents denied that their actions amounted to a lack of integrity and a failure to put clients' interests first contrary to r.5 of the Code of Conduct.

Assessing the case, the Board was advised to adopt the definition of integrity as set out in *Wingate v SRA* [2018] 1 W.L.R. 3969, whilst paying close regard to r.5 of the Code of Conduct for further definition in the context of IPReg proceedings. It was submitted that the test for lack of integrity in the context of the Code of Conduct amounts to "risking some harm to your client in circumstances where it is unreasonable to expose your client to such risk."

The Board found that in addition to the breaches of rr.11,12,17 and 20 which had been admitted by the respondents, the actions of the respondents also amounted to a lack of integrity under r.5.

The first respondent was removed from the register of trade mark attorneys for a period of eight months with recommendations sent to UK-IPO and OHIM recommending that his recognition and authorization to act before those offices should be withdrawn for a like period and that he should be suspended from membership of CITMA and disqualified for acting an employee or manager of a registered body for a similar period. The same sanctions were imposed on the second respondent but with the period of suspension/disqualification being six rather than eight months. Each of the respondents was ordered to pay £26,391 in costs.

As is noted above, in applying disciplinary sanctions for breaches of the Code of Conduct, IPReg will consider case law arising from the courts and other regulatory bodies. In that respect, patent attorneys should be aware of the recent decision in *Glencairn v Product Specialities* [2020] EWCA Civ 609 which concerns the extent to which "Chinese walls" could permit a firm of solicitors to act on behalf of a party in litigation where the same firm had previously acted in similar litigation on behalf of another client which had been concluded by way of a confidential mediation and settlement. In that case the court ruled that as different teams of solicitors were acting on behalf the clients and the firm was acting for two different parties against the same opponent rather than on behalf of a client opposed to a former client, the information barriers put in place by the firm were sufficient to protect any confidential information that might have been obtained in the previous mediation and the firm was permitted to continue to act.

HISTORY OF UNITED KINGDOM PATENT LAW

The present current patent law of the United Kingdom

—The "European and Euro-PCT routes"

Replace the penultimate paragraph with:

Although there is EU legislation in place, likely to enter into effect in 2023, which would also allow **A13** for a European patent to be designated shortly after grant as a "European patent with unitary effect", applying to those EU member states which had both participated in the "enhanced procedure" by which the EU established this and had ratified the Agreement on a Unified Patent Court, it can no longer apply to the UK since its withdrawal from the EU. The Unified Patent Court would also, subject to transitional provisions and opt-outs, have jurisdiction over traditional European patents in so far as they were in force in those EU Member States that had ratified such Agreement.

To the end of the last paragraph, add:

The economic benefits of the EPC for the UK are discussed in Tony Clayton, The European Patent Convention (EPC) and its Impact on the UK Economy and Innovation, The Chartered Institute of Patent Attorneys and the IP Federation (2020), available on the CIPA website.

The Paris International Convention

In the first paragraph, replace "(then called "industrial property" as it did not cover copyright protection)" with:

(then called "industrial property" as it did not cover copyright) **A14**

—The changes to United Kingdom patent law initiated by the 1977 Act

At the end of the second paragraph, replace "but now, also to appear before the IPEC" with:

but now, as patent attorneys, also to appear before the IPEC **A15**

—The differing systems of procedural law and judicial background

Replace the fifth paragraph with:

A limited degree of harmonisation as to court procedures and remedies amongst EU and other EEA **A16** Member States has been brought about by Directive 2004/48/EC ("the Enforcement Directive"), as to which see §61.02. This continues to apply to the UK even after completion of the process of withdrawal from the EU at the end of 2020 as "retained EU law" and will remain so unless and until UK legislation to the contrary is enacted or the UK Supreme Court (and possibly certain other specified UK courts in certain circumstances) rules otherwise.

Major changes made subsequent to the 1977 Act

—"Supplementary Protection Certificates" and the Biotechnology Directive

After the last paragraph, add new paragraph:

This EU legislation, subject to modifications made to the "supplementary protection certificate" for **A19** the UK by the Patents (Amendment) (EU Exit) Regulations 2019 (SI 2019/801) continues to apply to the UK even after completion of the process of withdrawal from the EU at the end of 2020 as "retained EU law" and will remain so unless and until UK legislation to the contrary is enacted or the UK Supreme Court (and possibly certain other specified UK courts in certain circumstances) rules otherwise.

The future for patent law in and for the United Kingdom

In the last paragraph, after "no other system", add:

A24   of relatively general application

THE TREATY ON THE FUNCTIONING OF THE EUROPEAN UNION
(TFEU)

Scope of this Appendix

After the first paragraph, add new paragraph:

The UK ceased to be a Member State of the EU on January 31, 2020 (European Union (Withdrawal) **D01**
Act 2018, as amended by the European Union (Withdrawal) Act 2018 (Exit Day) (Amendment) (No.3)
Regulations 2019 (SI 2019/1423)), known as "exit day." The 2018 Act, as amended by the European
Union (Withdrawal Agreement) Act 2020, also provided for a transition period from February 1, 2020
to December 31, 2020 (at 23:00 GMT), which is referred to as the "Implementation Period" during
which, in effect, the EU *acquis* (which impacts upon patents through supplementary protection
certificates, competition matters and the biotechnology directive) continued to apply to the UK. The end
of the implementation period on December 31, 2020 is now termed "IP completion day".

Replace the second paragraph with:

The 2018 Act as amended also repealed, as from the IP completion day, the European Communities
Act 1972 and made other provision in connection with such withdrawal. This includes converting,
subject to necessary modifications to be made by statutory instrument, directly applicable EU regulations into UK law and preserving laws made in the UK to implement EU directives, all with the aim of
ensuring that the law on the day before IP completion day is the same as the law the day after as far as
possible. Accordingly the EU acquis as at IP completion day, referred to as "retained EU law," will
continue to form part of UK law after IP completion day except in so far as it is subsequently amended
by UK legislation or departed from by the UK Supreme Court or other UK appellate courts. UK courts
have no longer been able to refer matters to the Court of Justice of the European Union since IP completion day.

After the second paragraph, add new paragraph:

In competition terms all previous commitments and undertakings given to the European Commission continue to be enforceable (art.95(1) Withdrawal Agreement (2019/C 384 I/01, OJEU 2019, C384/
1). On IP completion day the Competition (Amendment etc.) (EU Exit) Regulations 2019 (SI 2019/93)
and the Competition (Amendment etc.) (EU Exit) (No. 2) Regulations 2019 (SI 2019/1245) entered into
force, amending the UK Competition Act 1998 which in its Chapter I and Chapter II prohibitions parallel arts 101 and 102 TFEU discussed below, and providing, inter alia, for the continued application in
the UK of the EU block exemption regulations also discussed below as "retained block exemption
regulations".

RELEVANT ARTICLES OF THE TFEU

Commentary on the EU Treaty

Incorporation of the Treaty into United Kingdom law

In the first paragraph, replace "This provides in s.2(1) that" with:

This provided in s.2(1) that **D10**

To the end of the last paragraph, add:
As noted above, the Treaties ceased to apply to the UK after IP completion day on December 31, 2020, even though much EU law remains in place domestically in the UK as retained EU law.

The EEC, EC and EU Treaties

D11

In the first paragraph, replace "There are currently 28 Member States in the European Union." with:
There are currently 27 Member States in the European Union (the UK having left on January 31, 2020).

Interpretation of the Treaty by the European Court of Justice

D12

In the second paragraph, after "Member States. However,", delete "because of its relative youth,".

Replace the fourth paragraph with:
The great majority of cases relevant to intellectual property reach the CJEU in Luxembourg because of requests made by national courts for preliminary rulings concerning the interpretation of the TFEU under art.267 TFEU. Under this article, any court of a Member State may request the CJEU to give a ruling when it considers this to be "necessary" so that the national court itself can give judgment on the case before it. A court of final jurisdiction in the Member State must make such request if a question of interpretation regarding any of the Union Treaties arises.

Delete the last three paragraphs (i.e. from "The first cases in which art.267 TFEU" to "the law as laid down by the CJEU.").

The principle of free trade between EEA Member States (arts 34–36 TFEU)

—Free movement of goods within the EEA

D13

In the second paragraph, replace "EU Member State are treated in the same way" with:
EU Member State were treated in the same way

Replace the third paragraph with:
A further consequence of requiring intra-Union trade to be treated on the same basis as domestic trade is that those provisions in ss.48 and 50 of the 1977 Act, which provided a distinction between working an invention within the United Kingdom and elsewhere with regards to the possible grant of compulsory licences, were held, whilst the UK was an EU Member State, to be contrary to European Union law (*EC Commission v United Kingdom* (C-30/90) [1993] R.P.C. 283; [1992] E.C.R. I–829). The matter was probably dealt with in the amendments made to ss.48 and 50 under the Patents and Trade Marks (World Trade Organisation) Regulations (SI 1999/1899) promulgated to bring ss.48–54 into conformity with the TRIPS Agreement (for which see the commentaries on these sections).

—The "existence" and "exercise" of intellectual property rights under EU law

D14

In the first paragraph, second sentence, replace "the free movement of patented products and to competition within the Community." with:
the free movement of patented products and to competition within the Union.

—"Exhaustion of rights" in intra-EU trade

D15

In the second paragraph, penultimate sentence, replace "suffering from an inequality in patent law within the Community." with:
suffering from an inequality in patent law within the Union.

Change title from ""Exhaustion of rights" in international trade and the effect of **D16**
Brexit" to:

—*"Exhaustion of rights" in international trade and the effect of EU exit*

Replace the last paragraph with:
   Since IP completion day on December 31, 2020, the Intellectual Property (Exhaustion of Rights) (EU   **D17**
Exit) Regulations 2019 (SI 2019/265) have provided for the UK, at least for the time being, to continue
to apply existing EU law as to exhaustion of rights in relation to goods first placed on the market in the
EU (or the rest of the EEA), even though the Member States of the EU (and the rest of the EEA) will
not so treat goods first placed on the market in the UK by or with the consent of the rights holder and
so it will be possible in the EEA to assert patents and other intellectual property rights against the import
of such goods from the UK. The position in the UK as to patents and other intellectual property rights
will thus in this respect remain unchanged.

After the last paragraph, add new paragraph:
   The UK Government consulted on the UK's future regime for exhaustion of IP rights, the consultation period ending on August 31, 2021. The consolation document and a summary of responses is accessible via *https://www.gov.uk/government/consultations/uks-future-exhaustion-of-intellectual-property-
rights-regime.* That web page currently indicates that there is not enough data available to understand
the economic impact of any of the alternatives to the current UK+ regime and that, as a result, it has not
been possible to make a decision based on the criteria originally intended.

Anti-trust provisions of the TFEU (arts 101 and 102 TFEU)

Replace the last paragraph with:
   Also, the Competition Act 1998 (c.41), in force from March 1, 2000, makes domestic behaviour car-   **D18**
ried on within the United Kingdom likewise objectionable if it is of the type which would have been
contrary to either of arts 101 or 102 TFEU if carried on across national borders within the EEA, see the
commentary on repealed s.44. Any agreement, etc. exempted under an EU Block Exemption Regulation is automatically exempted under the Competition Act 1998 s.10. Since IP completion day on
December 31, 2020 such Block Exemption Regulations have continued to form part of domestic UK
law as "retained block exemptions" by the Competition (Amendment etc.) (EU Exit) Regulations 2019
(SI 2019/93) the Competition (Amendment etc.) (EU Exit) (No. 2) Regulations 2019 (SI 2019/1245 and
the Competition (Amendment etc.) (EU Exit) Regulations 2020, but as the retained block exemptions
expire the Competition and Markets Authority consults on and makes recommendations as to their
replacement by block exemption orders in the UK.

The Technology Transfer Block Exemption

To the end of the first paragraph, add:
   The TTBE remains part of UK retained legislation.   **D20**

In the second paragraph, first sentence, replace "the new TTBE is more prescrip-
tive" with:
   the 2014 TTBE is more prescriptive

Key concepts in the TTBE

—*Scope*

Replace the third paragraph with:
   The concept of a market is not always easy to define, as in pending cases C-176/19 P and C-201/19   **D22**
P *Commission v Servier SAS* (on appeal from the General Court—T-691/14), arising out of a patent set-
tlement agreement in which the Commission is challenging before the CJEU a decision of the General
Court which, inter alia, had found the Commission's definition of the product market, albeit in the context
of art.102 TFEU, to be wrong. In the case of patents, the view sometimes taken by competition authorities is that the market is defined by reference to the claims of the relevant patent. However, in *Genzyme
Ltd v OFT* [2004] CAT 4, Sir Christopher Bellamy QC at [197]–[221] said that the question was one of
fact. *Genzyme* was followed in *Chemistree Homecare Ltd v Abbvie Ltd* [2013] EWHC 264, Roth J.,
where he said at [27]:

"It is, of course, very possible for a single patented drug to be dominant in a market and it is conceptually possible for such a drug to constitute a distinct market of its own, although that is rare (see, for example, the discussion [in *Genzyme*]). Everything depends on the facts."

Application of the TTBE to particular provisions

—No challenge clauses

D23

In the second paragraph, after "not necessarily contrary to art.101 TFEU", add:
, especially in the context of a royalty free licence,

Agreements for collaborative research and development

D24

Replace paragraph with:
Agreements for joint ventures are generally outside the scope of this Work, but, as noted in the EPH, there are other Block Exemption Regulations of possible relevance to the subject-matter of this Work. These include: (1) Reg.217/2010 for research and development agreements and (2) Reg.1218/2010 for "specialisation" agreements. These both expire at the end of 2022 and the Competition and Markets Authority, after a consultation, has published its recommendations for their replacement, as to the UK, by two block exemption orders of broadly equivalent scope—see *https://www.gov.uk/government/ consultations/retained-horizontal-block-exemption-regulations-rd-and-specialisation-agreements- consultation*. The vertical agreements block exemption Reg.330/2010, which addressed certain agreements of a "vertical" nature, usually concerned with arrangements for product sales made via intermediaries, expired at the end of May 2022 and was replaced as to the UK by the Competition Act 1998 (Vertical Agreements Block Exemption) Order 2022 (SI 2022/516).

Decisions of relevance to the application of Article 101 TFEU

D25

After the last paragraph, add new paragraph:
Several pharmaceutical patent settlement agreements entered into by innovators and prospective generic entrants involving payments by the innovator patentee have been held by the European Commission to be in breach of art.101, which determinations have to date been largely upheld by the General Court and the Court of Justice. Such issues were also the subject of a reference from the English courts to the CJEU in *Generics (UK) Ltd v Competition and Markets Authority* (C-307/18) EU:C:2020:52 (Court of Justice, January 30, 2020), which related to a patent settlement concerning the drug paroxetine, in which the court formulated the following principles as to both arts 101 and 102 in relation to such agreements:

1. Article 101(1) TFEU must be interpreted as meaning that a manufacturer of originator medicines who is the holder of a manufacturing process patent for an active ingredient that is in the public domain, on the one hand, and the manufacturers of generic medicines who are preparing to enter the market of the medicine containing that active ingredient, on the other, who are in dispute as to whether that patent is valid or whether the generic medicines concerned infringe that patent, are potential competitors, where it is established that the manufacturer of generic medicines has in fact a firm intention and an inherent ability to enter the market, and that its market entry does not meet barriers that are insurmountable, which it is for the referring court to assess.

2. Article 101(1) TFEU must be interpreted as meaning that a settlement agreement with respect to pending court proceedings between a manufacturer of originator medicines and a manufacturer of generic medicines, who are potential competitors, concerning whether a process patent (for the manufacture of an active ingredient of an originator medicine that is in the public domain) held by the manufacturer of originator medicines is valid and whether a generic version of that medicine infringes the patent, whereby that manufacturer of generic medicines undertakes not to enter the market of the medicine containing that active ingredient and not to pursue its action for the revocation of that patent for the duration of that agreement, in return for transfers of value in its favour by the manufacturer of originator medicines, constitutes an agreement which has as its object the prevention, restriction or distortion of competition:

    • if it is clear from all the information available that the net gain from the transfers of value by the manufacturer of originator medicines in favour of the manufacturer of generic medicines can have no explanation other than the commercial interest of the parties to the agreement not to engage in competition on the merits;

[212]

- unless the settlement agreement concerned is accompanied by proven pro-competitive effects capable of giving rise to a reasonable doubt that it causes a sufficient degree of harm to competition.

3.   Article 101(1) TFEU must be interpreted as meaning that if a settlement agreement, such as those at issue in the main proceedings, is to be demonstrated to have appreciable potential or real effects on competition, and, therefore, is to be characterised as a "restriction by effect", that does not presuppose a finding that, in the absence of that agreement, either the manufacturer of generic medicines who is a party to that agreement would probably have been successful in the proceedings relating to the process patent at issue, or the parties to that agreement would probably have concluded a less restrictive settlement agreement.

4.   Article 102 TFEU must be interpreted as meaning that, in a situation where a manufacturer of originator medicines containing an active ingredient which is in the public domain, but the process of manufacturing which is covered by a process patent, the validity of which is disputed, impedes, on the basis of that process patent, the market entry of generic versions of that medicine, there must be taken into consideration, for the purposes of definition of the product market concerned, not only the originator version of that medicine but also its generic versions, even if the latter would not be able to enter the market legally before the expiry of that process patent, if the manufacturers concerned of generic medicines are in a position to present themselves within a short period on the market concerned with sufficient strength to constitute a serious counterbalance to the manufacturer of originator medicines already on that market, which it is for the referring court to determine.

5.   Article 102 TFEU must be interpreted as meaning that the strategy of a dominant undertaking, the holder of a process patent for the production of an active ingredient that is in the public domain, which leads it to conclude, either as a precautionary measure or following the bringing of court proceedings challenging the validity of that patent, a set of settlement agreements which have, at the least, the effect of keeping temporarily outside the market potential competitors who manufacture generic medicines using that active ingredient, constitutes an abuse of a dominant position within the meaning of art.102 TFEU, provided that that strategy has the capacity to restrict competition and, in particular, to have exclusionary effects, going beyond the specific anticompetitive effects of each of the settlement agreements that are part of that strategy, which it is for the referring court to determine.

Abuse of a dominant position (TFEU art.102)

After the sixth paragraph (beginning "In 2009, the Commission imposed a large fine"), add new paragraphs:

It can be argued that by its nature, a patent that is "essential" to a standard, i.e. it is infringed by the practice of a standard, confers, by itself a dominant position on the rights holder. Thus art.102 has especial potential application to the enforcement of standards-essential patents ("SEPs"), and a body of case law has developed as to this. Standards are usually established by standards setting organisations ("SSOs") such as the European Telecommunications Standards Institute ("ETSI"). Membership by a patent owner of an SSO is not mandatory but any person wishing to be a member, who has one or more SEPs must usually agree to licence their patent on FRAND terms (see below). In the case of ETSI this is required by the ETSI IPR Policy. But even those who are not members are subject to art.102.

D26

In 2009, in Case COMP/38.636—RAMBUS, the Commission reported on its investigation of concerns as to the claiming of potentially abusive royalties for the use of certain patents for "Dynamic Random Access Memory" ("DRAM") chips subsequent to allegedly intentional deceptive conduct in the context of the standard-setting process. The alleged deceptive conduct related to the non-disclosure of the existence of patents and patent applications which were later claimed to be relevant to the adopted standard. The Commission concluded its investigation by accepting commitments from Rambus as to maximum royalty rates on its patents that were essential to the standards in issue.

Replace the seventh paragraph with:

The extent to which art.102 could be applied to disputes over patents that have been declared essential to telecoms standards, and as to which the holders of such patents are obliged to offer licences on fair, reasonable and non-discriminatory ("FRAND") terms, was considered by the Court of Justice in *Huawei Technologies Co Ltd v ZTE Corp* (C-170/13) EU:C:2015:477 in which the court held:

1.   Article 102 TFEU must be interpreted as meaning that the proprietor of a patent essential to a standard established by a standardisation body, which has given an irrevocable undertaking to that body to grant a licence to third parties on FRAND terms, does not abuse its dominant position, within the meaning of that article, by bringing an action for infringement seeking an

injunction prohibiting the infringement of its patent or seeking the recall of products for the manufacture of which that patent has been used, as long as:

- prior to bringing that action, the proprietor has, first, alerted the alleged infringer of the infringement complained about by designating that patent and specifying the way in which it has been infringed, and, secondly, after the alleged infringer has expressed its willingness to conclude a licensing agreement on FRAND terms, presented to that infringer a specific, written offer for a licence on such terms, specifying, in particular, the royalty and the way in which it is to be calculated, and
- where the alleged infringer continues to use the patent in question, the alleged infringer has not diligently responded to that offer, in accordance with recognised commercial practices in the field and in good faith, this being a matter which must be established on the basis of objective factors and which implies, in particular, that there are no delaying tactics.

2.   Article 102 TFEU must be interpreted as not prohibiting, in circumstances such as those in the main proceedings, an undertaking in a dominant position and holding a patent essential to a standard established by a standardisation body, which has given an undertaking to the standardisation body to grant licences for that patent on FRAND terms, from bringing an action for infringement against the alleged infringer of its patent and seeking the rendering of accounts in relation to past acts of use of that patent or an award of damages in respect of those acts of use.

Replace the eighth paragraph with:

The need for a contractual clause or obligation of like effect between buyer and seller of an intellectual property right to ensure that the FRAND commitment is transferred has been emphasised in the European Commission's Guidelines on the applicability of art.101 to horizontal co-operation agreements (OJ EU, 2011/C 11/01)—para.285; see also *Google/Motorola Mobility* (Case No COMP/ M.6381) before the European Commission. However, it seems to be accepted law (and certainly was in the case of *Unwired Planet International Ltd v Huawei Technologies Co Ltd* [2015] EWHC 2097, [2015] Info. T.L.R. 95, Birss J.) that a FRAND obligation followed a patent, and thus could be imposed upon subsequent purchasers without more (upheld in that respect at [2016] EWCA Civ 489; [2016] E.C.C. 21, CA).

Delete the ninth paragraph (beginning "Birss J. was upheld (in that respect)").

Replace the tenth paragraph with:

The legal notion of FRAND and its history and purpose were reviewed by Birss J. in *Unwired Planet International Ltd v Huawei Technologies Co Ltd* [2017] EWHC 711 (Pat); [2019] 4 C.M.L.R. 7 at [89]– [97]. The concept originated in US anti-trust law (see Jorge Contreras, "A Brief History of FRAND: Analyzing Current Debates in Standard Setting and Antitrust Through a Historical Lens" 80 *Antitrust Law Journal* 39 (2015)). The first public formulation by the European Commission of a specific requirement for FRAND terms in the context of IP and standardisation had been in a paper entitled *Communication on Intellectual Property Rights and Standardisation* on October 27, 1992 (COM (92) 445 final at 4.3.3). Its most recent paper on the subject was its Communication entitled *"Setting out the EU approach to Standard Essential Patents"* of November 28, 2017 (COM (2017) 712 final).

Delete the eleventh paragraph (beginning "The view of Birss J. was that the concept").

Replace the twelfth and thirteenth paragraphs with:

In *Unwired Planet International Ltd v Huawei Technologies Co Ltd* [2017] EWHC 2988 (Pat); [2018] 4 C.M.L.R. 17, [2017] R.P.C. 19, Birss J. settled the terms of a FRAND licence after certain patents had been held to be valid and essential to the relevant standards. He rejected Huawei's submission that a UK portfolio licence would be FRAND and held that a FRAND licence between Unwired Planet and Huawei would be a worldwide licence. Where a proprietor of a standard essential patent (SEP) was in a position to licence a global portfolio (because the technology was usually only licenced on a global basis, the parties being globally orientated) then it was not a breach of competition law for the proprietor of an SEP to insist upon a licence which does that.

The terms of the licence which were eventually settled by Birss J. are attached to a further judgment of his at [2017] EWHC 1304 (Pat) in which he granted a "FRAND injunction", namely an injunction in respect of those patents that had been held to be valid and essential to the relevant standards but which the defendants could avoid by taking the global FRAND licence that he had settled. The primary matter in these judgments that was the subject of appeal by the defendants at [2018] EWCA Civ 2344 was the FRAND injunction—whether a UK court has jurisdiction and may properly exercise a power, without the agreement of both parties, to (a) grant an injunction to restrain the infringement of a UK patent where the patented invention is an essential component in an international standard of telecommunications equipment, which is marketed, sold and used worldwide, unless the implementer of the patented invention enters into a global licence of a multinational patent portfolio, and (b) determine royalty rates and other disputed terms of such a global licence. The only other two matters the subject of such appeal were the nature of the non-discriminatory aspect of the FRAND licence and whether the court should refuse to grant the owner of such a SEP an injunction on the ground that it had breached art.102 TFEU because it had not complied with the guidance given by the Court of Justice in *Huawei v ZTE* (see above). The Court of Appeal ([2018] EWCA Civ 2344; [2018] R.P.C. 20 CA) rejected the appeal in each respect, as did the UK Supreme Court on a subsequent appeal to it at [2020] UKSC 37; [2020] Bus. L.R. 2422; [2021] 4 C.M.L.R. 3, *The Times*, October 16, 2020, SC which was heard together with an appeal from the decision of the Court of Appeal in *Huawei Technologies Co Ltd v Conversant Wireless Licensing SARL* [2019] EWCA Civ 38 CA as to whether England is the appropriate forum to determine those matters. The Supreme Court also rejected both appeals in all the respects canvassed in the Court of Appeal, and also rejected a further ground of appeal by Huawei, albeit one that had not been canvassed in the lower courts, namely the circumstances in which it is appropriate for an English court to grant a prohibitory injunction or to award damages instead.

After the last paragraph, add new paragraph:
As to the art.102 issue the Supreme Court interpreted the Court of Justice ruling in *Huawei v ZTE* (above) as not mandating the protocol that it set out in order to avoid breaching art.102, and that on the facts, what mattered was that SEP holder had shown itself to be willing to grant a licence to the defendants on whatever terms the court decided were FRAND. The Supreme Court did however accept that the Court of Justice in *Huawei v ZTE* had made it clear that bringing an action for a prohibitory injunction without notice or prior consultation with the alleged infringer will infringe art.102, although the Supreme Court did observe that the nature of the notice or consultation required will depend on the circumstances of the case. For other issues relevant to the competition issues aspect of the dispute between Unwired Planet and Huawei see §§61.21, 61.34 and 61.59.

—Mere exercise of rights

In the penultimate paragraph, replace "the negotiation process (conducted in good faith) is complete—see MEMO/14/403 & 322, IP/14/49 & IP/13/403" with:
the negotiation process (conducted in good faith) is complete—see IP/14/49 & IP/13/403 **D27**

THE CIVIL PROCEDURE RULES

THE OVERRIDING OBJECTIVE

Replace clause (1) with:

(1)   These Rules are a procedural code with the overriding objective of enabling **E01**
the court to deal with cases justly and at proportionate cost.

Replace clause (2)(a) with:

    (a)   ensuring that the parties are on an equal footing and can participate
fully in proceedings, and that parties and witnesses can give their best
evidence;

PART 63 OF THE CIVIL PROCEDURE RULES

Replace Note "5." with:

Notes

5.   Part 63 was further amended by the Civil Procedure (Amendment No.3) Rules 2016 (SI 2016/788 r.12(b)) as from October 3, 2016, the Civil Procedure (Amendment) Rules 2017 (SI 2017/95 r.11(1)) as from April 6, 2017 and the Civil Procedure Rules 1998 (Amendment) (EU Exit) Regulations 2019/521 reg.13(2) as from December 31, 2020.

Rule 1— Scope of this Part and interpretation

Replace 63.1 with

63.1— Scope of this Part and interpretation

(1)   This Part applies to all intellectual property claims including–   **F63.01**
   (a)   registered intellectual property rights such as–
      (i)   patents;
      (ii)   registered designs; and
      (iii)   registered trade marks; and
   (b)   unregistered intellectual property rights such as –
      (i)   copyright;
      (ii)   design right;
      (iii)   the right to prevent passing off; and
      (iv)   the other rights set out in Practice Direction 63.
(2)   In this Part –
   (a)   "the 1977 Act" means the Patents Act 1977;
   (b)   "the 1988 Act" means the Copyright, Designs and Patents Act 1988;
   (c)   "the 1994 Act" means the Trade Marks Act 1994;
   (d)   "the Comptroller" means the Comptroller General of Patents, Designs and Trade Marks;
   (e)   "patent" means a patent under the 1977 Act or a supplementary protection certificate granted by the Patent Office under Article 10(1) of Council Regulation (EEC) No. 1768/92 or of Regulation (EC) No. 1610/96 of the European Parliament and the Council and includes any application for a patent or supplementary protection certificate;
   (f)   "Patents Court" means the Patents Court of the High Court constituted as part of the Chancery Division by section 6(1) of the Senior Courts Act 1981;
   (g)   "Intellectual Property Enterprise Court" means a specialist list established within the Chancery Division of the High Court;
   (h)   "enterprise judge" means a judge authorised by the Chancellor of the High Court to sit in the Intellectual Property Enterprise Court;
   (i)   *omitted*

(j) "the register" means whichever of the following registers is appropriate –

    (i) patents maintained by the Comptroller under section 32 of the 1977 Act;

    (ii) designs maintained by the registrar under section 17 of the Registered Designs Act 1949;

    (iii) trade marks maintained by the registrar under section 63 of the 1994 Act; and

    (iv) *omitted*

    (v) *omitted*

    (vi) plant varieties maintained by the Controller under regulation 12 of the Plant Breeders' Rights Regulations 1998; and

    (vii) *omitted*

(k) "the registrar" means –

    (i) the registrar of trade marks; or

    (ii) the registrar of registered designs, whichever is appropriate.

(3) Save as provided in r.63.27, claims to which this Part applies are allocated to the multi-track. Rule 26.3(1) applies save for the modification that the court will send the parties a notice requiring the parties to file proposed directions by the date specified in the notice. For a claim which is allocated to the multi-track by this rule, r.26.3(1B) and r.26.4 to 26.10 do not apply.

I
PATENTS AND REGISTERED DESIGNS

Replace 63.2 with:

Rule 2— Scope of Section I and Allocation

63.2— Scope of Section I and Allocation

F63.02 (1) This Section applies to–

    (a) any claim under–

        (i) the 1977 Act;

        (ii) the Registered Designs Act 1949;

        (iii) the Defence Contracts Act 1958; and

    (b) any claim relating to–

        (i) *omitted*

        (ii) semiconductor topography rights; or

        (iii) plant varieties.

(2) claims to which this Section applies must be started in–

    (a) the Patents Court; or

    (b) the Intellectual Property Enterprise Court.

Replace 63.8 with:

Rule 8— Case management

63.8— Case management

F63.08 (1) Parties do not need to file a directions questionnaire.

(2) The following provisions only of Part 29 apply –

(a) rule 29.3(2) (legal representatives to attend case management conferences);

(b) rule 29.4 (the parties must endeavour to agree case management directions); and

(c) rule 29.5 (variation of case management timetable) with the exception of paragraph (1)(b) and (c).

(3) As soon as practicable the court will hold a case management conference which must be fixed in accordance with Practice Direction 63.

III
SERVICE OF DOCUMENTS AND PARTICIPATION BY THE COMPTROLLER

Replace 63.14 with:

Rule 14— Service of documents

63.14— Service of documents

(1) Subject to paragraph (2), Part 6 applies to service of a claim form and any document in any proceedings under this Part. **F63.14**

(2) A claim form relating to a registered right may be served –

   (a) on a party who has registered the right at the address for service given for that right in the appropriate register at—

      (i) the United Kingdom Patent Office,

   provided the address is within the United Kingdom; or

   (b) in accordance with 6.33(1) or 6.33(2) on a party who has registered the right at the address for service given for that right in the appropriate register at –

      (i) the United Kingdom Patent Office.

(3) Where a party seeks any remedy (whether by claim form, counterclaim or application notice), which would if granted affect an entry in any United Kingdom Patent Office register, that party must serve on the Comptroller or registrar –

   (a) the claim form, counterclaim or application notice;

   (b) any other statement of case where relevant (including any amended statement of case); and

   (c) any accompanying documents.

PRACTICE DIRECTION—INTELLECTUAL PROPERTY CLAIMS

Replace 16.1 with:

Section II— Provisions about Registered Trade Marks and Other Intellectual Property Rights

Practice Direction 63.16—Allocation (rule 63.13)

Allocation (rule 63.13)

F63PD
.16
16.1 The other intellectual property rights referred to in rule 63.13 are –
(1) copyright;
(2) rights in performances;
(3) rights conferred under Part VII of the 1988 Act;
(4) design right;
(5) Community design right;
(6) association rights, including the right of the Birmingham Organising Committee by virtue of section 3(4) of the Birmingham Commonwealth Games Act 2020 to take action for breach of section 3(1) of that Act (prohibition of unauthorised association with the Games);
(7) moral rights;
(8) database rights;
(9) unauthorised decryption rights;
(10) hallmarks;
(11) claims in respect of technical trade secrets;
(12) passing off;
(13) protected designations of origin, protected geographical indications and traditional speciality guarantes;
(14) registered trade marks; and
(15) Community trade marks.

16.2 There are Chancery district registries at Birmingham, Bristol, Caernarfon, Cardiff, Leeds, Liverpool, Manchester, Mold, Newcastle upon Tyne and Preston.

16.3 The County Court hearing centres at Caernarfon, Mold and Preston do not have jurisdiction in relation to registered trade marks and Community trade marks.

Section V— Provisions about proceedings in the Intellectual Property Enterprise Court

Replace 27.1 and 27.2 with:

Practice Direction 63.27—Scope of Section V

Scope of Section V

F63PD
.27
27.1 Except as provided for in paragraph 27.2 this Practice Direction, as modified by this Section, applies to claims in the Intellectual Property Enterprise Court.

27.2 Paragraphs 5.2, 5.10 to 9.1 and paragraph 9.2(3) do not apply to a claim in the Intellectual Property Enterprise Court.

Replace Note with:

Note.

Rules 45.01–45.29N and 45.33–45.44 are outside the scope of this work and are not here reproduced. Part 45 was amended by the Civil Procedure (Amendment) Rules 2017 (SI 2017/95) r.8(5) as from February 28, 2017; the Civil Procedure (Amendment) Rules 2018 (SI 2018/239) r.3(a) as from April 6, 2018; and the Civil Procedure (Amendment No.3) Rules 2019 (SI 2019/1118) r.3 as from October 1, 2019.

F45.01.
F45.40

Add new paragraphs §§F45.01.F45.40A—F45.01.F45.40C:

IV
SCALE COSTS FOR CLAIMS IN THE INTELLECTUAL PROPERTY ENTERPRISE COURT

45.30—   Scope and interpretation

(1) Subject to paragraph (2), this Section applies to proceedings in the Intellectual Property Enterprise Court.

F45.01.
F45.40A

(2) This Section does not apply where—
   (a) the court considers that a party has behaved in a manner which amounts to an abuse of the court's process; or
   (b) the claim concerns the infringement or revocation of a patent or registered design or registered trade mark the validity of which has been certified by a court or by the Comptroller-General of Patents, Designs and Trade Marks in earlier proceedings.

(3) The court will make a summary assessment of the costs of the party in whose favour any order for costs is made. Rules 44.2(8), 44.7(b) and Part 47 do not apply to this Section.

(4) "*Scale costs*" means the costs set out in Table A and Table B of the Practice Direction supplementing this Part.

45.31—   Amount of scale costs

(1) Subject to rule 45.32, the court will not order a party to pay total costs of more than—

F45.01.
F45.40B

   (a) £50,000 on the final determination of a claim in relation to liability; and
   (b) £25,000 on an inquiry as to damages or account of profits.

(2) The amounts in paragraph (1) apply after the court has applied the provision on set off in accordance with rule 44.12(a).

(3) The maximum amount of scale costs that the court will award for each stage of the claim is set out in Practice Direction 45.

(4) The amount of the scale costs awarded by the court in accordance with paragraph (3) will depend on the nature and complexity of the claim.

(4A) Subject to assessment where appropriate, the following may be recovered in addition to the amount of the scale costs set out in Practice Direction 45—Fixed Costs—
   (a) court fees;
   (b) costs relating to the enforcement of any court order; and

(c)   wasted costs.

(5)   Where appropriate, VAT may be recovered in addition to the amount of the scale costs and any reference in this Section to scale costs is a reference to those costs net of any such VAT.

45.32   Summary assessment of the costs of an application where a party has behaved unreasonably

F45.01.
F45.
40C

Costs awarded to a party under rule 63.26(2) are in addition to the total costs that may be awarded to that party under rule 45.31.

Delete paragraphs §§F45.41—F45.43.

INDEX

Russell-Clarke & Howe on Industrial Designs, 10ᵗʰ Edition

Martin Howe KC, James St. Ville and Ashton Chantrielle
978-0-414-08888-7
February 2022
Hardback/Westlaw UK/ProView

Russell-Clarke & Howe on Industrial Designs provides in-depth commentary on the protection of industrial designs and is the essential text for guidance on how to get the best from the vast bed of legislation surrounding industrial designs, ensuring that your designs are safeguarded and protected.

The tenth edition contains full coverage of changes to UK industrial designs laws following Brexit, including sections on the new rights which replace Community registered and unregistered design rights: "re-registered" UK rights, and "continuing" and "supplementary" unregistered design rights. There is full discussion of relevance of past and future case law of EU Court of Justice and General Court to interpretation of post-Brexit UK design laws, and up-to-date coverage of case law developments in UK and EU courts across the industrial designs field.

Copinger & Skone James on Copyright, 2ⁿᵈ Supplement, 18ᵗʰ Edition

Gwilym Harbottle, Nicholas Caddick KC and Uma Suthersanen
978-0-414-10973-5
December 2022
Paperback/Westlaw UK/ProView

A leading text in its field, *Copinger & Skone James on Copyright* offers thorough and comprehensive coverage of the main aspects of copyright and connected rights. The Second Supplement to the 18th edition updates the Main Work with the latest legislative and case law developments.

Contact us: Tel: +44 (0)345 600 9355   Order online: sweetandmaxwell.co.uk

Volume one contains commentary and analysis with Volume two featuring legislation and materials. The title takes a subject-by-subject approach to take you through Copyright, Rights in Performances, Rights in Designs, Moral Rights and a variety of Miscellaneous Rights.